Sorcerers' Apprentices

100 Years of Law Clerks at the
United States Supreme Court

Artemus Ward and David L. Weiden

NEW YORK UNIVERSITY PRESS
New York and London

NEW YORK UNIVERSITY PRESS
New York and London
www.nyupress.org

Library of Congress Cataloging-in-Publication Data
Ward, Artemus, 1971–
Sorcerers' apprentices : 100 years of law clerks at the United States
Supreme Court / Artemus Ward and David L. Weiden.
p. cm.
Includes bibliographical references and index.
ISBN-13: 978-0-8147-9404-3 (cloth : alk. paper)
ISBN-10: 0-8147-9404-1 (cloth : alk. paper)
1. Law clerks—United States.   2. Law clerks—United States—His-
tory.   3. Judicial process—United States.   4. United States.
Supreme Court.   I. Weiden, David L.   II. Title.
KF8771.W37   2006
347.73'16—dc22   2005037482

New York University Press books are printed on acid-free paper,
and their binding materials are chosen for strength and durability.

Manufactured in the United States of America

10 9 8 7 6 5 4 3 2 1

To the memory of my grandfather, Artemus Ward II
— A.W.

To the memory of my parents, Lawrence and Ramona
— D.W.

Contents

Illustrations

TABLES

Acknowledgments

This project has been ongoing for quite a long period—over ten years—and we have correspondingly incurred tremendous debts to those who were kind enough to assist us. We are grateful, first and foremost, to the many former clerks who spoke with us. We thank them for their candid and insightful comments and responses. We also thank those colleagues who commented on drafts of these chapters at a number of academic meetings, including the American, Western, Midwest, and Southwestern Political Science Association conferences. We also thank colleagues in our respective departments who not only supported our research financially but also were willing to offer constructive criticism and suggestions. We are also indebted to the archivists at the Library of Congress, Princeton University, and Washington and Lee University for their help with the papers of the justices. Finally, we thank the anonymous reviewers of NYU Press, who provided such excellent feedback on the manuscript. Of course, all errors in this book are ours alone.

Art Ward wishes to first thank Jeff Biggs and the American Political Science Association's Congressional Fellowship Program. I was fortunate to spend an amazing year living and working in Washington, D.C., while completing this manuscript. I also want to thank my colleagues on the House Judiciary Committee who taught me so much about American government—and who never knew that in between hearings and markups I regularly spent my lunch hours across the street in the papers of the justices at the Library of Congress. Also, the American Political Science Association's Centennial Center provided valuable space and resources. Steve Wasby, Tony Mauro, David Garrow, and Cornell Clayton were invaluable as I labored over successive drafts of this manuscript, and I thank them for their help and encouragement. Brian Frederick provided valuable research assistance toward the end of this project and I am grateful for his help.

David Weiden wishes to thank, first, former graduate student colleagues and faculty members in the Department of Government at the
University of Texas at Austin. Some very early drafts of the ideas in
chapter 1 of this book first surfaced in seminar papers for various graduate school courses at UT. H. W. Perry, Jr., was not only a tremendous advisor and mentor but also an invaluable source of knowledge
about the Court and its processes. Steve Wasby was kind enough to
read early versions of proposals for this research, as well as finished
drafts throughout the process. Howard Ernst gave excellent suggestions
on survey analysis. Special thanks must go to Curtis Bradley of the
Duke University School of Law, whose comments and conversations in
the mid-1990s provided the impetus for this research. Finally, I thank
Marina Rolbin for always being supportive of my research efforts, and
David L. B. Weiden, Jr., who cares little about the Court at this point
but is the light of my life nonetheless.

Preface
Awesome Responsibility and
Complete Subservience

Clerking for a U.S. Supreme Court justice is the most prestigious position a recent law school graduate can attain. Each summer,
three dozen clerks begin their year-long assignment with the nine justices. These highly coveted placements in turn lead to prestigious careers
in the legal and academic worlds. Indeed, the justices themselves are
routinely lobbied by various law firms, corporations, and academic institutions to provide lists of former clerks, make recommendations, and
even reserve rooms and schedule interviews for their current and past
clerks. For example, a typical letter that Justice Harry Blackmun received from a New York law firm stated, "We have decided to add
another associate in the fall of 1983 and would appreciate it if you
would pass this letter on to your clerks."[1] Another memo, this time addressed to all the clerks from a clerk to Justice Lewis Powell, explained,
"Dean Ernest Gellhorn will be in the S[olicitor] G[eneral]'s Office from
8 to 11 a.m. and from 2 to 6 p.m. on September 30 to interview clerks
for teaching positions."[2] Supreme Court law clerks, past and present,
are at the top of the legal profession.

Law clerks are part of the legal, political, and business elite. Their
former ranks include Secretary of State Dean Acheson, Attorney General Francis Biddle, U.S. Steel president Irving Olds, noted sociology
professor David Reisman, Secretary of Transportation William Coleman, Secretary of Defense Elliot Richardson, Federal Communications
director Newton Minow, Securities and Exchange Commission director
Roderick Hills, and *Washington Post* president Philip Graham, to name
a few. Many, such as Alexander Bickel, Andrew Kaufman, John P.
Frank, Laurence Tribe, and A. E. Dick Howard, went on to influential
careers in academia. The ranks of federal judges are filled with former

clerks, including Guido Calabresi, Richard Posner, Louis Oberdorfer, Henry J. Friendly, Harold Leventhal, and Calvert Magruder. Some clerks, however, have gone in a different direction. For example, Alger Hiss, former clerk to Justice Oliver Wendell Holmes, was accused of spying and convicted of perjury in a sensational Cold War–era case.[3]

A handful of clerks even went on to become justices themselves. Byron White clerked for Fred M. Vinson, William Rehnquist clerked for Robert Jackson, John Paul Stevens clerked for Wiley Rutledge, Stephen Breyer clerked for Arthur Goldberg, and John Roberts clerked for Rehnquist.[4] In a congratulatory note written to Rehnquist upon his appointment to the Court, Justice Wil-liam O. Douglas wrote, "I realize that you were here before as a member of the so-called Junior Supreme Court."[5]

Law clerks enjoy many perks while they are at the Court. They have a private dining room in the Court's cafeteria and attend lunches, receptions, and parties with the justices. Unlike other government employees in Washington, law clerks do not wear name badges or show identification when entering the Court. They are simply waved through each day by guards who have studied and memorized their photographs before their clerkships even began. Informal, life-long relationships develop right away between justice and clerk, resulting in such experiences as surprise birthday parties with Oliver Wendell Holmes, Thanksgiving dinner with William Howard Taft, tennis matches with Hugo Black, walks with Harlan Fiske Stone, Saturday lunches and baseball and football games with Earl Warren, golf with John Marshall Harlan, II, tests of athletic skill, including afternoon basketball games and in-chambers putting contests, with Byron White, and Halloween pumpkin-carving with Sandra Day O'Connor.

Relationships between justices and their former clerks continue long after their clerkships end. Clerks often organize annual reunions for their justice and former clerks. Chief Justice Warren's former clerks started the practice in his chambers in 1961 with a black-tie reception and dinner each year. The affair was held on a Saturday night, and during their presidencies, both John F. Kennedy and Lyndon Johnson stopped by. The next morning, Warren and his wife would have a brunch for the former clerks and their spouses at the Congressional Country Club.[6] Justice Stanley Reed had a similar practice for his former clerks.[7] Warren's former clerks played a key role after Warren's death when the former Chief Justice lay in state in the Great Hall of the Supreme Court building in 1974. Reed's former clerks placed a plaque in his honor at the University of Kentucky Law School, with each of their names listed below his.

Clerking for a U.S. Supreme Court justice has a dramatic effect on those who are selected. Laura Ingraham, who clerked for Justice Clarence Thomas in 1992 and went on to be a CBS News commentator, remarked, "It spoils you for any other legal job in the country."[8] Columbia law professor and 1991 clerk to Justice Anthony Kennedy, Michael Dorf, said, "It's a very strange mix of awesome responsibility and complete subservience. It's more responsibility than you'll ever have again."[9]

Law clerks perform a number of functions. Supreme Court scholar Bernard Schwartz called the work performed by law clerks "important and substantial."[10] While these duties can vary slightly from chambers to chambers, they essentially consist of legal research and writing. Clerks conduct research, prepare memoranda, and draft orders and opinions. Justice Harry Blackmun remarked, "Most of us have four full-time law clerks who put in 80-100 hours a week. It is all I can do to keep up with their output."[11]

The clerk's role shifts as cases move through the stages of the decision-making process. When someone seeks Supreme Court review of a case, clerks review the arguments, write memos, and recommend that the petition for review (a petition for certiorari, or cert) be denied or granted. This stage is crucial as the Court only decides to hear a small fraction of the number of cases petitioned to it. For example, during the 2002–2003 Term, the Court received 8,255 petitions and delivered only seventy-one signed opinions—less than 1 percent.[12] The clerks are the initial gatekeepers in this weeding-out process.

In those cases where review is granted, clerks draft bench memos for their justices to use during oral argument. In contrast to the memos on whether the Court should grant review, bench memos contain greater detail of fact and analysis of the case and often a recommendation from the clerk for a decision on the merits. Donna Murasky, who clerked for Justice Harry Blackmun during the 1975 Term, wrote the justice on the last day of her clerkship, "I have to apologize for the length of this bench memo. I was on page 13 when you called yesterday and told me to instruct the new clerks to limit theirs to 5 or 6."[13] The justices use bench memos during oral argument and in conference to help them make their decisions on the cases. Not every justice has had his or her clerks prepare bench memos on every case. Justice Powell, for example, felt that bench memos were not necessary in many cases, and he distinguished between "major research memos, full memos, and 'bob-tail' bench memos" depending on the importance and difficulty of the case.[14] He remarked, "I like for my clerks to devote a substantial part of the summer months to special study of the more important cases set for argument next Term."[15] Bench memos in general, however, are less important to the justices than the clerks' cert memos and opinion drafts. In 1973 Justice Rehnquist explained,

> The method of operation which I have come to favor during my short tenure does not rely heavily on bench memos. For reasons doubtless peculiar to my own way of working, I have tended to concentrate my time heavily in the area of reviewing records and briefs in the argued cases, feeling that the time of the law clerks could be more usefully employed in working on the certs and in the drafting of opinions when assignments begin coming around.[16]

Law clerks may attend oral argument but generally do not. Eugene Gressman, clerk to Justice Frank Murphy, explained, "My duties as law clerk precluded attendance at most oral arguments."[17] Justice Powell encouraged his clerks to attend the arguments for the cases they were responsible for:

> It is usually desirable for the responsible clerk to hear the oral argument of the cases assigned to him. Of course, clerks are welcome to hear any arguments, and every clerk in the building is likely to be present for the occasional "big case." As the Term goes on, and time becomes more precious, there is little profit in hearing oral arguments in the average case unless it is "your" case.[18]

Clerks discuss the merits of cases with justices. For example, 1991 Blackmun clerk Andrea Ward wrote her justice regarding *New York v. United States*, "This is a highly political case, and the conservatives granted the case only to limit or overrule your decision in *Garcia* and Justice Brennan's in *Baker* regarding the 10A or federalism-based limits on Congress' power to regulate under the Commerce Clause."[19]

During the voting and coalition-formation stage, clerks act as informal ambassadors across chambers and make recommendations based on information they get through this "clerk network." For example, in *Eisenstadt v. Baird*, 1971 Blackmun clerk John T. Rich briefed his boss on three other justices' opinions being circulated by other justices and ultimately made a recommendation as to which to join: "Justice Douglas's ingenious opinion is the narrowest of all. . . . Justice White's opinion has the virtue of being simple. . . . Justice Brennan's opinion is much more confusingly organized. I can't help but think that his opinion is much more difficult than Justice White's, and recommend that you concur in the latter."[20]

Clerks also routinely draft opinions. For example, 1991 Blackmun clerk Molly McUsic wrote her justice concerning the religious establishment case *Lee v. Weisman,*

> As we discussed yesterday . . . I have developed an outline for the dissent, and collected research in support of each of the points. I have also attempted to draft various sections. . . . As I see the dissent now, it will make the following points. . . . It will take at least two weeks of solid work after the majority comes out to get something to you.[21]

The following study is the first comprehensive examination of law clerks at the U.S. Supreme Court. By analyzing each facet of the role they play, from screening cases to writing opinions, we hope not only to better understand their role but also to provide a different lens through which we can understand the thinking and behavior of the justices. Clerks have become an integral part of the functioning of the Supreme Court, so much so that even the justices admit that the institution could not operate without them. A detailed analysis of the clerks' role provides a unique view of the day-to-day processes that take place at the Court. Furthermore, even the leading accounts of the behavior of the justices scarcely mention the influence of clerks on their thinking and decision making.[22] A clerk-centered approach can provide an important supplement to these studies.

The standard account of clerks at the Supreme Court is that the institution was introduced to help with the Court's growing workload. In this examination of those important actors in the judicial process, we refute that account by analyzing clerks historically. We suggest that clerks were an outgrowth of the apprentice model of legal education, where learning the law took place at the feet of a practitioner rather than in a classroom. But the institution was transformed on a number of occasions as both the numbers of clerks allotted to each justice and the responsibility delegated to them by their justices increased. In the chapters that follow, we discuss this transformation, addressing the way clerks are selected to serve at the Court, their role in the process of deciding which cases merit review by the justices, the part they play in the drafting of judicial opinions, and their influence in the decision-making process of the justices they serve. In all, we suggest that the collective influence of clerks is increasing.

Previous Literature

In 1957, a young former clerk wrote an article that appeared in *U.S. News and World Report*. The clerk worked for Justice Jackson and charged that the justices were delegating too much authority to clerks. For their part, the author said that the clerks were "unconsciously" placing their own views of the law into their memoranda and draft opinions. The author of this early critique of law clerks was William H. Rehnquist, who returned to the Court as a justice in 1971 and became Chief Justice in 1986.

The Rehnquist article touched off a long-standing debate on the role of law clerks. There have been countless anecdotal studies of clerks, mostly first-person accounts from single clerks recounting the personality of their justice, the important cases of the term, or both. Two of these have been book-length treatments that focused on the politics of judicial decision making and the role clerks play in that process. Bob Woodward and Scott Armstrong's 1979 book *The Brethren* and Edward Lazarus's 1998 book *Closed Chambers* were highly controversial, and each sparked debate over the role of Supreme Court clerks.[23] While these books charged clerks with exercising undue influence on the Court, both have been criticized for their lack of empirical rigor.

There have been only three book-length empirical treatments of the role of clerks.[24] John Bilyeu Oakley and Robert S. Thompson's 1980 book *Law Clerks and the Judicial Process*[25] explored the role of law clerks from the perspective of sixty-three judges of federal courts and appellate courts in California. They found that increases in public funding for judicial staff necessarily determined the rise in law clerk usage by judges. While Oakley and Thompson's work was an important first step in exploring this understudied area, their study was lacking in a number of important ways. Primarily, they failed to systematically address the issue of clerk influence on judicial decision making. Furthermore, our work differs from that of Oakley and Thompson in that we focus exclusively on U.S. Supreme Court law clerks and their role at the Court, though much of what we have to say applies to law clerks generally.

H. W. Perry's excellent study of the certiorari process, *Deciding to Decide: Agenda Setting in the United States Supreme Court*, though not an examination of clerks per se, provided valuable insight into their role at the Court. Perry had unprecedented access to the Court's proceedings and procedures, and conducted interviews with five justices and sixty-four former clerks.[26] In detailing the cert process in general, Perry noted, "The clerks are not Richelieus or Rasputins, but that they play an important role in the cert. process simply cannot be denied."[27] Perry's data on clerks in this process is rich and illuminating. However, what distinguishes our inquiry from his is that we examine their role from an institutional perspective rather than a procedural one. That is, where Perry sought to use clerks to explain how the cert process functioned, we use the cert process to explain the role of clerks.

The recent book by Bradley J. Best, *Law Clerks, Support Personnel, and the Decline of Consensual Norms on the United States Supreme Court, 1935–1995*, argued that the rising influence of law clerks has played an important role in coalition forming and opinion writing.[28] Best's book was important because he highlighted the increasing influence of clerks in the decision-making processes of the justices. But Best's book did not take a comprehensive look at each stage of the judicial process. Focusing on the increase in the number of individual concurring and dissenting opinions issued by justices, he neglected the certiorari process as well as the substantive and stylistic role that clerks play in opinion writing. His book is still an important addition to the overall portrait of clerks at the Court and highlights the need for a more complete account.[29]

This study fills the gap between the numerous anecdotal works that charge clerks with undue influence and the three systematic full-length studies that focused on the perceptions of lower court judges and on specific areas of Supreme Court law clerk influence. Our findings are based upon an empirical analysis of clerk perceptions of their role at every stage of the Supreme Court decision-making process as well as a historical analysis of the development of the law clerk. The following chapters comprise the first complete account of the role and influence of law clerks at the U.S. Supreme Court.

Overview

In chapter 1 we examine the creation of the law clerk and suggest that the origin of this position reflected the legal apprentice/mentor model of legal education that was imported from England, and was not a response to the growing workload of the Court, as is commonly thought. The institution of the law clerk underwent successive transformations as the justices changed the way they did their work and the number of clerks was increased. With each transformation, greater responsibilities were delegated to the clerks, and in turn, their influence grew. Today's clerks bear little resemblance to the early clerks, who began their service over a century ago.

In chapter 2 we discuss clerk selection and find that academic performance at elite law schools as well as prior clerkship experience with top "feeder" judges on the courts of appeals are the two most important selection factors. We also discuss geographical, racial, gender, and ideological considerations. We found that, in general, justices and clerks did share the same ideology, and we suggest that informal cues such as the prospective clerk's recommenders, prior clerkships, and memberships in organizations allow justices to select clerks who are ideologically similar to them. Still, in recent years, as prospective clerks began applying to an increasing number of justices and the number of applicants exploded, clerks have become less ideologically aligned with their justices. In all, we argue that while the institution of the law clerk has undergone important changes, clerkships are still largely the province of white males from elite law schools.

In chapter 3 we discuss the role of clerks in the agenda-setting process. Early on, clerks had little responsibility and influence as caseloads were manageable and the justices discussed every potential case in conference. With the introduction of the "dead list" and increasing numbers of cases no longer being discussed as a group, the justices turned to their clerks for an initial review of the petitions. We describe how the number of cases petitioned to the Court rose dramatically in the 1970s and discuss how the justices responded by pooling their clerks to deal with the increased workload. We analyze the extent to which clerks and justices disagreed on when cases should be granted review and discuss how likely clerks were to change the mind of their justice on a decision to grant or deny hearing of a case. Contrary to conventional wisdom, we suggest that the practice of pooling clerks has diluted their individual influence rather than bolstered it. At the same time, given their formal responsibility in the agenda-setting process, the collective impact of clerks as an institution has never been more important.

Do clerks influence justices in the decision-making process? In chapter 4, we address this question by discussing how the "clerk network" is used in forming coalitions across chambers. We found that clerks play a crucial role in both substantive and strategic negotiations among the justices. To highlight this process, we provide a detailed analysis of the abortion case *Planned Parenthood v. Casey*.[30] We also suggest that clerks have been able to change their justices' minds about particular cases or issues before the Court. While this phenomenon is by no means commonplace, over time clerks have become increasingly successful at persuading justices on cases and issues. We discuss how clerks are most persuasive in deciding which cases merit review, in fashioning the legal and substantive content of opinions, and in influencing the more stylistic aspects of opinion writing. Where clerks have less influence is in changing their justices' minds on the outcomes of cases. When weighed with other factors considered by the justices in making their decisions, clerk influence is ultimately less important than more traditional aspects of judicial decision making such as the justices' jurisprudential philosophy, specific case facts, and precedent.

In chapter 5 we argue that the opinion-writing process can take place in different ways, with justices giving clerks greater or lesser responsibility for the actual writing of the finished product. We also show that the process has changed over time, with justices ceding greater responsibility to clerks in recent years. This evolution was largely caused by the equalization of opinion assignment, which began under Chief Justice Vinson. We discuss how drafts written entirely by clerks are often released as opinions with little or no changes made by justices. We also discuss how practices vary from chamber to chamber, with certain justices ceding greater authority to clerks than others. Ultimately, these findings raise a number of important questions concerning the role that clerks play in this process, and we discuss these in light of what clerks and justices say about the process.

In chapter 6 we analyze our findings and what they mean for the institution of Supreme Court law clerk. Ultimately, we suggest that on the whole law clerks are not the scheming usurpers that some accounts suggest, nor are they merely the agents of the justices. Instead, clerks play a more complex, and increasingly influential, role. Ultimately, their high level of responsibility, coupled with their intimate relationships with the justices, has given rise to the increasing danger that clerks could exploit their positions in order to shape outcomes. Indeed, some of the data included here suggests that in some situations, this may have already happened. As a result, we suggest that the justices, and particularly the clerks themselves, should adopt standards to limit clerk influence and thereby stem this potential for abuse.

Sources

This book is based on a variety of primary and secondary sources. The primary sources include the U.S. Supreme Court's virtually complete list of former clerks, which indicates the term when the clerk served and the clerk's justice, law school, and prior clerkship experience; the papers of various justices available at the Library of Congress and elsewhere; and a mail survey and personal interviews with former clerks. Secondary sources included the numerous judicial biographies written about the members of the Court, the relatively few books and scholarly articles written by and about former law clerks, and newspaper and periodical accounts of clerking at the Court. In all, these sources have allowed us to paint a rich and detailed account of the institutional development of the Supreme Court law clerk from the inception of this position in 1882 to the present day.

For our survey, we compiled a database of over fifteen hundred former Supreme Court law clerks and mailed to a random sample of six hundred of them a self-administered survey instrument, which contained a range of questions, from demographic queries to inquiries about clerk selection, certiorari, opinion writing, and decision making (see appendix G). After two mailings, we achieved a response rate of 28 percent.[31] The respondents ranged from a clerk who worked for Justice Harlan Fisk Stone in the 1930s to clerks who served as recently as the late 1990s. Given the nature of our questions, we were not surprised that many more clerks declined to speak with us than accepted our invitation. Many clerks declined participation because it would violate what they felt was a confidential relationship between clerk and justice. Still, the fact that 160 clerks spanning more than fifty years did participate suggests that quite a few clerks feel that it is appropriate to discuss their first-hand experiences of the Court's inner workings—at least with academics.[32] And while some may criticize us for basing some of our findings on the responses of 160 clerks, we have supplemented this data through personal interviews, archival research, and previously published works, including many by the justices and clerks themselves. Thus, the arguments we present in the following chapters are based on a combination of sources.

Secrecy

The Court prides itself on secrecy, and the clerks are held to a high standard. Since clerks began working at the Court, they have learned both through formal conversations with their justices and through informal Court norms that the Court's internal deliberations are not for public consumption. As soon as clerks arrive, they hear about the legendary "ninety-second rule": any clerk caught talking to a journalist for more than ninety seconds will be fired.[33] For example, after 1984 Blackmun clerk Vicki Been was selected for a clerkship, the *New York Daily News* sought an interview with the former New York University law student. Justice Blackmun wrote, "When this information reached my desk, I called Vicki Been and told her that under no circumstances should she grant an interview. I advised her of the Chief Justice's attitude about law clerks speaking to reporters. She said that this was all brought about by a friend of a friend who was well meaning and that she had turned the interview down."[34]

Clerks are also introduced to the "burn bags," paper sacks where they are told to throw away all drafts, notes, and other discarded documents for regular shredding.[35] For example, in 1993 Chief Justice Rehnquist wrote the other justices,

> About two weeks ago, the Clerk's Office discovered dozens of discarded cert. pool memos in the bins used for recycling cert. petitions and briefs. This was the first time that the Clerk's Office was aware that this happened, although it may have happened before. The Court's recycling program should not be used to dispose of any sensitive material, including cert. pool memos or draft opinions. We have no control over what is done with the recycled material once it leaves the Court, and it is possible that sensitive material could be compromised through the recycling process. "Burn bags" should be used for all material of this sort.

As part of a follow-up to last month's incident with a draft opinion, we will be looking carefully at our procedures for disposing of sensitive material and will be instituting new procedures or circulating additional advice. In the meantime, I believe we need to bring this incident to the attention of our messengers, secretaries, and law clerks and remind them that the recycling bins should not be used for cert. pool memos.[36]

Rumors of leaks have been around since the inception of law clerks, but only one clerk in the institution's history, Ashton F. Embry, who served for nine years as clerk for Justice Joseph McKenna, was fired in 1919 for "leaking" an opinion not yet officially released.[37] Former McReynolds clerk John Knox recalled that midway through his clerkship year, "I was by then so afraid that I might inadvertently blurt out some Court secret, even in conversation with another law clerk, that I thought it best to avoid even looking at the voting result [in the Justice's docket book]."[38]

Concerns over clerks speaking with reporters were present throughout the Burger Court. In 1971, Chief Justice Burger wrote the other justices,

It has come to my attention that a reporter of the Wall Street Journal is seeking to interview Law Clerks on a wide range of subjects regarding the work of Clerks. I have categorically directed that none of my staff have any conversation on any subject with any reporter. This directive was really not necessary since this is a condition of employment. I know of no one who is skilled enough to expose himself to any conversation with a reporter without getting into "forbidden territory." The reporter will inevitably extract information on the internal mechanisms of the Court, one way or another, to our embarrassment.[39]

In 1973, Burger appointed Justices Potter Stewart and William Rehnquist as an ad hoc committee on Court security. He wrote, "Although I assume the internal security of each Chamber is exclusively a matter for each Justice, I for one, would regard it as helpful to have recommendations for improvement."[40] Justice Powell wrote his clerks,

This is *not* an investigative committee intended to detect sources of leaks or to check up on individual Chambers. . . . It appeared from the Conference discussion that we may have been a bit more lax in these

Chambers than in some others. . . . I think I should have a locked cabinet of some kind in my office, in which I can place at night the boxes which contain the circulated opinions and the files on assigned opinions on which we are working. In other words, I do not want any of us to leave draft or circulated opinions open and available to an unauthorized person to pick up.[41]

In 1974, Justice Blackmun wrote Burger, "At the NYU Seminar, Bill Erickson told me of his concern about an oath for a law clerk. He feels they should be required to take an oath. Attached is a copy of what he has worked out. Perhaps it needs a reference to the media."[42]

In 1976, Justice Powell wrote a memo to his clerks about security and confidentiality:

The Conference agreed, several years ago when there was [*sic*] serious breaches of security by unidentified personnel, that each Justice would stress the importance with incoming clerks (as well as other new personnel) of preserving confidentiality with respect to the work of the Court. Although this seems unnecessary, I repeat the self-evident proposition that the rule of confidentiality applies broadly to all action by the Court and to what Justices do or say about Court business (or each other!). Some elements of the media, particularly where pending cases are of large public interest, are persistent, resourceful and sometimes devious in attempting to obtain information as to the outcome of a case, when it will be brought down, how the Justices voted at Conference. For example, a well-known columnist sought last Term, through clerical personnel and even one or more law clerks, to ascertain in advance the Court's decisions in the capital cases. It may be more pertinent to note that the rule of confidentiality applies also with respect to what transpires within our Chambers, where we have no secrets from each other. My files, also, are open to you at all times, although when opinion writing is in process the relevant files should be kept in cabinets at night or otherwise out of sight.[43]

Seven months later, Powell returned to the subject, writing his staff,

In view of recent events, I think it desirable to have a policy in our Chambers that all of us follow scrupulously. If any newspaper or media reporter calls and wishes to talk to you about me or any business of the

Court, I suggest you say that you are: "Not authorized to talk, either on or off the record, about Justice Powell or the Court to any representative of the press." If the person calling wishes to speak with me, say that you will see if I am available to talk. I will then make the decision as to whether or not to speak on the telephone (or in my Chambers) with the press representative. We also should be more careful about leaving our files out of the cabinets at night, and the cabinet that contains the files on pending cases should be locked each night. . . . The last individual to leave the Chambers at night should check to see whether the cabinet containing the files is locked.[44]

It appears that at least some of Powell's clerks got the message. Outgoing 1977 Powell chief administrative clerk, Sam Estreicher, wrote the incoming clerks,

I would like to emphasize the craftiness of the press. If you get calls from members of the "Fourth Estate," it is recommended that you refer the caller to the Press Officer, and say nothing more. Even if the inquiry is innocuous seeming—one local reporter called this year to ask whether the Justice was in town—the safest course is one of courteous noncooperation. You also should be careful not to say anything to friends or relatives about the internal workings or deliberations of the Court; they are likely to be persistent. At the end of the year, [the secretaries] will tell you of the "burn bag" procedure; every copy of a draft opinion or a memorandum prepared during the year will be destroyed.[45]

With the 1979 publication of Woodward and Armstrong's *The Brethren*, the Court revisited the topic of secrecy. The authors provided a behind-the-scenes account of the first seven years of the Burger Court through a review of internal Court documents and interviews with five justices and 170 former clerks. Woodward has revealed that Justice Potter Stewart was his initial primary source and that he also spoke with Justices Powell and Blackmun.[46] But even Powell and Blackmun were concerned about the information apparently revealed by law clerks. Powell wrote his former clerk from the 1977 Term, Jim Alt,

I particularly appreciate your remarks about the Woodward book. You voice my sentiments quite accurately when you express distress that law clerks—and perhaps other personnel here at the Court—have violated the implicit trust of confidentiality that over the years has been observed rather admirably. I cannot imagine any of my clerks having talked, and yet in view of what is said in the book I cannot be sure. This is more than a little troubling to me personally. The two messages which the book strives to convey are that: (i) the Chief Justice is wholly inadequate for his job, and (ii) the Court is so torn by discord and dissension that it cannot function effectively. Both of these messages are wrong. Yet, for purveying this misinformation, the authors no doubt will reap millions. What a degrading way to become rich![47]

Powell wrote the other justices, "There always have been rumors of personal dissention within the Court. . . . I suppose all that is really new (apart from a change in the actors) is that some clerks—I believe only a few—betrayed extensively and imaginatively the confidentiality that has been honored here over the decades."[48] Justice Blackmun noted, "The book, unfortunately, is bound to have an adverse effect, to some degree at least, on the relationships among us and with our law clerks."[49] In response to the book, the justices moved to prevent clerks from leaking documents. Burger wrote his colleagues,

My calendar tells me that this is the time of the year when the Conference agreed that each of us would emphasize to all law clerks that no papers of any kind relating to their work in the Court may be removed from the building. I would add that even though an individual member of the court might elect to make exceptions with reference to his own internal files, that there should be no exceptions with respect to any communication or material received from any other member of the Court. That, of course, would follow on the ancient doctrine that a written communication remains the property of the sender, not the recipient. I will place this on the Conference agenda.[50]

After the publication of *The Brethren*, some former clerks were asked about their involvement with the authors. For example, 1973 clerk John Jeffries said he declined to speak with the authors.[51] George Rutherglen, who served as a Douglas-Stevens clerk in 1975, said, "I told them that they should look at the opinions of the Court if they wanted to confirm or falsify their beliefs, which is apparently the one place they didn't look. . . . [The book] follows the gossip I heard when I was a clerk. So, I'm pretty sure it's fairly inaccurate."[52] Marshall clerk Stephen Saltzburg said of his meeting with Armstrong, "He told me what he had and I told him when I thought something was wrong. I made them double-check some things I thought they had wrong. I noticed some things were corrected in the book. . . . Most of the critics are nitpicking because some dates or legal terms are wrong. It's about as correct as could be gotten by an outsider."[53]

During the 1981 Term, the Court once again focused on security. Powell wrote his outgoing clerks,

> It also is well for incoming clerks to be told about the "security flaps" we have had this Term. There is talk (with which I disagree) of having police officers accompany the cleaning women, not only to keep an eye on them, but—I suppose—to see whether a Justice or clerks have left drafts of opinions exposed. I am told that some Chambers lock up all drafts and files. In my view, this is impractical and unnecessary. But I am now more careful about leaving opinion drafts exposed. The same level of care is not necessary with respect to cert petitions memos or even bench memos.[54]

At their initiation tea each fall, the Chief Justice swears clerks to secrecy. Early in the term, Rehnquist typically writes the clerks, "I request all of you to meet with me in the East Conference Room in order that I may acquaint you with your obligations with respect to security and confidentiality in your present positions."[55] If Rehnquist is unable to be present during orientation, he ensures that one of the other justices makes the speech, as Justice Byron White did at the beginning of one term.

While clerks are expected to follow the Code of Conduct for Federal Judicial Employees, on March 3, 1989, the Court specifically adopted its own written Code of Conduct for Law Clerks, which states,

> The law clerk owes the Justice and the Court complete confidentiality, accuracy, and loyalty. The Justice relies upon the law clerk's research in reaching conclusions on pending cases. The Justice relies on confidentiality in discussing performance of judicial duties, and the Justice must be able to count on complete loyalty.
>
> Separate and apart from the duty owed by each law clerk to the appointing Justice is the duty owed by each law clerk to the Court as a

body. Each law clerk is in a position to receive highly confidential circulations from the chambers of other Justices, and owes a duty of confidentiality with respect to such material similar to the duty owed to the Justice employing the clerk.

The relationship between a Justice and a law clerk is essentially a confidential one. A law clerk should abstain from public comment about a pending or impending proceeding in the Court. A law clerk should never disclose to any person any confidential information received in the course of the law clerk's duties, nor should the law clerk employ such information for personal gain. The law clerk should take particular care that Court documents not available to the public are not taken from the Court building or handled so as to compromise their confidentiality within chambers or the Court building in general.[56]

The controversy surrounding the decision of the Library of Congress to open the papers of Justice Thurgood Marshall upon his death, and only a year and a half after his retirement from the Court, further rankled the justices. Marshall gave the library discretion to make the decision upon his death. Members of the Court were upset that they were not consulted by the library and concerned that their recent internal deliberations were available for public consumption.[57] The Court revisited this issue again in 1993 when Rehnquist wrote his colleagues,

> Recently, the Supreme Court Historical Society received a donation (many boxes) of the papers of a former law clerk to Retired Chief Justice Burger. Several of the boxes were said to contain "papers" from the clerk's tenure at the Supreme Court. Although no one from the Court has gone over to examine these "papers," and hence we do not know exactly what they consist of, the notion of law clerk "papers" is a bit disquieting. In light of the recent events regarding the Thurgood Marshall papers, I wanted to inform you of this development and seek your views at our next Conference.
>
> I have been reminded that during the tenure of former Chief Justice Burger rules were promulgated forbidding law clerks from taking any official papers out of the building. Although we many not choose to impose so Draconian a rule, it might be wise to consider whether we should make some mention of this subject in the Law Clerk Code of Conduct.[58]

After the justices met to discuss Rehnquist's concerns, he wrote the law clerks, "The Conference has decided that law clerks, when they leave the employ of the Court, should not take with them any material which originated in a chambers other than the one in which they work. Retention of materials originating in the chambers for which they work is to be determined by the individual justice."[59]

Clerks were once again the center of controversy with the 2004 publication of an article in *Vanity Fair* detailing the behind-the-scenes decision making that took place during the 2000 election case of *Bush v. Gore*.[60] A number of liberal law clerks who opposed the ruling spoke to the article's authors and are quoted anonymously throughout the piece. In response, nearly one hundred mostly conservative former clerks and lawyers who argue cases before the Court signed a letter that appeared in the *Legal Times* condemning the clerks who spoke out. This resulted in still further articles about whether clerks should divulge what they saw during their clerkships.[61]

It is apparent that throughout the Court's history, justices have been very concerned about what clerks might divulge to outsiders. Indeed, it has only been recent practice for the Court to make public the names of the current clerks, and even now it is still up to each justice to allow this information to be made available. A 1979 memorandum to Justice Blackmun from his secretary noted,

CJ [Burger] does not release the names of clerks because of their delicate work with opinions and possible press harassment. T[hurgood] M[arshall] is reluctant to release names also. J[ohn] P[aul] S[tevens] feels their names are a matter of public record and releases their names as a general rule. Most Justices have no objection concerning past clerks and release those names and schools, etc. (although no current addresses), but feelings differ among chambers concerning current clerks. [Supreme Court Press Officer] Mr. [Barrett] McGurn mentioned some chambers leave this decision to the clerks themselves.[62]

These stories and safeguards have proved generally effective while clerks are at the Court. Clerks do on occasion, however, talk to academic researchers and the press, sometimes anonymously and sometimes not, but almost always after they leave the Court. Clerks have always published first-person accounts of Court processes, cases decided during their tenure, and recollections of the justice they clerked for.[63] This was always done after their clerkships were over. While the bibliography for this book shows that there are many such resources, overall, most clerks have not made their experiences public. In most cases this is probably due to their view of the job, and in particular their working relationship with their justice, as largely confidential. But ultimately, the issue of whether to discuss their experiences or not is a matter for each clerk to decide.

Do clerks inflate their importance? It has been suggested that the transition from U.S. Supreme Court law clerk to private practice may lead clerks to romanticize their time at the Court or inflate their influence. Justice Stevens explained, "You get an inappropriate idea of your importance in the world for a year, and then you're out doing mortgage foreclosures. After you leave, there's a real letdown."[64] After her year clerking for Justice Harry Blackmun, Karen Nelson Moore wrote the justice,

> I was fascinated to read in the New York Times this week the reports of the Conference's decisions concerning the granting of cert. It is a bit strange, however, to read about the decisions rather than to be observing them first-hand as we did last year. It is especially strange for those cases which I worked on last summer at the cert memo stage. As I suspected, it is hard to adjust to being separated from the Court, and I miss the excitement and stimulation of last year.[65]

Similarly, following his term with Justice Powell, 1980 clerk Paul Cane wrote, "I have been following the Court's initial orders (e.g. *U.S. v. Ross*!) with a great deal of interest; yet I also feel somewhat left out. My year with you at the Court was so exciting that I am somewhat apprehensive that the practice of law will be a letdown."[66] Powell responded, "There probably will be some letdown, as a good deal of what one does in the practice of law seems unimportant compared to the work of this Court."[67]

A number of clerks who spoke to us were also concerned about this potential problem. For example, a former clerk to Chief Justice Burger told us, "Law clerks generally flatter themselves about their influence, at least when compared with my experience." Another former clerk told us,

> In my own case, as law clerk to Justice Douglas, I always felt free to express my own opinions. Yet there was never any doubt as to who was

the Justice and who was the law clerk. Justice Douglas's decisions and opinions were always his own, regardless of the magnitude of my assignments. I would respectfully suggest that reports of substantially different experiences you receive, regardless of the Justice involved, should be treated with great skepticism.[68]

We recognize that there is always a danger with survey research that the respondents will fail to be sincere. Furthermore, we take seriously the charge that clerks lack perspective and are generally "full of themselves," as one former clerk put it, because of their prestigious clerking positions. As a result, we offer our survey data with these caveats in mind. But it should be noted that the former clerks we spoke with were guaranteed anonymity and therefore had relatively little to gain personally.[69] Also, we were surprised that our data showed that the clerks largely downplayed their importance. Our survey instrument contained numerous opportunities for clerks to sing their own praises regarding their influence in the cert process, in decision making, or in opinion writing. In every case, clerks were careful to highlight their contributions in the context of other factors. Furthermore, our survey and interview data is supplemented by other primary sources such as judicial papers and previously published first-person accounts, as well as countless secondary materials. But despite these safeguards, we recognize that law clerks still may overstate their influence.

Are the clerk disclosures found in the following chapters a betrayal of the Supreme Court? While there will undoubtedly be some who decry the very existence of this book, it is our position that this research will ultimately serve to strengthen the Court. It is up to the clerks, justices, and ultimately the American people to decide how the Court conducts its business. Toward that end, we feel that research that helps inform the debate over improving the Court's functioning can only be beneficial.

1

Introduction
The Institutionalization of the Supreme Court Law Clerk

I believe that it would greatly facilitate the business of the Supreme Court if each justice was provided by law with a . . . law clerk.
— Attorney General A. H. Garland, 1885

Often [Justice Gray] would ask his [law clerk] to write opinions in . . . cases.
— Samuel Williston, law clerk to Justice Horace Gray, 1888

The law clerk is a vitally important yet poorly understood component of the U.S. Supreme Court. These personal assistants to the justices draft opinions, research questions of law, and play a vital role in the decision to grant certiorari, the process by which the Court sets its agenda. The role of the law clerk in the judicial process has garnered increasing amounts of scholarly attention, from both the legal and the social science communities.[1] Public controversy regarding the proper role of the law clerk at the Court seems to wax and wane according to the appearance of journalistic reports concerning the operations of the Court. Despite the recent accounts, only a few scholarly works have discussed the historical development and context of the law clerk, while the institutional arrangements have been ignored altogether.[2]

In this book we attempt to remedy that deficiency by examining the Supreme Court law clerk from an historical and institutional perspective.[3] Recently, many scholars have shown that institutions, broadly defined, shape and constrain the choices made by political actors and that the institutions in question are in turn altered by those decisions.[4] Stephen Skowronek notes, "Institutions do not simply constrain or channel the actions of self-interested individuals, they prescribe actions, construct motives, and assert legitimacy. That indeed is how institutions perpetuate the objectives or purposes instilled in them at their founding; that is what lies at the heart of their staying power."[5]

With those principles in mind, we examine the historical formation of the institution of law clerk and the institutional framework in which it developed. Specifically, we offer a new explanation for the genesis of the institution, which refutes the standard account. It is often thought that clerks were established as a response to the increasing workload faced by the justices. We suggest, however that the institution of the law clerk is rooted in the apprentice model of legal education. Furthermore, we argue that the institution was also transformed on several occasions. Changes in the way the justices conducted their work, as well as the number of law clerks allotted to the justices, caused one law clerk regime to be replaced by another. While there is some overlap and carryover from one regime to the next, each era of clerks had distinct characteristics that differentiated it in important ways from the previous eras. It is with this historical understanding of the institution that we lay the groundwork for the chapters that follow on clerk selection, the certiorari process, decision making, and opinion writing. Just as the Court has transformed and remade itself, so has the institution of the law clerk. Today's clerks bear little resemblance to the early clerks, who began their service over a century ago.

Table 1.1 shows the institutional development of the Supreme Court law clerk. The *recurrent structures*, such as research assistance and drafting opinions, reflect the most important routinized behaviors of clerks over time. These shared behaviors became more or less dominant at certain points in time because of the *emergent structures* that were imposed on the institution. Specifically, as the law clerk was introduced and the number of clerks allotted to each justice increased, the institution of the law clerk was transformed on each occasion, creating different time periods or "regimes." Each law clerk regime is constituted by an emergent structure, such as the doubling of the number of clerks and the introduction of the dead list, and gives rise to certain recurrent structures, or routinized behaviors, such as opinion writing, that dominate clerk responsibilities in that era.

On three occasions, the numbers of clerks were expanded by congressional statute, largely as a result of the justices delegating increasing amounts of responsibility to their clerks. In 1919, clerks went from per-

TABLE I.I
*Regime Changes and Dominant Structures of Law Clerks in the
U.S. Supreme Court*

Years	Regime	Emergent Structures	Recurrent Structures
1882–1918	Secretaries	Clerks Introduced Funded by Justices	Secretarial Duties Learning the Law
1919–1941	Research Assistants	"Law Clerk" Established Funded by Congress	Research Assistance
1942–1969	Junior Justices	Clerks Doubled in Number Dead Listing Opinion Equalization Clerk Network	Bench Memos Certiorari Memos Opinion Drafting
1970–present	Sorcerers' Apprentices	Third and Fourth Clerks Added Explosion of Clerk Applications Cert Pool Established	Pool Memos Opinion Writing

forming largely secretarial duties, such as taking dictation and typing, to research assistance on cases. Clerks edited opinion drafts, added footnotes, and began reviewing certiorari petitions, still relatively few in number compared to recent years. In all, clerks performed these duties more for an advanced education in the law than because their justice needed the help. In 1942, the clerk was transformed from being primarily a research assistant to being an active decision maker. The number of cases petitioned to the Court exploded and each clerk was responsible for reviewing a larger number of cert petitions than ever before, or since. It was also in this period that bench memos became the norm. In bench memos, which are used in oral argument and in conference, clerks analyzed cases and provided recommendations for their justices. Once again, in 1970, the institution was transformed. Clerks went from largely being decision makers—making recommendations on cert petitions and in bench memos—to being opinion writers. This evolution was caused by the addition of a third clerk (later four) per justice and the creation of the cert pool. Each clerk actually reviewed fewer petitions than in the previous regime, and with more clerks per justice, they devoted more time to opinion writing.

These regime changes in the institution of the law clerk have given rise to a modern law clerk that barely resembles its first incarnation.[6] Modern Supreme Court law clerks receive a formal orientation when they begin their clerkships, receive a "Supreme Court Law Clerk Manual" covering court-wide administrative matters, and are held to their own code of conduct drafted by the justices.[7] The successive transformations that have culminated in the modern law clerk have also led to increased criticisms of the institution. While calls for reform have been persistent, the only changes in the institution in its 120-year history have been to further integrate the clerk into the workings of the institution by ceding the clerk more responsibility. Modern clerks are trusted decision makers who work alongside the nation's highest officials deciding important political and legal matters. In the following section, we show how the Supreme Court law clerk was created and transformed over time.

Creating the Supreme Court Law Clerk

In the 1850s, the justices of the Supreme Court sought approval from Congress to hire "investigating clerks" to aid them in such tasks as copying opinions.[8] But Congress failed to act and some of the justices turned to employees of the Court clerk's office for assistance. The first "law clerk," however, was introduced to the Supreme Court in 1882 upon the appointment of Justice Horace Gray, who was continuing a practice he originated as Chief Justice of the Massachusetts Supreme Court. The young men who served as clerks were referred by Gray's half-brother, Harvard law professor John Chipman Gray, and Justice Gray initially paid their salaries himself. This experiment proved successful, and in 1885, Attorney General A. H. Garland recommended to Congress that the practice of providing clerks to the justices be extended: "I believe that it would greatly facilitate the business of the Supreme Court if each justice was provided by law with a secretary or law clerk, to be a stenographer, to be paid an annual salary sufficient to obtain the requisite qualifications, whose duties shall be to assist in such clerical work as might be assigned to him."[9] Congress met Garland's challenge in the Sundry Civil Act of August 4, 1886, and provided for a "stenographic clerk" for each justice of the Court to be paid a salary of sixteen hundred dollars.[10] After the act's passage, Justices Blatchford, Field, Harlan, and Matthews joined Gray and promptly hired their first clerks. The next year Justice Lamar followed suit, and with Justices Bradley and Miller and Chief Justice Fuller appointing clerks for the 1888 Term, the institution of the clerk was firmly established.

While there appears to be no debate as to the circumstances sur-

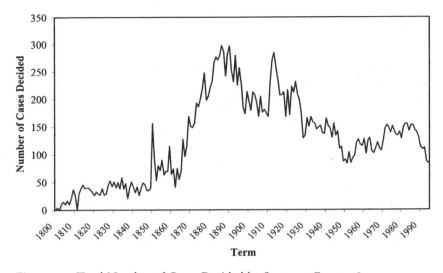

Figure 1.1. Total Number of Cases Decided by Supreme Court: 1800–1994

rounding the introduction of law clerks at the Supreme Court, the answer to the question of why the law clerk was created and why the institution formed as it did is less clear. The standard account is that the development of the law clerk was a response to the increasing workload of the Court. For example, Baier asserts, "From the data it appears the introduction of the law clerk in the early 1880's was no historical accident; rather the clerkship sprang up as the Court's protective response to its burgeoning docket."[11] This explanation is initially appealing in light of the fact that the Court in the 1880s was deciding far more cases than it ever had before or would since.

Figure 1.1 shows that, in 1856, the Court issued signed opinions in just sixty-three cases; in 1886, this number was at an all-time high of 298. Of course, the opinions were substantially shorter in length and contained far fewer citations and footnotes than judicial opinions in the modern era, but it is clear that the workload of the Court was rapidly growing in the late nineteenth century. It seems rational to surmise that the justices were receptive to any form of assistance by way of additional staff.

However, mitigating against the workload theory is the fact that Judge Gray initiated the custom of using a law clerk in 1875 when he was Chief Justice of the Massachusetts Supreme Judicial Court and continued the practice when he was appointed to the United States Supreme Court in 1882. As no firm data appear to exist for the Massachusetts Supreme Court in this period, it is impossible to speculate as to whether Gray began the custom in response to increasing docket pressures in that court. It is possible that the creation of the law clerk was much more of an historical accident than Baier allowed for. Our account of the creation of the law clerk is consistent with previous literature suggesting that institutions are greatly influenced by random processes.[12]

There is no question that the workload thesis helps to explain the *growth* of the institution of the clerk. It largely explains the increase in numbers of clerks provided to the justices and, as we will discuss in chapter 3, the increasing responsibility given to clerks for initially reviewing cases petitioned to the Court. However, the workload explanation is not helpful in explaining the *form* that the institution of the law clerk initially assumed. We argue that the origin of the law clerk reflected the legal apprentice/mentor model of legal education that had been imported from England and was not a response to the growing workload of the Court.

The traditional English model of legal training involved, first, obtaining a general education followed by a lengthy period of time "reading the law" at one of the Inns of Court. Then, a period of further apprenticeship in the office of a barrister ensued.[13] Friedman notes that early American legal training followed the English model, although there was no American equivalent to the Inns of Court.[14] In America, the apprentice model typically required an undergraduate education, although this was not uniformly practiced or required, followed by a substantial period reading the standard legal treatises and commentaries as an apprentice to a practicing attorney. Stevens observes that the formalized apprenticeship varied from state to state, but that Massachusetts was typical in requiring a five-year apprenticeship period, with a one-year reduction if the apprentice possessed a college degree.[15] Although apprenticeships varied considerably among the practitioners who sponsored these young men, it seems clear that the apprentices balanced the formal study of legal treatises with clerical assistance. Stevens notes, "The only way that most articled clerks differed from copying clerks was that the former were expected to comprehend Coke on Littleton with normally only the most marginal of assistance from their masters."[16]

Private law schools did exist. However, they were not schools in the

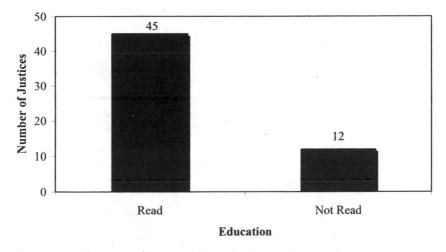

Figure 1.2. Education of Supreme Court Justices: 1789–1898

modern sense but rather training sessions held in the offices of popular practitioners. Gradually, the private law schools began to operate under the umbrella of established colleges, starting around the early 1820s. However, the status of lawyers began to wane in the Jacksonian era, and the movement toward college-connected law schools slowed considerably. Predictably, the requirements for study as an apprentice also eased, as only nine out of thirty-nine jurisdictions required formal apprenticeship periods by 1860.[17] The law school model of legal education was revitalized in 1870 with the appointment of Dean Langdell at Harvard. Langdell revolutionized legal training through the introduction of casebooks and the Socratic method by which he presumed to teach law as a science; the English apprentice model was doomed. By 1890, the number of law schools had grown to sixty-one with over seven thousand students enrolled.[18]

Figure 1.2 presents a graphic illustration of the form of legal education obtained by U.S. Supreme Court justices of the late eighteenth and nineteenth centuries, starting with John Jay, appointed in 1789, and ending with Joseph McKenna, appointed in 1898. Of the fifty-seven justices appointed in the eighteenth and nineteenth centuries, forty-five obtained their legal training by reading the law with a mentor. Of those forty-five, three both read the law and graduated from an early law school, and ten read the law and attended a law school but did not

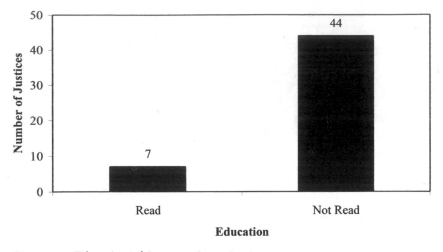

Figure 1.3. Education of Supreme Court Justics: 1902–1994

graduate. Twelve justices did not read the law with a mentor in that period, although eight of those were self-taught. Two justices attended a law school and also taught themselves the law. Thus, in both Figure 1.2 and Figure 1.3, we have included in the category "Read" only those justices who were confirmed to have studied law as an apprentice with a master. In the period 1789–1898, it appears that only Justice Benjamin Curtis, who served on the Court from 1851 to 1857, received his legal education solely through law school, with no self-teaching or apprenticeship involved. Of course, this was later to become the dominant model, but it was unusual for the midnineteenth century.

The apprentice model of legal training was almost completely replaced during the early years of the twentieth century, and the education of the justices reflects this. Figure 1.3 shows that, from 1902 to 1994, only seven justices received their legal education through reading the law with a mentor. Thirty-nine justices graduated from modern law schools, four attended law school but did not graduate, and one justice in this period was self-taught. The last justice to read the law with a mentor was Pierce Butler, who read with J. W. Pinch and John Twohy in Minnesota from 1887 to 1888.

This analysis suggests that the Supreme Court law clerk emerged in 1882, just as the traditional apprentice model of legal education was being supplanted by the law school system. However, there was still a strong tradition of mentor/student training in the legal profession, and the genesis of the law clerk reflected this. Samuel Williston's comments regarding his clerkship with Justice Gray are extremely valuable, for they suggest that Gray conceptualized the law clerk as an apprentice and student, and not as just another member of the clerical staff—although the clerk did in fact perform various clerical duties, just as apprentices did:

> His colleagues generally appointed as their clerks stenographers and typewriters, but Judge Gray continued his practice of securing each year a member of the graduating class from the Law School at Cambridge. . . . Before Saturday morning, therefore, Judge Gray would take up the week's budget of cases with his secretary, whose duty it was to have given them a study requisite for a mastery of the essential facts and of the authorities cited in the briefs. In doing this he would generally make his secretary state the points of the case as best he could before he himself would say much, but before the discussion closed the conclusions of the tyros were severely tested. . . . Often he would ask his secretary to write opinions in these cases, and though the ultimate destiny of such opinions was the waste-paper basket, the chance that some suggestion in them might be approved by the master and adopted by him, was sufficient to incite the secretary to his best endeavor.[19]

It is interesting to note that the originator of the law clerk was also the first justice to graduate from law school *and* read the law as an apprentice. Gray graduated from Harvard Law School in 1849 and then read the law with Judge John Lowell and at the firm of Sohier and Welch.[20] It may be that Gray's dualistic legal training—formal law school education coupled with experience as an apprentice—influenced and colored his use of the law clerk. We suggest that the origin of the clerk was strongly affected by the apprentice model of legal education. Indeed, one of the clerks in this period, Stephen Day, who clerked for Chief Justice Fuller in 1906, passed the bar exam after his clerkship apparently without attending law school or reading the law with another attorney.[21]

Thus, we suggest that it is the apprentice/student model that best explains the creation of the institution and the early role conceptualization of the clerk. The law clerk is a manifestation of the last vestiges of the apprentice model in American law; as such, the clerk occupied a dualistic position—that of student as well as secretary and clerical assistant. However, the role of the clerk would not remain static. Just as the legal profession itself was being reshaped, so was the institution of the clerk. As the model of legal education shifted to the more formalized and institutionalized methods of the law schools, the law clerk also modernized and became institutionalized, although the origins of the clerk apprentice would remain. Indeed, we suggest that justices still view clerks as apprentices in many ways. For example, in his first year on the Supreme Court, Justice Hugo Black met with Harvard Law School dean and former clerk to Justice Louis Brandeis, John M. Landis, to discuss the matter of law clerks. After their meeting, Landis wrote Black about the importance of clerkships for recent graduates:

> I have thought over considerably the subject matter of our conversation. My interest in the matter, as you know, is that of an academician trying to further the training of young men in the law. Apart from the tremendous services rendered individually by such men as Mr. Justice Holmes and Mr. Justice Brandeis, they rendered an abiding service to the law by yearly sending out men into the profession who had had the advantages of association with them. Those secretaryships, as well as the secretaryships with Mr. Justice Stone and Mr. Justice Cardozo, are the greatest fellowships in the law that this country has to offer. It is primarily for this reason that I urge upon you the desirability of following the tradition set by these men. . . . If year by year young men went to the Bar who had had the privilege of association with you, I think that your influence for good would be magnified that many times.[22]

Landis's notion of clerkships as apprenticeships benefiting both justices and young lawyers has been the dominant view of clerks since their inception.

Law Clerks in Historical Context

The Birth of Clerks: 1882–1918

Initially, Congress provided funds for a single stenographer for each justice. As a result, some justices paid for clerks themselves. Using the term "law clerk" when referring to these early assistants is somewhat misleading because they were commonly referred to as "secretaries,"

TABLE 1.2
Law Clerk Tenure on the U.S. Supreme Court

Terms Served	Number of Clerks
9 or more	12
6	8
5	6
4	6
3	13
2	106
1	1,585
	Total = 1,736

SOURCE: U.S. Supreme Court.

and that denomination also largely describes the duties of clerks at that time. These assistants performed primarily clerical and stenographical services for the justices, and they had little authority or autonomy. They typed, took dictation, proofread documents, and also attended to personal matters for the justices, such as paying their bills and even cutting their hair![23] Of course, it must be noted that the use of the early clerks apparently varied considerably by individual justice, and that some clerks did perform legal tasks. Eventually, an informal norm developed on the Court with regard to the tenure of law clerks. The career appointments that were common in the early years of clerks soon gave way to term appointments, with tenure becoming increasingly shorter until virtually every clerk worked on the High Court for a single year. However, in the early years of clerks, it appears that career clerks carried out the legal work.

From 1882, when the practice was started, through 2002, a total of 1,736 people served as U.S. Supreme Court law clerks. Only 151, less than one-tenth of 1 percent, worked at the Court for more than one term. Table 1.2 shows that of the 151, 106 served an additional year, thirteen served for three years, six clerks served for four years, six served for five years, eight clerks served for six years, and the remaining twelve clerks served for nine years or more.

The longest-serving clerks were career clerks from the institution's early years. Table 1.3 shows the longest-serving clerks in the Court's history. At seventeen consecutive terms each, Clarence M. York and Frederick J. Haig top the list. Each clerked for nearly the entire tenure of their justices, Fuller and Brewer, respectively, though York took one year off in the middle of his tenure with the Chief Justice to assist

TABLE 1.3
Longest-Serving U.S. Supreme Court Law Clerks: 1882–2002

Clerks	# Terms Served	Justice(s)	Terms
Clarence M. York	17	Fuller	1889–1895, 1897–1905
		Field	1896
Frederick J. Haig	17	Brewer	1893–1909
Albert J. Schneider	15	Roberts	1930–1944
James Cecil Hooe	14	McKenna	1897–1910
S. Edward Widdifield	12	Peckham	1904–1908
		Lamar	1910–1911
		Clarke	1919–1921
		Sutherland	1922–1923
John E. Hoover	11	Peckham	1904
		Harlan I	1906–1910
		Lamar	1912–1915
Wendell Mischler	10	Taft	1921–1929
		Hughes	1929
Jesse C. Ball	9	Peckham	1895–1903
Ashton F. Embry	9	McKenna	1911–1918
William R. Loney	9	Sanford	1922–1929
		Roberts	1930
John T. McHale	9	Van Devanter	1929–1936
		McReynolds	1937
Irwin B. Linton	6	Field	1889–1894
A. B. Hall	6	Brown	1890–1895
Rufus Day	6	Day	1907–1910, 1917–1918
M. D. Kiefer	6	Van Devanter	1914–1918, 1923
John J. Byrne	6	E. White	1918–1920
		Taft	1921–1923
Robert G. Cogswell	6	McKenna	1919–1923
		Stone	1924
John F. Cotter	6	Butler	1923–1928
Reynolds Robertson	6	Taft	1929
		Hughes	1929–1933
William R. Harr	5	Harlan I	1896, 1898–1901
Gray, Alan E.	5	Sutherland	1924–1928
Arthur J. Mattson	5	Van Devanter	1924–1928
Maurice J. Mahoney	5	McReynolds	1927–1928, 1931–1933
Harry Shulman	5	Brandeis	1929–1933
Eugene Gressman	5	Murphy	1943–1947

NOTE: Table reflects clerks who served five terms or more.
SOURCE: U.S. Supreme Court.

declining Justice Stephen J. Field during his last year at the Court. Albert J. Schneider came to the Court with Justice Owen Roberts from their private law practice in Philadelphia and was essentially the only clerk Roberts had for fifteen years. Schneider's wife was Roberts's secretary during the same time. James Cecil Hooe clerked for Justice Joseph McKenna during his first fourteen years on the bench. In his twelve years clerking at the Court, S. Edward Widdifield served more justices than any other clerk in the institution's history. Between 1904 and 1923 Widdifield spent terms with Justices Peckham, Lamar, Clarke, and Sutherland. An amazing fourteen years after his last term with Justice Sutherland, Widdifield sought to return to the Court. From his Maryland home, he wrote newly appointed Justice Black in 1937,

> I respectfully apply for the position as law clerk and secretary to you as an Associate Justice of the Supreme Court of the United States. I served Mr. Justice Joseph R. Lamar and Mr. Justice John H. Clarke in that capacity, and enclose a letter of endorsement from the latter, who now resides in San Diego, California. I am a stenographer, typewriter and lawyer—a member of the bar of the above Court—and familiar with the duties of the position.[24]

What is plain from Table 1.3 is that over time, even the longest-serving clerks had increasingly shortened tenures. Indeed, since 1947, the last term of Justice Frank Murphy's long-time clerk Eugene Gressman, only one clerk served for three years on the High Court: John W. Nields, who clerked for Justice Byron White from 1974 through the 1976 Term.[25]

Another hallmark of the early clerk is that, before 1935 and the creation of the present Supreme Court building, the clerks typically performed their duties at the private residences of the justices, and some clerks even lived with their justices. Justice Charles Evans Hughes discussed the role of early clerks:

> My secretaries . . . were fine young men who had been admitted to the bar, but as I kept them busy with dictation, hating to write in longhand, they had little or no time to devote to research and whatever was necessary in that line I did myself. Occasionally, the question of providing law clerks in addition to secretaries was raised, but nothing was done. Some suggested that if we had experienced law clerks, it might be thought that they were writing our opinions.[26]

Interestingly, it appears that Justice Gray was also the first to utilize his clerks beyond clerical duties exclusively, presaging the coming era of law clerks when all justices would follow Gray's lead and Congress would formally recognize clerks. Williston's recollections of his clerkship with Gray reveal that a prototype of the modern law clerk existed in Gray's chambers. Gray was the first to request that his clerks draft opinions for cases, although the drafts were only used to stimulate Gray's own writing. Gray also debated his clerks regarding the cases before the Court, and expected the clerks to defend their views. The Gray clerks also read and commented on opinions that were provided by other justices.[27] The use of clerks by Gray foreshadowed the way in which the law clerk later developed. However, it appears from the historical record that all of the justices did not adopt these practices until much later.

It was up to the individual justice to decide how to use his assistants in this early period, and there was often little distinction between law clerks and secretaries. Indeed, at their own expense, a number of justices decided to employ more than one assistant to cover both clerical work and legal research. In 1888, Chief Justice Fuller was the first member of the Court to take on two "clerks," employing both T. H. Fitnam and James S. Harlan. In 1889, Justice John Marshall Harlan I had three assistants: Henry M. Clapp, Blewitt H. Lee, and Edgar R. Rombauer. Even Justice Gray used two clerks, employing two recent Harvard graduates in 1892: Moses Day Kimball and James M. Newell. Others, like Justice Louis Brandeis and Justice Oliver Wendell Holmes, decided to use their assistants as law clerks. Each year, both took a Harvard Law School graduate chosen by Professor Felix Frankfurter. Brandeis's third law clerk, Dean Acheson, said that both Holmes and Brandeis "believed that these young men, fresh from the intellectual stimulation of the law school, brought them constant refreshment and challenge, perhaps more useful in their work than the usual office aides."[28]

Clerks Established: 1919–1940

The year 1919 marks the first transformation of the institution. Specifically, law clerks became differentiated from stenographic clerks and career appointments gave way to term appointments. In 1919, Congress provided for a "stenographic clerk" to be paid two thousand dollars annually, and a "law clerk" to be paid thirty-six hundred dollars per year.[29] With the passage of this legislation, justices routinely employed two assistants—at least one of whom was a law clerk acting largely as a research assistant. With a clear division of labor, the law clerk role of solely doing legal research was firmly established. For example, Dean Acheson, who clerked during the 1919 Term, described the division of labor between himself and Justice Louis Brandeis as a matter of the justice writing the opinion while he wrote the footnotes.[30] Similarly, during the 1925 Term, Brandeis clerk James M. Landis did research for the justice on the case of *Myers v. United States*. Landis immersed himself in Senate publications regarding the Tenure of Office Act, calling his work "as thorough a piece of historical research as you would find in the Supreme Court Reports anywhere."[31]

Holmes's clerks discussed cases with the justice, checked citations, and suggested changes in opinions for the sake of clarity. Working at the justice's house, clerks often had time to themselves to read and study on their own. Holmes once summoned a clerk, who was reading a novel in the next room, to discuss a case. When the clerk suggested the justice consider a particular precedent he had read while at Harvard, Holmes responded, "Do you think you might spare me a moment from your cultivated leisure to look out that citation?"[32] In *Danovitz v. United States*,[33] Holmes wrote, "The decisions under the revenue acts have little weight as against legislation under the afflatus of the Eighteenth Amendment." One of his clerks questioned using the word "afflatus," noting that many people thought he purposely picked obscure words. Holmes replied, "Yes. I felt myself that it was rather a cabriole word" and left it in. When the same clerk objected to what he felt was an unclear paragraph in another opinion Holmes was writing, the justice responded, "What the hell do you mean—not clear! Give it to me. Well, if you don't understand it, there may be some other damn fool who won't. So I would better change it." But on another occasion when a clerk suggested that a certain phrase the justice had included in an opinion would only be understood by one man in one thousand, Holmes answered, "I write for that man."[34]

During this period, clerks began writing memos on the cases petitioned to the Court. Initially, this was part of the clerks' apprenticeship and not an essential function performed for their justice. John Knox, a clerk for Justice James McReynolds in 1936, recalled,

> Only gradually did it dawn upon me that the Justice regarded all of my work on these petitions as little more than a mental exercise to keep me busy and out of mischief. It was undeniably true that a great many petitions were without merit, and even without any of my summaries before him in conference McReynolds could have held his own with the other Justices.[35]

Hugo Black began his service on the Court in 1937 and noted that the norm for law clerk tenure was for career appointments:

> Each of the Justices has a law clerk. It is my understanding that Justice Brandeis and Justice Holmes when he was on the bench, have ordinarily obtained the services of a Harvard graduate each year. Other Justices do not change so often. I have a young man with me who graduated at Harvard and who has been with me since I assumed my duties.[36]

Black's first clerk, Jerome A. Cooper, served for three years. But career appointments soon gave way to term appointments for a number of reasons. First, an informal norm developed that clerkships should last only a single year. Justices were concerned that clerks who remained too long could gain some measure of undue influence and saw limiting the clerkship as an important check on this potential abuse. Also, limiting clerkships to recent law school graduates provided an additional safeguard. When an experienced attorney wrote Black about a possible clerkship in 1944, the justice replied, "It is the custom of the Judges of this Court to appoint Clerks who have only recently come out of law school, and I am certain that no one of the Justices would be willing to take a Clerk who had been engaged in the practice of law for many years."[37]

Today, even those who choose to clerk have little desire to serve more than one or two years. This is largely due to financial and professional reasons. Clerks serve on a lower court before coming to the Supreme Court. With oftentimes heavy student loans to pay back and the virtual guarantee of more prestigious and financially rewarding career choices when they move on, clerks feel a strong pull to make their clerking years relatively few. In 2003, the base salary for law clerks with one year of experience clerking on a lower court was $51,927.[38] Given their background, this is considerably less than the clerks could make in private practice, where salaries for top law school graduates are double what they make as clerks.

The Rise of the Modern Clerk: 1941–1969

The second major transformation occurred in 1941 when the number of clerks was doubled to two per justice. Chief Justice Stone took advantage of the new legislation and immediately added another law clerk as well as another secretary. Justice William O. Douglas also added a second clerk but found that the two had little to do. He reverted back to his practice of using a single clerk the following term. In 1965, Justice Douglas explained, "I tried two one year and discovered they spend about half their time writing memoranda to each other. I work pretty well with only one man. If he is married his wife ends up hating me because she never sees her husband."[39] In 1942, Justice Hugo Black tried using a second clerk but also found that he preferred one and went back to selecting only one clerk the following year. In 1948 Black explained, "At the present time it is not my intention to have a second law clerk for the next term of court. In fact, it would be necessary for the Court to ask for an increased appropriation should I change my mind on this subject. We ask the Appropriations for only enough money to provide clerks for those judges who desire them."[40] One of Black's clerks from the 1940s told us, "Justice Black needed a clerk about as much as I need a third leg. I was useful, but marginal." Justice Wiley B. Rutledge also tried doubling his clerks in both 1942 and 1943. But like Douglas and Black, he too went back to a single clerk in 1944. Except for these experiments by Douglas, Black, and Rutledge, Chief Justice Stone was the only member of the Court to consistently use two clerks per term until Chief Justice Fred Vinson succeeded him in 1946. When Vinson joined the Court, he immediately added a third law clerk, prompting Judge Learned Hand to dub him "Vinson Incorporated." A former clerk thought that "Vinson Limited" was a more appropriate description.[41] Vinson's addition caused most of his colleagues to follow suit and move to two clerks each.

As we discuss in chapter 3, the creation of the "dead list" under Chief Justice Hughes prompted the justices to rely more heavily on their clerks for certiorari memos. Previously, every case petitioned to the Court was discussed in conference, with the Chief Justice summarizing the facts and issues involved. When Hughes started circulating a "dead list" of cases he would not discuss in conference unless one of the other justices requested it, justices who had previously relied on the chief's summaries to familiarize themselves with the cases now turned to their clerks for assistance. The practice expanded under Chief Justices Stone and Vinson as the number of cases placed on the dead list climbed.

Accounts from Chief Justice Vinson's clerks confirm that the duties of clerks had broadened considerably from secretarial work. While some clerks continued to assist their justices with correspondence, the preparation of speeches, and other clerical tasks, they were much more involved in the certiorari process.[42] The clerks were required to prepare brief and informal memoranda regarding the petitions for review, which included the clerk's recommendation as to whether or not to accept the case. The statement of facts was of paramount importance and some clerks felt their recommendations were of little value. A clerk for Vinson said, "We soon learned that our recommendations as such were given little weight by the Chief."[43] But perceptions of influence varied as the review of petitions was handled independently by each justice and his clerks. Memos written by Vinson clerks were only read by Vinson and not circulated to the other justices, as would later be the case.

The exception, however, was the Miscellaneous Docket, which included capital cases in the form of in forma pauperis (IFP) petitions. One clerk described them as "that handwritten garbage" because they often came to the Court scrawled on scraps of paper, usually by prisoners claiming violations of their constitutional rights.[44] Beginning with the chief justiceship of Charles Evans Hughes, these petitions were only screened by the Chief's clerks, who wrote brief memos on each. Initially only Hughes reviewed the memos, but subsequent Chief Justices circulated the memos to all the chambers for review. If the clerk felt the petition had merit, he included it with his memo for circulation, but this happened only rarely.

Felix Frankfurter was "concerned" about "the potential inadequacies and dangers" of the IFP procedure. In a 1954 memorandum, he recounted the history of IFPs and charged that the Court was not considering these cases with the same level of review given to non-IFP petitions: "In few instances was the kind of examination made of these *in forma* records that is made as a matter of course of the cases having printed records and briefs."[45] Frankfurter said that he too was guilty of relying too heavily on these memos and cited one petitioner, in particular, who had filed several different petitions beginning in 1950 only to be denied by the High Court each time. Frankfurter pointed out how the most recent clerk-written memo was incorrect in its interpretation of the prior litigation in the case and its recommendation, "I see no reason to take this case," was probably mistaken. Chief Justice Warren was sensitive to Frankfurter's concerns and instructed his clerks to take extra care with these cases: "Inasmuch as the IFP petitioners generally do not have counsel, it is necessary for you to be their counsel, in a sense."[46]

The petition in *Gideon v. Wainwright* came to the Court in this form and ultimately led to the landmark ruling that indigent defendants have

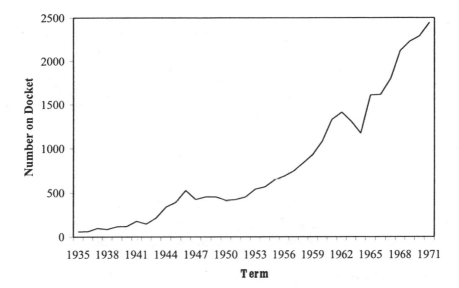

Figure 1.4. Petitions for Certiorari, In Forma Pauperis: 1935–1971

a constitutional right to proper counsel. This unique role performed by the Chief Justice's clerks gave them considerable discretion over the Court's Miscellaneous Docket and continued until the Court abolished the Miscellaneous Docket in 1971 and placed all cases, including IFPs, on a single docket for review by every justice. Indeed, as Figure 1.4 shows, this rule change immediately eased the enormous burden the Chief's clerks were under with the IFPs.

The clerk's role in the certiorari process transformed the institution during this period. As the number of petitions increased, clerk influence grew. Clerks now constituted a Court-within-a-Court as justices relied on them more and more. Growing dockets meant that justices were less able to read the petitions themselves as a check against their clerks. In most cases, the only check in place was that each chambers had at least one clerk reviewing each case for his or her justice. Litigants could rest assured that at least nine different clerks would look at their case. Of course, with IFP petitions, only one clerk in the Chief's chambers would review each case.

F. Aley Allen, who clerked for Justice Stanley Reed in 1946, discussed his role in light of the increasing dockets and the new legislation authorizing two clerks per justice:

> I'm sure that the temptation to use the clerks even more than the justice did in my day, must have grown with the burden of the Court. . . . In my day . . . with the burden just growing [to] the point where they needed a second law clerk, there wasn't quite that same need, if you will. So, my role and my predecessor's role was pretty much confined to writing these memoranda on petitions for certiorari and having long discussions with the justice on legal issues, and going off to the library to research in-depth points of law that he wanted to investigate. I think there was only one time that I ever was given the opportunity to actually write an opinion for the justice.[47]

Another significant innovation in this era was the introduction of bench memos. Justice Harold Burton and several other justices began requiring their clerks to prepare short summaries of the cases that were to be argued before the Court and discussed in conference. These memos outlined the relevant facts and issues of the case, suggested questions to be put forth during oral argument, and, depending on the justice, occasionally made recommendations on the merits of the case.[48] Arthur Rosett, who clerked for retired Justices Harold Burton and Stanley Reed as well as Chief Justice Warren during the 1959 Term, recalled, "Burton always wanted a bench memo, and the Chief, of course, relied heavily on bench memos."[49] A clerk for Justice Clark from the 1960s told us, "Justice Clark was less a user of bench memos than a number of the other justices. But we did them from time to time." In a note to Justice John Marshall Harlan, Justice Felix Frankfurter expressed his concern over the justices who "have mind all made up on basis of law clerk's bench memos, as I see the C.J. reading those bench memos."[50] Writing bench memos became a standard clerk function during this period and continued with nearly every justice into the next era. For example, a Blackmun clerk from the 1970s informed us, "We wrote [bench] memos for the Court before oral arguments and we did that until the very end of the year." The 41-page bench memo prepared by 1971 Blackmun clerk John T. Rich in the case of *Moose Lodge No. 107 v. Irvis* was a typical example of the kind of detail Blackmun expected.[51] One former clerk said that the clerks who "worked by some considerable measure the hardest" were those of Justices Blackmun and O'Connor. The clerk continued, "Both had clerks writing fairly substantial memoranda on each case that was to be argued. I think from early September until May I had one day away from the office."[52] Powell felt that his chambers was so overburdened that he even farmed out some of his bench memo work to staff clerks on the Fourth Circuit Court of Appeals![53]

After reading the bench memos, it was not uncommon for justices to discuss the case orally with their clerks prior to oral argument. Justice Kennedy explained that he likes "to talk through the cases with my clerks" and models his interaction with them at this stage on the "discursive" exchanges between barristers and judges in England, where informal oral argument can last days as the precedents are consulted and discussed.[54] Similarly, one of Justice Blackmun's clerks from the 1970s that we spoke with said, "I can remember him coming out and wanting to ask a question or get at something—an added view on something."

As with bench memos, clerks were sometimes directed to write lengthy memoranda on particular areas of the law. In 1954, Justice Frankfurter asked his clerk Alexander Bickel to write a memo on segregation. Bickel, who went on to become a highly respected and widely published law professor, produced a 91-page analysis of the issue.[55] Justice Robert Jackson asked his clerk, William H. Rehnquist, for a memo on the same topic. At the end of his analysis, entitled "A Random Thought on the Segregation Cases," Rehnquist concluded, "I realize that it is an unpopular and unhamanitarian position, but I think *Plessy v. Ferguson* was right and should be reaffirmed."[56]

Having been granted considerable influence in the cert process and with bench memos, clerks were treated with a new level of respect by their justices. For example, Bickel commented on the level of equality Frankfurter cultivated with his clerks: "This striking egalitarianism—that was meant quite seriously. . . . There was no hierarchy in this business. You were as good as he was, depending on what you had to say." Frankfurter said of his clerks,

> They are, as it were, my junior partners—junior only in years. In the realm of the mind there is no hierarchy. I take them fully into my confidence so that the relation is free and easy. However, I am, they will tell you, a very exacting task-master; no nonsense, intellectually speaking, is tolerated, no short-cuts, no deference to position is permitted, no yessing, however much some of them in the beginning be awed.[57]

Clerks were expected to debate Frankfurter. Andrew Kaufman, Frankfurter's clerk for both the 1956 and 1957 Terms, said, "I didn't feel the

slightest compunction that I was on forbidden ground." Another Frankfurter clerk added, "We regarded it as part of our job when we disagreed with him."[58] Similarly, Charles Nesson, who clerked for Justice
John Marshall Harlan, II, in 1964, said, "I can remember spending
hours in his office, arguing back and forth. . . . He would state his tentative conclusion and offer the framework of his analysis, then open
each problem for response and discussion."[59]

The stature of clerks had never been higher. As they demonstrated
high levels of competence in the cert process and in drafting bench
memos, justices felt more comfortable allowing their clerks to draft
opinions, sometimes rarely or occasionally as with Justices Black and
Douglas, and sometimes regularly as was the case with Chief Justice
Vinson and Justices Frankfurter, Murphy, and Burton. Burton codified
his expectations in a memorandum to his clerks in which he explained
that he wanted them "to feel a keen personal interest in our joint product" and expected "the most complete possible exchange of views and
the utmost freedom of expression of opinion on all matters to the end
that the best possible product may result."[60]

Beginning with Fred Vinson's chief justiceship and becoming fully real-
ized under Earl Warren, the opinion-writing process changed dramatically, and with it the role of clerks. Douglas recalled the transformation:

> Hughes had a custom of never assigning an opinion to a man who al-
> ready had an opinion that was unwritten. He made his assignments to
> those who had nothing to do. As a result, those who turned out work
> like Stone and Black and myself . . . each of us got more than a ninth of
> the load. And I think Stone continued that practice and I think Vinson
> did. . . . When Earl Warren came on as Chief Justice he instituted a
> different system. He decided that every member of the Court should
> pull the same size oar and row as hard as anybody else. And so he has
> roughly allotted the opinions one-ninth to each judge and he has tried
> to level it out so if a judge gets a big, complicated case the next time
> around he gets a simple case. He's tried to even out the workload.[61]

This new method of assigning opinions was followed by subsequent
Chief Justices and had an important long-term effect on the Court. Justices who were accustomed to writing very few opinions each term under
Chief Justices Taft and Hughes, and in the early years of Vinson's tenure, were suddenly expected to greatly increase their opinion output, and

they turned to their clerks for help. Clerks for justices who wrote their own opinions at a relatively quick pace, like Black and Douglas, were unaffected while clerks for more methodical writers like Frankfurter and Reed found themselves writing virtually all of their justice's opinions.[62]

During this time clerks also took on a crucial role in coalition formation. Clerks were expected to comment on the memoranda and opinions from the other chambers. Justice Powell told his clerks,

> Each of you has been most helpful in giving me memoranda analyzing and making recommendations with respect to opinions circulated by other chambers. This is important work, as it will be impossible for me personally to review each of these opinions with the meticulous care which they merit before I decide finally whether to join, concur or dissent. While you may be reasonably sure that I will not agree with your recommendations in all instances, I promise to consider them carefully and respectfully.[63]

As we detail in chapter 4, the "clerk network" developed when the Court moved to its own building and clerks saw each other on a daily basis. Clerks became an important resource to their justices in obtaining information about the positions of their colleagues. Clerks became informal ambassadors in negotiations across chambers. For example, the memo from 1977 clerk Bob Comfort to Justice Powell regarding "Possible Common Ground with Justice Brennan in *Bakke*" illustrates this phenomenon:

> I explored this issue informally with [Brennan clerk] Dave Carpenter today. After our conversation, I was pessimistic about the possibility that Justice Brennan would join substantial portions of an opinion you authored. I should make it clear, however, that Dave has not sounded Justice Brennan out on this issue for some time. Also, I get the impression that Dave may be less flexible in his approach to making up a Court opinion than Justice Brennan himself might be. If anything breaks in their Chambers, Dave will let us know.
>
> As to specific issues separating your position from Justice Brennan's, Dave was convinced that our differences were over "small points." I was not so convinced, primarily because Dave's view seemed to be not so much that the points themselves were small, but that our positions on them were not seriously defensible. First, Dave believes that Justice

Brennan will maintain his proposition that stigmatizing and non-stigmatizing discrimination can be differentiated and should be treated differently in terms of judicial review. This does not seem to be a small point to me, since much of our memo is directed to the idea that, in cases such as this, it is too difficult for a court to attempt to sort out who is stigmatized and who is not. This is the thrust of Justice Douglas's *DeFunis* dissent, from which we quote at length. If this classification is non-stigmatizing, and if such classifications do not trigger "strict" scrutiny, then our entire memo evaporates.

Second, Dave believes that Justice Brennan will refuse to agree that under the facts of this case, the only compelling state interest advanced by the University was integration of the student body, i.e., diversity. According to Dave, Justice Brennan believes that correcting "societal discrimination" is a compelling state interest, and one that the University plausibly could serve without guidance from the legislature or other state entities. I suggested that our memo left open the possibility that if the legislature or some other body charged with remedying the effects of some broad-based notion of discrimination investigated the problem and made a judgment based on some relevant evidence, this might be considered a compelling state justification. Dave refused to concede that there was any federal interest in preventing the states from delegating decision-making authority in any way it sees fit. This, despite my assertion that such a principle underlay *City of Lafayette*! Dave dismissed that as a "statutory" case, for whatever relevance that has. Again, this point seems to be a linchpin of our memo, because if you accept the idea that the University is in a position to redress the wrongs perpetrated by society at large on blacks as an undifferentiated group, then once more our less restrictive alternative analysis melts away.

Third, Dave thinks that Justice Brennan could agree to apply less restrictive alternative analysis to this case, though he would disagree that our "case-by-case consideration" alternative actually is less restrictive. I think that is the weakest chink in our armor, but I do not understand why, given Justice Brennan's purported positions on the previous two issues, he even has to reach a less less-restrictive-alternative inquiry. In any event, since he would conclude that the existing Davis plan is the least restrictive alternative, it is not clear what it would mean to join a section of your opinion applying such analysis.

Dave says that it is Justice Brennan's belief that you will be assigned the opinion announcing the judgment of the Court, assuming that Justice Blackmun ends up somewhere on our side of the fence. This belief is based on the fact that yours would be the narrowest ground for reversal, and it would be reversal only in part. Because of that fact, Justice Brennan concludes that it would be your opinion to which courts and schools would look for guidance, since you would state the actual judgment and *ratio*. For that reason, says Dave, Justice Brennan is eager to join as much of your opinion as he can. Yet Dave gave little indication that his boss could join anything of significance in our memo as it now stands.[64]

Modern Clerks: 1970–Present

In 1970, Congress once again increased the number of clerks to three and then to four in 1974, and the justices immediately took advantage of the allotment. The cert pool was created in 1972 and once again the institution of the law clerk was transformed. Up to this point, each chambers was responsible for separately reviewing each case petitioned to the Court. The two or three clerks in each chambers divided the petitions among them so that each justice had a memo on each case written by one of his own clerks. In order to reduce the growing workload caused by the increasing number of cases filed, Justice Lewis F. Powell, Jr., suggested the Court pool its clerks to reduce the duplication of effort by the clerks in each justice's chambers. A number of justices agreed to participate in the "cert pool" and over time, an increasing number of new justices joined. The idea was a simple one. Rather than have nine clerk-written memos on each case, the pool of clerks would divide up all the petitions and produce only one memo on each case for all the justices who chose to participate. After the retirement of Justice Thurgood Marshall in 1991, only Justice Stevens remained outside the pool, choosing to have his clerks review all the cert petitions themselves, as was the practice before the creation of the cert pool. One reason Stevens decided to remain outside the pool was to provide a check against what he saw as a dangerous practice that ceded too much authority to a single clerk.

The creation of the cert pool, the addition of a third and fourth clerk, and the creation of the Legal Office in 1973, which is staffed with semi-permanent lawyers who assist the justices and clerks with the cert pool, have considerably lightened the workload of each clerk.[65] Except for the clerks who worked for justices not participating in the pool, most clerks had more time to devote to other tasks—principally opinion writing. In the years since Earl Warren began equally assigning opinions, it became increasingly common for justices to delegate opinion writing to clerks, and an institutional norm developed. After the cert pool was created and expanded, the number of separate concurring and dissenting opinions issued by the justices exploded. We argue that this was largely caused by the combination of the norm of clerk-written opinions that developed under Warren and the fact that modern clerks are spending less time on cert petitions than clerks from the previous era. As we will show in chapter 3, because of the cert pool, each clerk reviews fewer petitions than his or her counterpart did thirty years ago, leaving clerks more time to devote to other tasks—namely, opinion writing.

The most prominent and certainly most controversial task that the modern law clerk performs is the drafting of judicial opinions, and correspondingly, participating in the decision-making process. The degree to which the nonappointed and nonelected law clerks influence the final output of the Court has been the subject of periodic and intense debate.[66] Whatever the merits of judicial delegation of opinion drafting to law clerks, it is clear that this is a crucial feature of the modern law clerk. Oakley states that "the drafting of opinions by law clerks is prevalent, and increasingly so, to the point where it is seen as something of a quaint idiosyncrasy when a judge attempts to draft his or her own opinions."[67] As we will show in the chapter on opinion writing, it was during this modern era of the law clerk that it became routine practice for justices to delegate the drafting of opinions to their clerks. This was a marked change from previous eras when justices wrote first drafts and clerks added footnotes and citations, edited, and suggested small changes. We suggest that the modern law clerk is directly responsible not only for the dramatic increase in separate concurring and dissenting opinions now issued by the Court but also for the increased length and detail of the opinions. Indeed, in one instance when Chief Justice Burger's concerns were met by the writer of the majority opinion, he still issued the concurrence written by one of his law clerks because to withdraw it "would break [the] law clerk's heart."[68]

In sharp contrast to the institution's early years, in nearly every case modern law clerks only spend one year at the Court. There are exceptions, however, such as Margo J. Schlanger, who clerked for Justice Ginsburg during her first two years on the Court. Table 1.4 lists the Rehnquist Court clerks who served for two terms. The reasons for clerks serving two terms vary. One reason is continuity. The senior or

TABLE I.4
Two-Term Rehnquist Court Clerks: 1986–2002

Clerks	Terms Served	Justice(s)	Terms
Troy A. McKenzie	2	Stevens	2001–2002
Deanne E. Maynard	2	Powell	1993
		Breyer	1994
Margo J. Schlanger	2	Ginsburg	1993–1994
Pamela A. Harris	2	Stevens	1992–1993
Julius Genachowski	2	Brennan	1992
		Souter	1993
Henk J. Brands	2	Souter	1991
		Breyer	1994
Jeffrey F. Pryce	2	White	1991–1992
Peter J. Rubin	2	Souter	1991–1992
Hugh W. Baxter	2	Brennan	1991
		Ginsburg	1993
Christopher Landau	2	Scalia	1990
		Thomas	1991
Gregory E. Maggs	2	Kennedy	1989
		Thomas	1991
R. Hewitt Pate III	2	Powell	1988
		Kennedy	1989
Richard A. Cordray	2	White	1987
		Kennedy	1988
Ronald A. Klain	2	White	1987–1988
Randolph D. Moss	2	Stevens	1987–1988
Abner S. Greene	2	Stevens	1987–1988
Paul T. Capuccio	2	Scalia	1987
		Kennedy	1988
Harry P. Litman	2	Marshall	1987
		Kennedy	1988
Peter D. Keisler	2	Kennedy	1987–1988
Miguel A. Estrada	2	Kennedy	1987–1988
Flanagan, Timothy	2	Burger	1986–1987

SOURCE: U.S. Supreme Court.

"chief" clerk is able to ease the transition from old clerks to new by providing experience and guidance to new clerks. In 1955, Chief Justice Warren wrote, "If possible, I would like to have one of my present three clerks remain another year as head law clerk if it fits in with their plans."[69] When the justices moved from three to four clerks per chambers, Justice Lewis Powell wrote,

> As I indicated to the Conference when we were discussing our needs, I consider the "fourth clerk" an experiment just as you and Byron do with respect to your "experienced" clerk. I have no doubt as to the desirability of greater depth of professional assistance. My only uncertainty,

so far as my chambers are concerned, is whether this is more likely to be achieved successfully by retaining an "experienced" clerk, by a fourth clerk for the customary one year term, or perhaps by some "staff clerk" concept such as that now widely employed among the Courts of Appeals.[70]

A second reason is promotion, where a clerk may move up from clerking for a retired justice to clerking for an active one. This was the case with Deanne E. Maynard, who went from clerking for retired Justice Lewis Powell in 1993 to clerking for Justice Breyer the following term. The reverse can also be true: a clerk may switch from working for an active justice to working for one who is retired. This was the case for Dennis J. Hutchinson, who clerked for Justice White in 1975 and then for retired Justice William O. Douglas the following term. Clerks may also serve an additional year if their justice begins in the middle of a term. This was the case for Justice Anthony Kennedy's first clerks, as he did not gain Senate confirmation until February 3, 1988. The final reason clerks may serve two years is personal. A clerk may stay on simply because of the personal rapport between him- or herself and the justice. Indeed, justices often speak of clerks as part of their extended family. Justice O'Connor remarked, "You feel close to them for a lifetime."[71] It is also interesting to note that except for McKenzie, no clerk has served for two years since the early 1990s, further proof that this practice has all but disappeared.

Role Perception in Historical Context

As we will show in the following chapters, these historical transformations of the institution of the law clerk had important effects on the Court. At the same time, these changes also altered the way law clerks viewed their role in the larger institution. For example, it is often thought that having new clerks arrive at the Court each year would provide the justices with a fresh perspective. Robert von Mehren, former clerk to Judge Learned Hand and Justice Stanley Reed, remarked on this perception:

[Clerks] bring a continual infusion of the latest thinking of the law schools to the bench and bring the enthusiasm and the new perspectives of younger people to judges who, in many ways, are quite isolated from what's maybe going on at the universities, etc. So, I think it's a uniquely valuable function in that regard, and I think you lose a part of the importance of the function if you keep a law clerk certainly any more than two years. There are some judges who like to keep them for two years because it's a little bit easier. In a certain sense, part of the first year is a learning process for the clerk. But from the point of view of personal experience, I view my own two clerkships as really the ideal sort of situation: two very exciting years in two different courts with two very different judges. And if I were a judge, for example, I think I would opt for the one-year system.[72]

Similarly, Justice Louis Brandeis justified having to train a new clerk each year: "It's good for me. It keeps me from getting lazy."[73] How have clerks from different eras conceptualized their role? Figure 1.5 shows that where at one time clerks saw their role as that of bringing a fresh perspective to the Court, this is no longer the case. For example, a Douglas clerk from the 1960s told us that he "sometimes" saw this as

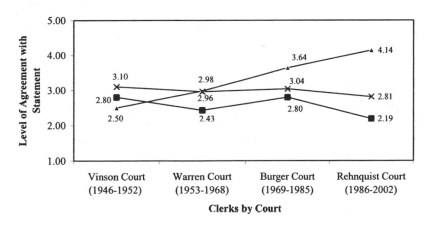

Figure 1.5. General Role Perception of Supreme Court Law Clerks

his role. A Burger clerk from the 1970s said, "Get serious!" A Rehnquist clerk from the 1990s said, "Most of the 'current intellectual and legal ideas' to which we are exposed at law school are nonsense that have no bearing on what statutes or a constitution written more than 200 years ago mean."

Similarly, we wondered whether clerks saw their role as that of playing devil's advocate (providing opposing viewpoints) to their justice. In 1972, Justice Lewis F. Powell remarked, "the law clerks perform an indispensable role—not only in assisting Justices with various duties but in providing stimulation, challenge and testing of ideas and positions."[74] Powell made a similar remark in discussing a prospective clerk with a recommender: "Obviously I want someone of an independent mind who will test, as well as stimulate, my own thinking."[75] Powell wrote his clerks at the start of each term,

> I respect, and desire to know, the views of my clerks. These are routinely given, at least in capsule form, with respect to cert petitions in the memoranda circulated by the pool. I particularly value your views on the argued cases. Most of these present close and difficult issues as to which the ablest lawyers and judges may well differ. I do not want my clerks to be "result oriented" any more than I would wish myself to be (although I recognize that a certain measure of this is inevitable in all of us). It is most helpful, therefore, to have a clerk—in the bench memo or in verbal discussion—present the best view that can be taken to each side of a case. In the end, of course, I have to cast a vote and often support it in a written opinion. When my decision is made, our common talk is to implement it in the most effective and lawyer-like way. But until I have "come to rest" my office, and my attentive ear, is open to each of you.[76]

Clerks generally did not feel that providing opposing viewpoints was their role, modern clerks even less so than their predecessors. For example, a Minton clerk from the 1950s said, "I certainly didn't think of myself as a devil's advocate. I thought of myself as basically doing something very interesting. It was advisory, or clerk-like, not making any decisions." A Warren clerk from the 1950s told us,

> We did some of that. But in those sessions after the Chief had finished up with the clerk of the Court and he was just talking to us about what

had gone on during the week, we weren't just sitting there saying "yeah," it was a fairly wide discussion about interesting cases. Each of us had ideas about things and felt free to express them but we knew we were not influencing the Chief Justice. This guy did not get to become Chief Justice by being easily influenced by kids.

A Douglas clerk from the 1960s said, "That was not a role WOD wanted his clerks to play. I would have done so otherwise." A Rehnquist clerk from the 1970s did not feel that this was his role. Instead, he felt he was expected "to act as a lawyer-adviser."

As H. W. Perry found in his interviews with clerks, many were uncomfortable with the characterization "devil's advocate." Still, they did say that they often felt free to express their own views. A Stewart clerk from the 1970s told us,

> In the discussion before the decision, people could say their own views but it wasn't necessarily playing devil's advocate. It wasn't taking the other side to see what his answer would be. But rather saying, "this seems like this brief made a good point. This is good reasoning here. You should go this way," and he'd agree, but not always, if it was not to his own view.

Similarly, a Rehnquist clerk from the 1990s told us, "My role was to offer my view as to the correct legal view, identifying counterarguments to and/or weaknesses with that view." However, 1982 O'Connor clerk Gary Francione said, "I won't say she was the easiest person to work for, because she is extraordinarily demanding. We disagreed on a number of issues, but there was always a clear understanding that she expected us to challenge her. She was concerned that the opinion be intellectually defensible."[77]

Instead of bringing new ideas to the Court, or playing devil's advocate, modern clerks were more likely than their predecessors to act as surrogates or agents for their justice in the myriad activities they perform, from certiorari recommendations to opinion writing.[78] For example, a Black clerk from the 1940s told us that he thought of his role this way when he wrote "second drafts" for the justice. A recent study of the memos Rehnquist wrote for Justice Jackson during Rehnquist's year as a law clerk provided "no evidence that Rehnquist used his cert or appeals memos to further his conservative goals, and only occasionally did he employ his bench memos for this purpose."[79] Instead, he largely acted as Jackson's surrogate, tending to "anticipate the views" of Jackson when writing memos.[80] A Clark clerk from the 1960s told us, "My basic role was to do the research the justice requested." Justice Powell routinely wrote his incoming clerks, "You are perhaps generally familiar with many of my decisions. You should be thoroughly familiar at least with the major ones by the time you 'join up.'"[81] As a result of his instructions, Powell's clerks knew that he was often searching for moderate position in tough cases. For example, in Bob Comfort's 71-page bench memo on *Bakke*, he begins by saying that it is an attempt "to map out a middle ground which will avoid the dire consequences each side predicts if it should lose."[82] But a Rehnquist clerk from the 1970s said that acting as a surrogate was not the role Rehnquist wanted his clerks to play: "We were encouraged to say what we thought."

As the following chapters demonstrate, in each area of clerk responsibility the distinction between devil's advocate and surrogate depends on the circumstances involved. A Clark clerk from the 1950s explained, "Depending on the case, depending on the particular justice, depending on the particular clerk, depending on the relationship between the justice and the clerk and any given clerk and any given term, depending on the relationship between the clerks and the justices, there are all sorts of variables."

We suggest that the addition of a third and fourth clerk per chamber had a chilling effect on the extent to which clerks felt they could introduce new ideas and generally express a different position to their justice. A Blackmun clerk from the 1970s commented on the changing dynamics caused by more clerks: "The experience isn't as close when they had only one clerk or two clerks. I suspect that was a substantially closer relationship. Three is starting to be up there and with four clerks I think is it easy to be the one who hasn't got a very close relationship. So there are costs to continuing to expand the clerkship pool." As clerks have taken on greater amounts of responsibility, they have also increasingly seen themselves as surrogates for their justice.

Overview

In the following chapters, we explore clerk selection, the certiorari process, decision making, and opinion writing in the context of the historical development of the Supreme Court law clerk. While justices wield formal power to decide important legal and political issues, the role of clerks in this process has been largely invisible to public scrutiny. Do clerks make decisions, or are they simply research assistants that carry out the instructions of the decision makers—the justices? In the following chapters, we answer this important question and argue that clerks do make decisions about cases that are often unseen by those outside of their justice's chambers. Should clerks have this power? Are the American people best served by a Supreme Court where clerks are given important decision-making responsibilities on key issues of public concern?

Ultimately, we suggest that the institution of law clerk, once created as part of the now-outdated apprentice model of legal education, has been transformed into a key part of the Court's inner workings. Law clerks have taken on many of the functions that were only performed by federal judges for over a century, until clerks were introduced in 1882. Because of this development, there exists a very real danger of clerks using their positions to influence judicial decision making. We contend that both justices and the clerks themselves could adopt standards to limit the clerks' role, and the potential for abuse, particularly in the area of opinion writing.

2

A Great Ordeal
Selecting Supreme Court Law Clerks

> As I am sure is the case with every law school in the country, we are exceedingly anxious to place our best graduates as law clerks to the Justices of the Court.
> —Dean Edward H. Levi, University of Chicago Law School

> I wouldn't hesitate to hire anyone who I believed had the requisite capabilities. But it is harder to assess that package on cold paper than it is to take the top five or 10 people from Harvard or four or five other top law schools. I'd be delighted if someone in that group turned out to be a black woman or a black male.
> —Judge J. Michael Luttig, U.S. Court of Appeals
> for the Fourth Circuit

Initially Supreme Court clerkships were the province of young white males who graduated at the top of their class from the nation's top law school. Certainly this described the Court's first clerks, who began the institution in 1882. But how well does it describe more recent clerks who joined the Court over a century later? In some ways, the faces of clerks have changed considerably while in many other ways today's clerk could easily be yesterday's. In recent years the selection of U.S. Supreme Court law clerks has garnered much attention. The focus of this attention was on the racial and gender composition of the clerks.[1] While diversity among Supreme Court law clerks is an important issue, our focus is on the selection process in all its aspects.

In this chapter we explore the backgrounds of and selection criteria for Supreme Court law clerks. We discuss the path they take to gain a clerkship, including law school and prior clerking experience, and how this path has changed over time. We also discuss other factors that the justices consider in selecting their clerks, such as geography, gender, race, and personal compatibility. Our survey results suggest that there is a remarkable ideological congruence between justices and clerks. What ultimately emerges is a portrait of Supreme Court law clerks as a relatively homogeneous legal elite who matriculate at top law schools, secure prestigious clerkships with prominent judges and justices, and embark on careers of power and reward. Indeed, Justice Sandra Day O'Connor commented, "We have a luxury of riches when it comes to applicants."[2] For the most part, this group is a small club composed of recurring players. And while the group has been transformed in some ways, it is still largely the elite enclave of privileged associations that it has been since its inception. We conclude with a discussion of the implications of having a selection process and a clerking corps that largely resembles its earlier incarnations.

The Path to a Supreme Court Clerkship

The road to becoming a clerk begins early in a lawyer's career. Being admitted to the right law school, usually Harvard or Yale, is the first hurdle. End-of-first-year grades and making law review are the next steps, as applications for clerkships at the U.S. courts of appeals are sent out in the second year. Justice Harry Blackmun wrote a prospective clerk, "In the final selection process grades are very important, as is law review work."[3] Justice Powell remarked of an applicant, "I had been disinclined to interview him because he did not serve as an officer of the Stanford Law Review."[4] Justice O'Connor said, "It takes considerable time to look [the applications] over with extreme care. I look at the courses they have taken, their grades, the honors achieved."[5] Steve Smith, a clerk for Justice Clarence Thomas during the 1991 Term, explained, "It's not enough to be from Harvard. You have to be on law review, too. There's a good old-boy network at work. It's hard for other schools, like Howard University, to get into the loop."[6]

In the third and final year of law school, with acceptances from the courts of appeals judges, students apply for and are hired by Supreme Court justices for clerkships that are a year and a half to two years away.[7] Letters of application vary, but most contain brief descriptions of qualifications and any personal association the applicant may have with the justice or someone the justice might know. Many are short—only one or two paragraphs—and most are less than a page long (for example, see appendix B). A typical letter begins, "I am a third-year Stanford law student who will be graduating in June and clerking for Judge Abner Mikva of the D.C. Circuit Court of Appeals beginning in early July. I am offering to you my law school record, recommendations, and writing samples, in hope that I might have the honor of clerking for you next year."[8] Some applicants flatter the justice by praising certain opinions, law review articles, or speeches the justice has authored. One applicant wrote Justice Douglas, "My wife and I named one of Per Stirpes' kittens after you. Since we didn't like the name Douglas for a cat, we named her Orville. P.S. I'd like to be your clerk next year."[9]

With the applications sent, prospective clerks speculate on their competition and nervously await responses from the justices. The number of applications the justices received from prospective clerks and their recommenders was generally manageable from the institution's inception through the Warren Court. In the early years, the application process was haphazard and idiosyncratic, as is evidenced by a number of applications that arrived each year after the justices made their selections. For example, a typical late-arriving letter came to Justice Black at the end of June and he customarily wrote back, "My clerk was appointed some months ago and it is now too late to give consideration to any other applications."[10] Often it was the justice who actively sought a clerk through contacts with friends, colleagues, law professors, and judges. Black selected his clerk for the 1948 Term on the basis of a detailed three-page letter sent to him by Yale Law School Dean Wesley A. Sturges. Dean Sturges highlighted the qualifications of three candidates, but stated, "We all appreciate that you may prefer a boy from your home State of Alabama, and I am placing an Alabama boy before you for first consideration. His name is Truman McGill Hobbs."[11] Black immediately wrote back, "While ordinarily I do not select my clerk until a much later period than this, I see no reason to delay decision further this year. If Truman Hobbs desires to be my clerk, I should be glad to have him. Were he not from Alabama, I confess that my selection would be a far more difficult one."[12]

What is perhaps most surprising, however, is that each justice received very few applications and had very few applicants recommended to them during this period. For example, Justice Hugo Black's application files contain only a handful of letters from applicants and recommenders for each year he was on the bench through the 1940s. In the

1950s, the number of applications began increasing. For example, for the 1958 Term, Black received twenty-nine applications for two spots.[13] For the 1960 Term, Justice John Marshall Harlan received twenty-eight applications for his two clerkships. The Chief Justice often received more applications than his colleagues, which is understandable considering that the Chief generally employed more clerks than any other justice. For example, for the 1956 Term, Chief Justice Warren received forty-three applications for three spots.[14] Over a decade later, Warren was receiving more than twice as many. For the 1967 Term, Warren sent formal rejection letters to forty-eight applicants, but his screening committees of former clerks considered dozens more.[15] For the 1964 Term, Justice Black considered thirty-six applicants for two spots.[16] Four years later, Black received sixty applications for his two clerkships.[17] Black always took pride in corresponding with each applicant personally. But as the number of applications doubled, and tripled, he could not meet the demand. In 1968 he wrote, "so many applications have come to me this year that I have reluctantly been driven to writing a form letter in reply . . . the job of selecting clerks is probably my most difficult one, simply because I have to turn down so many well qualified people."[18] Justice Harlan received fifty applications for the 1970 Term.[19] In 1971, Justice Douglas selected two clerks out of what he reported were "30 odd applications" screened by his committee—though the amount was probably more.[20] In 1974, Justice Harry A. Blackmun wrote, "This is always an excruciating process. Over 150 apply each year for the three positions and nearly every applicant is highly qualified."[21] In 1977, Justice Powell wrote, "The selection process becomes both more difficult and 'chancy' each year, as the number of applicants increases. There will be well over 200 of these for the 1978 Term."[22] In 1989, Justice O'Connor said, "I usually end up with somewhere in the neighborhood of fifty."[23]

For most of the institution's history, prospective clerks singled out a few justices to send their applications to. These justices were usually ideologically aligned, though not always. For example, one applicant wrote Justice Thurgood Marshall, "I am also applying to Chief Justice Warren and Justice Fortas. It is my understanding that as Stanford's sole nominee for a clerkship with Chief Justice Warren, I am obligated to remain available should he decide to accept me for that position." Marshall noted on the letter, "probably not so."[24] In 1968, Professor John K. McNulty of the University of California, Berkeley School of Law, and former Supreme Court law clerk, wrote Justice Black about Berkeley's strategy for placing their top students at the Court: "The three best students in the class are making a number of applications to Justices of the Supreme Court. They are trying not to conflict with each other or to hurt each other's chances. The net result is that one student . . . is applying to you."[25]

The number of applicants exploded during the Burger and Rehnquist Courts, and now more than one thousand applicants apply each year for less than a handful of spots per chamber.[26] This is not surprising, as a growing number of law schools have taken to the practice of formally recommending a slate of candidates each year for federal clerkships. For example, in 1966 Paul R. Dean of Georgetown Law School wrote Chief Justice Warren, "Sixteen of the thirty-four students recommended by the Committee last year were selected and have, during this term, served with distinction as law clerks on the United States Courts of Appeals and the District Courts throughout the nation and the Court of Appeals of New York."[27] Clerkship committees are usually composed of former clerks who become law professors. They conduct interviews, rank students, and decide who will be recommended for particular clerkships. An applicant described Yale Law School's recommendation process in his application to Justice Thurgood Marshall:

> A law school committee selects certain third year students to recommend to the various justices of the Supreme Court. The committee recommended me to five justices, but not to you. When I asked why I had not been recommended to you, the head of the committee admitted that once a student was selected to be recommended to the Court, the further process of sending his name to particular justices was conducted somewhat at random. He indicated that the school has no objection to our applying on our own to other justices.[28]

Over time, prospective clerks have applied to a greater number of justices. In recent years it has become increasingly common for applicants to apply to all nine. For example, after his interview with a prospective clerk, Justice Powell noted that the applicant "has interviewed [with] Justice Rehnquist and applied to all other Justices."[29] This should not come as a surprise considering the intense competition and huge career rewards that a High Court clerkship guarantees. A recent clerk said, "I was selective—I applied to only nine justices."[30] Currently, con-

TABLE 2.1
Number of Justices Applied To:
Blackmun Clerks 1975–1993

Measure	Burger Court 1975–1985 (n = 33)	Rehnquist Court 1986–1993 (n = 29)
Median	7	9
Average	6.8	7.4
Standard Deviation	2.1	2.2

SOURCE: Blackmun Papers, Boxes 1553–1568.

servative appeals court Judge J. Michael Luttig encourages his clerks to apply to all nine justices, even though he has never placed a clerk with the Court's liberal members.[31] Former 1996 Kennedy clerk John P. Elwood counseled, "Candidates should apply to all the Justices."[32]

The detailed notes kept by Justice Blackmun during his interviews with prospective clerks illustrate this phenomenon. Table 2.1 shows that the average number of justices that Blackmun's clerks applied to increased from 6.8 to 7.4 from the Burger to the Rehnquist Courts. The increase in the median number of justices applied to from seven to nine is a further indication of this phenomenon. To be sure, some candidates limit their applications, even in this competitive climate. For example, in 1983 Scott R. McIntosh only applied to Justice Blackmun. Blackmun was surprised to learn this during the interview, and noted, "Me only!"[33] He selected McIntosh to be one of his four clerks that term, despite the myth recounted by former Kennedy clerk Elwood: "In the old days, Justice Blackmun supposedly wouldn't hire people who didn't apply to all the Justices. I think he didn't like the idea of the clerk making that choice based on ideology."[34]

Law schools have also decided to send their recommendation lists out to an increasing number of justices, if not all nine. As early as 1968, Yale said in its letter to Justice Hugo Black that their top students were "also being recommended to the Chief Justice and Justices Harlan, Stewart, Marshall and White. (Justices Brennan and Fortas have, I think, selected their clerks for next year; and Justice Douglas prefers clerks from law schools in the Ninth Circuit.)"[35]

In the past, there were occasions when a clerk was selected solely on the basis of recommendations, with no formal application being sent. These recommendations came from current clerks, family friends, lower court judges, law professors, and even other justices. For example, Justice

John Marshall Harlan wrote newly appointed Justice William J. Brennan, "Unless I am mistaken, one of the problems that must be besetting you in your move down here is the selection of Law Clerks. . . . I know one young man who would be well worth considering."[36] After he had chosen his clerks, Justice Powell's habit was to send a memo to some of his colleagues listing "the names of several clerk applicants whom I thought were fully as well qualified as the four whom I engaged."[37]

Justice Stanley Reed selected his second clerk for the 1947 Term, Robert von Mehren, on the basis of a recommendation from the first clerk he selected for that year, John Spitzer. Similarly, after Justice John Marshall Harlan was confirmed by the Senate, 1954 Burton clerk Bill Matteson wrote the new justice recommending E. Barrett Prettyman, Jr.:

> Mr. Justice Jackson, while he was here, adhered to the practice of having one clerk. Last Term his clerk was Barrett Prettyman, Jr., a man of most unusual ability. Although the usual practice is for a law clerk only to stay around for one Term, Barrett stayed on for a second Term as a matter of choice and I imagine on the Justice's urging. Since the Justice's death Barrett has been kept on the pay roll and has kept himself busy doing work on special projects, particularly for Mr. Justice Frankfurter (who, by the way, thinks he is one of the best clerks he has found on the Court). Barrett is thus here and would be most agreeable to continuing on as your law clerk.
>
> There is no reason why you have to adopt the law clerks left by other Justices. I would want to emphasize that I do not think any body would look upon it as strange if you did not. The Chief Justice did last year but I am not sure he was the happier for it. However, I did want you to know the situation down here, that you are entitled to two law clerks and that there is an exceptional fellow here who could become your second for the balance of the Term. By the way, the above remark about the Chief Justice stems only from the quality of clerks Chief Justice Vinson had when he died.
>
> I do hope you do not think this is at all presumptuous of me. I would not do it if I did not think so highly of Barrett, and of you, for that matter. You are certainly free to do whatever you wish. As far as Harvard is concerned, you could continue to get your law clerks from the Dean in the future but I am sure no difficulty would arise over this interim term. Moreover it would probably be most difficult to get anybody at this time of year.[38]

In addition to these informal recommendations, occasionally, current clerks are formally included in the selection process. For example, 1995 Blackmun clerk Mike Wishnie wrote the justice, "I have pulled the attached 12 applications for your review. There were 82 in all. These 12 are arranged in alphabetical order; I would be happy to rank them if you wish."[39] Justice Blackmun replied, "Yes—please rank them."[40] Justice Powell's clerks always played an important role in finding their successors. They examined the applicant files, met with those selected for interviews, wrote memos outlining their views, and discussed the candidates with Powell.[41] For example, he wrote, "My present clerks are reviewing applications, and they . . . tell me that this is a bumper year—with an unusually large number of apparent superstars."[42] Similarly, he remarked, "My own clerks give Gene [Comey] 'high marks' after they spent some time with him."[43]

In 1974, Powell outlined the criteria his current clerks should use in picking their successors: "I prefer candidates who have attended strong colleges and law schools, with good records at both, with experience as an officer of a quality law review, and with service preferably with a strong circuit court judge. . . . As you know, I consider the human qualities of personality, character and congeniality to be quite as important as first rate scholarship."[44] Similarly, in 1982 he told his clerks,

> What my clerks have done in the past, I believe, is to divide up the applications. . . . Each of you might indicate your views on the files assigned to you, and then put together a composite list. The credentials are familiar to you, since they are your credentials: strong college and law school records, from the better colleges and law schools; law review or some fairly comparable experience, with a plus given for service as a top officer of a good law review; and pluses for graduate degrees other than law, and work or summer clerking experience that broadens one's capacity to function here. Last summer, for example, I took some fifty to sixty files—selected by my clerks—to review in setting up an interview list. We interviewed twenty-three people last September. I would like to reduce this to about fifteen.[45]

One of Justice Reed's choices for the 1955 Term, Julian Burke, was made on the basis of a recommendation in the form of a phone call from his friend and appeals court Judge E. Barrett Prettyman, whom Burke was clerking for at the time. Burke recalled,

I was in the room, indeed, when Judge Prettyman called Stanley Reed and it was a friendly, easy conversation between two people who obviously knew each other quite well. Two days later I got a call at Judge Prettyman's chambers from Mr. Justice Reed, whom I had never met, and he introduced himself to me and he said that after having talked to Judge Prettyman he found it totally unnecessary to interview me or to see me—that he would like me to become his law clerk for the coming Term.[46]

Such instances were not the norm, however, not even for Justice Reed, who generally felt that interviewing prospective clerks was important.

Despite the obvious benefits, there are a number of potential problems in having current clerks participate in the selection of their successors. Justice Powell recognized this when he informed his current clerks,

As former clerks have done, I would like for you to review the applications received to date, and make a priority list of not more than two dozen applicants who appear to have the strongest credentials. The list should include any information or personal knowledge which you may have, in addition to the bare statistical data. I would, everything else being equal, like to include in next year's "crop" at least one clerk from a "new" law school. I have tended—perhaps too much—to rely on the recommendations of incumbent clerks who, in turn, naturally know more about their own law schools and their successors on the law reviews.[47]

Prospective clerks routinely state in their letters of application that they are available for interviews. Applicants have often given dates and times that they will be in Washington, D.C., because they must pay all travel costs themselves. For example, when asked by Justice Blackmun's secretary if she was available for an interview, Helane Morrison said, "Can I ask you how many people he is interviewing? Don't get me wrong. I'd really like the job, and I'm very thrilled and honored to be asked to come for an interview. It's just that I've had two interviews with Justices and it adds up, you know."[48] Financial concerns are often heightened for applicants who must travel a significant distance. For example, Justice Blackmun's secretary wrote him,

Ms. [Corey] Streisinger called again this morning. She has been contacted for an interview with Justice O'Connor. . . . Ms. Streisinger said that if you would possibly be interested in arranging an interview, she would be happy to be in Washington a day or so before or after her interview. . . . She added that her reason for calling was an effort to minimize the expense of interviewing for positions on the East coast.[49]

While most justices interviewed candidates personally, some delegated the task to others. The first justice to have clerks at the Court, Horace Gray, allowed his brother, John Chipman Gray, a professor at Harvard Law School, to make the selections. Justice Felix Frankfurter made the selections for Justices Holmes and Brandeis. The latter explained his reasons for delegating the selection to Frankfurter:

> There isn't one chance in a thousand for any graduate of the Harvard Law School to come to the Court these days without Professor Frankfurter's approval. . . . Of course a Justice can appoint a law clerk if he wishes. It is more convenient, however, for some of us to have a professor make the choice because he knows many of the students and associates with them for several years. Down here in Washington I don't get to see any students—from Harvard or from any other school.[50]

When he joined the Court, Frankfurter followed the practice. He commented, "Not merely formally, but without qualification, I have nothing whatever to do with the selection of my law clerks."[51]

Chief Justices Earl Warren and Warren Burger and Justices William O. Douglas and Thurgood Marshall delegated the task of selecting their clerks to a committee. Currently, Justice Kennedy follows that practice, relying on a committee composed of his son Gregory, a New York lawyer, and a number of former clerks. Justice William O. Douglas wrote a prospective applicant, "A former law clerk of mine, now residing in California, makes the selection for me."[52] In 1964, Douglas wrote another applicant, "I use only one Clerk and he is chosen for me from among the graduates of the schools of the Ninth Circuit by an ex-Law Clerk, Stanley E. Sparrowe. . . . I would suggest that you get in touch with him promptly, as they are usually chosen by the end of the year."[53] In another letter to a prospective clerk, Douglas explained why he decided to delegate the selection to Sparrowe:

> For a while I tried to process the selection myself, but since I could not get to the Far West until usually late in June, I discovered that many of

the men who were eligible had already taken other jobs, and the few hours I had for the interviewing were not adequate. So I changed to the present system, which works very satisfactorily. Sparrowe does not go on grades alone. I think he has sometimes selected a person with lower grades but better overall capacity.[54]

For many years Chief Justice Warren did the screening of applications, interviewing, and selection of clerks on his own, ultimately winnowing down the applicants to a single list he drew up in pencil on a yellow legal pad. He listed schools and their applicants, ranked the candidates, made notes in the margin after phoning recommenders, and checked on each applicant's availability, as some had accepted other positions by the time Warren got to his files in January, February, or sometimes later each year.[55] In his first three years, he consulted with Justice Frankfurter on the matter and each year chose a clerk from Harvard Law School. But when Warren's and Frankfurter's relationship soured, he never again selected a clerk from Harvard, believing that a Harvard clerk might discuss the activities in his chambers with their former law professors, who in turn might relay that information to their old colleague, Frankfurter.[56]

Warren was always happy to meet with any applicant, as long as his schedule permitted it. He routinely informed applicants and their recommenders, "I will be happy to consider [his] application. . . . If he is in Washington for other reasons and will call my secretary . . . I will be glad to see him if my calendar permits."[57] But what is said in these meetings and interview sessions is largely unknown. When Warren would write the recommenders about his interviews with prospective clerks, he was vague: "Mr. Skornia was in to see me recently, and we had a very pleasant chat. He seems like a very serious, capable young man, and I will be glad to consider him."[58]

Eventually, Warren delegated the task to two committees of his former clerks, one in Washington, D.C., and one on the west coast, who screened applicants, conducted interviews, and made recommendations to the chief.[59] A former Warren clerk from the 1950s told us, "I remained close to the Chief Justice until his death, working with him on extra-judicial matters and sorting through the applications for his clerkships in order to make recommendations as to two of those positions. Mike Heyman filled the same role with respect to the third clerkship, which the Chief Justice invariably awarded to someone from the West."

In 1966 Warren wrote Dean Arthur M. Sammis of the Hastings College of Law about the process, "I suggest [the applicant] get in touch with Prof. Ira Michael Heyman at the Law School, University of California, Berkeley. Prof. Heyman and another one of my former clerks, Mr. Henry J. Steinman, who is practicing law in Los Angeles serve as a committee to screen the West Coast applicants for me."[60] He further elaborated in a letter to Dean Samuel D. Thurman of the University of Utah College of Law,

> I now have a committee of some of my former clerks in Washington and another one on the West Coast to screen the applicants for me. Because we thought it was unfair to ask an applicant from your section of the country to come all the way to Washington for an interview at his own expense, the two committees got together and decided that the States adjacent to or close to California would be considered by the West Coast committee. They do not have time to interview all those who are interested, but they do talk to the ones whom they expect to recommend to me.[61]

Each year, Justice Harry Blackmun interviewed a short list of up to ten prospective clerks. He used a numbered list of talking points, kept brief notes of each candidate's answers, and sometimes even graded the applicant. For example, 1993 clerk Sarah Cleveland received an "A+" from the justice. Blackmun's papers contain a well-worn single master list of talking points that he apparently reused each year he conducted interviews, making additions, subtractions, and notations on the list as the years progressed (see appendix D). While Blackmun asked some obvious questions, such as, "Why does he want a clerkship," he also included a number of not-so-obvious topics, such as "Attitudes toward the lower courts" and "Favorite branch of law." Blackmun discussed personal issues like "Room tidiness," "Health," and "Smoking," and asked if interviewees were "Ever in trouble [with the law]?" Perhaps most intriguing are the points "Where else applied," "n[umber of] interviews," and "No comment about the Justices or their division." While it is unclear whether Blackmun was reminding himself not to comment on his colleagues or whether he was referring to the applicants, it is plain that the partisan divide among the members of the Court was something he was concerned about in interviewing prospective clerks.

Like Blackmun, Justice Powell also interviewed a short list of candidates, from one to two dozen, and made a formal record of his interviews with them.[62] He also graded them, but did that prior to the interview as he went through the files. For example, he rated 1976 clerk Charlie Ames an "A prospect."[63] Powell was particularly concerned with finding applicants he could get along with on a personal level. He wrote a recommender about 1973 clerk John J. Buckley,

> I am . . . interested primarily in an appraisal . . . of Mr. Buckley's personality and personal characteristics. We have to live on a fairly intimate basis with our law clerks, working long hours together. . . . It is important to have a law clerk who works well with the other clerks and with me. . . . Jo and I also see a good deal of our clerks and their wives socially, and therefore we hope for attractive and congenial young people.[64]

But instead of keeping handwritten notes during the interview, as Blackmun did, Powell orally recorded his impressions and had his secretary type up a "CONFIDENTIAL . . . Memorandum on Interview." For example, Powell said,

> Jim Alt made a favorable impression in our interview. He has been with Judge Morgan since the middle of June; has worked with him on three opinions for the court, including two signed opinions; and thinks he is having a fine experience. Although a political science and economics major in college, Alt is a self-educated history scholar. He is particularly interested in early American history, and recently has read the Jefferson/Madison papers. He has been a student of the Court since the latter part of his college days. He exhibited a fair familiarity with some of my recent opinions. He is essentially reserved in demeanor, but conveys sincerity and candor. His wife also is a lawyer. She is with him in Georgia, but is exploring the possibility of practicing in Chicago. Without having seen other applicants as of this date, I would rate Alt as a fine prospect.[65]

Justice O'Connor said, "After I have winnowed the number down to ten or less, I make what is the hardest decision I make every year, and that is selecting four from among the extraordinary people I have interviewed."[66] O'Connor said that she looks for an overall balance among different law schools, geographical areas, race, sex, and backgrounds in

TABLE 2.2
Number of Interviews with Justices:
Blackmun Clerks 1974–1993

Measure	Burger Court 1974–1985 (n = 22)	Rehnquist Court 1986–1993 (n = 24)
Median	3	2
Average	3.4	2.0
Standard Deviation	1.9	1.1

SOURCE: Blackmun Papers, Boxes 1553–1568.

general. "One thing I do look for is the person who has the ability to remain unruffled and get along." She explained,

> Maturity, stability and congeniality are important to me because we work long hours and every weekend and holidays, other than Christmas Day and New Year's Day. It is a very intense year and because of the intensity and pressure of all the deadlines that have to be met, we really don't have time around here to solve many personal problems. We need to concentrate on the work.[67]

How common is it for prospective clerks to interview with more than one justice? Again, Blackmun's notes provide some idea. The interview data compiled by Blackmun probably reflects the total number of interviews for each applicant. It is reasonable to assume that few, if any, interviews were conducted after Blackmun's since he made his selections later than nearly all of his colleagues. He wrote, "I am always about the last of everyone here to make clerkship appointments. I usually defer this to near the end of the calendar year when I have input from the judges for whom thy are currently working."[68] Of the forty-six Blackmun clerks that he noted this information for, the median number of interviews was two and the average was 2.7. Table 2.2 shows the decline in the number of interviews from the Burger to the Rehnquist Court. During the Burger Court, Blackmun's clerks interviewed with three or four justices on average. During the Rehnquist Court, however, Blackmun's clerks interviewed with Blackmun and only one other justice, on average. This lends further support to our suggestion that the selection process has become increasingly competitive.

When clerks accept an offer from one justice, they withdraw their applications with the others. For example, an applicant for the 1955

Term wrote Chief Justice Warren, "It is necessary for me to withdraw that application as I have accepted a position as law clerk to Mr. Justice Clark for the coming term."[69] Similarly, in 1974 an applicant wrote Justice Douglas, "Would you please withdraw my application for a position as one of your law clerks for the October Term, 1975. I have just accepted a position with Mr. Justice Rehnquist for that same period."[70]

Factors in Clerk Selection

In a 1974 letter of recommendation sent to Justice Douglas, law professor Thomas F. Bergin noted, "I believe you should know that I am sending this letter to every member of the Court."[71] There are necessarily a number of factors that each justice weighs in selecting law clerks. It is understood that when making a selection justices consider certain law schools, geographic regions, prior clerking experience, and personal compatibility. But there are other factors that may or may not be important to the justices but have garnered much controversy among the public and the press. In addition to the previous factors, we will discuss the sex, race, sexual orientation, and ideology of the clerks and explore whether the justices have considered or ought to consider such factors in choosing their clerks.[72] While letters of recommendation from professors and judges have always carried a certain amount of weight, an increasingly important factor are the word-of-mouth, and sometimes more formalized, recommendations and general input of current clerks. Judge Luttig noted that law school recommendations do not carry much weight because "the professors don't really know the students."[73]

Furthermore, the influence of various factors has changed over time, as securing a lower court clerkship has become the norm for virtually all Supreme Court clerks. The courts of appeals judges, therefore, have come to provide an important screening function. The clerks who end up at the Supreme Court are first selected by certain "feeder judges" on the courts of appeals who weigh the factors discussed here, such as class ranking and law school attended, letters of recommendation from law school faculty, and other factors. Because the race to secure a Supreme Court clerkship has led to applications being submitted to the justices before their clerkships on the lower courts even begin, recommendations from lower court judges have come to be less important. Instead, just securing a clerkship with a lower court feeder judge, and

TABLE 2.3

Factors in Law Clerk Selection by Clerk Ranking

Selection Criteria	"1"	"2"	"3"	Total
Law School Academic Performance	69	31	17	117
Recommendation of Professor or Judge	55	23	21	99
Quality of School	13	20	25	58
Prior Clerking Experience	23	16	16	55
Rapport with Justice during Initial Interview	14	9	16	39
Other	6	3	9	18
Similar Political Views as Justice	2	0	3	5

Respondents were asked to rank the top three factors, regarding their selection, that they felt were most important to their justice, with "1" being the most important factor.

noting this in an application to a Supreme Court justice, has become crucial.

We asked former clerks to rank the factors they thought were most important to their justice in making their selection. Table 2.3 shows that the most important factor was law school academic performance, with sixty-nine clerks in our response group ranking it the most important factor and 117 placing it among the top three. The second, and almost equally important factor, was the recommendation of a professor or judge, with fifty-five clerks ranking it the most important criteria. The next two key factors were the quality of the law school and prior clerking experience, with fifty-eight and fifty-five clerks, respectively, placing these two factors in the top three. Interestingly, only five clerks placed "similar political views" among the top three factors, and only two said it was the most important criterion for their selection.

Law School

The law school the clerk graduated from as well as recommendations from the dean and faculty are perhaps the key factors for the justices. Indeed, some schools make a determination each year—sometimes through a formal clerkship committee, and sometimes through formal interviews with students—whether or not to nominate anyone for a Supreme Court clerkship.[74] If they do, then often the dean will write the justices with recommendations for one or more candidates. For example, in 1955 Dean Russell D. Niles of the New York University School of Law wrote Chief Justice Warren, "I should like to recommend a few [of our students] for your consideration as possible law clerks. I enclose the resumes of five men. . . . If you would be willing to interview any of these men they could go to Washington at any time."[75] In 1962, Warren wrote Columbia Law School Dean Gerald Gunther,

> Because I rarely have an opportunity to become personally acquainted with the applicants, I have come to rely more and more on the recommendations of the deans and professors of the law schools. I am grateful to you for your continued cooperation in this respect. . . . I find that choosing three law clerks from the large group of well qualified persons who apply is becoming a greater ordeal for me each year.[76]

The competition among law schools to place their top students at the Court is fierce. Faculty and deans continually lobby the justices for consideration of their candidates. For example, in 1954 Dean Edward H. Levi of the University of Chicago Law School wrote Chief Justice Earl Warren,

> As I am sure is the case with every law school in the country, we are exceedingly anxious to place our best graduates as law clerks to the Justices of the Court. . . . I realize that many factors enter into the selection of a law clerk but I hope you will be willing to consider our graduates. Mr. James Ratcliffe, who is Assistant Dean of the Law School, will be in Washington next week. I very much hope that you will be willing to permit him to see you for a few minutes. Mr. Ratcliffe will have full information on such present members of our senior class as we would be willing to recommend.[77]

In 1955, Dean Harold C. Havighurst of Northwestern University School of Law wrote Chief Justice Warren, "I would be less than frank if I did not tell you that it means a great deal to our School to have a graduate as one of your law clerks."[78]

The first Supreme Court law clerks came exclusively from Harvard Law School. Justice Horace Gray began the tradition and was followed by Oliver Wendell Holmes, Louis Brandeis, Felix Frankfurter, and, to some extent, William Brennan. While some justices preferred Harvard graduates, others did not. In 1936, Justice James McReynolds allowed his colleague Justice Willis Van Devanter to select his clerk for the coming term. Van Devanter selected John Knox, a recent Harvard graduate. McReynolds was suspicious and told Knox,

I suppose you know that Washington is full of impractical lawyers, and I must say that many of them seem to have come from Harvard. You might as well realize right now that I think the Harvard Law School is highly overrated! I also hope that you did not come under the influence of Frankfurter when you were in law school. There was some doubt in my mind about Justice Van Devanter's selection of any law clerk who graduated from a school where Frankfurter teaches. He is certainly one man not to be trusted. . . . He is dangerous to the welfare of this country.[79]

Other justices have had a similar practice of choosing their clerks from particular schools. For example, Justice Potter Stewart preferred Yale graduates, as did Hugo Black (as long as they were originally from the South), Justice Frank Murphy selected his clerks from the University of Michigan, Justice Sherman Minton preferred Indiana University, and Justice John Marshall Harlan II usually chose one of his clerks from Harvard and the other, often from Columbia. Chief Justice Vinson favored Northwestern, and Chief Justice Stone's clerks came from Columbia. One former clerk told us that Justice Clark tried to choose his clerks from "underprivileged law schools." Justice Powell generally selected one of his clerks each term from the University of Virginia. Still, he recognized that diversity was important. He remarked,

I accept the view that clerkships should be rotated among law schools to a certain extent, and that qualified people are available from other law schools. Yet, in view of the way we work in our chambers and the close relationship among us, a clerk's personality and human qualities are extremely important. My impression in one interview corroborates testimonials in this respect from a number of my friends on the faculty at U. Va.[80]

Some justices strive for diversity in school representation. For example, each year Chief Justice Warren had only one clerk from a particular school and tried to balance his clerks by taking one from the western states. In 1962 he wrote, "I try to take clerks from different schools each year, and this time I have selected graduates of the University of California, Harvard and Yale."[81] When Warren chose to delegate screening to committees of ex-clerks, they made recommendations on the basis of Warren's criteria. In the 1966 Washington, D.C., committee recommendation, Warren was advised, "to take Nathan would be to

TABLE 2.4
Law Schools Attended by Supreme Court
Law Clerks: 1882–2002

Law School	Number of Clerks	Percentage of Clerks
Harvard	461	28%
Yale	270	17%
Chicago	125	8%
Columbia	106	6%
Stanford	94	6%
Virginia	72	4%
Michigan	69	4%
California—Berkeley	48	3%
Pennsylvania	47	3%
Georgetown	31	2%
Northwestern	31	2%
New York University	30	2%
Texas	30	2%
California—Los Angeles	17	1%
George Washington	12	1%
Indiana	12	1%
Duke	11	1%
University of Washington	10	1%
Brigham Young	9	1%
Southern California	8	1%

NOTE: Percentage based on 1,635 clerks.
SOURCE: U.S. Supreme Court.

have two from Yale in one year (although to take Kranwinkle would be to have three in a row from Michigan)."[82] Similarly, when Hugo Black started employing two clerks, he was careful not to choose both from the same school. In 1950 he wrote a prospective applicant from Yale, "I have written several other applicants from Yale that I would not appoint a second clerk from that law school."[83]

Over time, the dominance of Harvard soon gave way until ultimately seventy-seven different law schools were represented with at least one Supreme Court clerkship. But twenty-three of those schools have had only one clerk, fourteen had two, and ten had three. Beginning with Gray's first clerk in 1882, Table 2.4 shows the percentage of clerks who came from the top twenty Supreme Court–clerk-producing law schools.[84] Overall, nearly one-third (461, or 28 percent) of all clerks came from Harvard. Yale was a distant second with 17 percent. But these two schools combine for nearly half (45 percent) of all clerks. Following Harvard and Yale, Chicago and Columbia have each placed over one hundred clerks at the High Court. Stanford, Virginia, and Michigan have also enjoyed considerable success. These seven schools alone account for nearly three out of every four (73 percent) law clerks in Supreme Court history.

Have these percentages changed over time? Is Harvard losing ground to other schools in law clerk placement, and is the process becoming more heterogeneous? Table 2.5 shows that over time Harvard has increasingly lost ground to the other top seven clerk-producing schools. Also, clerks have become a slightly more heterogeneous group—at least with respect to law schools attended. Still, Harvard's dominance in the

TABLE 2.5

Law Clerk Placement by Court and Top Seven
Clerk-Producing Schools: 1882–2002

Court	Harvard	Yale	Chicago	Columbia	Stanford	Virginia	Michigan	Top 7 Total
Waite								
(1874–1888)	100%	0%	0%	0%	0%	0%	0%	100%
n = 5	(5)	(0)	(0)	(0)	(0)	(0)	(0)	(5)
Fuller								
(1888–1910)	83%	0%	0%	0%	0%	0%	0%	83%
n = 18	(15)	(0)	(0)	(0)	(0)	(0)	(0)	(15)
White								
(1910–1921)	94%	0%	0%	0%	0%	0%	0%	94%
n = 16	(15)	(0)	(0)	(0)	(0)	(0)	(0)	(15)
Taft								
(1921–1930)	67%	5%	0%	5%	0%	0%	0%	76%
n = 21	(14)	(1)	(0)	(1)	(0)	(0)	(0)	(16)
Hughes								
(1930–1941)	59%	4%	0%	15%	0	0%	0%	78%
n = 46	(27)	(2)	(0)	(7)	(0)	(0)	(0)	(36)
Stone								
(1941–1946)	38%	14%	5%	19%	0%	0%	5%	81%
n = 37	(14)	(5)	(2)	(7)	(0)	(0)	(2)	(30)
Vinson								
(1946–1953)	27%	24%	6%	4%	3%	1%	4%	69%
n = 100	(27)	(24)	(6)	(4)	(3)	(1)	(4)	(69)
Warren								
(1953–1969)	34%	15%	5%	4%	4%	3%	4%	69%
n = 278	(94)	(43)	(13)	(12)	(11)	(8)	(11)	(192)
Burger								
(1969–1986)	22%	15%	6%	6%	7%	7%	6%	69%
n = 528	(114)	(79)	(32)	(34)	(36)	(38)	(30)	(363)
Rehnquist								
(1986–2002)	24%	19%	12%	7%	7%	4%	4%	77%
n = 600	(142)	(116)	(72)	(41)	(44)	(25)	(23)	(463)

NOTE: n = 1,649 as fourteen clerks worked on two different Courts and are therefore counted twice in this total.
SOURCE: U.S. Supreme Court.

early years is striking. From the Waite Court through the White Court, Harvard was the only top seven clerk-producing school represented. The few clerks during this time who did not come from Harvard instead graduated from Georgetown, George Washington, and Detroit. Harvard clerks continued to dominate the Taft Court, but the first clerks from Yale and Columbia were selected. During the Hughes Court, these two schools continued to make gains, but Harvard was still dominant, with 59 percent of the clerks. The dominance of Harvard and Yale was decried by many, such as law professor Floyd A. Wright from the University of Oklahoma, who wrote each justice in 1938:

> [Our] graduates are as well trained as the young men graduating from Yale, Harvard, or Columbia, or any other law school in the country. The matter that has impressed me is the relatively low percentage of the graduates from the law schools of the great state universities given responsible positions in our national government. In other words our graduates are severely discriminated against. If a man is from Harvard or Yale, the men in the executive departments of our national capital seem to think such [a] man possesses superior abilities and training. That is extremely erroneous. I am a graduate from Yale and I am fully familiar with the relative standards in these schools. We have a wide interchange of students between this school and the eastern schools and there is nothing to indicate superiority among students coming to us from Harvard and Yale. In fact we have an industry, sincerity, and earnestness among our law students here which is much less intense on the campuses at Cambridge, Mass., and New Haven, Conn. Many of the boys who go there do so because they have money.[85]

Justice Black replied, "The members of the Court make individual selections of their law clerks. I do not believe that all of the law clerks are graduates of Yale or Harvard."[86] Technically, Black was correct, but he could not deny the dominance of these elite schools. Black's own clerk during his first three years, Jerome A. Cooper, was a Harvard Law graduate.

By the time of the Vinson Court, Yale made great strides in placing its students at the High Court, nearly equaling Harvard and thereafter besting every other school, except its Ivy League rival, by a considerable margin. It was also during the Vinson Court that the other five schools

TABLE 2.6
Final Rehnquist Court and Law School Attended

Justice	Law School
William H. Rehnquist	Stanford
John Paul Stevens	Chicago
Sandra Day O'Connor	Stanford
Antonin Scalia	Harvard
Anthony Kennedy	Harvard
David Souter	Harvard
Clarence Thomas	Yale
Ruth Bader Ginsburg	Harvard/Columbia
Stephen Breyer	Harvard

in the top seven reached parity in placing clerks at the High Court. While these schools continued this relative equality through the Burger Court, recently Chicago pulled away from the others and moved closer to the top. But despite the gains made by the other top seven schools in recent years, Harvard and Yale have continued to battle for supremacy, with Harvard out-placing Yale by a relatively comfortable margin through the recent Burger and Rehnquist Courts. For example, Justice Powell wrote a former clerk, "I have now finished interviewing for the 1984 Term and have engaged clerks from the University of Maine Law School (believe it or not!), Harvard, Yale, and Virginia."[87] Also of note is the overall decline and then leveling off at 69 percent of top-seven school placements through the Burger Court and the dramatic reversal back to 77 percent during the Rehnquist Court.

A number of factors contribute to the disparity among law schools. First, as with lower court judges, Supreme Court justices have developed relationships with particular schools and oftentimes personal relationships with faculty at those schools. And since faculty recommend students to the justices, it is not surprising that clerks would continue to come from the same recommenders and therefore the same schools. Indeed, the justices themselves often came from the same law schools and even had the same professors as their clerks. Table 2.6 shows the law schools attended by the final members of the Rehnquist Court. Each one attended a top-seven clerk-producing school, with Harvard's dominance once again plain.

Though Harvard and Yale have continually dominated the selection process, some justices have consciously tried to diversify the pool. For example, Justice Douglas always took his clerks from a competition among schools in the Ninth Circuit. In 1959, he explained to a recommender that his practice ensured that "the western schools are represented whereas otherwise Harvard, Yale, and Columbia would have the Court pretty well covered."[88] Similarly, in 1965 he said, "it gives broader national representation to our Court."[89] Informed that he was not eligible for a clerkship with Douglas, one applicant wrote the justice, "I admit that I am now rather unhappy that I chose to attend Yale rather than Boalt [California-Berkeley] or Stanford."[90]

Prior Clerkship Experience

Another key factor is prior clerking experience and the letters of recommendation that clerks have written for them from lower court judges. Chief Justice Warren wrote to Dean Eugene V. Rostow of Yale Law School, "I do consider it good training for an applicant to have served as a law clerk on the Court of Appeals."[91] For example, Stanley Silverberg clerked on a lower court before he applied to several justices for a clerkship during the 1943 Term. Appeals Court Judge Jerome Frank wrote to Justice Douglas on Silverberg's behalf, "Dear Bill: Stanley Silverberg is Judge Learned Hand's law clerk and has expressed to me an interest in working for a Supreme Court Justice. . . . I am writing to you, rather than having Judge Hand do so, because of my closer acquaintance with you. . . . I have sent a similar letter to Justices Jackson and Black."[92] Douglas replied, "Dear Jerry: I will be happy to see Silverberg. My practice, however, has been to take as a law clerk only a graduate of a law school in the Ninth Circuit. I want to continue that practice. It means much to the western schools."[93] Ultimately, Silverberg also applied to Justice Frankfurter and was selected by him for the 1943 Term. F. Aley Allen, former clerk to Judge Learned Hand and then Justice Stanley Reed, explained how he came to the Court: "Justice Reed, as the other justices do, made a practice of asking various law schools if they had any recommendations of persons who might be interested in becoming law clerks, and my name was given to him [by Yale] and he then got in touch with Judge Hand and asked Judge Hand whether he could recommend me."[94]

But, on occasion, a "recommendation" is not so positive. For example, Judge Jerome Frank wrote Justice Black about an applicant whom Black felt looked excellent on paper:

Unquestionably the lad has a good mind but he is, in my opinion, a first-rate neurotic, having the devil's own time in adjusting himself to life, and accordingly a very unpleasant fellow to have around. I wouldn't be surprised if, at any moment, he had a nervous breakdown. I would think he'd be the last person in the world that you'd want to have as your secretary.[95]

But such letters were the exception, as nearly every applicant was extremely well qualified and highly recommended.

In recent years, recommendations from lower court judges have become less crucial as prospective Supreme Court clerks now send their applications to the Court before they even begin clerking for a lower court judge. As a result, the letter has been replaced by the clerkship itself. As we will show, simply securing a clerkship with one of the top feeder judges on the courts of appeals virtually guarantees the applicant a Supreme Court clerkship.

It is extremely rare for the modern law clerk to come to the Court without prior clerking experience on a lower court, usually on the courts of appeals. Table 2.7 shows that 98 percent (589 of 600) of Rehnquist Court clerks had prior clerking experience. But historically, this pattern was less common. The first law clerks generally came to the Court straight out of law school. While the data is somewhat incomplete on this point for the early years of clerks, by the 1930s, clerks were coming from lower courts to the Court in increasing numbers. For example, Ambrose Doskow clerked for Judge Ainsworth of the Court of Appeals for the Fifth Circuit in 1932 before working for Justice Benjamin Cardozo on the Supreme Court the following year. But in

TABLE 2.7

Percent of U.S. Supreme Court Law Clerks with Lower Court Experience by Prior Clerkship: 1969–2002

Court	Number of Clerks with Lower Court Experience	Courts of Appeals	U.S. District Courts	State Courts
Burger (1969–1985)	361	85% (308)	12% (42)	3% (11)
Rehnquist (1986–2002)	589	92% (543)	7% (44)	0.3% (2)

NOTE: Reliable data not available prior to Burger Court.
SOURCE: U.S. Supreme Court.

general, in the early years of clerks, the norm was to spend only one year clerking after law school, whether it was on a lower court or on the Supreme Court. For example, Robert von Mehren, who clerked for Judge Learned Hand on the court of appeals, was ready to move to a private firm after his year with Hand. Von Mehren explained, "Some of the partners at this firm felt that one shouldn't spend more than one year clerking. That was enough."[96] Still, he was offered and accepted a clerkship with Justice Stanley Reed for the 1947 Term. A Clark clerk from the 1960s told us, "At that time it was uncommon for a clerk to clerk on a federal district court or court of appeals. . . . It was more common for a clerk to go directly from law school to the Court."

Why has prior clerkship experience become so commonplace for Supreme Court clerks? One reason is that over time, the competition among recent law school graduates for Supreme Court clerkships intensified. As clerkships grew in prestige as stepping stones to promising careers in prestigious law firms, government agencies, and the legal academy, applicants sought ways of improving their chances of landing a position on the Court. Graduating at the top of one's class from an elite law school no longer guaranteed a spot on the High Court. By gaining experience on a lower court, and securing a favorable recommendation from their judge, applicants became more attractive to the justices.

Also, as clerk responsibility expanded over time, the justices valued candidates who had worked on lower courts. Experienced clerks could hit the ground running and provide immediate support to their justice with comparatively little training and start-up time. Justice Powell wrote one applicant, "I have a policy of engaging clerks who have had a year's experience clerking in a federal court or a state supreme court. I judge from your letter that you do not contemplate this intermediate step."[97] Similarly, Justice Blackmun typically wrote applicants, "I have reached the point . . . where I feel that one must have a prior year's clerkship with a federal court of appeals judge or with a state supreme court judge. This is excellent training for the pressures that are present in the Supreme Court."[98]

Not only does nearly every modern Supreme Court clerk spend a year clerking on a lower court, but they also almost always spend it on one of the courts of appeals. Table 2.7 shows how this has become increasingly the case. During the Burger Court, 85 percent of law clerks with prior clerkship experience worked on the courts of appeals. That number increased to 92 percent during the Rehnquist Court. Conversely, the percentage of clerks who spent time on the U.S. district courts has decreased from 12 percent under Burger to 7 percent under Rehnquist. The number of clerks who spent time on state courts has also decreased to the point that it is extremely rare, from 3 percent during the Burger Court to less than 1 percent during the Rehnquist Court, where only two clerks out of 589 had state court experience.

The increasing trend toward prior clerkships on the courts of appeals suggests that it is the primary step toward a clerkship on the Supreme Court. Prospective clerks know that their best chance of securing a spot on the High Court is to spend a year on one of the courts of appeals. The case of John H. Mansfield is instructive. In his third year at Harvard Law School, Mansfield applied for a clerkship on the High Court for the 1956 Term. Dean Erwin Griswold wrote a glowing recommendation: "During the fall I have been looking for the outstanding one of our students and recent graduates to recommend to you for one of your law clerkships next year. I believe I have found him. In terms of legal training, all around qualifications, personality, and maturity, I think he is well up to the qualifications of both Mr. Gunther and Mr. Stern." Chief Justice Warren replied to Dean Griswold, "I eventually decided on one of your former graduates, Mr. Martin T. Richman, who is presently serving as law clerk to Judge Magruder." Mansfield graduated from Harvard that spring and went on to clerk on the courts of appeals. He reapplied to the High Court and was selected by Justice Frankfurter for the 1957 Term.

Warren admitted in his rejection letters to prospective clerks and their recommenders, "Choosing three law clerks from the large number who applied was a very difficult task for me. There are so many young law graduates of apparently equal abilities and qualifications that it was impossible to follow any real pattern of selection."[99] But a pattern was developing. As faculty and applicants saw that recent graduates with lower court clerkship experience had an advantage in the process, prospective clerks waited until after graduating and after securing a placement on a lower court before applying to the justices.

Since the work that clerks perform on appellate courts more closely resembles the work that they will do on the Supreme Court, it is not surprising that they would seek clerkships there as opposed to trial courts. Still, there are merits to having prior clerkship experience on trial courts. After Justice Blackmun selected a clerk for the U.S. District

Court, Deborah C. Malamud, for the 1988 Term, U.S. District Judge David Hittner wrote Blackmun, "I believe that clerks on United States District Courts are uniquely exposed both to the writing and theoretical experience of an appellate court together with the 'people aspect' [of] the trial court. They observe trials, meet with attorneys, attend pretrial conferences, and participate in the day to day decisions which characterize the practice of law in the courtroom."[100] Blackmun replied, "While the temptation always is to go to court of appeals clerks, I have found that district court clerks bring a wealth of experience and a refreshing point of view."[101] While there have never been very many Supreme Court clerks who trained on state courts, the decline from eleven during the Burger Court to only two during the Rehnquist Court suggests that this is no longer an option for prospective High Court clerks.

Even among clerks who come from the courts of appeals, there is considerable variation. Of the twelve circuits that comprise the appeals courts, the D.C. Circuit is by far the most prevalent stepping stone for High Court clerks. Table 2.8 shows the circuit breakdown of Supreme Court clerks with prior clerkship experience on the courts of appeals. More than one-third of all Supreme Court clerks come from the Court of Appeals for the D.C. Circuit. This is not surprising given that the D.C. Circuit is widely considered the most prestigious appellate court. It routinely handles precedent-setting cases that involve the role of federal agencies, the separation of governmental powers, and broad matters of business and trade. Indeed, as with clerks, a disproportionate number of the current justices—Scalia, Thomas, Ginsburg, and Roberts—have come to the Court following their service on the D.C. Circuit.

The variation among circuits is largely caused by the disparity in the number of judges, and therefore the number of clerks, in each circuit. For example, since 1984 there have been only six judges in the First Circuit (New England and Puerto Rico) while there have been twenty-eight in the Ninth Circuit (the Pacific). With three law clerks for each judge, the pool of Ninth Circuit clerks to draw upon is considerably larger. Therefore, it is not surprising that, excluding the D.C. Circuit, more Supreme Court clerks, currently one in five, come from the Ninth Circuit than from any other. The reason the percentage of clerks coming from the Ninth Circuit has doubled from the Burger Court to the Rehnquist Court is the general growth of the Pacific states and, concurrently, the federal court systems with their jurisdictions.[102] Similarly, the de-

TABLE 2.8
*Supreme Court Clerks with Prior Court of Appeals
Experience by Circuit: 1969–2002*

Court	DC	1st	2nd	3rd	4th	5th	6th	7th	8th	9th	10th	11th
Burger	39%	7%	19%	5%	6%	9%	1%	4%	1%	9%	0%	0.6%
(1969–1985)	(121)	(21)	(59)	(14)	(17)	(29)	(3)	(11)	(3)	(28)	(0)	(2)
n = 308												
Rehnquist	36%	6%	12%	2%	11%	4%	0.4%	5%	1%	19%	1%	2%
(1986–2002)	(197)	(31)	(66)	(13)	(59)	(20)	(2)	(27)	(7)	(103)	(8)	(10)
n = 543												

NOTE: Reliable data not available prior to Burger Court.
SOURCE: U.S. Supreme Court.

crease in the number of clerks coming from the Fifth Circuit (from 9 percent to 4 percent) was due to the 1980 Fifth Circuit Court of Appeals Reorganization Act, which divided the circuit in half, creating the new Eleventh Circuit.

But not all the variation can be explained by size alone. For example, what accounts for the dramatic rise in clerks ascending to the Supreme Court from the Fourth Circuit, which includes Maryland, West Virginia, Virginia, North Carolina, and South Carolina? Unlike the Ninth Circuit, the Fourth Circuit did not have a dramatic increase in the number of judges and clerks during the period under study, though they did gain four judgeships in 1990. The data suggests that the increase has been caused by the general conservative shift that the Supreme Court has undergone in recent years and the higher number of conservative clerks now working there. Far and away, the Fourth Circuit judge who is the most successful at placing his clerks at the Supreme Court is conservative J. Michael Luttig, former clerk to Justice Scalia when he was on the D.C. Court of Appeals and to Chief Justice Burger on the Supreme Court. Through 2002, Luttig placed thirty of his clerks on the Rehnquist Court. By comparison, his closest rival on the Fourth Circuit for Supreme Court placements was Chief Judge J. Harvie Wilkinson, III, who had eighteen during the same period. What makes Luttig's success so remarkable is that he did not begin his service on the Fourth Circuit until 1991. With essentially every one of his former clerks gaining a spot on the High Court every year since then, it is clear that Luttig's ascension to the Fourth Circuit has had a major impact on Supreme Court placements. Furthermore, all of his clerks have been placed with

TABLE 2.9
Supreme Court Law Clerk Placement Success Rate
by Lower Court Judge: 1962–2002

Judge	Court	Tenure	Years of Service*	No. of Clerks Placed	Per Term Average
J. Michael Luttig	4th Circuit	1991–	11	30	2.73
Guido Calabresi	2nd Circuit	1994–	8	17	2.13
Laurence Silberman	DC Circuit	1985–	17	30	1.76
David S. Tatel	DC Circuit	1994–	8	14	1.75
Alex Kozinski	9th Circuit	1985–	17	27	1.59
Abner J. Mikva	DC Circuit	1979–1994	16	24	1.50
Stephen F. Williams	DC Circuit	1986–	16	21	1.31
Michael Boudin	1st Circuit	1992–	10	13	1.30
Robert Bork	DC Circuit	1982–1988	7	9	1.29
Harry T. Edwards	DC Circuit	1980–	22	28	1.27
James Skelly Wright	DC Circuit	1962–1988	27	31	1.15
J. Harvie Wilkinson	4th Circuit	1984–	18	20	1.11
Ruth Bader Ginsburg	DC Circuit	1980–1993	14	15	1.07
Patricia Wald	DC Circuit	1979–1999	21	19	0.90
William A. Norris	9th Circuit	1980–1997	18	16	0.89
James L. Oakes	2nd Circuit	1971–	31	26	0.84
Douglas Ginsburg	DC Circuit	1986–	16	13	0.81
Malcolm R. Wilkey	DC Circuit	1970–1985	16	13	0.81
Stephen Breyer	1st Circuit	1980–1994	15	12	0.80
Richard A. Posner	7th Circuit	1981–	21	14	0.67
David B. Sentelle	DC Circuit	1987–	15	9	0.60
Carl E. McGowan	DC Circuit	1963–1987	25	15	0.60
Louis H. Pollak	District Court	1978–	24	14	0.58
Pierre Leval	Dist Ct & 2nd Cir.	1977–	25	14	0.56
J. Clifford Wallace	9th Circuit	1972–	30	16	0.53
Ralph K. Winter	2nd Circuit	1981–	21	11	0.52

* Through 2002.

only five justices: Rehnquist, O'Connor, Scalia, Kennedy, and Thomas—the Court's five most conservative members—with twenty-three of his former clerks (77 percent) working for either Scalia or Thomas.

Table 2.9 shows the lower court judges who have had the most success at placing their clerks on the Supreme Court. Judge Luttig tops the list with an average of nearly three of his clerks (2.73) being place at the High Court each year. Judge Guido Calabresi has also had considerable success, with two or more of his clerks on average (2.13) ascending to the Supreme Court each term. As the top feeder court, the D.C. Circuit has had a number of judges who have had considerable success: Laurence Silberman, David S. Tatel, Abner J. Mikva, Stephen F. Williams, Robert Bork, Harry T. Edwards, James Skelly Wright, and Ruth Bader Ginsburg. On average, each of these judges placed at least one clerk on the High Court each year. In other circuits, Alex Kozinski, Michael Boudin, and William A. Norris had similar success at placing their clerks with one of the justices. Interestingly, while it is rare for district court judges to place their clerks with Supreme Court justices, both Louis Pollak and Pierre Leval have each placed fourteen clerks at the High Court.

Why have certain lower court judges had more success than others? Certainly one important factor is the personal relationships that these judges have with their colleagues on the Supreme Court. For example, given Luttig's close ties with Scalia and Thomas, it is not surprising that three-fourths of his clerks who gain Supreme Court clerkships end up with these two justices. After meeting with a number of former Powell clerks, incoming clerk Paul Cane wrote the justice, "I had no idea that so many of Judge McGowan's clerks had gone on to spend the following year in the Powell Chambers."[103] Powell responded, "It will be good to have another McGowan clerk. You will be following in a very distinguished line."[104] Another reason is reputation. The judges with success at placing clerks are well known and well respected in their professions. The list includes two current justices, over half the judges have been on the federal bench for more than fifteen years, and many are active leaders in the legal profession. Another factor is the quality of training that these judges provide their clerks and the recurring ability of those clerks to contribute to the work of the Court. If certain judges routinely produce top-notch clerks, it is not surprising that the justices would return to these judges for more.

While all of these reasons probably play some role in the success rate of these lower court judges, ideology is crucial.[105] It has been argued that "most justices choose clerks for their legal training and experience and not because of ideological affinity with particular federal judges."[106] While legal training is important, we suggest that ideology largely determines which judges place their clerks with particular justices. Table 2.10 shows the top ten clerk-placing lower court judges (in terms of the number of clerks placed) and the justices their clerks were placed with on the High Court. The ideological congruence between judge and justice is striking. Nineteen (61 percent) of James Skelly Wright's thirty-one clerks who were placed at the Court were selected by two liberal justices, William Brennan and Thurgood Marshall. Twenty-two (79 percent) of Harry T. Edwards's twenty-eight placements went to liberal justices, including Brennan and Marshall. James Oakes, Abner Mikva, and

TABLE 2.10
Supreme Court Law Clerk Placement, Lower Court Judge & Justice: 1962–2002

Judge	Court	Tenure	Number of Clerk Placements	Justices Clerks Placed with (n =)
James Skelly Wright	DC Circuit	1962–1988	31	Brennan (10), Marshall (9), O'Connor (3), Stevens (3), Stewart (2), White (2), Blackmun (1), Powell (1)
J. Michael Luttig	4th Circuit	1991–	30	Thomas (12), Scalia (11), Kennedy (4), Rehnquist (2), O'Connor (1)
Laurence Silberman	DC Circuit	1985–	30	Thomas (9), Scalia (8), Kennedy (4), O'Connor (4), Breyer (3), Rehnquist (2)
Harry T. Edwards	DC Circuit	1980–	28	Marshall (5), Brennan (4), O'Connor (4), Souter (4), Stevens (4), Blackmun (2), Ginsburg (2), White (2), Breyer (1)
Alex Kozinski	9th Circuit	1985–	28*	Kennedy (13), O'Connor (10), Ginsburg (2), Scalia (2), Rehnquist (1)
James L. Oakes	2nd Circuit	1971–	26	Marshall (9), Blackmun (4), Brennan (4), Powell (2), White (2), Breyer (1), Burger (1), Rehnquist (1), Souter (1), Stevens (1)
Abner J. Mikva	DC Circuit	1979–1994	26*	Blackmun (7), Brennan (6), Marshall (4), O'Connor (2), Powell (2), Stevens (2), Kennedy (1), Rehnquist (1), Souter (1)
Stephen F. Williams	DC Circuit	1986–	21	Scalia (8), Souter (5), Ginsburg (2), Brennan (1), Kennedy (1), Marshall (1), O'Connor (1), Rehnquist (1), Thomas (1)
J. Harvie Wilkinson	4th Circuit	1984–	21*	Kennedy (7), O'Connor (5), Thomas (5), Ginsburg (1), Powell (1), Rehnquist (1), Scalia (1)
Patricia Wald	DC Circuit	1979–1999	19	Blackmun (5), Stevens (5), Ginsburg (2), O'Connor (2), Souter (2), Breyer (1), Marshall (1), White (1)

* A single clerk placed with two justices in two different terms was counted twice for the purpose of this analysis.
SOURCE: U.S. Supreme Court data.

Patricia Wald had similar congruency with the liberal members of the Court. On the other side of the spectrum, every clerk J. Michael Luttig has placed at the High Court has been with a conservative justice. Laurence Silberman has placed twenty-seven (90 percent) of his thirty Supreme Court clerks with conservative justices like Clarence Thomas and Antonin Scalia. Even the moderate conservative justices on the Supreme Court, O'Connor and Kennedy, draw from the same lower court judges: Alex Kozinski, who has placed 82 percent of his clerks with them, and J. Harvie Wilkinson, who has placed 57 percent of his Supreme Court clerks with the Court's two swing justices. Of the top ten clerk-producing lower court judges, only Stephen F. Williams has a somewhat mixed record, placing a mere 57 percent of his High Court clerks with conservative justices, though eight have been selected by Justice Scalia.

Geography

Geography is another consideration for many justices who routinely select clerks from the area of the country they are from or from the circuit they preside over. Justice Stevens has had a large number of clerks from midwestern schools, and said of his criteria, "I don't have any affirmative action program for hiring clerks except maybe geographic."[107] This was the practice of Justice Douglas, who ran a competition in the Ninth Circuit for his clerks. In 1965 he noted, "Other Justices take clerks from around the country. But they have no rhyme or pattern about it. They merely interview likely candidates."[108] Like Douglas, Justice O'Connor looks for clerks who hail from the western United States, particularly her home state of Arizona. But O'Connor has chosen as many clerks from both Harvard and Yale as she has from her alma mater, Stanford. Chief Justice Warren had his search committees choose at least one clerk from the West and one from the East. Warren also left instructions that Douglas should always have first choice of a clerk from the West.[109]

Justice Hugo Black wrote of his criteria, "My custom is to make my selection of a Clerk wholly on the basis of merit and qualifications, except that I prefer to get someone from Alabama or the South, other things being equal."[110] Black felt it important to hire southerners who would return to the South. In 1952, he explained to Dean Erwin Griswold why he chose two southerners:

Both intend to make their permanent residence in the South. . . . The determining factor with reference to both the young men selected is that they are not only natives of the South but intend to live there. It may be wrong in the viewpoint of some for me to take this factor into consideration, but I do have a particular interest in that section to the extent that I think it can well utilize men of broad national views.[111]

Black also wanted his clerks to engage in public service. In 1957 he explained to New York University law professor Edmond Cahn that he was looking for an applicant

who gives the greatest promise of being the most outstanding contributor to the public welfare. . . . I do not mean by this to limit myself to persons who want to hold public office. I do feel, however, that those young men who are selected to serve as clerks in this Court should have greater aspirations than that of becoming the most successful lawyer, meaning by that the most highly paid lawyer.[112]

One of his former clerks said, "The perfect clerk for Justice Black was an Alabama boy who went to Alabama Law School. If that wasn't possible, then someone from the South who went to a leading law school."[113] In fact, only one Black clerk went from Alabama Law School directly to the Court—David J. Vann, who clerked for Black in 1953—and only eight other Black clerks came directly from southern law schools: Virginia, Texas, and Washington and Lee. Though they may have originally been from the South, or attended an Alabama school at some point, as with nearly every other justice, the vast majority of Black's clerks, thirty-three out of fifty (66 percent), came from Harvard and Yale. Such was the case with Louis Oberdorfer, who graduated from Yale and clerked for Black in 1946 but originally hailed from Birmingham, Alabama.

Personal Compatibility

Perhaps the most nebulous selection factors are those personal traits or circumstances that a particular justice finds appealing and that might tip the scales in favor of a particular candidate. Justice Gray's use of his first clerks as barbers, Justice Black's attraction to clerks who could offer him a competitive tennis match, and Justice O'Connor's interest in clerks who could exhibit a particular talent at the Court's annual holiday party are but a few of the idiosyncratic intangibles that can come into play in the selection process. A former clerk told us,

> I was hired by Hugo Black, as far as I can tell, based upon the fact that I had a history of stuttering. He thought he could help someone that stuttered. I saw very little evidence that he was interested in either my academic background (University of Texas; 4th in class; Editor in Chief —*Texas Law Review*) or in my prior clerking experience with the Honorable Carl McGowan who, I think, gave me a decent recommendation. Black liked to hire clerks he thought he could help. (He hired A. E. Dick Howard because he thought anyone who had an initial for a first name was pretentious; he hired Steve Susman because he was overweight . . . or so the stories go.)

Another clerk said, "I was also hired by Lewis Powell as his first law clerk because, almost entirely, I happened to be there waiting for him at the Court when he arrived." One clerk remarked, "It was truly a lightning strike. Justice Blackmun owed my judge a favor. I knew two prior clerks personally. My year he favored Oxford and Cambridge graduates, perhaps because of prior work of [the] Hon. Keith Ellison."

There were a number of other intangible factors that former clerks told us about. For example, one clerk said that he was "available in [the] middle of [the] Term and from Missouri." Also, graduate school or professional experience sometimes helped, as well as a connection through a "family friend," being on the law review, "recommendation of prior law clerk," "interview with professor and former clerk," "quirks in personal history," "maturity as demonstrated by other life experiences, i.e., military service," and "prior government service (with the C.I.A.)." One clerk said that a contributing factor was that "I didn't take myself too seriously."

Gender

In 1961, Ruth Bader Ginsburg was clerking for a federal district judge in New York when she learned that Harvard Law School was recommending her for a clerkship with Justice Felix Frankfurter. Like nearly every one of his colleagues, Frankfurter had never selected a female clerk and decided not to "take a chance" on Ginsburg when he found out that she had a five-year-old daughter.[114] At a forty-year reunion of 1962 clerks, Robert O'Neil, who clerked for Justice William J. Brennan, remarked, "We told Justice Ginsburg that, had there been justice at the time, she would have been one of us."[115]

Gender has always been a factor in law clerk selection—though mostly because historically women were automatically excluded from consideration.[116] For example, in 1943 Justice William O. Douglas wrote Dean Judson F. Falknor of the University of Washington School of Law, "I am wondering whether or not you will have any candidates from your School whom you and the faculty could recommend to me. . . . I also realize that you may not have any one whom you could recommend. But I want to continue my practice of drawing from the law schools of the Ninth Circuit."[117] Falknor replied, "I deeply regret that I am compelled to report that there appear to be no available graduates, or prospective graduates of our school whom my colleagues and I feel we can recommend for appointment as your clerk."[118] Douglas wrote back, "When you say you have 'no available graduates' whom you could recommend for appointment as my clerk, do you include women? It is possible that I may decide to take one if I can find one who is absolutely first-rate."[119] Falknor replied,

> The top-ranking graduate of our 1942 class was a girl, Nona Fumerton now Mrs. Kenneth Cox. She is absolutely first-rate in every respect, and upon the receipt of your letter . . . it was my intention to recommend her to you. However, I found on inquiry of her that she was not in a position to go to Washington and she has advised me definitely that she is not available. . . . There is no other woman graduate of our school whom my colleagues and I feel we could recommend for this appointment. I cannot begin to tell you how disappointed we are at this turn of affairs, but I know that you would prefer that we confine our recommendations to those whom we believe to be absolutely first-class.[120]

In 1950, Sarah Livingston Davis, a graduate of Columbia Law School, applied to Justice Black for a clerkship. She wrote, "Some judges do not like women in their chambers, but perhaps you have different views on this subject."[121] Black replied, "I should have no objection whatever to appointing a woman clerk provided she met the qualifications desired."[122] Similarly, Adrian Kragen, former clerk to Earl

Warren, professor at the University of California School of Law, and a member of Warren's clerk selection committee, wrote the Chief,

> One question has arisen in regard to one of the individuals who we may interview. This individual is a woman whose Dean says she is very unusual and outstanding. However, we did not know whether you felt that with the background of all male clerks, which I understand has been the practice, a woman would fit in even though she might be extremely capable. For our guidance this time and in the future, I shall appreciate your comment in this regard. I know, of course, that you have no personal prejudice against the use of women clerks, but thought it might be that the character of the entire group working as law clerks might be such as to make it impossible or impractical to fit in a woman.[123]

Warren wrote a note to his secretary, "Wire him it is OK." Still, like nearly every one of his colleagues, the Chief never did select a female clerk. One of his colleagues who did, however, was Justice Douglas. In a 1971 reply to a female applicant, Douglas wrote, "the two [clerks] which have been chosen for this next Term by my committee are both women. I mention this fact to indicate that there is no reason at all why you should not be considered here. I have had a woman law clerk before, and so have some of the other Justices."

Table 2.11 shows the first female law clerks to work at the High Court. The first female law clerk was Lucille Lomen of the University of Washington School of Law, selected by Justice Douglas for the 1944 Term. But the Court would not have a second female clerk for another twenty-two years, when Justice Black selected Margaret J. Corcoran, a graduate of Harvard Law School and the daughter of former Holmes clerk and influential lobbyist Tommy Corcoran. Two years later, Justice Abe Fortas selected Martha F. Alschuler of the University of Chicago Law School for the 1968 Term. No female clerks were selected for the 1969 Term, and the 1970 Term would be the Court's last without at least one female law clerk.

On October 19, 1971, Ruth Bader Ginsburg, an attorney for the American Civil Liberties Union, argued the case of *Reed v. Reed*[124] before the all-male Supreme Court that had denied her a clerkship. She suggested that government policies, like the one in question, which automatically preferred males to females for the purposes of administering estates, were unconstitutional under the Equal Protection Clause of

TABLE 2.11
First Female Law Clerks in the U.S. Supreme Court: 1944–1976

Clerk	Law School	Justice	Term
Lucille Lomen	Washington	Douglas	1944
Margaret J. Corcoran	Harvard	Black	1966
Martha F. Alschuler	Chicago	Fortas	1968
Barbara D. Underwood	Georgetown	Marshall	1971
Carol S. Bruch	California	Douglas	1972
Janet Meik	Southern California	Douglas	1972
Fredericka Paff	Stanford	Rehnquist	1973
Karen N. Moore	Harvard	Blackmun	1974
Marsha Berzon	California	Brennan	1974
Karen Hastie Williams	Catholic	Marshall	1974
Julia P. Clark	Texas	Powell	1974
Donna M. Murasky	Chicago	Blackmun	1975
Candace S. Kovacic	Northeastern	Burger	1975
Christina Brooks Whitman	Michigan	Powell	1975
Sharon Baldwin	Chicago	Stevens	1975
Diane Pamela Wood	Texas	Blackmun	1976
Susan Low Bloch	Michigan	Marshall	1976
Judith A. Miller	Yale	Stewart	1976

SOURCE: U.S. Supreme Court.

the Fourteenth Amendment to the U.S. Constitution. In conference, the Court voted unanimously to strike down the policy. While the case was an important constitutional victory for women's rights, it may also have caused a number of justices to question their own practices in selecting clerks. After *Reed* was decided, Justice Douglas selected two female clerks for the upcoming term—the first time the Court had ever had more than one female clerk at the same time. In 1973, Ginsburg returned to argue another sex discrimination case, *Frontiero v. Richardson*.[125] Again, the Court struck down a government policy that discriminated against women and again the justices were personally affected. Justices Blackmun, Brennan, and Powell promptly hired their first female clerks for the following term. By 1977, every justice had hired his first female law clerk.

Were the justices wary of hiring their first female clerks? The case of Justice Harry Blackmun's first female clerk, Karen Nelson Moore, is instructive. She clerked for Judge Malcolm R. Wilkey of the U.S. Court of Appeals for the District of Columbia, and he wrote Justice Blackmun on her behalf, "She is the first girl clerk I've had, there's no difference in her work from my previous clerks', except hers is better than most of her predecessors and equal to any so far."[126] Blackmun's file on Moore, including the justice's handwritten notes taken during their interview, contain no mention of concern about hiring a female clerk. In 1998, when she was a judge on the Sixth Circuit Court of Appeals, Moore wrote to Blackmun on behalf of prospective clerk Jennifer Hendricks, "I can hardly believe that I am writing to you with a recommendation for my own clerk. It was just yesterday that I applied to you for a clerkship . . . or was it 25 years ago almost?"[127] Blackmun replied, "You mention that it was just yesterday when you applied here for a clerkship. It seems so to me, too. I am proud of your accomplishments in the last twenty plus years, both personally and professionally."[128]

Justice Powell was conscious of his choice in hiring female clerks. He wrote a former clerk in 1983, "For the first time, I am taking two women."[129]

Since the Court's landmark sex discrimination decisions of the 1970s, there has been a steady, but uneven, increase in the percentage of female clerks serving at the Court (see Figure 2.1). The percentage of female clerks reached an apex in the 1998 Term at 39 percent. After two terms of decline, the percentage has rebounded to near 1998 levels, with females comprising 37 percent of all clerks in 2002. These percentages have generally mirrored the percentage of women obtaining law degrees. According to the American Bar Association, women received 37 percent of juris doctorate degrees awarded in 1984. In 1994, women

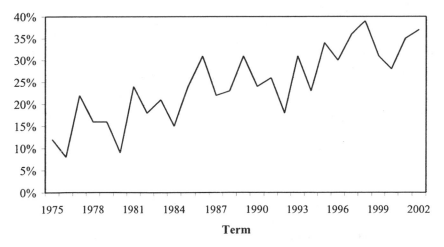

Figure 2.1. Percentage of Female Law Clerks in the U.S. Supreme Court; 1975–2002

TABLE 2.12

Percentage of Female Clerks by Justice through 2002

Justice (Total # Clerks)	Per Term High	% Female Clerks
Stephen Breyer (36)	3	50% (18)
Sandra Day O'Connor (88)	3	45% (40)
Ruth Bader Ginsburg (40)	2	40% (16)
John Paul Stevens (79)	2	29% (23)
Clarence Thomas (49)	3	27% (13)
David Souter (52)	2	21% (11)
William H. Rehnquist (91)	1	16% (15)
Antonin Scalia (68)	2	15% (10)
Anthony Kennedy (67)	2	13% (9)

NOTE: Data through 2002–2003 Term.
SOURCE: U.S. Supreme Court.

received 43 percent of these degrees. By 2001, the percentage reached 47 percent. As more women have graduated from law schools, and finished at the top of their classes, they have also made gains in Supreme Court clerkships.

Many of the inroads that women have made since the 1970s at gaining clerkships at the High Court resulted from the hiring practices of specific justices. For example, Justice Harry Blackmun did much during his years at the Court in this regard. In all, Blackmun selected thirty-four female clerks—37 percent of all clerks who worked for him. He was also the first justice to select three women as his clerks during the same year when he chose Beth Heifetz, Pamela Karlan, and Helane Morrison for the 1985 Term. Table 2.12 shows the percentage of female clerks selected by the final members of the Rehnquist Court through the 2002 Term. Justice Stephen Breyer has selected the highest percentage of female clerks (50 percent) since he joined the Court in 1994. Second was Justice Sandra Day O'Connor with 45 percent, though she selected the largest number of female clerks overall, with forty. Justice Ruth Bader Ginsburg also selected a relatively high percentage of female clerks (40 percent) during her tenure. At the opposite end of the spectrum, Justice Anthony Kennedy only chose nine female clerks (13 percent) through his first sixteen years on the High Court. Similarly, Justice Antonin Scalia has selected ten female clerks (15 percent) since he joined the Court in 1986, and Chief Justice Rehnquist only had fifteen female clerks while choosing seventy-six males during his three-decade-long service on the bench. Three female clerks have worked together in the chambers of Justices Breyer, O'Connor, and Thomas, while Chief Justice Rehnquist never selected more than one female clerk in a term.

Race

In June 1946, William T. Coleman, Jr., an African-American law student at Harvard, wrote Justice Hugo Black about a possible clerkship. Coleman outlined his impressive credentials, including his high class ranking, law review editorship, and military service. He then wrote, "Despite my training, due to the fact that I am a negro I have encountered considerable difficulty in getting a suitable position."[130] Black replied, "My clerk was selected some months ago, and I have no prospect of a vacancy until he finishes his job with me. You have made an excellent record, and I congratulate you on it."[131] Coleman did not gain a High Court clerkship for the 1946 or 1947 Terms.

In 1947, the Court's nine law clerks, Irving J. Helman, William Joslin, Albert J. Rosenthal, Stanley E. Sparrowe, John B. Spitzer, John Paul Stevens, Stanley L. Temko, John A. Thompson, and Robert B. Von Mehren—all white males—decided to throw the first Christmas party in the institution's history. The invitations were to go out to all Court employees, including the janitorial staff—comprised almost entirely of African-Americans. When Chief Justice Vinson was informed of the clerks' proposal, he raised the issue with the other justices in conference. Justice Stanley Reed said that he would not attend if African-Americans were invited. One of the justices replied that Reed's absence would place the Court in "a terrible position after all the noble utterances of the Court publicly against racial discrimination." Reed explained, "This is a purely private matter and I can do what I please in regard to private parties." Justice Felix Frankfurter joined the debate: "The very fact that we have been sitting here for nearly an hour discussing the right to hold the party makes it difficult to regard it as purely private. The Court is entangled no matter what way you look at it."[132] The party did not take place and the Court would not hold its first holiday gathering for another twelve years.

Soon after the conference where the Christmas party was discussed, Justice Frankfurter received a letter from Paul Freund of Harvard Law School, who selected Frankfurter's clerks. Freund recommended Coleman to the justice. Frankfurter wrote back, "I don't have to tell you that I don't care what color a man has, any more than I care what religion he professes or doesn't."[133] When Coleman's selection was announced in the spring of 1948, a number of people wrote Frankfurter, praising the appointment and its breaking of the racial barrier. But Frankfurter saw Coleman's receipt of the appointment solely as a matter of merit. He wrote back, "Mr. William T. Coleman was named as one of my law clerks for next year precisely for the same reason that others have been named in the past—namely, high professional competence and character. You are kind to write me, but I do not think a man deserves any praise for doing what is right and abstaining from the wrong."[134]

The first African-American clerk in the Court's history, Coleman was selected as one of two Frankfurter clerks for the 1948 Term—sixty-five years after the Court's first clerk and eight years before the Court's landmark decision in *Brown v. Board of Education*.[135] Table 2.13 lists the African-American Supreme Court law clerks from 1948 to 1996 and shows that the second African-American clerk was not selected until 1967, when Tyrone Brown clerked for Chief Justice Warren. Justice Marshall selected the Court's third African-American clerk, Karen Hastie Williams, in 1974. When the Court was considering the 1978 affirmative action case *Regents of the University of California v. Bakke*, Marshall wrote his colleagues, "As a result of our last discussion on this case, I wish also to address the question of whether Negroes have 'arrived.' Just a few examples illustrate that Negroes most certainly have not. In our own Court, we have had only three Negro law clerks."[136]

Despite the *Bakke* case and Marshall's comment about clerks, no justice, other than Marshall, selected an African-American clerk for nearly a decade. Marshall selected the Court's next three African-American clerks, two in 1980 and one in 1983. The next African-American clerk worked for Justice Stevens in 1987. Justice Blackmun's first African-American clerk joined the Court in 1990, twenty years after he joined the Court. Three years later, Justices O'Connor and Thomas selected their first clerks who were African-American. Justices Ginsburg and Breyer followed suit in 1995 and 1996, respectively.

When the justices opened the 1998 Term, representatives from the NAACP and others protested the lack of minority clerks by demonstrat-

TABLE 2.13
African-American Law Clerks in the U.S. Supreme Court: 1948–1996

Clerk	Gender	Law School	Justice	Term
William T. Coleman, Jr.	Male	Harvard	Frankfurter	1948
Tyrone Brown	Male	Cornell	Warren	1967
Karen Hastie Williams	Female	Catholic	Marshall	1974
Stephen Carter	Male	Yale	Marshall	1980
Adebayo Ogunlesi	Male	Harvard	Marshall	1980
Randall Kennedy	Male	Yale	Marshall	1983
Teresa Wynn Roseborough	Female	North Carolina	Stevens	1987
Sheryll Cashin	Female	Harvard	Marshall	1990
Scott Brewer	Male	Yale	Marshall	1990
Alan Jenkins	Male	Harvard	Blackmun	1990
Crystal Nix	Female	Harvard	Marshall	1991
Michelle A. Alexander	Female	Stanford	Blackmun	1993
James Forman, Jr.	Male	Yale	O'Connor	1993
Stephen Smith	Male	Virginia	Thomas	1993
Paul Watford	Male	UCLA	Ginsburg	1995
Olati Johnson	Female	Stanford	Stevens	1996
Robin Lenhardt	Female	Harvard	Breyer	1996

SOURCE: Adapted from list titled "African American Law Clerks," Blackmun Papers, Box 1569.

ing at the Court. They left twenty-one resumes: three addressed to Chief Justice Rehnquist, one addressed to Justice Souter, and seventeen with no cover letter. On instructions from the Chief Justice, his administrative assistant, James C. Duff, forwarded a summary of the applicants to the other justices. Duff wrote, "Nine of the candidates are either first or second year law students; two of the candidates have not attended law school; none of the candidates have federal clerkship experience, nor do any indicate that they will have a federal clerkship. One candidate is clerking for the Alaska Supreme Court and was a member of the California Law Review."[137] Duff also included a copy of a letter written on NAACP letterhead to Chief Justice Rehnquist from Cheryl Thompson:

> As you begin a new session of the Supreme Court, I want to share with you my personal concern about the under representation of minority law clerks on the staffs of Justices of the Supreme Court. It has been brought to my attention that: In the 112 years of cumulative service of the current Justices, only 7 African American law clerks have been employed out of a total of 394, in the same period 4 of 394 have been Hispanic, and 0 have been Native American. . . . 4 of the nine Justices have never appointed an African American law clerk and only one Justice has appointed more than one African American; only three Justices

have appointed Hispanic American law clerks and none has appointed more than one Hispanic. The law clerk plays an extremely important role in informing the Supreme Court decision process and in actually helping to shape the Court decisions which impact the entire Nation. I am certain, therefore, that you would agree that the Court should more fully reflect the diversity of the Nation. Accordingly I ask that you, as the Chief Justice, as a matter of urgency, provide the leadership for the development and implementation of policies and strategies that will encourage and enhance diversity among Supreme Court law clerks.[138]

A 1998 study of every clerk hired by the current nine justices during their tenures found that clerks have been overwhelmingly white and male. Fewer than 2 percent were African-American, 5 percent, Asian-American, and 25 percent, women (see Table 2.14). Through 1998, Chief Justice William Rehnquist and Justices Anthony Kennedy, Antonin Scalia, and David Souter had never hired an African-American clerk.[139] William J. Brennan, one of the Court's most liberal justices, never hired an African-American clerk in his three decades on the bench. Souter remarked, "There is no one on the court who would not like those numbers to change."[140] Justice Thomas, who has only hired one African-American clerk, said, "I look forward to the day when all four of my clerks are minorities and hold their heads proudly at the court."[141]

Pressured by a storm of controversy in the press, as well as protests outside the Court building, the justices sharply increased the number of minority clerks in the October 1999 Term, from one Hispanic clerk the previous year to two African-Americans and three Asian-Americans.[142] In 2002, the Court had a record nine minority clerks out of thirty-five.[143]

Why the lack of diversity? One argument is that the pool of potential clerks is narrow. Clerks are "stars" who graduate at the top of their class from the nation's most prestigious law schools. Justice Scalia said, "I think we should have the best and the brightest law clerks we can get."[144] Two law schools alone, Harvard and Yale, account for half of all clerks.[145] Also, minorities may not be applying or may decline a clerkship in favor of a high-paying job. Margaret Tuitt, who works on placing Harvard graduates, explained, "People are self-selective. Finances are a factor, and a lot of people feel the burden is too high. There is a bonus after the fact, but many people cannot afford to wait. I don't know if the numbers (of minorities in clerkships) are ever going to be huge."[146] Judge Luttig had a similar observation, reflecting on

TABLE 2.14
U.S. Supreme Court Law Clerk Racial
Composition: 1971–1998*

Race	% (N = 428)
White	92.9
	(398)
Asian-American	4.2
	(18)
African-American	1.6
	(7)
Hispanic	1.2
	(5)

* Includes all clerks selected by Chief Justice Rehnquist, and Justices Stevens, O'Connor, Scalia, Kennedy, Souter, Thomas, Ginsburg, and Breyer through 1998.
SOURCE: Table derived from Tony Mauro, "Court Justices Defend Hiring Record," *USA Today*, December 8, 1998.

an African-American Harvard graduate who declined a clerkship with him and a likely spot at the Supreme Court: "He went with an investment banking firm instead."[147] Justice Thomas spoke of one potential law clerk who in "no way" could have clerked for him because of his $160,000 student loan debt.[148]

What do the current justices think about the issue of race in selecting clerks? Justice Breyer said the current situation reflects "a world in which there has been considerable underprivilege, and that underprivilege is something that has to be corrected over time."[149] Souter recognized that there was a problem but did not think it was calculated: "I see something incomplete. There has been no hint that anyone on the current court is engaging in ethnic or racial discrimination. We are creatures of our feeder system. They are going to push minority high achievers in a way they have not before. We are going to see the fruits of some pushing."[150] Justice Scalia said that he was against "a system in which we have sort of racial quotas for these jobs."[151] Justice Thomas said that he would look beyond the Ivy League to a wider range of schools for his clerks. Chief Justice Rehnquist explained that he selected clerks on the basis of "superior professional achievement in law school, together with an appraisal as to how well we would work together. I have never excluded consideration of anyone because of that person's race or nationality."[152] Justice O'Connor said, "We do not discriminate here on the basis of gender or race or anything else. We try to get the best we can. I have had black clerks, I have had Asian clerks, I have had Hispanic clerks."[153]

For their part, recommenders often highlight a candidate's status as a racial minority. For example, Michelle Alexander's three recommenders from Stanford Law School made reference to her racial status. Dean Paul Brest wrote Justice Blackmun, "More generally, I want to say that, for whatever reasons, very few minority students at Stanford have achieved so high an overall average to be elected to the Order of the Coif."[154] Professor Gerald P. Lopez noted in his recommendation, "I have heard lavish praise of Michelle [Alexander] from many quarters —from other African-Americans."[155] Professor Barbara Allen Babcock wrote, "she may not be able in the short run to resist the law firms' blandishments (heightened in the case of a brilliant black woman)."[156]

One way to increase the number of minority clerks would be for the Court to adopt a loan forgiveness program, rewarding top graduates for going into public service. When Representative Frank Wolf, a Virginia Republican, made this suggestion in 2003, Justice Kennedy replied, "This is a revelation. You are teaching me."[157] Both pledged to explore the matter.

Sexual Orientation

There are no completely accurate statistics on the number of gay and lesbian former law clerks. In their 2001 book *Courting Justice*, Joyce Murdoch and Deb Price found twenty-two gay former Supreme Court clerks—eighteen men, four of whom died of AIDS, and four women. Historically, gay clerks kept their sexual orientation private, only choosing to come out after their justice retired. According to Murdoch and Price, the earliest discovered gay clerk worked for Justice Harlan in the 1950s. Jim Graham, who clerked for Chief Justice Warren during the 1973 Term, did not disclose his sexual orientation to the retired Chief. Justice Powell, who provided the fifth vote in *Bowers v. Hardwick* to uphold a state law criminalizing sodomy, unconsciously hired at least one homosexual clerk for six consecutive terms in the 1980s.[158] During the conference discussion of *Bowers*, Justice Blackmun noted, "Clerks!" while Powell was discussing his views.[159] Blackmun recalled a conversation he had with his colleague after Powell had initially provided the fifth vote in conference to strike down the state law only to change his mind a week later: "I remember him telling me, 'Harry, I've never known a homosexual in my life.' Well, when he said that, there were two in his chambers."[160]

But in recent years, some gay clerks have come out to their justice. For example, Michael Conley, a 1990 Blackmun clerk, recalled a typical conversation between Blackmun and his clerks: "One of my co-clerks would say, 'Well, my husband, Sean, and I are going here or there.' "And I would say, 'Yeah, Mark and I have been there.'"[161] Bill Araiza, a 1991 Souter clerk, recalled coming out to the justice: "I tried to explain to him why I thought it was appropriate that I tell him—that it is important for people in authority to realize that people who work for them and who are their trusted confidants are gay."[162]

While sexual orientation may not be a criterion used by justices in selecting clerks, the evidence provided by Murdoch and Price demonstrates that a number of justices have had openly gay clerks. Still, they suggest that Court traditions have limited their impact on the institution:

> Justices' isolated work environment makes it very difficult, if not impossible, for them to know how much of their court's work has been done by gay people. Most of today's justices are unlikely to be aware, for example, of Powell's long string of gay clerks. There is no Gay and Lesbian Former Supreme Court Clerks Association filing briefs or inviting justices to dinner.[163]

Ideology

Do justices choose clerks who are ideologically similar? If so, how do they go about determining a clerk's political leanings? Do justices ask potential clerks questions related to politics in an attempt to gauge their attitudes? Do clerks state their political affiliations in their letters of application? Or are there more subtle ways of determining ideological congruence? Justice Scalia explained his selection criteria: "All I have are the grades from law schools, the law school that the person graduates from and the recommendations of the law professors, and I pick my law clerks on the basis of that."[164] But John Fee, a Scalia clerk from 1997, remarked, "Justice Scalia considers [ideology], but he likes to have clerks with a variety of perspectives."[165] Blackmun's notes on a phone call to appeals court Judge Herbert Choy reflect that they discussed a prospective clerk's ideology. In addition to noting the applicant's

toughness and other qualities, Blackmun wrote, "lib–conservative."[166]
Justice O'Connor said,

> I am the one who has to make the decisions around here, so I am not
> concerned or interested in the individual's particular philosophy. How-
> ever, I don't want to hire someone who has a particular ax to grind in
> terms of legal structure. I am more interested in finding people who can
> be objective. So I look for the skills that any good lawyer should have—
> the ability to pull apart a legal problem, break it down to its logical
> components and analyze it.[167]

There is considerable evidence to suggest that some clerks limit their
applications to particular justices for partisan reasons. As we discussed
earlier, most clerks apply to all nine justices. However, we were interested in examining which justices were excluded for those clerks who
applied to only eight or seven justices. Table 2.15 suggests that, at least
for the clerks who accepted a clerkship with Justice Blackmun, certain
justices are regularly excluded. For those clerks who applied to every
justice but one, Chief Justice Rehnquist was excluded by four clerks and
Justice Thomas by three. For those who applied to all but two justices,
Rehnquist was excluded by seven clerks and Chief Justice Burger by
seven. While all three of these justices are conservative, the data suggests that clerks may have excluded them for other reasons. Both Burger
and Rehnquist served as Chief and clerks may have excluded them because of the additional duties performed by the Chief's clerks, such as
coordinating the cert pool. Thomas may have been excluded because of
the controversy surrounding his confirmation. Still, Rehnquist was excluded by six of the Blackmun clerks who applied to seven or eight justices before he became Chief Justice. Similarly, in 1979, Virginia law
professor Peter W. Low wrote Justice Powell, "Susan [Lahne] is applying to all of the Justices except Rhenquist."[168]

In general, applicants do not overtly state their political or ideological leanings when applying for clerkships. But on occasion, eager applicants looking for an advantage over others have been direct. For
example, a prospective clerk wrote Justice Hugo Black in 1937, "Although I know that your selection will not hinge on these factors, I suppose that I should state that politically I am a liberal Democrat; my
religion, Jewish."[169] In his application to Justice Black for the 1958
Term, Arthur R. Miller explained that he desired a clerkship "with a

TABLE 2.15
Justices Not Applied to for Clerkships by
Blackmun Clerks: 1975–1993

Number of Justices Applied To	Justice(s) Excluded	Number of Clerks Excluding Justice
8	Rehnquist	4
	Thomas	3
	Brennan	2
7	Rehnquist	7
	Burger	7
	Scalia	1
	White	1
	Stevens	1
	Brennan	1

SOURCE: Blackmun Papers, Boxes 1553–1568.

justice with whose views I have sympathy."[170] And on occasion, a rec-ommender has made subtle hints at ideological congruence. For exam-ple, Judge Learned Hand wrote Justice Hugo Black about an applicant, "you would find him, I believe, in entire accord with your own general approach and outlook."[171] In another letter of recommendation to Jus-tice Black, Judge David Bazelon of the D.C. Circuit Court of Appeals described an applicant as having "mature and liberal insights."[172] And even justices have been overt that ideology is important. Justice Douglas wrote University of California, Berkeley, law professor Max Radin, in asking him to take on the task of selecting his clerks, "I do not want a hide-bound conservative fellow."[173]

We asked former clerks whether they discussed policy or political issues with the justice during their interview. One clerk said that during her interview with one of the Court's liberal members, she "told him I had not applied to Justice Burger." Another clerk said that he discussed "judicial philosophy" but "no political issues." A former clerk for Stan-ley Reed said of his interview, "I think, with all honesty, we hit it off. [The interview] was very important with Stanley Reed because he was very much a man who relished talking to his law clerks and arguing with his law clerks."[174] Another clerk told us, "In my meeting with Jus-tice Powell he stressed his commitment that our views as law clerks on matters of policy and political issues were irrelevant—as were his."

As a rule, Chief Justices Vinson and Warren and Justices Frankfurter, Brennan, and Douglas did not interview prospective clerks. One Frank-furter clerk explained, "Justice Frankfurter did not select his law clerks.

He delegated that decision at the time of my selection to Professor Sacks at Harvard Law School. There was no interview with anyone. Sacks picked only Harvard Law School students whom he knew." A former Douglas clerk explained that he "did not interview with Justice Douglas directly. I was interviewed by Stan Sparrowe, one of his former clerks." A Brennan clerk told us that he had "no interview. Justice Brennan selected mostly based on recommendations, transcript, law review position, etc." In 1956, Justice Black explained, "So many applications are received that I have found it impossible to interview all applicants. My regular method of selecting is to look over applications and select two persons for interviews."[175] It was also not uncommon for other justices to hire clerks without interviews. One of Burger's clerks said that he had "no interview with the Chief." Another said that the "Chief had a panel that interviewed. He did not." Two of Clark's clerks said that they had "no interview." One of Reed's clerks said he had "no interview." Though fewer interviews were conducted as the number of applications increased, in general, justices continue to interview prospective clerks to this day.

Figure 2.2 shows that only 14 percent of clerks (sixteen of 114) discussed policy or political issues during their interview. There is no discernable pattern among the justices as to which discussed politics and which did not, except in the case of Justice Powell. Of the six Powell clerks we spoke with, though this was admittedly a small number, four said that they discussed politics in their interview with Powell. Powell wrote that he sought clerks who were "more dedicated to high quality professional work than to any particular social or political viewpoint."[176] After he interviewed 1974 clerk Penny Clark, he said that she "has no ideological commitment to any cause or causes."[177] Similarly, after his interview with 1974 clerk Ronald Carr, Powell commented,

> I discussed with him whether he would be happy working with a Justice who is characterized as being "conservative" after working with a Circuit Judge who is generally considered quite "liberal." He gave me a satisfactory answer to this, indicating his desire to decide cases on the law and the facts, with due regard to ultimate consequences (where these may properly be considered).[178]

Coupled with Justice O'Connor's remarks about not wanting clerks who have "an ax to grind" and Justice Blackmun's interview question about

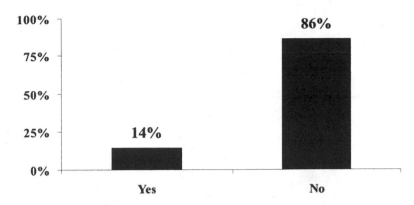

Figure 2.2. During your interview with the justice for your selection as law clerk, did you discuss policy or political views? (N = 114)

the "division" of the justices, we submit that while ideology is not entirely absent from the interview process, in general it does not come up at this stage of the selection process, at least not in an overt way.

Still, ideology can play a role in clerk selection. A former clerk said of Justice Brennan, "He's developed a system that brings to him very liberal, very talented clerks who think as he does. They do for him what he would do for himself."[179] We were interested in the ideological composition of the clerks and whether there was a relationship with the ideological composition of the justices. Table 2.16 shows that there is a remarkable congruence. Overall, law clerks tend to be moderately liberal (3.5), but there is variation in the data as the standard deviation is 1.02. And while our per-justice responses are lower than we would like, the results are suggestive. The data suggests that most liberal clerks worked for Justices Douglas, Warren, Marshall, and Brennan. Within this group, the clerks for Douglas, Warren, and Marshall were more consistently liberal (standard deviations of 0.45, 0.58, 0.63, respectively) than were Brennan's clerks (0.99). The most conservative clerks worked for Justices Rehnquist, Blackmun, Burger, and Clark. Within this group, the clerks for Rehnquist and Clark were more consistently conservative (standard deviations of 0.92 and 0.88, respectively) than were Blackmun's and Burger's clerks (1.17, 1.46). Overall, the justices who had clerks with the most consistent ideology were Douglas and Frankfurter, with standard deviations of 0.45 each. On the other end of the spectrum, Justice White and Chief Justice Burger had the most

TABLE 2.16
Clerk Ideology by Justice

Justice	Mean Clerk Ideology (n =)	Standard Deviation
Douglas	4.20 (5)	0.45
Warren	4.00 (7)	0.58
Marshall	4.00 (7)	0.63
Brennan	3.87 (15)	0.99
Frankfurter	3.80 (5)	0.45
Stewart	3.80 (5)	1.10
Black	3.75 (12)	0.75
White	3.75 (8)	1.58
Powell	3.50 (6)	1.05
Clark	3.27 (15)	0.88
Burger	3.13 (8)	1.46
Blackmun	2.83 (6)	1.17
Rehnquist	2.38 (8)	0.92
Overall Mean & Stdev =	3.50	1.02

5 = extremely liberal, 4 = slightly liberal, 3 = moderate, 2 = slightly conservative, 1 = extremely conservative.
NOTE: Justices with fewer than five respondents are omitted from the table but included in the overall mean & standard deviation (n = 137).

overall variation in clerk ideology, with standard deviations of 1.58 and 1.46, respectively.

Table 2.17 compares the ideology of the justices, as measured by liberal policy output, to clerk ideology as reported on the survey instrument. Similarly, Figure 2.3 shows the relationship between justice and clerk ideology. Justice ideology is measured by the average percentage of liberal policy decisions on criminal procedure, civil rights, and First Amendment cases. Clerk ideology is measured on a scale from one to five, with five being "extremely liberal." Each data point on the scatter plot represents a justice and shows that there is a strong correlation between the ideology of a justice and the ideology of his or her clerks (R^2 = 0.6).[180]

TABLE 2.17
Justice Ideology and Law Clerk Ideology

Justice	Justice Ideology*	Mean Clerk Ideology
Douglas	92.1	4.20
Marshall	84.5	4.00
Brennan	83.0	3.87
Warren	80.0	4.00
Black	67.8	3.75
Blackmun	59.0	2.83
Stewart	54.5	3.80
Frankfurter	52.1	3.80
Clark	43.4	3.27
Whittaker	43.1	3.00
Powell	39.2	3.50
Burger	29.1	3.13
Rehnquist	18.4	2.38

* Justice Ideology is average percentage of liberal policy output on criminal procedure, civil rights, and First Amendment cases as reported in Jeffrey Segal and Harold Spaeth, *The Supreme Court and the Attitudinal Model* (New York: Cambridge University Press, 1993), 245–51.

Law Clerk Ideology scale: 5 = extremely liberal, 4 = slightly liberal, 3 = moderate, 2 = slightly conservative, 1 = extremely conservative.
NOTE: Justices with fewer than five respondents are omitted.

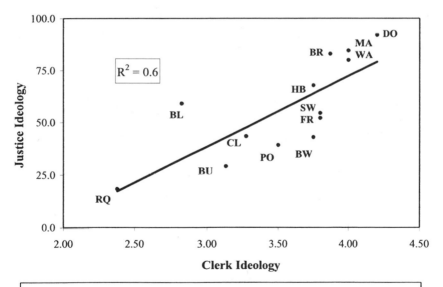

Note: HB=Hugo Black; BL=Harry Blackmun; BR=William Brennan; BU=Warren Burger; CL=Tom Clark; DO=Douglas; FR=Felix Frankfurter; MA=Thurgood Marshall; PO=Lewis Powell; RQ=William Rehnquist; SW=Potter Stewart; WA=Earl Warren; BW=Byron White.

Figure 2.3. Justice Ideology by Clerk Ideology

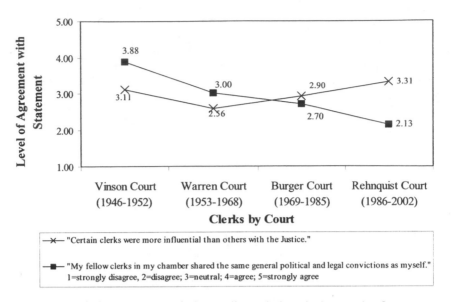

Figure 2.4. Clerk Perceptions of Their Fellow Clerks' Ideology and Influence

Figure 2.4 shows clerk perceptions of the ideology and influence of the other clerks they worked with in their chambers. In general, through the Warren Court, clerks were ideologically aligned and had the same level of influence with their justice as their fellow clerks. Beginning with the Burger Court and most dramatically into the Rehnquist Court, clerks were much less ideologically aligned and certain clerks were more influential than others. On the question of whether they shared the same ideological and political views as their co-clerks, a Vinson clerk from the 1940s said, "One did. I didn't." A Clark clerk from the 1950s said, "The other clerk was a moderate Republican. We rarely, if ever, disagreed on issues." A Burger clerk from the 1970s said, "Two did. I didn't." A Rehnquist clerk from 1970s said, "It was never relevant what we thought, so I don't know."

We suggest that these changes were a direct result of the change in the application process. Through the Warren Court, clerks were selective in targeting specific justices to apply to. In general, liberal clerks limited their applications to liberal justices and conservative clerks targeted conservative justices. But as the process got more competitive and a greater number of recent law graduates sought High Court clerkships, applicants began targeting every justice regardless of ideology. This made it more difficult for justices to determine the ideological persuasion of prospective clerks. For their part, liberal clerks accepted offers from conservative justices, as did conservative clerks with liberal justices. This is why the level of ideological agreement among clerks has declined. Similarly, this phenomenon has also led to certain clerks, presumably those more closely aligned ideologically with their justice, having more influence than others.

Conclusion

The preceding analysis suggests that while many factors come into play in the selection of Supreme Court law clerks, some factors are more important than others. While clerks come from a handful of elite schools, it is their academic achievement at these schools, such as attaining high class ranking and making law review, that makes them viable candidates for positions at the High Court. Similarly, securing a clerkship on the courts of appeals with one of the top "feeder" judges has become a virtual requirement. For particular justices, geographical considerations are considered. While gender diversity is very important to a few justices, most chambers are composed of male clerks. Lagging even further behind gender is racial diversity, though recent criticisms have caused some justices to begin to diversify their clerking corps.

Perhaps our most interesting finding, however, is the general ideological congruence between justices and clerks, with liberal justices generally selecting liberal clerks and conservative justices selecting conservative clerks. Since modern clerks generally apply to all nine justices, and political and ideological persuasions are generally not discussed overtly in application letters and interviews, we conclude that informal cues have led to the ideological alignment between justice and clerk. Specifically, application cues such as memberships in conservative or liberal organizations and, more importantly, the ideology of the lower court judge, allow justices to quickly assess the clerk's partisan alignment. This is not to say that ideology is more important than other factors, such as academic performance and prior clerkship experience; rather, ideology is simply another criterion, like geography or even gender, for the justice to use in further narrowing the enormous pool of applications they receive from top students who clerk for "feeder" judges. This should not be surprising given the level of responsibility that modern clerks have been given by the justices, such as making recommendations on certiorari petitions and bench memos, and writing opinions. At the same time, because most clerks apply to every justice, the process of achieving ideological congruence has been made more difficult and has resulted in increasing partisan differences among clerks who work for the same justice, which in turn has led to certain clerks being more influential than others.

Overall, clerks are still a relatively homogenous group reaping the professional rewards and personal influence of a now-outdated apprentice model of legal education. They are still largely white males who graduated at the top of their classes from a handful of elite law schools and went on to secure prestigious clerkships on the courts of appeals with a small group of judges who place a large number of clerks at the High Court. For a process that is conducted independently by nine different people, there is remarkable cohesion. In a letter to members of Congress, Chief Justice Rehnquist defended the current process:

> Each justice of course acts independently in deciding whom to employ as law clerks. The importance of preserving this independence makes it inappropriate for the court as an institution to play a role in the selection of law clerks by individual justices. The same interest in preserving the independence and impartiality of the judicial process also makes it inappropriate for any justice, in performing official duties, to seek guidance from special constituencies. That said, all of the justices are pleased to consider recommendations and comments from all segments of the bar with respect to the qualifications and credentials of an applicant.[181]

Still, the relatively unchanged face of the century-old Supreme Court law clerk does not bode well for an institution that has been criticized for wielding too much power. In the following chapters, we address the concern over the growing influence of law clerks by discussing the cert process, decision making, and opinion writing.

3

The Junior Court
Deciding to Decide

If I made all the rules, I don't think I'd want it.
—Justice John Paul Stevens on the cert pool

This issue is factbound. I recommend that you vote to deny.
—Typical law clerk cert memo

For most of the nation's history, each justice personally reviewed every petition that came to the Court. In his testimony before a House committee in 1925, Justice Willis Van Devanter stated, "Each judge examines [the petition, brief, and lower court records] and prepares a memorandum or note indicating his views of what should be done."[1] The earliest clerks reviewed petitions too, but merely as part of their advanced apprenticeships in the law, as the nine justices always discussed every case in conference. But as the number of petitions increased, from eight a week when Van Devanter was on the Court to over 150 a week at present, and the justices stopped formally discussing every petition, they started relying on their clerks to review the cases and prepare memos. What began as a learning exercise developed into necessary work. In the mid-1950s, Justice Robert Jackson wrote, "A suspicion has grown at the bar that the law clerks constitute a kind of junior court which decides the fate of certiorari petitions. This idea of the law clerk's influence gave rise to a lawyer's waggish statement that the Senate no longer need bother about confirmation of justices but ought to confirm the appointment of law clerks."[2]

Julian Burke, who clerked for Justice Stanley Reed in 1955, said,

Reed was not as interested in full-blown, thorough analyses of cert petitions as some of the other justices were. He wanted you to, in as few words as possible, tell him what the issues were and tell him what the turning issue was. He really wanted you to synthesize then as much as possible to give him a sense of how important it was or wasn't. He was more interested in learning how important the matter was than whether or not it had been decided correctly below. As a consequence, our cert memos were significantly less long than almost any other clerk's. And he could go through those very, very quickly. And then he would end up with a much smaller group, and then he'd want broader, longer, analytical memos. I always thought that it was exactly what he should be doing, exactly the focus he should give to you, and as a consequence we had much more time to spend with him on his opinions. And we even had a lot of time to go to oral arguments. A lot of clerks never would show up in court because they were constantly researching on all these cert petitions.[3]

In this chapter we discuss the role of law clerks in the certiorari process. Specifically, we argue that, contrary to conventional wisdom, the creation of the cert pool drastically reduced the amount of time clerks devoted to reviewing cert petitions and writing cert memos and also diluted their individual influence in the certiorari process. Because they reviewed fewer petitions, and sometimes had their memos checked by clerks from other chambers, clerks felt that their recommendations were less influential with the justices than before the cert pool was created. Still, some clerks were more influential in this process with their justice than were clerks for other justices. The implications of clerks reviewing fewer petitions are at least twofold. First, they can delve more fully into the cases they do review, and second, they are free to devote more of their time to opinion writing. Given these findings, we suggest that the addition of three and subsequently four clerks per chamber, as well as the creation of the cert pool, radically transformed the institution of law clerk, affording clerks greater responsibility and enhanced opportunity for overall influence.

Exploding Dockets and Pooling Clerks

Clerks have reviewed cert petitions since the institution's inception. Samuel Williston, the first clerk, was instructed by Justice Horace Gray to review all the cases filed at the Court and make recommendations in oral discussions with Gray before conference.[4] When Congress formally appropriated funds for the first law clerks in 1919, more justices began using clerks to review the certiorari petitions and draft memos. C. Dickerman Williams, who clerked for Chief Justice William Howard Taft during the 1924 Term, recalled his initial conversations with the Chief: "My duties, he said, would be to digest, i.e., summarize, the facts and issues in petitions for certiorari . . . and then send them on to him."[5] Initially, justices did not use their clerks out of necessity but instead involved them in teacher-student relationships, with the clerks being engaged in a unique study of the law at the nation's highest court. Clerks wrote memos on cert petitions not as an aid or shortcut for their justice so much as for a learning exercise.[6] Some justices, however, began using clerk-written memos in conference. Justice Harlan Fiske Stone's secretary wrote, "[Justice Stone] takes [to the conference] only the typed memoranda prepared by the law clerk in connection with the certs."[7]

Until the 1935 Term, the Court formally considered every cert petition in conference. For example, Chief Justice Taft routinely sent memoranda to his colleagues informing them of the upcoming conferences. A typical letter to the "Brethren" from Taft briefly stated, "I am calling for a conference for next Saturday . . . we should dispose of motions and certioraris [then]."[8] Charles Evans Hughes continued the long-standing practice in his first few years as Chief Justice. For example, he wrote the other justices in 1931,

> The Clerk is sending each member of the Court a complete list of all applications for writs of certiorari which will be submitted on Monday, October 5th. Unless a different course is desired, I suggest that the Court hold a Conference on Tuesday, October 6th, at noon, at which the first 100 cases on the clerk's list, that is, Nos. 47 to 206, both inclusive, will be considered, and such further Conference or Conferences later in the week as the Court on Tuesday shall decide upon.[9]

This procedure greatly minimized the need for law clerks to review petitions, except perhaps the Chief's clerks. But Hughes was aware that his colleagues were using their clerks to prepare memos. He recalled,

> There was a large amount of work to be done during each summer in preparation for the October Term of the Court. This was in examining the host of applications for certioraris, the jurisdictional statements

upon appeals, and the applications to be heard *in forma pauperis*. The law clerks of the Justices did the preliminary work in examining records and briefs and preparing copious memoranda. I had highly competent law clerks. Reynolds Robertson, Francis R. Kirkham, Richard W. Hogue, Jr., and Edwin McElwain served in succession with great ability. But, while availing myself of their memoranda, I made it a practice to check them by my own examination of the records and briefs and I made my own notes, which were as succinct as possible. I presented each case with my views to the conferences of the Court which were held in the opening week of the Term, when we passed upon the various applications.[10]

Because the Chief Justice would summarize every case on the docket before calling for a vote, justices could rely on the conference discussion to help them decide whether or not to grant a case, even if they had never read the briefs, let alone a law clerk's memo. For example, John Knox, who clerked for Justice James McReynolds in 1936, wrote,

I became more and more puzzled as to why the Justice never seemed to care whether I was going to finish reading all of the petitions or not. I failed to realize that all of my reading and typing was really quite unimportant after all. Even if I had not read and briefed a single petition, it would not have been too much of a loss for the Justice. I overlooked the fact that McReynolds and Van Devanter were the ranking senior Justices of the Court. McReynolds was next to the senior Justice in point of service, which meant that he had the privilege of voting next to the last at every conference of the Court—unless Hughes exercised his privilege of voting last by virtue of being Chief Justice. The youngest Justice in point of service had to vote first, [and so on up the seniority ladder]. So McReynolds and Van Devanter always had the benefit of the votes of at least six Justices, and perhaps seven, before they needed to cast their own ballots. Therefore, any recommendations which I might make in my digests of the petitions for certiorari were more or less superfluous. In a pinch, all McReynolds really needed to do was to listen to the Chief Justice's discussion of the facts of each petition and then wait for the Justices to vote. With his more than twenty years of experience on the bench, it was only natural that by 1936, petitions—even hundreds of them—would leave McReynolds quite unmoved.[11]

Justice William O. Douglas echoed Knox's characterization of Mc-Reynolds: "McReynolds didn't participate much in the life of the conference. He was very curt and short and would say, 'It is obvious this should be affirmed. I need not state my reasons.' And let it go at that. He never would argue with anybody."[12]

Evidence suggests, however, that Chief Justice Hughes changed the conference procedure in 1935. Justice Douglas recalled,

> Hughes would send around before a conference a list of cases that he put on a special list. On the special list were cases that were, in his mind, patently frivolous cases that didn't present any substantial question, that were not even worthy of conference discussion. Anyone, theoretically, if he wanted to discuss a case on Hughes' special list could have the case removed from the special list and brought up and discussed and voted upon. But it hadn't been done, at least very often, when I came on the Court. Hughes used the special list as an efficiency device to get through by four-thirty and to speed up the work of the conference.[13]

The "special list" became known as the "dead list" since cases left on it were neither discussed nor voted on, and were therefore automatically denied. On September 30, 1935, Hughes wrote the other justices, "I enclose a list of petitions for certiorari to be presented to the Conference (week of October 7) simply by number and title. If you desire one of the cases on the list to be stated to the Conference, kindly let me know."[14] Similarly, he wrote his colleagues in 1938, "I hand you herewith Special List of certioraris for the Conference to be held during the week of October the third. If there are any cases on this list which you think should be presented for discussion, kindly advise me so that I may go over the cases again and prepare to make an appropriate presentation."[15]

Dead listing was an outgrowth of the procedure for handling in forma pauperis cases, which were the sole responsibility of the chief justice. Douglas recalled the conference procedure for IFPs:

> Hughes would bring them all to conference and he would not discuss the facts of all of them. He would say, "Gentlemen, there are only two this week in the miscellaneous group that I think need mention. One is a capital case . . . from South Carolina and the other is a felony case

from Michigan," or whatnot. And he would summarize very briefly and if anybody was interested in seeing the record, he would say, "I will distribute it." Once in a while somebody would say, "Would you mind if the case would go over so I can look over the record?" And he would say, "Certainly." So he would send the record around to those who wanted to see it. But those cases were handled by Hughes himself and . . . the law clerk that Hughes paid out of his own pocket . . . all during the Hughes regime.[16]

When Knox informed Justice Louis Brandeis of the certiorari work he was doing for McReynolds, Brandeis was surprised and said, "You digest all of the petitions in writing?"[17] When another McReynolds clerk complained about the heavy workload and suggested that he needed an assistant, McReynolds replied, "You'll do this work alone and like it. Furthermore, if I weren't afraid the Chief would suspect me, I'd make you write my opinions, too."[18] Knox recalled Justice Mc-Reynolds's instructions:

> "There will be hundreds of petitions for certiorari coming in during the summer, and I want you to read each one. Then summarize each petition in one page of typing, single-spaced. Give me the facts of each case, the question of law presented, the holding of the lower courts, and your own personal recommendation whether you think the petition should or should not be allowed."[19]

After the creation of the dead list, clerks took on an increasingly crucial role in case selection. A clerk for Justice Hugo Black from the 1940s told us, "I made recommendations re: all cert petitions. Usually, he agreed, but not because of my recommendation." Edwin M. Zimmerman, one of two clerks for Justice Reed during the 1950 Term, said,

> My recollection is that a basic function was, of course, to write the cert memos, and in looking through these files that I resurrected this morning, I find an enormous volume of cert memos which we all wrote for, I guess, the conference in those days on certs was Saturday morning. And we would be particularly busy Friday afternoon trying to finish up the stuff that had to be finished up for the justice to read, or maybe we had to get it in to him in time for him to read it on Friday—

these single spaced typed memos which [were] really in the hundreds of pages. So an important function, there were two of us, two clerks, he relied heavily on us to summarize the cert petitions. He would make his own judgments, though. He would go over them very carefully and, I think, essentially use our memos as a way of getting into the facts more quickly.[20]

The dead list had the practical effect of elevating the importance of clerks in screening petitions for possible conference discussion. In 1950, Chief Justice Vinson stopped circulating the dead list.[21] Since then, the justices have only worked from the discuss list, with each justice being able to place a case on the list at any time and as many times as he or she likes. As a result, by the 1950s, justices who still did their own cert work were rare. A Frankfurter clerk from the 1950s told us, "Clerks for Frankfurter did not participate in cert decisions." In a letter to Justice Potter Stewart, Frankfurter said that cert decisions are "so dependent on a seasoned and disciplined professional judgment that I do not believe that lads—most of them fresh out of law school and with their present tendentiousness—should have any routine share in the process . . . however tentative and advisory their memos on what is reported in the record and what is relevant to our taking a case may be."[22] Like Frankfurter, Justice William Brennan also largely reviewed cert petitions himself. But Frankfurter and Brennan were somewhat unique during this period when many justices had two clerks and had to find something for them to do.

As dockets grew, and a greater number of cases failed to make the discuss list, the justices were forced to rely more heavily on their clerks. The clerks were expected to write brief memos on the lengthy cases. Chief Justice Earl Warren told one of his clerks, "I just read your memos and I don't think you need twenty pages to convince me that those are cert-worthy cases. I hope you can be more brief in the future, because I have to wade through an awful lot of these memos for each conference."[23] In 1961, Justice Douglas said, "My law clerk writes a memorandum on all the certioraris and appeals that come in—a very useful record. I make some notes on his memoranda and they are good reference material, particularly if the case comes up for argument or if it comes back for a rehearing."[24] Justice Lewis F. Powell, Jr., wrote his 1973 clerks,

I have observed from my short experience here that the Chief Justice and the more senior members of the Court almost invariably include on the discuss list all cases which I think merit discussion. The Justices vary considerably in their degree of "liberality" as to what should be discussed, and I personally think that the discuss list frequently includes a number of quite meritless cases. I would prefer to see us concentrate—with greater deliberation—on the relatively small number of cases arguably quite important in terms of the issues presented. Nevertheless, when the discuss list circulated by the Chief Justice is received do not hesitate to bring to my attention any case which you think should be discussed and which is not on his list.[25]

An example of the kind of analysis a clerk might give in a cert memo on a controversial case is 1970 Blackmun clerk Robert E. Gooding, Jr.'s discussion of the sex discrimination case *Reed v. Reed*: "Appellant makes a strong case that the statute violates equal protection. . . . It cannot be denied that the question is important. On the other hand, it might be argued that the issue arises in a somewhat trivial context and that the Court ought to await a more compelling fact situation before it speaks to the issue of unconstitutional discrimination against women."[26] An example of a typical analysis in a noncontroversial case is the following cert memo, in which Justice Marshall wrote a large, red "D" in the upper right corner to indicate that he would vote to deny the petition. The memo was written by Marshall clerk Michael S. Davis, who put his initials on the memo after his recommendation to "DENY":

> 90-8030   timely/response waived
> Johnson v. Longview School Dist.
> Cert to CA5 (Politz, *Davis*, Barksdale)
> Petr, an Afro-American school teacher, brought a complaint under Title VII and §§1981 and 1983 after she was terminated from her position. The DC found that racial bias might have played a role in her dismissal, but that the motivating factor was petr's poor job performance and that, with or without any racial bias, petr would have been dismissed because of her job performance. The CA5 affirmed. Petr challenges the factual findings below. She maintains that the testimony of her evaluators as to her poor job performance was not credible. This issue is fact-bound. I recommend that you vote to deny.
> DENY md   June 23, 1991   June 27 List, p. 9[27]

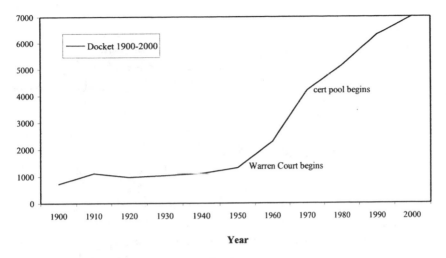

Figure 3.1. U.S. Supreme Court Caseload: 1900–2000

Figure 3.1 shows that the Court's docket was relatively stable at around one thousand cases a year from the beginning of the century until the 1950s, when the docket exploded. During the Warren Court, in forma pauperis petitions increased dramatically and Congress passed environmental, civil rights, consumer, safety, and social welfare legislation. Justices and clerks strained to meet the burden, with clerks taking on a more active role. In a stunning incident of clerk influence as early as 1948, Justice Wiley Rutledge wrote Chief Justice Vinson, "After discussion with Justices Black and Douglas and Justice Murphy's clerk, Mr. Gressman, it has been agreed that I should inform you that the four of us" agree that the cert petition should be granted review and that "the case should be set for argument forthwith."[28] But Gressman's extraordinary influence was unique. One clerk described them as "Murphy-Gressman, because it was hard sometimes to distinguish between the two—the law clerk and the justice."[29] By 1970 the Court was receiving over four thousand petitions a year.

In response to the growing caseload, the cert pool was created in 1972 to expedite the processing of petitions for certiorari. Justice William H. Rehnquist noted,

The first term in which I served on the Court, there was no "cert pool," and each chambers did all of its own certiorari work as well as its other work. I could not help but notice that my clerks were frequently pressed for time, scrambling between having memos describing the certiorari petitions ready when they should be, and drafts or revisions of Court opinions or dissents ready when they should have been.[30]

Similarly, Justice Powell was shocked when he arrived at the Court, commenting to his clerks, "These ubiquitous things will be with us always."[31] In private practice at Hunton Williams, Powell had managed a large team of partners and associates and found his small Supreme Court staff of two clerks and a secretary distressing. He wrote one of his clerks,

> In view of the caseload here, we all know that regardless of the hours worked a thorough, scholarly performance is simply impossible. Something is drastically wrong with a system in which a petition for certiorari, involving vastly important matters for the parties involved, and which may have been worked on for many weeks by distinguished counsel, can be "deadlisted" here with no Justice giving the case more than the "back of his hand."[32]

At a conference of the justices in June 1972, Powell suggested they pool their clerks to eliminate the repetition of nine clerks writing nine memos on the same case for each of their justices. Instead, one clerk would write the memo on a case for all the justices to review. Four clerks from different chambers were selected to study the mechanics of running the cert pool and to draft a proposal.[33] Their draft proposal was circulated on July 12, 1972, and included, among other things, a provision for objectivity:

> The final paragraph will consist of a brief and objective analysis of the issues presented by the case, including an analysis of any jurisdictional issues, and a determination whether there really is a conflict in the circuits if the parties claim there is, and comment on the significance of the conflict. The memo will include no recommendations. . . . It is assumed that each chambers will have a clerk assigned to examine and review each memo and supplement it if necessary.[34]

Also included in the circulated proposal was an outline on "Memo Format" as well as a sample pool memo. The proposal's call for "objective analysis" and "no recommendations" suggests that the clerks were concerned that pool writers might use their new platform to influence justices outside their own chambers.

Nevertheless, Justices Powell, Rehnquist, Byron R. White, Harry A. Blackmun, and Chief Justice Warren E. Burger agreed to participate in the cert pool. Justice Blackmun's files contain a document from 1972 titled "Recurring Issues in Cert Petitions" written by one of Blackmun's clerks. The document lists eighteen "recurring issues" for clerks to consider in preparing their memos, for example,

(1) Overruling *Bartkus v. Illinois*, 359 US 121 (separate prosecutions for "same offense" under state and federal law, double jeopardy). The Court seriously considered granting cert on this issue during the 1971 term, but ultimately did not. Simply note the issue when it appears.

(2) California indeterminate sentencing. This is regularly attacked on every conceivable constitutional ground; cert has regularly been denied. . . .

(4) The "same transaction" test for the Double Jeopardy Clause. At present only Brennan, Douglas and Marshall would adopt this rule. Justice Blackmun is on record against it (e.g., 403 US at 384). . . .

(12) *Miranda* itself. Don't spend much time on contentions that *Miranda* should be extended, or on interstitial questions about *Miranda*-like details. The Court has been presented with most of these, is familiar with the issues, and is not eager to review this controversial area.[35]

Despite the cert pool's approval by a majority of the Court, four of the most senior members, Justices Douglas, Brennan, Potter Stewart, and Marshall, chose not to participate. Justice Douglas was particularly adamant in his opposition, writing Chief Justice Burger,

I like to go over these petitions personally. They are interesting and absorbing, and for me much more meaningful than when they are reduced to a memorandum written by someone else. . . . I think the Court is overstaffed and underworked. . . . We were much, much busier 25 or 30 years ago than we are today. I really think that today the job does not add up to more than about four days a week. I think that the more Justices who look at these petitions, the better the end product will be. Different eyes see different things, and the merits of these petitions obviously cannot be routed through a computer. The law clerks are fine. Most of them are sharp and able. But after all, they have never been confirmed by the Senate and the job here is so highly personal, depending upon the judgment, discretion, experience and point of view of each of the nine of us that in my view the fewer obstacles put in our way, the better. Pooling of the cert memos is, in my view, a rather major obstacle.[36]

But many clerks at the Court knew that Douglas's own clerks were terribly burdened by the cert petitions, particularly when Douglas only had one clerk when the other chambers had two. A former clerk for Justice Reed recalled,

As a consequence, Douglas' clerk never had time to deal in any depth at all on the cases that were actually before the Court. And, moreover, Douglas really didn't have much time for his clerks. He wasn't interested in that whole institution . . . he didn't have a desire to teach his clerks and to spend time with them. He needed them badly but he didn't offer them much, except a lot of work.[37]

Douglas wrote his incoming clerks for the 1971 Term about what he expected of them in writing cert memos:

The best I have had in recent years were prepared by [Thomas C.] Armitage in the 1969 Term and I suggest that you go over what he did to see the quality that they have. The memos done in the 1970 Term were some of the poorest I have ever seen. I have asked [Dennis] Brown to preserve and show to you some of the real horribles that he, himself, perpetuated. The purpose of the cert memo is to prepare an accurate summary of the issues in the case which can be used three months or a year from the time it is written so as to give a rather complete conception of what the case involves without going back to the original briefs and records. The flow of cases is so great that it is difficult to carry in mind even during one Term the precise issues raised in each case. Some of the cases in which you prepare cert memos will be discussed that very week but others will go over from Conference to Conference and a final vote and discussion may not be had until some months later. In that time the case may very well become dim in the memories of everyone in the office. The cert memo need not always cover every single point raised because some of the cases are just plain frivolous. But they should contain the main points with pros and cons relevant to granting the cert petitions or noting the appeal or granting the motion to dismiss or affirm. During the summer I go over the cases in the Far West and merely send back my votes attached to each numbered case. I make no separate notes. During the winter, while I am here, I go over each case separately from the law clerks' memos. But I repeat, the law clerks' memo is a very important point of reference in every Conference discussion especially those where the Conference discussion comes some weeks or even months later.[38]

Burger defended the cert pool against Douglas's critiques:

From Bill Douglas' memo, I think he misreads the operation of the "pool experiment.". . . The experiment is not a *substitute* for each Justice's individual study and treatment of the incoming cases; it is a *supplement* designed to save *law clerks time.* Whether it saves the time of a Justice, depends entirely on how he deals with these cases. As applied to my own situation, it will not save time for me; my own consideration will be precisely as it was before and I suspect this is generally true as to all of us. In short, Justices will continue to examine each case personally. For these reasons . . . I fail to see the relevance of the law clerks not having "been confirmed by the Senate." If the law clerks were doing something new or different, that might be relevant. I contemplate giving each case individual study and consideration as I have been doing for nearly 17 years as a judge and for 20 years as a practitioner.[39]

Like Justice Douglas, Justice Stewart declined to join the pool. He wrote Chief Justice Burger, "For a variety of reasons, some of them similar to those expressed by Bill Douglas, I have decided not to participate in the law clerk 'pooling' project."[40] Justice Brennan wrote Chief Justice Burger,

Since Bill Douglas, Potter and Thurgood have decided not to participate in the proposed Law Clerk Pool, I have decided that I should not participate. You'll recall that since I prefer doing my own certs when I can, I agreed only to participate on the premise that nine or at least eight of the offices would be involved. Since that apparently is not the case, I think I'll proceed as I have in the past.[41]

Brennan never did participate in the pool. He said that he would find three to four cases a year that the clerks had missed.[42] But eventually even Brennan had to relinquish some of the review process to his clerks due to the incessant pace and large numbers of petitions that came to the Court. Brennan wrote,

> I try not to delegate any of the screening function to my law clerks and to do the complete task myself. I make exceptions during the summer recess when their initial screening of petitions is invaluable training for next Term's new law clerks. And I also must make some few exceptions during the Term on occasions when opinion work must take precedence. When law clerks do screening, they prepare a memorandum of not more than a page or two in each case, noting whether the case is properly before the Court, what federal issues are presented, how they were decided by the Courts below, and summarizing the positions of the parties pro and con.[43]

One clerk wrote Brennan during the summer before the justice arrived to start the term, "We are all fascinated by the certs and shudder to think that when you get back you may take some of them away from us. But if you're very nice we won't fight too hard."[44]

The cert pool was viewed as an immediate success by those justices who participated. After only its second month of operation, Justice Powell wrote the participating clerks and their justices,

> Now that we have had a reasonable trial period with the cert pool, I write to commend each and all of you on what seems to me to be a satisfactory and constructive arrangement. On the basis of the first week or two, I had some concern that the memoranda tended to be longer than necessary and sometimes a bit repetitious. But the more recent circulations have a better balance in this respect, and reflect an appropriate discrimination between cases that are presumptively certworthy and those that are clearly not. Even when the memoranda may have seemed unnecessarily long, they have been educational for me. . . . The plan also is accomplishing its principal purpose: conserving, for other vital work, a significant part of the time of the Law Clerks who participate.[45]

Powell echoed his praise six months later as the term drew to a close and he lobbied for a continuation of the pool through the summer months as new clerks arrived:

My assessment of the merits of the Pool during this Term is quite affirmative. Although it has not lessened the time I personally devote to certs (and possibly added to it a bit), the advantages have been significant: (i) the Pool has reduced by at least 50% the time devoted by my clerks to certs, freeing them for other important work; (ii) as each Cert Memo written in another Chambers is nevertheless reviewed by one of my clerks before I see it, I have the benefit—in effect—of a double review with the additional assurance that anything important will be surfaced; (iii) my clerks are enthusiastic about the Pool and think the resulting allocation of their time is more productive in the areas that count the most. From what I have heard in the "corridors," the clerks in other participating Chambers have substantially the same view as to the continuation of the Pool next Term.[46]

Justice Rehnquist agreed with Powell:

I unqualifiedly concur in your favorable appraisal of the pool's performance during the Term. My clerks too, by their participation in the pool have had more time to devote to other work which is more important to me and more interesting to them. I have followed your practice of asking my own law clerks for their recommendations in those cases where they had not prepared the pool memorandum, and have similarly benefited from what you describe as the "double review." I am 100% in favor of the continuation of the pool next Term.[47]

Justice Blackmun too followed Powell's suggestion, having his own clerks mark up the pool memos and make recommendations in pencil. Blackmun then marked up the memos himself. He wrote the other justices in the pool, "It tends to conserve time for the clerks and to free them for other important work."[48] Chief Justice Burger responded, "I believe it has been a great success; memos prepared for five or more Justices tend to get a more careful treatment. The author knows he must clear five 'hurdles.'. . . I hear some rumors that others may want to join the pool."[49]

It is interesting to note that the "double review" concept of having one's own clerks mark up the pool memo and make a second recommendation was not new. When Chief Justice Stone, and subsequent Chief Justices, circulated their clerk written memos on the IFP cases, there is evidence that the justices who delegated the initial cert review to their clerks had them mark up the IFP "flimsies." For example, Justice Harlan's files contain handwritten recommendations from his clerks on each IFP memo circulated by the Chief Justice.[50]

As the cert pool began for the second time in 1974, Justice Powell wrote the Court's legal officer, Ken Ripple, who was organizing the pool, asking him to review the basic outline pool memos should follow. Powell noted that the memos should conclude with "the clerk's analysis or comment, with his recommendation where he wishes to make one."[51] Interestingly, this is contrary to the suggestion by the original clerk committee charged with setting up pool mechanics that "the memo will include no recommendations."[52] Indeed, our examination of the pool memos from their first year shows that no formal recommendations were made by pool clerks. However, even without a formal recommendation, the discussion section of the memo often performed the same function. For example, in one of his pool memos, 1974 Rehnquist clerk John E. O'Neill wrote, "Both issues are simply too narrow to be certworthy."[53] Similarly, 1974 Powell clerk Ronald G. Carr wrote in the discussion section of one of his pool memos, "There is nothing here."[54]

But as Powell suggested, some clerks began including formal recommendations at the end of their pool memos. Ultimately, pool clerk recommendations became so institutionalized that they were formalized in 1984 and placed in a separate final section of the pool memo after the discussion section. With formalization, consistent abbreviations became mandatory. Jan Horbaly, special assistant to the chief justice, wrote the pool clerks, "Please also watch your recommendations of appeals. A number of memos are coming into the Cert Pool with recommendations of 'DENY' on appeals. The recommendations on appeals should be 'AFFIRM,' 'REVERSE,' 'NJP,' 'X-DFWSFQ,' 'DFWSFQ,' 'X-DandD,' 'DWJ,' 'DFWPPPFQ' (Dismiss for want of a properly presented federal question), etc."[55]

Like many new clerks, Justice Powell was mystified by the shorthand. When he first joined the Court he wrote his clerks,

> I would like a tabulation of the various dispositions which may be made of petitions for appeal and certiorari by this Court, with an explanation as to the meaning of each. The most frequent action we take is to "deny" which I understand. I also understand what is meant when we "note probable jurisdiction." I think I know what we are doing—at

least what I am doing—when I vote to "dismiss for want of a substantial federal question." But when do we simply "dismiss"? When do we "dismiss and deny"? And what in the world is the difference between these two? There is certain additional jargon with respect to dispositions (such as DIG). What I would like is a simplified chart or table that I could keep in the back of my cert book (until I become fully familiar with it), to assist me with the nuances of this terminology.[56]

To be sure, having formal, standardized recommendations, as opposed to only discussion, greatly facilitates the review of cert memos. The danger, of course is that rather than review the discussion section, the entire memo, or the original petition, clerks and justices who are supposed to provide a check against the pool clerk may simply look to the formal pool recommendation and go no further.

Despite the refusal of Douglas and the other justices to join, the cert pool grew as opposition justices retired and were replaced. In 1981, Justice Sandra Day O'Connor joined the pool, and Justices Antonin Scalia, Anthony M. Kennedy, David H. Souter, Clarence Thomas, Ruth Bader Ginsburg, and Stephen Breyer have also added their clerks, leaving Justice Stevens as the only current justice outside the pool.

Cert Pool: Operation and Effects

The flow of cert petitions is constant. The cert pool procedures involve randomly dividing up all of the petitions for review among the participating chambers. In 1989 Justice O'Connor commented, "We receive close to 5,000 petitions for certiorari each year, which means we are reviewing some each day. It is a little like getting up in the morning and doing your exercises. You know you are going to have some petitions to review."[57] The petitions are further divided among each chambers' clerks. Each clerk then prepares a formal memorandum, the "pool memo," summarizing the issues and facts of the case and making a recommendation as to whether to grant cert. On average, each pool clerk writes nearly five memos each week.[58] This memo is then forwarded to all justices in the pool. While some justices have one of their clerks review the pool memo and "mark it up," others review pool memos without a markup being performed.[59] The markup memo may simply note that it agrees with the pool memo's recommendation or it may analyze the issue further and disagree with the recommendation contained in the pool memo. Over the years, it has become increasingly common for justices to base their certiorari decisions on what they read in the pool memo. In 1989, Chief Justice Rehnquist explained to the pool clerks, "The theory behind the cert pool is that the pool memos will save the time of the Justices because in many cases the Justices, after reading the pool memo, will not find it necessary to read the underlying petition and response."[60]

After all the memos have been prepared, the Chief Justice prepares a list of cases called the "discuss list." This list contains the cases that the Chief wishes to have discussed in conference. Any other justice can have cases added to the discuss list by merely informing the Chief's administrative clerk. On conference day, the justices discuss the petitions on the discuss list and announce their votes informally. Any case that receives four votes is granted certiorari, meaning that it will ultimately be heard by the Court and decided on the merits.[61]

Justice Stevens has opted out of the pool because he feels that he and his clerks provide an important check against potential mistakes. But how are they able to deal with the huge volume of petitions? Stevens has his clerks screen about 75 percent of all the petitions and only draft memos on those cases that they think are worthy of consideration. Stevens explained, "I have found it necessary to delegate a great deal of responsibility in the review of certiorari petitions to my law clerks. They examine them all and select a small minority that they believe I should read myself. As a result, I do not even look at the papers in over eighty percent of the cases that are filed."[62] Similarly, in detailing how his clerks were responsible for informing him when a potential conflict of interest might arise and he might have to recuse himself from a case, Justice Powell wrote his clerks, "I have to rely on each of you. This is especially true as to petitions for certiorari, appeals, stays, etc., as you see all of the briefs and petitions—many of which I never see."[63] He elaborated, "I have now found from experience that, where the quality of the cert notes is good, it is necessary for me to look at relatively few of the petitions and briefs."[64] When Powell was ailing, he further downgraded his level of review for cert memos. He explained to his clerks,

I will review initially only the cert memos that you think should make the discuss list. . . . I still have to conserve my strength. The great majority of petitions are not certworthy, and you have demonstrated ability to identify cases likely to make the Discuss List and cases in which you think I am likely to be interested. One exception to the foregoing is that I would like to take a look at the cert memos on all capital cases.[65]

In 1995, former Stevens clerk Sean Donahue elaborated from the clerk perspective, "While Stevens clerks have to read ten times as many petitions as do the cert pool clerks (amounting last year to about 45 a week per clerk), they write memos on only a fraction (perhaps 20–25 percent). They can also refer petitions directly to the Justice without protracted memo-writing or worrying about form."[66] Also, the cert memos that Stevens's clerks do write are more detailed than the memos written by the clerks in the pool. "When a clerk writes for an individual justice, he or she can be more candid," Stevens said.[67]

The importance of the law clerk in this process is readily apparent. Given that each year, over eight thousand petitions for review are filed with the Court and less than one-hundredth of 1 percent of these are decided on the merits, the justices must rely on the clerks to make the initial determination as to the "cert-worthiness" of a case. Table 3.1 illustrates the level of agreement on cert petitions between Chief Justice Vinson and his clerks long before the advent of the cert pool and the explosion in number of certiorari petitions filed with the Court. Vinson

TABLE 3.1
*Divergence of Chief Justice Vinson's Vote from
His Law Clerks' Recommendations: 1947–1952*

Term	Number of Cases Disposed	Percentage of Divergence: Vinson Vote from Clerks' Recommendations
1947	1,331	2.8% (38)
1948	1,434	3.6% (53)
1949	1,308	3.9% (52)
1950	1,216	4.1% (51)
1952	1,286	3.5% (46)
Total =	6,575	3.6% (240)

SOURCE: David M. O'Brien, *Storm Center*, 2nd ed. (New York: Norton, 1990), 168.

only had to dispose of some thirteen hundred petitions per year, compared to the nearly eight thousand received by the Court in 2003.

The law clerks are the initial gatekeepers for access to the Court in the cert process. Justice Rehnquist explained,

> As soon as I am confident that my new law clerks are reliable, I take their word and that of the pool memo writer as to the underlying facts and contentions of the parties in the various petitions, and with a large majority of the petitions it is not necessary to go any further than the pool memo. In cases that seem from the memo perhaps to warrant a vote to grant certiorari, I may ask my law clerk to further check out one of the issues, and may review the lower court opinion, the petition, and the response myself.[68]

Rehnquist's comments indicate an important caveat to the importance of the clerks in the certiorari process, though. In landmark or controversial cases, the justices are unlikely to rely upon the clerk's recommendation much, if at all. In general, then, the clerk's influence is likely to be greatest where the justice does not have a strong preference.[69]

The Decline of Candor and the Rise of Circuit Conflict

Although clerk influence in the cert process is not total, it is considerable, to say the least. The institutionalization of the law clerk has shaped the ways in which the cert pool operates. First, there is a culture of high achievement and competence among the clerks, accompanied by a corresponding status competition. Former Blackmun clerk Dan Coenen noted, "Law clerks are, by and large, hard-driven high achievers who develop profound loyalties to their own Justices; to such persons, producing written work that brings disrepute upon themselves and their chambers is little less than a heart-stopping prospect."[70] This culture of competitiveness, ability, and expertise is hardly surprising, given that the clerks are almost uniformly chosen from the elite law schools and are ranked at the top of their classes. Despite the tremendous workload that is imposed on them, the culture of the clerks that developed through the process of institutionalization ensured that they would expend a great deal of effort when preparing the pool memos, knowing that this signed memo would be widely distributed among other clerks and the justices.[71] Laura Ingraham, who clerked for Justice

Clarence Thomas in 1992, explained, "You're in perpetual fear of making a mistake. The fear factor keeps the work product reliable."[72]

Interestingly, this suggests that the substance of cert memos may have changed in other ways with the creation of the pool memo. There is some evidence that clerks who wrote only for their own justice were more candid in the past, particularly with political analyses and recommendations, than are current clerks who write one memo for eight justices who occupy different positions on the ideological spectrum. Justice Powell wrote his incoming clerks for the 1973 Term,

> While every petition, including the IFP's, merits careful consideration, it will be obvious to you fairly quickly that a substantial percentage—especially of the criminal IFP's—are without merit or frivolous. When this is perfectly clear, do not devote a great deal of time to writing a long memorandum. When you are writing for the Pool, you have to be somewhat more careful to "lay out" the pros and cons of a meritless or frivolous petition than when you are writing solely for me.[73]

One example of candid analysis from long before the cert pool began took place in November 1954, six months after the Court's decision in *Brown v. Board of Education*.[74] The Court was asked to consider the constitutionality of a state antimiscegenation law. In his cert memo, Chief Justice Warren's clerk wrote, "If students cannot be segregated on the basis of race, what of spouses? . . . Perhaps someday the court will have to [rule] on these questions. But review at the present time could only seriously aggravate the tensions stimulated by last term's segregation decision."[75] Justice Harold Burton's clerk made a similar analysis: "because of the political repercussions of the segregation decision, it would not be feasible politically to take this case at this time."[76] In another case prior to the pool, a clerk for Justice Douglas wrote, "It will begin to look obvious if the case is not taken that the court is trying to run away from its obligation to decide the case."[77]

A clerk from the 1970s explained his role in writing cert memos for Justice Stewart, who was outside the pool,

> On the cert petitions we had to learn what his views were about whether the cases were certworthy or not and you tried to do recommendations to reflect his views. You knew if it was an obscenity case he would want to have this recommendation or if it was another kind of

case you would have to go this way. Since it was only to one justice, we didn't have to spend the time the cert pool did. You could write a cert memo very short. Just by seeing the issue you knew he would say that he wasn't interested. Sometimes you didn't know so you had to make your best guess. And you didn't always agree—mostly [we did]. But it was not hard because you deny almost all of them so mostly you're right.

Stewart's concern for brief, candid memos was confirmed by Justice Powell, who wrote his clerks, "I recall [former clerk] Larry Hammond saying that Justice Black would reprimand a clerk who gave him a cert memo of more than one page except in the quite unusual case. Obviously this reflected his enormous experience and knowledge. Justice Stewart has remained out of the pool primarily because he likes brief cert memos."[78]

Pool writers generally take an opposite approach, attempting to incorporate every possible argument in an objective fashion. For example, 1988 Blackmun clerk Kevin M. Kearney wrote the pool memo in the abortion case *Webster v. Reproductive Health Services.*[79] Though clerking for the author of *Roe v. Wade*, Kearney wrote, "The seventh question presented is whether the Court should reconsider *Roe v. Wade*. It is not necessary to reconsider *Roe* in order to decide the other issues presented. However, should the Court wish to revisit that opinion this case is an adequate vehicle for doing so."[80] After the memo was circulated to the other justices in the pool, Kearney added a handwritten note: "(not that I think my recommendation counts for very much in this case.) I hope I have not taken objectivity too far."[81] In another example, 1990 O'Connor clerk Iman Anabtawi's pool memo in the religious establishment case *Lee v. Weisman* stated in the discussion section, "First, it is not so clear under the Supreme Court's cases when the *Lemon* test must be applied and when it need not. . . . I cannot agree with petrs, however, that there is a circuit split . . . I note that the fragmented opinion below in this case may not make it the best vehicle for consideration of the issue presented. . . . Recommendation: Deny."[82] While she agreed with the pool clerk, Blackmun clerk Ann Alpers's comments were much more candid when she marked up the pool memo for her boss two days later: "I think this is a hard case. But I hope the Court denies cert b/c I fear for what some justices would do if the case were granted."[83]

While still a proponent of pooling clerks, Justice Blackmun explained the notable difference in the cert memos he read after the first year of the cert pool:

> I am all in favor of the cert pool and the accomplishment of its intended purpose to conserve the time of the clerks. It has the opposite effect for me personally for, because of the extra length of the memoranda, the system takes more of my time than if the memos were prepared in my own chambers. This is partly due, I suspect, to the fact that each memo-writer, while he may know his own Justice, wishes to be sure that he covers every possible point in which any of the other Justices might be interested.[84]

In the early years of the cert pool Chief Justice Burger recognized, "Writing [a cert memo] for five justices is not a task one adjusts to overnight."[85] Indeed, some pool memos do not even contain recommendations. Instead, they provide analysis of what the Court might want to do and how they might go about doing it. For example, Samuel J. Dimon, who clerked for Justice White during the 1985 Term, wrote in the discussion section of his pool memo for *McClesky v. Kemp*,

> If the data base for the Baldus study is unreliable, as the DJ found it to be, there is no need to reach the 8th and 14th A. issues. If the Court *wants* to reach the underlying 8th A. issue, the DJ's findings do not pose an insuperable obstacle. . . . The *Giglio* issue turns very much on the facts, which weighs against granting cert on this question. On the other hand, the fact that this is a capital case weighs in favor of greater concern for the correctness of the decision below. . . . This case may present an opportunity to resolve the troublesome and frequently recurring question of whether a *Sandstrom* error can ever be harmless. . . . Having set out what I believe are the relevant considerations in the Discussion section, I prefer not to make a specific recommendation.[86]

The decline of candid analyses in pool memos is no doubt one reason why justices ask their own clerks to mark up the pool memo and do further research if a pool memo piques their interest. The case of *Regents of the University of California v. Bakke* illustrates this.[87] Powell clerk David A. Martin wrote his justice, "A clean grant. . . . This case presents with clarity an issue of great importance. . . . I recommend you assign one of us promptly to begin reading and thinking in preparation for this case."[88]

It should be kept in mind that the clerks, although in possession of top-notch academic credentials, do not typically have a broad vision of the Court's jurisprudential trends or a great deal of legal experience.[89] This point is underscored by a former clerk who noted that certain constitutional issues would not be given preference by the clerks, simply due to their lack of experience.[90] Given that the clerks wish to write a credible pool memo, they will naturally seek factors to justify their recommendations that are easily identifiable and defensible. The clerk culture has created an atmosphere in which clerks tend to emphasize the presence of a conflict between the circuit courts as a reason to recommend granting certiorari. To be sure, the presence of a circuit conflict has always been viewed as an important criterion in the decision to grant review. Commentators have noted the relevance of the role of the Court in assuring national uniformity of the law through the resolution of conflicts.[91] Previous research has shown that circuit conflict was the most significant predictor for certiorari decisions on the Vinson and Warren Courts.[92] Thus, it is certainly not novel to comment on the importance of conflict in the certiorari process.

But how important has circuit conflict been since the Warren Court, and particularly since the cert pool was created? We suggest that clerks, lacking institutional memory and a broad outline of the Court's trends, focused on the observable features of cases that could be justified as being "cert-worthy." With the creation of the cert pool in 1972, clerks increasingly emphasized circuit conflict. Knowing that they were writing for all of the justices in the pool as well as other law clerks, pool clerks gravitated toward a criterion that was easily defensible and not subject to attack by other clerks. This tendency then spread to nonpool clerks, and even attorneys, as normative isomorphic change occurred. For example, attorneys tell petitioners, "you are almost certainly going to need a conflict in the lower courts to convince the Supreme Court that your case is certworthy."[93] A former clerk told us that circuit conflict was the first thing clerks would look for in a petition for review, and that clerks would often research and look for conflicts even if one was not claimed in the petition for review. Indeed, this was the practice of clerks in Justice White's chambers. Kevin Worthen, 1983 White clerk, said, "Clerks were not allowed to rely on the parties' assertion that the conflict existed. They were not even permitted to take the word of clerks from other chambers who may have prepared the cert memo. Clerks had to read the cases themselves and certify whether the conflict was real."[94] Similarly, in his book on the certiorari process, H. W. Perry reported that all sixty-four former clerks he interviewed noted that a conflict in the lower courts was the factor that was most important to them when reviewing cert petitions.[95]

Partisanship and Strategy

Despite the incentives for pool clerks to write objectively, there is some evidence that they behave in partisan and strategic ways. One way that clerks exercise influence in the cert pool is through the substance and form of the cert memos themselves. Sometimes, the line between objective analysis and advocacy is blurred as clerks are charged with making recommendations. For example, Michael Conley, a Blackmun clerk from 1990 said, "To the extent that you are looking at pool memos from clerks indicating that a case shouldn't be taken, very often that's a defensive posture. You realize that it is much better for a case not to be taken. . . . There is room for judgment on whether it is now the right time."[96]

This suggests that some clerks may have crossed the line. For example, dissenting opinions from the lower court have often been omitted from pool memos. Indeed, Justice Blackmun made an annual plea to the chambers of his colleagues in the pool: "I have sensed . . . in the pool memos, a tendency to overlook dissents. I personally would appreciate it if clerks, in preparing the memoranda, would outline the position of dissenting judges. A dissent expresses judicial disagreement, and I, for one, want to know the opposing posture without having to dig back myself each time."[97] Were these omissions calculated? Chief Justice Burger replied, "Some clerks are plainly 'sloppy' on this. Please each of you, tell your clerks that we will set up some 'Williamsburg stocks' in the courtyards to discipline those who err."[98]

Another common omission that Justice Blackmun was concerned about was the absence of the names of the judges participating in the case. Blackmun wrote, "I have noted a tendency this year (as in some prior years) to omit the names of the judges participating in the decision below and to use, instead, a phrase such as 'per curiam' or nothing at all. I like to know who the judges below were, even when the petition or jurisdictional statement comes from a state court."[99] Whether pool clerks were behaving strategically or not, omitting the names of judges makes it more difficult to identify the ideological direction of the outcome, i.e., whether it was liberal or conservative.

A similar problem exists with the labels that are placed after the names of the parties to the case. One problem is omission. Clerks were reminded,

> When a case is styled "SMITH v. DOE, et al." and one of the parties is a senator, congressman, cabinet officer, judge, mayor, police officer, warden, school board member, inventor, husband or wife (in a divorce action), employer or employee (in a labor matter), etc., the party should be identified. For example, "SMITH (Attorney General) v. DOE (taxpayer), et al." This information is helpful to the Justices because it makes it easy to identify the party who lost in the Court of Appeals or the District Court.[100]

The following is a list of examples of labels on a group of IFP cert memos chosen at random from 1983: "sex offender," "prisoner," "prison officials," "murderer," "convicted of murder," "schemer," "sibling bank robbers," "criminal deft," "criminal," "car thief," "Sec'y HHS," "former guardian *ad litem*," "alien smuggler," "Prison Superintendent," "warden," "defrauder," "convict," and "counterfeiter."[101] Plainly, the labeling prerogative suggests the problem of "editorializing." For example, in the cross-burning case *R.A.V. v. St. Paul*, 1991 Rehnquist clerk Jeffrey L. Bleich labeled the petitioner, "R.A.V. (skinhead)."[102] Pamela Karlan, who clerked for Blackmun during the 1985 Term, wrote to her justice regarding *Kemp v. Drake* and the power of the Chief Justice's chief clerk, who collects and distributes the pool memos:

> I am sorry to bother you with this little matter, since I know right now is a very busy and stressful time. I wrote the pool memo in this case. . . . As you will no doubt notice, despite the fact that I indicated clearly that this is a former capital case and described resp, accurately, as a successful habeas petitioner, [Chief Justice Burger's clerk] Tim Flanigan (the superclerk) felt it necessary to add a parenthetical identifying resp as an accused murderer.
>
> I am furious at this clear editorializing. The *only* reason I can see for Flanigan's action is to suggest that the case warrants a grant because a defendant convicted of murder satisfied a unanimous *en banc* Court of

Appeals that his conviction and death sentence were unconstitutional. Flanigan's comment was wholly gratuitous. Moreover, despite the fact, which we have discussed at breakfast, that Matt Neumeier, one of the Chief's clerks and thus a pool memo writer clearly under Flanigan's jurisdiction, has repeatedly made disparaging and legally and factually incorrect remarks in *his* pool memos about *pro se*, i.f.p., and inmate petitioners, Flanigan has never, to my knowledge, done anything about this, either by talking to Neumeier privately (Anne Coughlin, one of Justice Powell's clerks told me that she had complained to Flanigan and he had defended Neumeier's work) or by writing his own editorial comments on Neumeier's memos before distributing them. I take my responsibility in writing pool memos quite seriously. If another Justice disagrees with my analysis, he or she is clearly free to reject it, and if my performance were unsatisfactory, I would imagine that he or she might take up the question with you. Similarly, if a clerk in another chambers, having read my memo, disagrees, it is his or her responsibility to make that disagreement clear to his or her Justice. But it is none of Flanigan's business how I analyze the cases assigned to me, and he certainly has no right to use my work to make editorial comments to other chambers. I would like to communicate my anger to Flanigan, but I wanted to talk to you and get your reaction first.[103]

There is also a danger that pool writers as well as the chief clerk may manipulate the timing of when pool memos are released to the justices before the conference vote. Of course, it may also be that pool clerks and the chief clerk are simply behind in their work. The files of Justices Blackmun and Powell contain numerous complaints from pool justices over the lateness of pool memos. For example, Justice Powell wrote Chief Justice Burger,

It seems to me that the cert memos are being circulated more slowly than in the past. I have understood that the "target date" for circulating them is no later than one week prior to the Conference, i.e. on or before the Friday a week before the Friday conference. This affords us (and here I certainly speak for myself) the opportunity to review the cert memos before moving into a week of arguments. I appreciate that we have a new "crop" of law clerks, and also that Jan was in the process of concluding his work here. Knowing Mike Luttig, I am confident that he will do his best to see that a reasonable schedule is met.[104]

TABLE 3.2
Law Clerk Workload I: Cert Petitions and Associate Justices

Year	Number of Clerks Per Associate Justice	Total Number of Cert Petitions*	Number of Cert Petitions Reviewed by Each Clerk
1940	1	814	824
1945	1	774	774
1950	2	640	320
1955	2	842	421
1960	2	789	395
1965	2	1,164	582
1970	3	1,903	634

* Does not include in forma pauperis petitions, as they were reviewed exclusively by the Chief Justice's clerks.

With the use of computers at the Court, there have even been suspicions that something as seemingly harmless as font style might be used to make it more difficult to read pool memos. In 1990, Blackmun clerk Andrea Ward wrote her justice,

> The following is a message sent to me on the computer from the Thomas clerks. I thought you might appreciate knowing that they are not intentionally printing their poolmemos too lightly. "It just dawned on me that last night I circulated a supplemental memo printed in the dreaded plain Courier 12 font. It was late, and I just forgot. Please convey my apology. Greg Katsas."[105]

Suspicions about partisan pool clerks have led the justices to place internal checks on pool memos to guard against outside influence. The mark-up memo is the most important formal check. In discussing the process of reviewing pool memos from other chambers, outgoing 1977 chief administrative clerk for Justice Powell, Sam Estreicher, wrote the incoming clerks, "You will quickly develop a mental list of the clerks who can be relied upon to write a fair, soundly reasoned memo. Where the cert. pool author recommends a 'grant' or a 'note,' I found it useful to go to the papers and at least read the opinion of the court below."[106] In 1986, Justice Blackmun began having his clerks add more information to the last name of the pool clerk appearing at the end of each pool memo. Blackmun's clerks added the first name, law school attended, the last name and circuit or district of the lower court judge he or she clerked for, and then the name of the justice he or she was currently working for.[107] For example, "Dunnigan" became "Vaughn Dunnigan (SOC, Browning, Columbia)."[108] Clearly such information would not be necessary if each pool clerk provided objective analyses.

Workload

But even with the important developments of the decline of candor, the rise of the use of circuit conflict, and strategic behavior, the key effect of the cert pool was the drastic reduction in the number of cases that pool clerks had to review. For the purposes of this analysis, we distinguish between clerks of associate justices and clerks of Chief Justices, as only the Chief's clerks were responsible for in forma pauperis petitions prior to the 1971 rule change that combined IFPs with other petitions on a single docket and the subsequent creation of the cert pool. Table 3.2 shows the number of cert petitions reviewed by clerks of associate justices prior to the inception of the pool. The data for the 1940s are telling. On the surface, it appears that the single clerk that each justice annually employed for most of the decade was terribly burdened by cert petitions. The reality, however, was that most of the justices helped their clerks in reviewing the cases, thereby reducing clerk workload. Indeed, as we have already pointed out, Justice Frankfurter, for example, handled all the cert petitions himself. It was the rare justice who completely delegated the review of all the petitions to his clerk. Justice McReynolds followed this then unusual practice. His clerk from 1936, John Knox, described his first day of work in late August:

> The floor of the entire room was literally filled to a depth of more than a foot with hundreds of statements of fact, briefs, answers, etc.—all comprising what seemed to be countless petitions for certiorari. There were at the time approximately five hundred petitions piled on the floor of that room.[109] All of these would have to be read before the opening of Court in October, and a page referring to each petition would then have to be typed. I had five weeks and two days in which to do this work.[110]

But by the late 1960s, clerks had largely taken over this task and, with growing dockets, were overwhelmed with work. In 1965, each clerk reviewed 582 cert petitions, or more than eleven petitions each week. By 1970, the last term before the rule change, each justice had

TABLE 3.3
Law Clerk Workload II: Cert Petitions and Chief Justices

Year	Number of Chief Justice's Clerks	Total Number of Cert Petitions**	Number of Cert Petitions Reviewed by Each Clerk
1940	1	934	934
1945	2	1,167	834
1950	2	1,055	528
1955	3	1,487	496
1960	4*	1,874	469
1965	4*	2,774	694
1968	4*	3,376	844

* Includes clerks for retired justices used primarily by the Chief Justice.
** Includes in forma pauperis petitions, as they were reviewed exclusively by the Chief Justice's clerks.

three clerks, but the non-IFP docket had expanded to almost two thousand cases. On average, each clerk reviewed 634 petitions for the 1970 Term, or more than twelve per week. This left little time for anything else, including opinion writing, which was less pronounced at this time.

As Table 3.3 shows, the Chief Justice's clerks were even more overworked as they had to review all the cert petitions for the Chief, as well as the petitions on the Court's Miscellaneous Docket, largely comprised of IFP petitions, for the entire Court. But Chief Justices devised ways to lighten the burden of reviewing the IFP petitions. First, the Chief almost always had one more clerk than the other justices. Justice Douglas recalled,

> Prior to the Stone Court, the Chief Justice himself processed all of the miscellaneous cases. Hughes put on the staff a man whose name I forget, but Hughes paid him out of his own pocket. He was preoccupied in large part in going over the cases in the miscellaneous docket. It is quite a cumbersome job because they come in, some of them in handwriting, most of them typewritten, and to go through the papers is quite a chore. . . . I think it started in 1942, the miscellaneous had increased in number to such an extent that Stone decided, quite wisely, to inaugurate a different method of handling. He got an additional law clerk, and this law clerk went over each of the miscellaneous cases and prepared a memo and had an original and eight carbons made and these were distributed to each judge. And that's what we call at Court the "flimsy." The flimsy appeared, I think, in 1942 for the first time, and then the, all capital cases were circulated, the record and the petitions and the briefs.

They were all circulated to all the Justices and that is the system that has continued since that time. . . . But we don't actually personally consider many of those miscellaneous cases apart from reading the flimsy that the law clerk prepares, except the capital cases, and we do look at those.[111]

But even with the additional clerk, the workload was extremely heavy. In 1955, Warren's three clerks reviewed nearly five hundred petitions each, an average of nearly ten per week. A Warren clerk from the 1950s told us,

> The Chief Justice wanted these people to have a fair shake and to have their cases considered fairly, even though as a group they are not terribly good at presenting their cases. So we did that and there were a lot of those and I thought that was important. . . . I used to write these prisoner's petitions up with some care. I did the lion's share my Term. I tried to see that each prisoner got a fair shake.

Warren was so stunned by the crushing workload that fell on his clerks that he sought additional help. Warren spoke to recently retired Justice Stanley Reed and they devised a plan. Former clerk Arthur Rosett explained, "It was during this period that the miscellaneous docket was growing rapidly. And they hit upon the scheme of putting in an appropriation line item for a clerk for the retired justices who, at that time, were Reed and Burton." In 1959, Rosett was the first clerk ever selected for a retired justice. But Reed and Warren came to an agreement whereby the Chief would primarily use the new clerk. Rosett continued,

> Justice Reed made it clear that he wanted me to treat the work for the Chief Justice as first call. . . . Reed/Burton clerks only worked for Reed and the Chief Justice, and gradually the Chief Justice took over the Reed/Burton clerk. . . . The Chief Justice had a lot of work which I did . . . and I used to spend a lot of time with the clerks, the Chief's clerks in particular.[112]

Warren's use of the additional clerk in 1960 kept the workload relatively stable. In 1962, Justice Douglas described the IFP process to writer James T. Brady:

All of the petitions that are filed *In Forma Pauperis* are screened by a law clerk in the offices of the Chief Justice, who sends a synopsis of the case to each of the Justices. These cases are not the long, involved matters that are involved in the run of litigation, but usually a few sheets which may be handwritten or maybe typed, making certain charges. Since there is only one copy, the synopsis makes the distribution easier than if each of the papers were sent through each of the offices. This is a matter of some importance because we get of the total 2,300 cases a year about 900–1000 in this group. Experience has shown that 90% of them are frivolous and deal with questions which present no aspect of federal law, and it is only federal law that our Court passes on, as you know. If any Justice has any question in his mind about any of the points covered in the synopsis he sends for the papers himself, and that is done in dozens and dozens of cases each Term. Moreover, as a matter of routine all capital cases, whether they are frivolous on their face or not, are circulated among all the Justices. We grant on the average not more than 2% of these cases. . . . The meritorious cases, however, are few and far between, and the screening system seems to work quite well.[113]

While the system may have worked well for Douglas and the other associate justices, by 1965, Chief Justice Warren's four clerks reviewed nearly seven hundred cert petitions each, an average of over thirteen per clerk per week. In Warren's last year, the four clerks reviewed nearly 850 petitions each, an average or over sixteen per week.

When Warren Burger became Chief Justice, he immediately changed the process. In 1969, he hired several additional clerks to help with IFPs. One month into his tenure, he wrote the other justices,

When I learned that the House had declined to authorize the nine additional Clerks requested, I explored the matter and then worked out an arrangement to "take what we could get," which was three Clerks. Even a cursory examination into problems of the Miscellaneous Docket had already satisfied me that the existing manpower arrangement was inadequate. And that we imperatively need help primarily for that work. . . . I appointed three men as General Law Clerks. These men have been assigned primarily the responsibility for the Miscellaneous Docket, along with the Clerk previously allocated to the office of the Chief Justice for that purpose. This should provide more than adequate manpower for the Miscellaneous Docket work.[114]

But Burger's "General Law Clerk" solution only lasted one term. He proposed three options for dealing with the miscellaneous docket and its growing number of IFPs: "(1) A revolving panel of Senior Judges acting as Special Masters, (2) having each Justice examine and prepare memos for the Conference on 1/9 of all petitions, (3) all IFP cases converted into nine-copy cases by Xerox."[115] Burger recognized the third alternative as "the simplest, most flexible and the one most readily subject to adjustment and change of the other two."[116] He continued,

> There is, indeed, some duplication of work in this system, but I am now persuaded that duplication is less a factor than appears at first glance. A Clerk preparing an internal memo for his own Justice can quickly determine just what is desired, whereas a single Clerk preparing a memo for all nine Justices has sought to cover every conceivable point, meritorious or not.[117]

Burger also successfully lobbied Congress to grant six more clerks in addition to the three "staff clerks" added the previous term. He wrote his colleagues, "In order to provide the needed additional manpower to take over the duties previously performed by 'Staff Clerks,' the six incoming (new) Law Clerks will be assigned to individual Justices."[118]

Burger's plan was put into effect on a trial basis. Despite his initial opposition to the plan, and his suggestion that the second alternative be used to avoid duplication of effort, Justice Douglas acquiesced.[119] He wrote Burger,

> I thank you for your effort to find the funds for my second law clerk. . . . My law clerk is moreover part of "a family" so to speak. A second one would not do IFP's only. He and the other and myself would rotate on a weekly basis, sharing all types of work, except opinion writing. My one law clerk and I are now handling all the IFP's and the regular certs. It means that I must do many of the IFP's. But the burden is not intolerable, and I rather enjoy it. But I must say it is a prodigious effort we are all making over such a few meritorious cases.[120]

When viewed through the lens of the IFP process, the creation of the cert pool was not too difficult a leap for the justices who joined.

Table 3.4 shows the radical transformation in clerk workload that took place beginning in 1972 with the creation of the cert pool. Over

TABLE 3.4
Law Clerk Workload III: Cert Petitions and Effect of Cert Pool

Year	Number of Justices in Pool	Number of Clerks in Pool*	Total Number of Cert Petitions	Number of Cert Petitions Per Pool Clerk
1972	5	18	4,619	257
1975	5	18	4,747	264
1980	5	19	5,120	269
1985	5	22	5,148	234
1990	7	29	6,758	233
1995	8	34	7,554	222
2000	8	29	7,851	271

* Includes clerks for retired justices who participated in cert pool.
SOURCES: Epstein, et al., *The Supreme Court Compendium*, 1997, 82–83; U.S. Supreme Court.

time, rising dockets have been balanced by the combination of increases in law clerks and the growing number of justices entering the pool. This has resulted in a relatively stable number of cert petitions assigned to each pool clerk: roughly 250 each, or an average of four to five petitions per week. In essence, the pool clerk's workload has been cut in half—an astonishing feat given that the Court's docket has almost doubled at the same time.

Clerks are spending far less time now on cert petitions than they did thirty years ago before the pool started. Former Stevens clerk Sean Donahue, who along with the other Stevens clerks did not participate in the pool, said, "I would estimate that cert petitions took up roughly a third of our work time. My guess is that this is more time than the average cert pool clerk spent on petitions, but only slightly more."[121] With Stevens's clerks reviewing far more petitions than the pool clerks, but spending nearly the same amount of time on the process, it is likely that pool clerks are able to delve more deeply into each case than clerks from the previous era. We can also deduce that clerks from the late 1960s were probably spending about two-thirds of their time reviewing cert petitions. We suggest that most of the additional time modern clerks gained by the creation of the cert pool has been spent on opinion writing and is probably a contributing factor in the explosion in the number of separate concurring and dissenting opinions now issued by the Court.[122]

Another implication of the increased use of clerks in the cert process is that the Court has granted certiorari in, and subsequently decided, fewer cases. Figure 3.2 shows the shrinking number of cases that the

Court has decided in recent years.[123] The most dramatic decreases, during the Rehnquist Court (1986–2002), coincide with the increasing number of justices and clerks joining the cert pool. It was initially thought by Justice Blackmun that the cert pool would make pool clerks more likely to recommend granting the cases they reviewed. As a result, he urged the other justices for a modification in the procedure:

> I feel . . . there is some merit in going "off" the Pool for three or four weeks during the summer. This enables the new clerks to get a heavy dose of certiorari applications and jurisdictional statements, something they do not have when they have only a one-fifth share. It gives them a feel for the business of the Court, and I think, makes them more appreciative and more selective when they pick up the Pool work.[124]

While the pool was "off" the first two summers, 1973–1974, the cert pool functioned year-round thereafter.[125] Contrary to Blackmun's concern, pool clerks did not overzealously recommend grants. Instead, the opposite occurred. As the number of justices and clerks joining the pool and reviewing pool memos increased, clerks became more cautious. Justice Stevens has recognized the decline in the number of cert grants and suggested that it is directly related to the Court's increasing reliance on

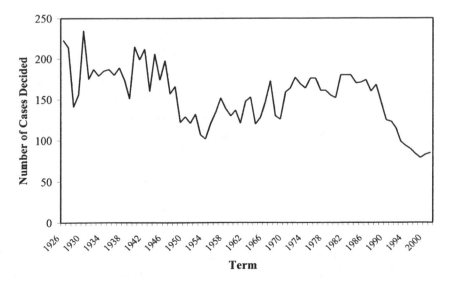

Figure 3.2. Cases Decided by U.S. Supreme Court: 1926–2001

law clerks to make recommendations on which cases to take.[126] Stevens explained, "You stick your neck out as a clerk when you recommend to grant a case. The risk-averse thing to do is to recommend not to take a case. I think it accounts for the lessening of the docket."[127] It has also been suggested by some like Kenneth Starr, a former federal judge and clerk to Chief Justice Warren Burger, that clerks fail to recommend seemingly uninteresting business cases.[128] Judge Richard Posner noted that "there seems to be a bias in favor of non-commercial cases."[129]

Clerk Influence

Because clerks make formal recommendations on cert memos, it is often thought that clerks have influence over cert decisions. Indeed, not only do clerks make formal recommendations on their cert memos, i.e., "GRANT" or "DENY," but they also often try to persuade in the body of the memo with political as well as legal analyses. For example, when asked whether he often attempted to convince his justice of his position on a case or issue, a Douglas clerk from the 1960s said that he did not, "except in cert memos." Indeed, one way of viewing the cert memo, and the mark-up memo in the case of pool memos, is that the clerk is attempting to persuade the justices to either take the case or not.

Along these lines, we asked the clerks if they were ever able to change the minds of the justices for whom they worked and, if so, when this was most likely to occur: with cert decisions, the substantive content of opinions, the stylistic content of opinions, the outcome of cases, or other ways. The highest response was in the area of cert petitions, with fifty of the 133 clerks (38 percent) who answered this question choosing this category (see Figure 3.3).[130] Since clerks are primarily responsible for reviewing these petitions, it should not be surprising that they believe their influence is most potent in this area.

Have clerk perceptions about their influence on the certiorari decisions of their justices changed over time? We asked the clerks how strongly they agreed or disagreed with the following statement: "The Justice and I often disagreed on when certiorari should be granted." Overall, the clerks said that they generally disagreed with the statement, meaning that, more often than not, clerks were in agreement with their justice about certiorari decisions. Figure 3.4 shows the level of disagreement between clerks and justices on granting certiorari. From the

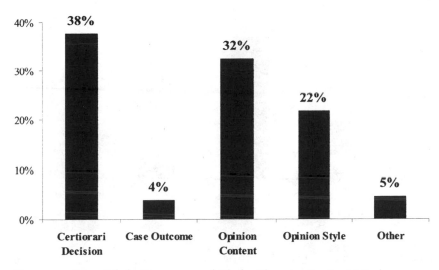

Figure 3.3. Most Likely Occurrence of Clerks Changing Justices' Minds

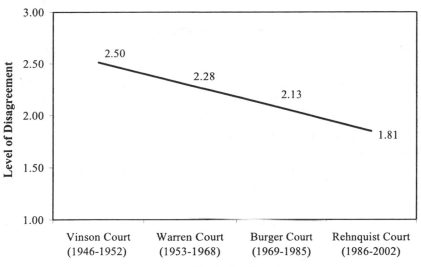

Statement: "The Justice and I often disagreed on when certiorari should be granted."
1=strongly disagree; 2=disagree; 3=neutral; 4=agree; 5=strongly agree

Figure 3.4. Level of Disagreement between Clerks and Justices on Granting
Certiorari by Court

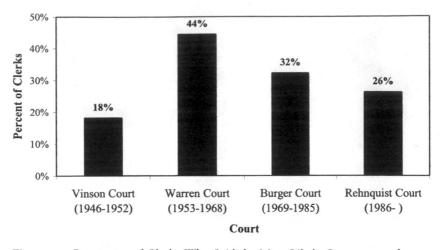

Figure 3.5. Percentage of Clerks Who Said the Most Likely Occurrence of Changing Their Justice's Mind Was in the Certiorari Process

Vinson Court through the Rehnquist Court, disagreement with the statement steadily declined. Hence, clerks have increasingly been in agreement with their justices on certiorari decisions. Given that modern clerks are personally reviewing fewer petitions than their predecessors, we suggest that modern clerks are becoming more like justices in the way they interpret cert petitions. That is, like justices, clerks have largely been forced to rely on cert memos from other chambers for the vast majority of cases that are petitioned to the Court. This has resulted in more conformity between clerks and justices regarding the decision to grant or deny.

We also asked the clerks whether, when they did disagree, they were likely to change their justice's mind on cert decisions. Figure 3.5 shows that there has been remarkable change since the cert pool was introduced. Only 18 percent of Vinson Court clerks (two of eleven) said that they were most likely to change their justices' minds in the cert process. But with the dramatic rise in the number of civil liberties cases reaching the Court, the clerks began to have a much more substantial effect on certiorari decisions. Forty-four percent of Warren Court clerks (twenty-four of fifty-four) said that they were most likely to change their justices' minds in this area. But as clerks began to be pooled in 1972, their influence declined, with 32 percent of Burger Court clerks (nineteen of fifty-nine) and 26 percent of Rehnquist Court clerks (five of nineteen) saying that their primary influence was in certiorari decisions.

Why has clerk influence in the cert process declined? Since its inception, an increasing number of justices have chosen to participate in the cert pool, and currently only Justice Stevens is outside the system. Prior to the cert pool there was always one clerk in each chambers who was intimately familiar with the case. Now clerks from other chambers write the memos for most petitions. Clerks feel their influence in this area has declined because they are simply reviewing fewer petitions— half as many as clerks reviewed prior to the cert pool. Contrary to what is commonly thought, the creation and expansion of the cert pool has led to a steady decline in individual clerk influence on the certioriari decisions of their justices. At the same time, the collective influence of the clerks as an institution on the certiorari process generally has increased as more chambers have come to rely on the pool memo.

Conclusion

What is evident from the above analysis is that the creation of the dead list, increases in the number of law clerks, and the creation of the cert pool completely transformed the institution of the Supreme Court law clerk. Clerks have become less like junior associates and more like junior justices. Critics have been vocal about this dramatic change. In 1993, Kenneth Starr wrote, "Selecting 100 or so cases from the pool of 6,000 petitions is just too important to invest in very smart but brand-new lawyers."[131] With the current caseload approaching eight thousand cases and no end in sight, the process will almost certainly continue to come under increasing scrutiny.

When cert petitions were relatively few in number during the early years of clerks, justices almost exclusively reviewed them with little or no clerk input. While clerks reviewed petitions from the institution's inception, it was largely part of their apprenticeship. With the creation of the dead list and the doubling of the number of clerks in the 1940s, some clerks began reviewing petitions in some chambers for actual use by their justices. By the 1960s, caseloads were exploding. Cert petitions were the primary responsibility of most clerks, and they spent the vast majority of their time on this task. They became the Court's experts in this area and felt they had a relatively high degree of influence on the decisions of their justices as to whether or not to vote to hear a particular case.

The cert pool, however, dramatically changed the role of the law clerk. It cut in half the number of petitions pool clerks had to review, freed up more time to research the cases more fully, and as we will discuss in chapter 5, gave them more time to devote to opinion writing. As more justices joined the pool in the 1980s and 1990s, the number of separate concurring and dissenting opinions increased dramatically. As clerks concentrated more on the declining number of cases that were granted cert, through bench memos and opinion writing, their individual influence over the cert process declined.

It has become increasingly difficult for the justices to be a check against clerk-written memos. Indeed, the clerks themselves have a difficult enough time checking the pool memos they receive from other chambers, relying on cues and shortcuts in an attempt to filter out shoddy work and biases. The cert pool has blurred the dividing line between justice and clerk in the long-standing battle against rising dockets. For their part, the justices have debated the cert pool's growth in recent years and some have expressed concern. In 1991, Justice Anthony Kennedy wrote Chief Justice Rehnquist,

> The cert pool is vital to our operations, and I think the Justice who succeeds Thurgood should be encouraged to participate. That would mean, though, that only John would be reviewing the petitions without the use of a pool memo. I propose we alter the system so that in each case one pool member does not receive the pool memo but instead performs an independent review of the petition by whatever in-chambers system he or she selects. To insure review isolated from the memo, perhaps the exclusion rotation should be designed so a clerk for the excluded judge has not prepared the memo for that case. This suggestion would impose a slight additional burden, but the benefit of an alternative form of review within the pool system may justify the extra effort.[132]

Original cert pool member Justice Blackmun wrote,

> For some years now, I, too have been concerned about the growth of the Pool. It seems that every time a new Justice arrives he almost automatically is assigned to the Pool. So long as there are four or three not

in the Pool, there was a brake against errors that might be committed by Pool writers. Now John is the only non-participant. I am not sure about Tony's suggested alternative, but I agree that the subject is something we ought to talk about at some conference in the near future.[133]

Blackmun returned to the topic three days later:

I add that I have benefited from an independent review and annotation by my clerks of all Pool memos circulated to chambers. I understand that this is the practice in some, but not all, of the other chambers. While this independent review entails extra work for my clerks, I feel that it constitutes a brake against errors by Pool memo writers. Moreover, my clerks report that it enhances their understanding of the Court's entire docket and helps make them better Pool memo writers in the process.[134]

Two months later, the justices discussed the matter in conference, and on his copy of Kennedy's memo, Blackmun wrote, "Our K now retreats from this. Now prefers to leave as is." He also noted that Justice O'Connor disagreed with Kennedy's idea and preferred to "use [her] own internal protective devices."[135] While the "exclusion rotation" reform suggested by Kennedy would provide, in addition to Justice Stevens's chambers, an additional check against the pool memo, it would not solve the larger problem of overall clerk influence in the certiorari process. Abolishing the pool, as some have suggested, would lead to an increase in individual clerk influence, as clerks who reviewed petitions prior to the creation of the cert pool reported that they had greater success in changing their justice's mind on certiorari decisions. We suggest that this would happen again if each chambers reviewed each cert petition, as was the practice prior to 1972. As we discuss in the concluding chapter, another solution would be for the justices to take the place of the clerks in a justice cert pool. Though their workload would necessarily increase, the justices would be assured that each case would be screened by one or more of their colleagues. One thing is certain, however. Absent any fundamental reform on the part of the justices, the only way the Court will be able to deal with continually rising dockets will be to do as they have done in the past: add more clerks and expand the cert pool.

4

Decision Making
Mission-Inspired Crusaders?

My principal reaction is that (at least in my era) *none* of the justices were as influenced by their clerks as some books would have you believe!
—Law clerk to Justice Tom C. Clark, 1950s

All of us discuss the matters which will be coming up at Conference with our law clerks.
—Chief Justice William H. Rehnquist, 1987

Do clerks influence justices in the decisions they make? As the institution of law clerks developed, their input on the decision-making process became formalized through recommendations on certiorari, bench memos, coalition formation, and opinion writing. Generally, it is more common than not for justices to solicit the views of their clerks on the merits of cases. For example, David Kendall, a former clerk from 1971, said that Justice Byron White "wasn't invested in an argument; if you could hit him back with a chair, intellectually speaking, he could be convinced."[1] In turn, clerks have taken this liberty to heart and many times set out to change their justice's mind. Herbert Prashker, one of Chief Justice Harlan Fiske Stone's clerks for the 1945 Term, recalled the preparation of Stone's dissent in *Girouard v. United States*:

On at least two occasions during the two-week period while the opinion was in preparation . . . the Chief made the long stomp from his office to our office on the other side of the conference room to talk about *Girouard*. [Co-clerk Eugene] Nickerson and I thought he was wrong, and I think Nickerson, who was helping on the dissent and who wrote parts of it, made an effort to get him to change his mind.[2]

Two highly publicized books on clerk influence recounted instances of clerks working on multiple fronts to change the minds of their justices. In *The Brethren*, Bob Woodward and Scott Armstrong detail clerk maneuverings to change the outcome in *O'Connor v. Donaldson*.[3] Similarly, in *Closed Chambers*, Edward Lazarus described the strategic actions of a clerk for Justice Anthony Kennedy in his attempts to influence the outcome in *Patterson v. McLean Credit Union*.[4]

In the following chapter, we suggest that, overall, clerks are not as influential as other factors are on the decision-making process of the justices. Still, clerks play a crucial role behind the scenes in forming coalitions and have been able to change their justices' minds about particular cases or issues before the Court. While it was never commonplace, over time clerks were increasingly successful at persuading justices on cases and issues. We detail how clerks and justices use the clerk network to aid in decision making, with clerks from different chambers routinely discussing cases with one another. The abortion case *Planned Parenthood v. Casey* is highlighted to illustrate clerk influence in the decision-making process.[5] We discuss how clerks are most persuasive with their justices in the certiorari process, in fashioning the legal and substantive content of opinions, as well as in the more stylistic aspects of opinion writing. Where clerks have less influence is in changing their justices' minds on the outcomes of cases. When weighed with other factors considered by the justices in making their decisions, clerk influence is ultimately less important than more traditional aspects of judicial decision making such as the justices' jurisprudential philosophy, specific case facts, and precedent. Still, when examined over time, clerk influence is on the rise, as are other factors in the justices' decision-making process, while other influences are on the decline. All of this suggests that clerks are an increasingly integral part of the judging process that takes place on the Court and begs the question of whether they ought to be.

Introduction

Asking clerks to comment on their own influence over the decisions of their justices is necessarily an imperfect strategy. Only the justices themselves can know for sure exactly how influential clerks are. While many clerks commented on their influence, some felt that they had no way of knowing. For example, one of Warren's clerks from the 1950s told us that he found it difficult to comment on the factors that influenced Warren's decisions:

> I worked closely with the C.J. both during and after my clerkship, and I
> was proud to count him as a good friend, but I have scant confidence in
> my ability to answer this question. The C.J. was in my view a very great
> man; and like other great men trained in the world of politics, he was in
> some respects very private. One respect was his decisional process.

Other clerks felt they were able to gauge their influence—or lack thereof. For example, John P. Frank, who clerked for Justice Hugo Black in 1942, said that he witnessed "my Justice ma[ke] approximately one thousand decisions, and I had precisely no influence on any of them."[6]

Still, clerks spend a large amount of time with the justices over the course of their year-long clerkship. Walter Gellhorn, who clerked for Justice Harlan Fiske Stone in 1931, said, "[Stone] made one feel a co-worker—a very junior and subordinate co-worker, to be sure, but nevertheless one whose opinion counted and whose assistance was valued."[7] Clerks discuss cases and work closely with their justices on opinions. They graduated at the top of their classes from prestigious law schools and clerked for lower court judges before coming to the High Court. Because of their background, training, and remarkably close relationship to their justices, clerks are in a unique position to comment on their decision-making practices. Robert von Mehren, who clerked for Justice Stanley Reed in 1947, said,

> Sometimes he found it hard to make up his mind and make his decision,
> and he'd like to talk at considerable length with both John [Spitzer] and
> myself, and sometimes with the two of us [together] if it were a particularly important case. And we would discuss in depth the problems and
> the approach he was taking to it. . . . We spent hours talking about a
> case and his views, and very often he would change his views after the
> discussion. Very often he wouldn't.[8]

Other justices, however, did not consult clerks in making their decisions. For example, a Black clerk from the 1940s observed, "When I was a law clerk, Justice Black had been on the Court for over a decade. Many of the cases had recurring themes, and he had decided views about them." The level of experience and quick work habits of some justices made decision making a relatively singular exercise. Another former clerk recalled, "The work was very easy for Douglas in a lot of ways. Douglas is a quick decider. He has an immediate view and writes so much more naturally as a consequence. He spent only fractional amounts of time in relation to the time [other justices] would spend on [their] work. I think too little."[9]

Blackmun clerk Edward Lazarus claimed in his book *Closed Chambers* that Justice Kennedy could be persuaded to vote against delaying executions when his clerks emphasized procedural flaws and persuaded him to make his decision early, before the other justices had a chance to weigh in. Lazarus said a group of conservative clerks "considered expediting executions a central part of their collective mission, and they pursued that goal passionately." Thomas Hungar, a former clerk, denied Lazarus's claims: "The idea that [Justice Kennedy] lets clerks dictate results is simply false and slanderous."[10] Still, Lazarus's overall argument that clerks often seek to influence their justices is difficult to ignore, in light of our findings. And while clerks rarely play a direct role in the result of a case, there are many ways in which clerks can influence a justice's decision.

Indeed, clerks are often encouraged to overtly give their views on the decisions their justices have to make. For example, Justice Lewis F. Powell, Jr., wrote one of his clerks before the start of the 1972 Term,

> I would like, before I have to vote, the benefit of your thinking on 71-863 [*CBS v. Democratic National Committee*], in which [co-clerk Hamilton] Fox prepared the memo. He was inclined to affirm, although recognizing that the question is a close one. I am uncertain, and will await the oral argument, further study, and possibly the Conference discussion before I come to a decision.[11]

Powell characterized Sam Estreicher's work on the landmark affirmative action case *Regents of the University of California v. Bakke* as "a major contribution."[12] Powell wrote Estreicher, "[I] relied a great deal on your views in some of the more difficult cases that came before us."[13]

Clerks have found strength in numbers. When all the clerks in a given chambers agree on a decision, they sometimes make their collective view known to their justice. For example, in *Bakke*, Estreicher wrote Powell, "Bob [Comfort] and I (and, possibly, Jim [Alt]) feel that a discretionary, one-track system which makes any use of 'racial' criteria must further a compelling or substantial state interest."[14] In his final memo to his justice before the Court voted in the gay rights sodomy case *Bowers v. Hardwick*, Powell clerk Mike Mosman wrote, "The three of us who worked on the [Eighth Amendment] theory last night—Ann [Coughlin], Bill [Stuntz], and I—continue to recommend that you use the theory to vote to reverse and write separately to introduce the argument, since it was not presented here. . . . We believe it would be a mistake to create a fundamental right to protect this conduct."[15]

And while clerks have been advocates for particular decisions, they have also found less overt ways to make their views known, such as ensuring that their justice is fully informed on all possible arguments. For example, regarding *McClesky v. Kemp*, 1986 Powell clerk Leslie S. Gielow wrote her justice,

> You should be informed that the Fourteenth Amendment theory which is now popular in the Marshall and Stevens chambers is based on the race of the *defendant*. . . . I recognize that this information will not change your thinking on the case, but I thought that you would like to be informed of the thinking in other chambers so that you would not be surprised at argument or at conference.[16]

It should also be pointed out, however, that the justices, many of them former clerks, know that clerks may try to change their minds on cases and issues. A former clerk to Justice Reed in the 1950s said,

> We would help him on particular opinions. And some opinions he would ask us to do a draft on, and sometimes he would do a draft and ask us to revise or comment. Mutual ways of mutual work. But ultimately, he was clearly in control of . . . he never truly delegated his judicial function to his law clerks. He used us, but he was very much in control, even though he always knew that the clerks were always conspiring to influence the justice and to . . . to write the opinions. And he was very aware of that and his eyes would twinkle and so forth.[17]

Chief Justice William H. Rehnquist commented on the deliberations that take place between justices and their clerks before the justices themselves meet in conference: "All of us discuss the matters which will be coming up at Conference with our law clerks. . . . But the knowledge that once in the Conference it is our own presentation, and not that of one of our staff, which must be depended on, does make a difference in the way the Conference functions."[18] The fact that only justices are allowed in the Conference room is an important check on clerk influence. Since they are on their own, the justices themselves must know the issues and arguments before deliberating and taking votes. Though there are many such procedural checks on clerk influence, it is ultimately up to the justices to decide how much leeway to give their clerks.

But clerks provide lengthy bench memos, which contain details of the facts, analysis, and recommendations on the cases argued in court and discussed in conference. Justice Powell paid particular attention to these recommendations on the merits. For example, after reading the bench memo in *Edwards v. Aguillard*, Powell noted, "Leslie [Gielow] has done well with a difficult subject to address. She would *affirm* generally on basis that the La statute's purpose is religious, that 'creation science' is not a 'science,' and that the statute limits *academic discretion* by making this 'teaching' mandatory."[19]

Indeed, justices take clerk-written memos with them to conference deliberation. So justices are never without clerk input, despite Rehnquist's assertions. After he had been on the losing end of a series of decisions in 1957, Justice Felix Frankfurter wrote another justice, "I wonder how many who are reversing out of hand in these cases have read the record and not relied merely on the memoranda of their law clerks. And, since my curiosity is very alert this morning, I wonder how many of the law clerks have read the whole record in these cases."[20]

Coalition Formation

After a draft is written and circulated to the other chambers, a clerk's job shifts from that of writer to that of negotiator. All nine justices must agree on the final wording of opinions, and clerks act as informal ambassadors for their justices in a process of negotiation and compromise. For example, a Rehnquist clerk from the 1980s told us, "Eight out of nine opinions were written by another justice, so [a] major part of [the] job was whether and how to join other opinions, request changes to others' opinions, etc. Here, [a] clerk's input was of influence." In 1973 Justice Powell wrote his clerks, "Each of you should read circulated opinions promptly, and give me your views where you think this is desirable. First take a look at my conference vote, and if the circulated opinion is in accord with my vote a memorandum from you will be unnecessary unless you think that the opinion is seriously flawed."[21] Powell elaborated on the procedure in a 1982 memo to his clerks:

> It is important for the responsible clerk to read the initial circulation from another Chambers quite promptly. If we are to make comments on it, it is desirable to submit them before other Justices have joined. Once a Justice has a "Court," he or she is not inclined to be responsive to substantive changes. You will rarely see an opinion that you would not like to "edit." It is not our function, however, to improve the writing style of other Chambers. I am primarily concerned, of course, with the substance of the opinion and particularly the analysis that results in the holding. Unless dicta is likely to be troublesome for me in the future, I do not worry too much about it. I resist the temptation to suggest changes that are not important enough to justify communicating with the author. If you think an opinion is satisfactory for me to join, simply write on it "OK to join." As we all work for the Court, if you see mistakes that you would like to have brought to your attention if you were the responsible law clerk, do not hesitate to talk to the clerk in the originating Chambers. I repeat that it is important for my responsible clerk to take a look at changes in draft opinions from other Chambers. I read the original circulation carefully, but rely primarily on my clerks to bring to my attention changes of substance.[22]

Along these lines, clerks routinely draft the memos, in the name of their justice, making requests to the other members of the Court to change their opinions. Outgoing 1977 chief administrative clerk for Justice Powell, Sam Estreicher, wrote the incoming clerks,

> In reviewing work from other Chambers which you determine requires some response from the Justice, whether suggestions for changes (where you recommend an ultimate join) or a decision to write separately, it is useful to offer the Justice a draft of the suggested changes or separate opinion as soon as possible after the draft in question has been received. This procedure not only improves your "bargaining power," but permits the Justice to see whether the suggested position will write before he decides how he will vote.[23]

Estreicher mastered the practice. Justice Powell wrote him about his influence that term in *Monell*:

> You are entitled to feel considerable satisfaction from the bringing down on yesterday of *Monell*. Although the "casebooks" will not reflect it, your contributions both to the result and the content of the opinion were not insignificant. Although you were advising me rather than Justice Brennan, your ideas—in large part—transmitted by my memoranda to the Conference and consultations with Justices, were constructive and effective.[24]

A 1950s clerk to Chief Justice Earl Warren commented on the circulated drafts from other chambers:

> They automatically made their way down to us and the person who worked on the case, we would read them and we would sort of volunteer, I don't recall any systematic thing about it, volunteer our notions about the quality of, not the quality in the aesthetic sense, but quality in the judicial workmanship sense, was more like the kind of opinions we saw coming across . . . so we volunteered that to the Chief on occasion, sometimes he would ask, sometimes he would call you in and sit around and chat about it. Sometimes we would all go and chat with him . . . he was the justice. We were there to help him if he wanted us to do so.

It was the rare case where the clerk actually made the decision on behalf of his or her justice. For example, Justice Frank Murphy's long-time clerk Eugene Gressman wrote Justice Wiley Rutledge, "I have tried in vain to reach Justice Murphy. But I know that he would want to join Black's statement if he files it. It certainly expresses his sentiments. I feel perfectly O.K. to put his name on it—he would want it that way, especially since you are putting your name on it."[25]

The common method of clerk input during this stage is analysis and recommendation, with clerks thinking strategically about the process. For example, in *Bakke*, Powell clerk Bob Comfort wrote his justice a memo regarding "Keeping Mr. Justice Blackmun in the Fold." He said,

> Here is a draft of a counterattack designed to tar Justice Stevens with the same brush he has used to daub your November 22 Memorandum to the

Conference. It is designed to indicate to (presumed) neutrals that your Memorandum is not a departure from the proper judicial role. This draft goes so far as to suggest that Justice Stevens is the one bending his judicial principles (which I think is true), and that if one does reject his rather naïve view of the evanescence of the constitutional dilemma, one would follow rather unprincipled statutory approach for no reason at all.[26]

In another memo on the case, Comfort wrote Powell regarding Justice Brennan's draft opinion, "In general, I think this is a rather poor effort, which will win friends only among those already committed to WJB's 'approved' result. It is not a well crafted piece of judicial workmanship. . . . WJB really begins to engage in flights of fancy."[27] Powell replied, "As you point out, the Brothers here on the Court who should be having a 'field day' rebutting WJB's social essay have silenced themselves by opting for the Title VI out."[28]

In attempting to fashion a majority coalition in *Roe v. Wade*, Justice Blackmun signaled that he was flexible on the key issue of the point at which the woman's privacy right gives way to the interest of the state.[29] He wrote the other justices, "You will observe that I have concluded that the end of the first trimester is critical. This is arbitrary, but perhaps any other selected point, such as quickening or viability, is equally arbitrary."[30] As the justices weighed in on this point, Justice Douglas informed the Court, "I favor the first trimester, rather than viability." Justice Powell's clerk Larry Hammond wrote Powell,

> I am shocked at Justice Douglas' note. The Justice, who more than anyone else on this Court stakes his judicial reputation on protecting the poor and the black (see his separate dissent in *Kras*), cannot fail to recognize that a first trimester rule falls most heavily on those classes. . . . I will find time to devote a day to seeing what empirical research is available on the question of how long it takes women—especially the young, the poor, and the minorities—to recognize their predicament.[31]

In another memo on the case, Hammond wrote Powell,

> What do you think will be HAB's personal reaction to your joinder? Do you think it will in any way hurt his feelings? When you write an opinion for the Ct it disappoints me to have others writing separately repeating what I had hoped we had said as fully and as completely as

necessary. Is it possible that HAB will view your decision to join PS as an indication that PS says something that he did not say adequately himself? On balance, I lean toward recommending that you not join PS, although if you think PS will be pleased none of the thoughts I have expressed seem preclusive.[32]

Despite this activity, it is difficult to determine the extent to which clerk comments on coalition formation are influential. A clerk for Justice Minton during the 1950s told us that he did not know what effect the comments he made on the drafts of other justices had on his justice: "I don't know. That was between him and the justices. I never sat in on any of his meetings with the other justices." However, a Warren clerk from the 1950s told us,

> [Warren] wrote a dissent. It was a strongly worded dissent. I didn't write it, no one else in the office wrote it. The Chief Justice wrote it. And he circulated it. One of the other justices had some comments on it. So the Chief called me in and passed along these comments and asked me to go up and do some research to see if there was any support for it, which I did. And I came back and reported. He had me report to this other justice. And he said to go ahead and modify the opinion. So I did that. We put that stuff in and the other justice joined the opinion and pretty soon all of them . . . it may have been five to four, it may have been seven to two, I don't recall the exact vote. So you got into negotiations with other offices on occasion.

Clerks not only have influence in the decisions their justices make about forming coalitions; they can also influence whether their justice should write separate opinions in cases they have not been assigned to write on.[33] For example, Justice Powell wrote his clerks, "It may well be that I will wish to write concurrences or dissents in some of the other cases on the December 15th list. As opinions circulate, I would welcome suggestions from any of you."[34]

The Clerk Network

Another important aspect of clerk influence on judicial decision making is the clerk network.[35] Clerks regularly talk to each other about their justices' as well as their own views and positions on cases and issues and then relay that information to their justices. Martha Minow, Harvard law professor and former clerk for Justice Thurgood Marshall during the 1980 Term, explained, "It's almost an ambassadorial role, trying to pick up information behind the scenes."[36] Clerks informally mine the network during the coalition-forming stage as votes are cast, opinions are joined, and requests for changes are made from chambers to chambers.[37] For example, 1957 Harlan clerk Norman Dorsen wrote, "The Court is still 5–4 on *Nilva*, although rumor has it that Justice Burton himself is wavering. Justice Frankfurter, it is said, is willing to consider amending Rule 42(b), but until it is amended would affirm. The clerks are about 18-0 for reversal, including both the Burton clerks."[38]

The clerk network started to emerge after the Supreme Court building was completed in 1935. At first, only Chief Justice Charles Evans Hughes and Justice Owen Roberts regularly used their chambers, while their colleagues preferred to continue doing their work at home.[39] Hugo Black's appointment in 1937 started the practice of new justices choosing to work primarily at the Court. With the exception of Chief Justice Stone, by 1941, every member of the Court was regularly using his High Court chambers. Stone remarked, "The place is almost bombastically pretentious, and thus seems to me wholly inappropriate for a quiet group of old boys such the Supreme Court of the United States."[40]

The Court was fully occupied by all the justices and their staffs beginning in 1946 when Chief Justice Fred Vinson was appointed. The result was that instead of working in the homes of their justices, geographically isolated from one another, every clerk worked in the same building, on the same floor, and in offices next to each other. The importance of this new working environment cannot be overstated. Clerks from different chambers saw each other on a daily basis: on the way to work, in the Court's parking garage, during lunch, and after work. Clerks began regularly lunching together, and the discussions frequently involved the cases they were working on. A Warren clerk from the 1950s told us,

> The clerks would all eat lunch together and they would talk about the cases. There was constant dialogue about the cases in there and it was very interesting. And so you knew a lot about what the clerks were thinking and to some extent the clerks disclosed what was known about

what their justice was thinking although I think they were all fairly circumspect about that.

Similarly, a Minton clerk from the 1950s said, "We always lunched together. We may or may not talk about cases. Often we did. Sometimes, if I had some question, and wanted to talk with one of the clerks, I might drop by and see what did he think about this and so forth. Except for the lunches, there was no fixed pattern."

When the Court established a separate dining room for the clerks, they saw even more of each other. For their part, the justices saw that they could benefit from the clerk network, and formally establishing a clerk's dining room was a way to foster it. Still, they recognized its potential dangers. For example, in 1983 Justice Powell wrote his clerks,

> At our conference a couple of weeks ago, the Chief Justice suggested that each of us invite our clerks' attention to the availability of the room set aside for use as a "dining room" for the clerks. Traditionally, law clerks have had a room set aside for their use at lunchtime. Apart from the social aspects, there are two principle purposes (i) to afford an opportunity for the clerks in each Chambers to know the clerks in other Chambers and to exchange ideas on pending cases; and (ii) to avoid the possibility, when such conversations go on in the public dining room, that newsmen or others will hear what was not intended for their ears. There have been examples—unfortunate ones—of newsmen overhearing conversations among clerks. The clerks made full use of the dining room last Term. But the year before, for unknown reasons, there was relatively little use. In view of the need for space, a decision almost was made to discontinue providing this room. Thus, it is to be hoped that this year's law clerks will continue the traditional practice of dining together most of the time. I add this caveat for my own clerks. While sharing views on pending cases may be constructive, it is prudent not to become clerk "politicians" who try to lobby the clerks of other Chambers. The line between lawyer-like discussion and "lobbying" is a fine one and not easy to draw. It becomes a matter of judgment. Another caveat, of course, is never speak *for* your Justice or *argue* for a view you know your Justice probably does not share.[41]

Because of the danger of activism, some justices discourage participation in the clerk network, particularly early in their tenures. For example, seven years before he wrote the preceding memo, Powell wrote his 1976 clerks,

> When I am writing in a case, whether for the Court or in concurrence or dissent, it is usually necessary for me to discuss with my clerk assigned to the case the views of other Justices. These must be taken into account, particularly in writing an opinion for the Court. But discussions of this kind are especially sensitive, and should not be discussed beyond our Chambers. I hardly need add that no Justice would like for his clerks to quote him to personnel from other Chambers, except where the views of the Justice have been circulated or are generally known.[42]

But like his colleagues, Powell ultimately encouraged the clerk network and used it to his advantage whenever possible. For example, regarding *McClesky v. Kemp*, 1986 Powell clerk Leslie S. Gielow wrote her justice,

> The other information which has come to me regarding the sentiment in other chambers is as follows (obviously this is mostly clerk sentiment). The Marshall and Stevens chambers have grasped on to the Fourteenth Amendment, and view it as a viable means for decision, but view the Eighth Amendment as more likely to appeal to a greater number of Justices. Justice O'Connor's clerk still thinks that some limit on prosecutorial discretion is the appropriate remedy. There is no indication as to the Justice's view, except that she is not at rest. Justice White returned the bench memo to his clerk and said, "This is a very nice memo recommending reversal. Now write one recommending affirmance." The Chief Justice favors affirmance, and does not want to write the opinion.[43]

At the start of his tenure, Chief Justice Warren Burger was also suspicious of the clerk network. Before the start of the 1969 Term, he instructed his chief clerk to write his other clerks explaining how they were prohibited from participation. The Burger clerks were informed,

> Some Clerks at times have had a tendency to develop a collective "Law Clerks" decision to resolve cases on the merits before the Justices themselves have worked out the answers. Of special importance in this regard is the conversation which takes place in the Law Clerk Dining

Room. Law Clerks generally view the lunch period as a unique opportunity to exchange insights and stories about their Justices. It has been customary for Law Clerks to discuss with one another the most intimate of matters relating to their Justices with the understanding that none of what is said shall go beyond the four walls of the Dining Room. While such conversations can be both educational and entertaining for the Law Clerks, the extent to which such information is not carried beyond the Dining Room is questionable. Any matters of a confidential nature which tend to place the Chief Justice in an unfavorable light should not be revealed to other Law Clerks. Despite the avowed confidentiality of the lunchroom, the possibility of unfavorable information being "leaked" to other Justices requires the Chief's Law Clerks to be reticent. It is likely that information received from a Justice's own Law Clerk will both diminish his effectiveness with his colleagues and damage his public image more grievously than information received from other sources if only because it will be more highly credited. The Chief's clerks are not to reveal which opinions they are personally working on. . . . The Chief Justice has a strict rule that suggestions are to be accepted from other offices only after another Justice has first considered the matter and then communicated directly and formally to the Chief Justice.[44]

Clerks generally begin their activity in the network after oral argument and prior to the initial conference vote as their justices are making decisions on the merits. A Stewart clerk from the 1970s told us, "There was interaction. There were lunches but also playing basketball and also on substantive things. Frequently the other clerks would come in and say something about the case. We might talk about the case before the vote. Just general talking about the issues, what do you think and why and what about this argument and stuff like that." Justice Powell explained to his clerks in the middle of the 1973 Term, "We can dispense with bench memos, although I will of course always want the views of each of you on each argued case before I go to Conference and, when feasible, prior to argument."[45] Instead of simply making their own recommendations on the merits of the case, clerks add their views on coalition formation via information gleaned through the clerk network. For example, 1991 Blackmun clerk Andrea Ward wrote her justice regarding *New York v. United States*, "I wanted to get back to you on this case prior to Conference. I continue to recommend that you vote to affirm the decision below. . . . From talking with other clerks . . . I think the vote is going to be 6–3 to find the statute (or at least the take-title provision) unconstitutional (the predicted dissenters being you, BRW, and JPS)."[46]

In general, the justices brief their clerks immediately following the conference deliberation and vote. In Chief Justice Warren's early years, he had a somewhat distant relationship with his clerks and failed to brief them on conference discussions. One of his clerks from that time explained, "We would go down to Justice Burton's to find out what happened, because he never told us what happened at conference, even the results, during that year."[47] Another former clerk continued,

> He had some very unusual rules that governed his chambers that the other clerks became aware of very early. . . . Rules like after every session with his clerks, he would decide whether or not his clerks could repeat or discuss whatever they had discussed, and if so, what part of this they could discuss with other clerks or with other justices.[48]

For example, Warren gave strict orders to his clerks not to "leak" information to Justice Felix Frankfurter and his clerks.[49] But in later years, Warren changed his mind and briefed his clerks extensively about the details of conferences. Justice William O. Douglas said that Frankfurter "used his law clerks as flying squadrons against the law clerks of other justices and even against the justices themselves. Frankfurter, a proselytizer, never missed a chance to line up a vote."[50] A clerk for Justice Minton in the 1950s told us, "He would drop in and discuss something. Occasionally it was a little embarrassing but I just didn't agree with him on some things. Justice Frankfurter was very much a politician in trying to get a majority of the Court any way he could." A Warren clerk from the 1950s told us, "Charles Whittaker got leaned on by Frankfurter a lot. Frankfurter was always trying to influence people, influence the clerks, trying to influence all the justices. . . . I think [Warren] resented Frankfurter's efforts of trying to persuade and cajole and proselytize the other justices. He thought it was inappropriate."

Negotiations across chambers are often delicate political matters. Justices rely on the clerk network as the least obtrusive means of gaining information about the views of their colleagues and ultimately of forming coalitions. A Stewart clerk from the 1970s told us,

When an opinion was circulated the clerks would often come in and say, "you know, this is a stupid point," or "can you make this change." Sometimes they'd be talking on their own behalf and sometimes they would be talking on their justice's behalf. Sometimes other justices would come in, usually to talk to Justice Stewart, although every once in a while, somebody, Justice White might come and talk to other clerks about a substantive issue but not very frequently. You negotiate back and forth, not a huge amount. Sometimes, on some issues a particular clerk would feel very strongly about [them]. I wrote one opinion where one of the other clerks felt very strongly that it was bad reasoning. The result was good, the reasoning was bad and he just would never stop about it. . . . He kept beating on me that this is stupid reasoning and you should use this other reasoning but we got a Court. Subsequently the opinion was fairly roundly criticized in the literature for the same thing that this guy had said. But we nevertheless got a Court.

Benjamin S. Sharp, a 1973 Blackmun clerk, wrote his justice concerning a majority opinion they circulated in *Renegotiation Board v. Bannercraft Clothing Co.*:

The vote in the case presently stands at 4–2 with the CJ, PS and TM having not yet voted. J Stewart has not read the opinion, but his clerks think that he is inclined toward the dissent. J. Marshall's clerks feel that he will join if some changes are made or that he will write a concurrence. The objections of J Marshall's clerks and J. Brennan's clerks are the same. . . . Most of J. Douglas' dissent is not too bad. . . . I think that he is wrong . . . where he states that we have erred. . . . I have spoken to J Douglas' clerks about this.[51]

In another example, 1993 Blackmun clerk Michelle Alexander wrote in a memo to her justice concerning *J.E.B. v. Alabama ex. rel. T.B.*,

I asked Justice Kennedy's clerk why Kennedy concurred in the judgment only, and he said that Kennedy just wanted to emphasize his "individual rights" theory. Apparently, Kennedy thought there were a few things in your opinion that were slightly inconsistent with his approach; rather than ask you to change your opinion, he decided to concur in the judgment since you already had five votes.[52]

Similarly, In *United States v. Fordice*, 1991 Blackmun clerk Andrea Ward wrote her justice about the politics of coalition formation around Justice White's majority opinion:

> This opinion has been in circulation for over a month. Aside from Justice Stevens' immediate joinder, nothing else has happened. Last week, however, the Chief circulated a memo to Justice White asking, in relevant part, that references to "racial identifiability" as a constitutional evil be removed. This is sure to stir up trouble. I am satisfied with the opinion as it now stands. . . . I think that it is very important not to kill this opinion from the "left" or to lose all your bargaining power by joining too quickly; thus, I've been waiting for movement from other chambers before recommending that you join. At this point, I continue to recommend that you wait, but that you be prepared to join quickly in the event that someone like Justice O'Connor or Justice Souter joins the draft. I'm not sure that any movement from the moderates will occur soon, however. Justice O'Connor has sent Justice White a memo asking for several changes which, if made, are sure to be acceptable to you and Justice Stevens. According to [O'Connor clerk] Crystal Nix, however, Justice O'Connor is still inclined to wait and has no plans to join anytime soon. Meanwhile, the conservatives have yet to weigh in on the Chief's suggested changes. I understand from Justice White's clerk that Justice White has no intention of removing the references to racial identifiability in the draft, and that he is going to try to find out how wedded the Chief is to these changes. I will keep you posted.[53]

It is plain that the justices not only tolerate but also welcome and even cultivate an active clerk network. Justice Brennan remarked, "The clerks get into the damnedest wrangles over some of these things, which is the way they most help me, and I get in the middle of a number of pitched battles, too."[54] In attempting to form coalitions during *Bakke*, Powell wrote a memo to his clerk Bob Comfort about two cases that bolstered their position. Powell concluded the memo, "You may have the opportunity, also, to use the cases in discussions with other clerks."[55] Justice John Marshall Harlan, II, wrote to one of his 1960 clerks, Phillip Heymann, concerning *Machinists v. Street*:

> I should like to have a full memorandum on the issues in this case. Your jumping off place should be Justice Black's draft of opinion, which,

of course, did not come down this Term. I know that one of Justice Frankfurter's new law clerks is going to be put on the job, and I suggest you coordinate with him. (For your information, I may say that Justice Frankfurter and I would have been in dissent on Justice Black's opinion.)[56]

One reason why justices allow their clerks to network across chambers is to foster educative experience. When one clerk is particularly learned in an area of the law, clerks from other chambers seek him or her out for help. For example, in extolling the virtues of former clerk Ronald Carr, Justice Powell noted his "special interest in and considerable depth of knowledge in economics." He continued, "He was particularly helpful to me in 'business' area cases: anti-trust and tax, in particular. . . . We considered Ron my principal adviser, during his clerkship, on federal jurisdiction. Indeed, I think it is accurate to say that Ron's reputation in the subjects I have mentioned attracted clerks from other Chambers who came to him for consultation."[57]

A second reason the clerk network is encouraged by the justices is that it helps them gain information about their colleagues' positions and aids in forming coalitions. Justice Powell explained to his clerks,

> After an opinion is circulated, we anxiously await responses from other Chambers. The happiest word is simply a note saying "Please join me." Less welcome communications include advice that "I will await circulation of the dissent," or a long memorandum suggesting major changes in our draft. Perhaps the most disquieting situation is to circulate an opinion, and receive no response at all. This means that even the Justices who voted with me in Conference do not like my draft. In this situation, negotiations may take place or the opinion may be reassigned to another Justice. Negotiations often occur at two levels: (i) by me with respect to proposed major changes, although the clerk will work with me in Chambers; and (ii) by my clerk directly with his opposite number. The latter situation occurs frequently with respect to editorial-type changes. For this, and other professional and personal reasons, it is helpful to maintain warm and cordial relations with the clerks in other Chambers.[58]

A Stewart clerk from the 1970s told us, "Some of the justices, and you could tell, put a lot more stock into what their clerks said. So that if those clerks were speaking it was a little more likely that was the justice's view." In the 1971 case *Boddie v. Connecticut*, Justice Harlan's clerk, Thomas Krattenmaker, urged one of Justice Marshall's clerks to try to persuade Marshall to join the majority. The clerk was successful and Marshall switched sides.[59] A former clerk for Justice Clark told us, "That's a very important part of the process. To some extent this is a political process of course. Consensus always is. You talk to other clerks about the drafts they had sent around and say 'You know I have trouble with that,' or 'explain this to me,' or whatever. It's a collegial process." When asked whether he would characterize this process as lobbying, the clerk said,

> Yes, absolutely. But again, remember that a lot of this depends on who the judge is, who the clerk is, and what their natures are. Some justices would say to their clerks, "I don't want you talking to other justices directly about my opinion or my draft, or so forth." Others didn't care. Some clerks by their nature wanted to impose their will on others and were very actively involved in it. It depended a lot. But was there lobbying? Absolutely. That's what you do. When you need five votes and you only have four, you go to somebody who you think you can win over and say, "What's it going to take?"

Powell clerk Bob Comfort wrote his justice,

> I had a long conversation this morning with Keith Ellison, one of Justice Blackmun's clerks, about the Bakke case. Their chambers have just begun to think seriously about the problems, but I gathered from Keith that Justice Blackmun is troubled about an aspect of the case not stressed in the bench memo. . . . The aspect in question is the recent amendment to the California constitution. . . . Frankly, I am not sure why this argument troubles Justice Blackmun. . . . The thinking in Justice Blackmun's chambers is still hampered by the inability to separate the decision on the proper level of scrutiny from the weighing of the various justifications for the Task Force program. It seems as though conflation of the various questions in the case is going to plague the Court in its attempt to produce a reasoned result in this case.[60]

The timing of circulation of opinions to the other justices is important not only so that clerks will know when they must complete their drafts but also as a strategic calculation in coalition formation. An example of the former occurred in *Edwards v. Aguillard*, when 1986 Powell clerk Leslie S. Gielow wrote her justice,

> I have not forgotten that you asked me to draft a concurrence in this case. I have spoken to Justice Brennan's clerk who says that he (the clerk) has just started work on the opinion and does not expect it to circulate for several weeks. I would expect to have a draft of the concurrence to you next week, in time for it to be edited and ready for circulation shortly after the Court opinion.[61]

Powell replied, "No hurry."[62]

Another way that justices and clerks benefit from the clerk network is that it makes it easier to gain information not only about the justices but also about the other clerks. Because clerks must work across chambers in reviewing pool memos written outside their chambers, forming coalitions, and writing opinions, clerks seek to learn as much as possible about the biases and reliability of their counterparts. Justices are concerned about clerks from other chambers as well. For example, midway through the 1985 Term, Justice Powell wrote his clerks,

> We do have some relief in sight for February and March, as [clerk to retired Justice Potter Stewart] Bob Stack has been made available to our Chambers for those two sessions of the Court. It is important to divide cert and bench memos with him for those two argument sessions. In view of his lack of experience with our Chambers, possibly he should not bear as heavy a load as each of you will. It may be desirable, in this connection, to check with friends in the Chambers of Justices Brennan and O'Connor to see the extent to which Bob has been helpful and in what ways. Justice Stewart's clerk also likes to have the opportunity to work with a Justice on at least one Court opinion.[63]

Because of its effectiveness, it should not be surprising when a justice makes reference to clerk input and the clerk network to the other justices. In 1957, Justice William J. Brennan wrote Justice Harlan, "I subscribe enthusiastically to what my clerks characterize, and I agree, is 'a magnificent opinion.'"[64] In 1965, Justice Harlan wrote Justice Black, "This is to say that I agree with your opinion subject to two matters which my law clerk has already discussed with yours. . . . As my thoughts have already been elaborated to your law clerk, I need not repeat them here."[65]

Case Swapping

In addition to the clerk network, another area where clerks exercise influence on decision making is in the choice of which clerk in a given chambers will work on a particular case. Since each chambers has multiple clerks, each justice must necessarily develop a procedure for dividing the workload. We found that procedures vary among chambers, and clerks are often given a great deal of leeway in making the choices themselves. This has led to the phenomenon of case swapping, where one clerk may trade an assigned case to a co-clerk for a different, perhaps more desirable case. This occurs with cert memos, bench memos, and opinions. While case swapping is almost exclusively practiced among co-clerks for a particular justice, it has also occurred, at least in the cert process, across chambers. In 1996, Chief Justice Rehnquist wrote the pool clerks about this issue:

> Pool memos are assigned to the various chambers participating in the pool on a random basis, partly because that is the easiest way to do it, and partly to avoid any temptation on the part of law clerks to select for themselves pool memos in cases with respect to which they might not be as neutral and detached as is desirable. There may be perfectly good reasons why a particular law clerk should not write a pool memo in a given case; the most obvious one would be if the clerk had worked on the case as a clerk in a court of appeals before coming here. But this sort of problem can, except in the rarest of circumstances, be handled by swaps within a chambers. It has been brought to my attention that not only this kind of swap, but swaps between chambers have on occasion occurred. This sort of trade has the potential for undermining the policy of random assignment of memos, and is, to put it mildly, "not favored." In the future, there are to be no trades of pool memos between chambers without my express permission, for good cause shown.[66]

To be sure, case swapping is necessary when a clerk may have a potential conflict of interest or when a clerk is overburdened with more work than his or her co-clerks. In such instances, assignments are routinely changed. Justice Powell wrote his clerks, "The argued cases will be divided among the three of you, and you will remain with the case assigned to you until all opinions have been written and it is 'brought down,' unless—to balance out the workload—the case is reassigned (which happens not infrequently)."[67] In one example of balancing the workload, Powell wrote his clerks,

> Three of the cases have been Larry [Hammond]'s responsibility. The Court views *Rodriguez* as a major constitutional case, requiring maximum effort to produce a satisfactory opinion. Accordingly, in a talk with Larry yesterday, I suggested that we ask Bill [Kelly] to assume initial responsibility for drafts of a court opinion in *Biggers* and a dissent in *Fuller*. This will free Larry to concentrate on *Rodriguez* which is a demanding assignment. If this is agreeable with Bill, both Larry and I can brief him at least sufficiently to give him a bit of a start.[68]

Similarly, 1992 Blackmun clerk Bill Dodge wrote his boss,

> We clerks have decided that I should keep the three writing assignments from October. However, Sherry [Colb] has agreed to take responsibility for the benchmemo in *District of Columbia v. Greater Washington Board of Trade*, one of the November cases. This seemed to be the most efficient solution. It means that I will have more time to work on opinions in the next few weeks and less chance of getting another writing assignment next month.[69]

Another example of workload issues affecting assignments is 1991 Blackmun clerk Molly McUsic's memo to her justice regarding *Kraft General Foods v. Iowa Dept. of Revenue*:

> You voted with the Chief in dissent on this case. Justice O'Connor has circulated a memo saying that she will wait for the dissent. The Chief's clerk sent me a message stating that the Chief was interested in knowing whether you were interested in writing. I think a dissent is important, because I am not convinced that the Court is correct. Before the end, I have to write a concurrence in *Lee v. Weisman*, (I have a draft nearly finished) and either our chambers or Justice Stevens must write a dissent in *Lucas v. South Carolina Coastal Corp.*, No. 91-453. At breakfast, we had discussed how I would draft the dissent in *Lucas*,

although you have not yet informed JPS. If I do both *Lee* and *Lucas* I do not think I could also write something in *Kraft*. Although I would be happy to write in *Kraft*, I would prefer to write in *Lucas*. But if you are interested in writing in both, we can simply divide it up among all the clerks. I do think a dissent written by us has a better chance of collecting SOC's vote than a quick job by the Chief. [Co-clerks] Jeff [Meyer] and Andrea [Ward] each have only one more opinion to write, and they have already started it. [Co-clerks] Steff [Dangel] and Hugh [Baxter] are overloaded. What should I tell the Chief's clerk about *Kraft*? Do you want to write the dissent in *Lucas*?[70]

But case swapping can be problematic when clerks are left unchecked by their justice to make their own assignments and trades. In discussing the status of opinions assigned to his clerks, Justice Powell wrote, "If in fact any one of you feels overburdened, please feel free to work it out with your colleagues—with or without my assistance."[71] Indeed, Justice Powell regularly deferred to his clerks on how to divide up cases. Powell's 1972 chief clerk, Bill Kelley, wrote him, "We have divided the cases for the Feb argument period as follows."[72] Paul Cane, Powell's chief administrative clerk for the 1980 Term, outlined the process he used of dividing up bench memo assignments:

> Under the watchful eye of [outgoing Powell clerk] Jonathan Sallet, I conducted a drawing today to assign summer bench memos. Everyone received at least his first choice, and Paul Smith did even better than that, raking in his top three choices. I will briefly explain the methodology used. I randomly established a "drafting order," which (unfortunately for me) turned out to be (1) Peter, (2) Paul S., (3) Greg, and (4) Paul C. During each round of the draft, each clerk was given his most-preferred case if it was still available; if it was not, he was given his next most-preferred case.[73]

Cane did the same thing for the incoming clerks the following term.[74]

The obvious solution to case swapping is to allocate work randomly. One benefit of random assignments is that it would prevent discord among co-clerks who might otherwise vie with each other for particular cases. Randomization is also a check on overzealous clerks who may want to work on a particular case for partisan reasons. The cost to the justices from such a system is that they might lose a particular clerk's expertise in a given area of the law. Indeed, some clerks are selected precisely because they are knowledgeable about certain topics. Justice Powell wrote his clerks about a swap in *Lloyd v. Tanner*, "Although originally Larry's case, Pete—an expert on 'company towns' from Alabama—will take this assignment."[75]

Abortion: A Case Study in Clerk Influence on Decision Making

The case of *Planned Parenthood v. Casey* is important to the study of law and courts for a number of reasons.[76] We focus on this landmark abortion rights case to highlight the role of law clerks at various points in the decision-making process, from the decision to grant cert to coalition formation, the clerk network, and opinion writing. *Casey* was the case that many thought would overturn *Roe v. Wade*.[77] As the author of *Roe*, Justice Blackmun was particularly invested in the outcome. For their part, Blackmun's clerks constantly lobbied their justice, provided strategic and political analysis as well as legal analysis, worked tirelessly behind the scenes with clerks from other chambers to gain information about what was happening with the other justices, and drafted Blackmun's opinion in the case. Their behavior reflects the way the institution has been transformed and the growing influence of clerks, particularly in important cases.

Molly McUsic was the first Blackmun clerk to work on *Casey*. She took the initial fifteen-page pool memo and marked it up with an important change. As was discussed in chapter 3, each pool clerk is required to list his or her name at the end of his or her pool memos. The Casey pool memo said "McAllister." McUsic, however, changed the memo to read, "Steve 'McAllister' CT/BRW/Kansas" in order to inform Blackmun that the writer was a former Kansas Law School student clerking for Justices White and Thomas. This change was plainly made to help reveal any biases the pool writer might have had in making his analysis. McUsic then composed a two-and-one-half-page legal, but mostly political, analysis on whether or not to grant the case (see appendix E). It stated in part, "If you believe that there are enough votes on the Court now to overturn *Roe*, it would be better to do it this year before the [presidential] election and give women the opportunity to vote their outrage."[78]

In thinking that he had enough votes to overturn *Roe*, Chief Justice Rehnquist wanted to delay the consideration of the case until after the presidential election. Blackmun threatened to release a dissent should the cases be relisted. Blackmun clerk Stephanie A. Dangel formally entered the fray four days later by talking to clerks in other chambers. After the morning conference where *Casey* was first brought up, she wrote Blackmun,

> Another piece of possibly good news. Peter Rubin, DHS's clerk, claims that DHS is trying to write the question in such a way as to *avoid* overruling *Roe*. His question presented will either focus on what the appropriate standard of review is (strict scrutiny or rational relation) and/or what role should considerations of stare decisis play in the case. Peter says he has confirmed this with his boss b/c DHS may not have been clear at the conference. Also, Peter says that DHS' desire for more time is due to his hope that he would have the summer to think about this question. Unlike the Chief and SOC, DHS is not concerned about the election. DHS (via Peter) has also expressed a tremendous amount of interest in what your vote will be. DHS is confused b/c he thinks that you will vote to deny on the Planned Parenthood petn, thus leaving him as the swing vote. While I know that your final decision will depend on the questions presented, do you want me to pass on anything to DHS about your inclinations that might help in framing the questions presented.[79]

Dangel's sources in the clerk network were correct. Five days later, the day before the conference vote, Souter submitted a memo to the other justices indicating that he might not be a vote the Chief Justice could count on to overturn *Roe*:

> The petition for cert presents this question: "Has the Supreme Court overruled *Roe v. Wade* . . . holding that a woman's right to choose abortion is a fundamental right." . . . At Friday's conference, I suggested that the question be rephrased . . . "Is . . . undue burden . . . the appropriate standard of review applicable to the regulation of abortion by the states? If so did the court of appeals correctly apply that standard to the challenged provisions of the Pennsylvania . . . Act?" I also asked that a question be added specifically addressing the issue

of precedent. The following would satisfy me: "What weight is due to considerations of stare decisis in evaluating the constitutional right to abortion?"[80]

Ultimately, the Court decided to be much less specific and simply order the parties to address the constitutionality of the various provisions of the Pennsylvania law. Then all the Blackmun clerks sent a joint memo lobbying their justice before the conference vote in *Casey*:

> We were reflecting on our breakfast conversation concerning this case. We know from talking to clerks that there is considerable interest among the other Justices about your views. For what it's worth, we all recommend that you take a clear stand at Conference tomorrow in favor of granting this case. . . . Moreover, we feel strongly that the case should be heard this spring, and that you should oppose efforts to relist the case any further.[81]

Blackmun took their memo to the conference, recorded the votes of his colleagues on it, and, for his part, voted exactly as his clerks suggested. As the clerks already suspected, only Chief Justice Rehnquist and Justice O'Connor voted not to hear the case because of the upcoming election. The other justices voted to grant.

Following oral argument, the justices voted 5–4 in conference to uphold the abortion restrictions in the state law and largely overturn *Roe*. Chief Justice Rehnquist circulated what he hoped would be the majority opinion, stating,

> the Court was mistaken in *Roe* when it classified a woman's decision to terminate her pregnancy as a "fundamental right" that could be abridged only in a manner which withstood "strict scrutiny." . . . A woman's interest in having an abortion is a form of liberty protected by the Due Process Clause, but States may regulate abortion procedures in ways rationally related to a legitimate state interest.[82]

After marking up the draft, Justice Blackmun wrote at the top, "*Wow*! Pretty extreme!"[83] Justice White immediately joined the Rehnquist opinion.[84] Justice Blackmun informed the other justices that he would be writing in the case.[85]

Meanwhile, Justice Kennedy had been discussing the case with Justices O'Connor and Souter and now wanted to speak with Justice Blackmun: "I need to see you as soon as you have a few moments. I want to tell you about some developments in Planned Parenthood v. Casey, and at least part of what I say should come as welcome news."[86] Meeting privately the next day, Kennedy explained that he was writing a joint opinion with Justices O'Connor and Souter. He said that *Roe* was sound, though not the trimester system. He said that they would uphold the Pennsylvania abortion restrictions except for spousal notification. He explained that Justice Souter was concerned about stare decisis and that they would use Justice O'Connor's "undue burden" standard from *Webster v. Reproductive Health Services*. Kennedy also spoke about his personal concerns. Blackmun recounted that Kennedy "seemed deeply concerned about being saddled with this issue for the rest of his career. He was especially worried about the attention he would get as a Roman Catholic reaffirming Roe."[87] Blackmun asked if he could join some of their opinion, and in his notes on the meeting wrote, "RC agony + traitor" and "election is unrel."[88]

While reading through the first circulated draft of the jointly authored opinion by Justices O'Connor, Kennedy, and Souter, Justice Blackmun noted in the margins the sections written by each justice. In particular, he noted "SOC's undue burden" standard and many other passages written by "SOC." Yet, at the end of the opinion, he wrote on the last page his objections to the parts of the opinion that he could not join and added, "Who wrote for SOC?"[89] Clearly, Blackmun was asking his clerks to mine the clerk network to find out.

The joint opinion demonstrated that Chief Justice Rehnquist's position could not command a five-member majority. Recognizing this, Justice Stevens immediately praised Justices O'Connor, Kennedy, and Souter, and offered to join substantial parts of it: "Your opinion is impressive; you are to be congratulated on a fine piece of work. I think I understand why you decided to write jointly, and I agree that your decision is a wise one."[90]

Dangel wrote Blackmun a memo outlining her view of the joint opinion's "sections . . . that I think that you can join" and added, "While I tend to agree with most of JPS' list, I tend to disagree with him on a few of the sections." She then proceeded to make a largely legal critique of the joint opinion with an eye toward what could be done to change it. For example, Dangel said,

Perhaps we can get the majority to tone do[w]n its language critical of *Roe*. . . . Section V . . . is very well done and has an almost "equal protection" sound to it that we can play up in our opinion. . . . I'd like to speak with the JPS' clerk before making any final recommendations. . . . I also plan to work on an outline setting out the sections in your concurrence/dissent. As a general matter, I think you should use your opinion to put the best possible spin on the SOC/AMK/DHS opinion and to attack the CJ's opinion.[91]

Two days later, Chief Justice Rehnquist sent a memo to all the law clerks:

The current issue of *Newsweek* at page 6 contains a purported account of what is happening within the Court in the case of *Planned Parenthood v. Casey*. While most of the story deals with matters of common knowledge to anyone who observes the Court, part of it does not. The story is attributed to "sources" and "clerks." Each of you is admonished to bear in mind the following portion of the Supreme Court Law Clerk Code of Conduct (page 4): "There should be as little communication as possible between the clerk and representatives of the press." In the case of any matter pending before the Court, the least possible communication is *none at all*.[92]

Dangel began drafting Blackmun's opinion and wrote the justice a memo on June 16:

I wanted to give you a brief summary of the approach I am taking in my draft. (I have cleared the approach with your other clerks, together with JPS' clerk) . . . I fear the decision may have the effect of removing abortion from the political agenda just long enough to ensure the reelection of Pres. Bush and the appointment of another nominee from whom the Far Right will be sure to exact a promise to overrule *Roe*. . . . I have no doubt that [the joint] opinion will have its cost for the troika. Once this opinion comes out, there will be no more speculation about a Vice President O'Connor or a Chief Justice Kennedy—and, as DHS himself recognized, I suspect Barbara Bush will find herself another most-eligible-bachelor to include on her White House invite list I think the tone in [the second section] cannot be harsh—it must be the more consoling tone of an older, wiser uncle, whose own views on abortion have evolved as he has faced this issue over and over again. . . . The third section attacks the position of the CJ and Co. While the specifics of this section cannot be worked out until AS has circulated his monstrosity, the format of this section should be a parade of the ever increasing horribles: first, the CJ's opinion, which overrules *Roe* without admitting it; second, AS' opinion which, by calling for the overruling of *Roe*, takes the ridiculous position that the answer to a question as fundamental as the right to choose should vary from State to State. . . . Now for the question of timing. . . . I think it is preferable to circulate *after* the conference on Friday. This opinion should ruffle some feathers on the right—better to give them a few days to cool off before you have to meet with them again. . . . As the other clerks are interested in this case and will be free next week, we can all spend the final week helping you polish your opinion. . . . As I mentioned the other morning at breakfast, JPS is considering writing an opinion staking out the equal protection basis for the right to choose. . . . Unfortunately, JPS' clerk has indicated that the Justice is now waffling on this idea, evidently because he feels that it might tread on territory you plan to cover. I've indicated to the clerk that we have no current plans to include this approach, but I bring this to your attention so that you can be prepared if JPS calls.[93]

As was his practice, Blackmun made brief comments on the memo such as "OK" and placed check marks throughout. For example, on Dangel's recommendation to release the draft after the conference on Friday, Blackmun wrote, "Yes." After her discussion of Justice Stevens's "waffling," Blackmun wrote, "Let JPS go free."[94]

Two days later, Dangel filled Justice Blackmun in on how the day's events would unfold:

While you should probably not let on that you know this, JPS is going to call you to discuss the possibility of getting the troika to make some modifications that would allow us to join the first three sections of the opinion. . . . It might be worth mentioning to Justice Stevens the general approach your [*sic*] going to take in your opinion. He will then be in a better position to assess whether he will have to write separately. . . . While we would surely welcome JPS aboard, our opinion may be too radical for him, at least in so far as you are inclined to strike down more provisions than he is. Again, you should probably act surprised when he calls. I did want to give you fair warning.

Just as Dangel had predicted, Justice Stevens continued to work with Justices O'Connor, Kennedy, and Souter to reach agreement:

> You have indicated that you would welcome suggestions that will enable Harry and me to join as much of your opinion as possible. Although I am conscious of the reasons why you have included criticism of the trimester approach early in the opinion, I would like to suggest that the entire opinion would be immeasurably strengthened by placing that discussion in a later section, thereby making it possible for Harry and me to join Parts I and II, and . . . Part III as well. In my view, an opinion that begins as an opinion of the Court and continues to speak for a Court for 25 pages would be far more powerful than one that starts out as a plurality opinion and shifts back and forth between a Court opinion and a plurality opinion.[95]

Justice Kennedy replied, "My initial inclination is that what you propose is quite feasible and I will recommend to Sandra and David that we accomplish your change in the next draft to see how it looks. In some significant respects what you suggest would improve the opinion."[96]

The joint authors made the suggested changes and sent around another draft. Dangel wrote Blackmun about the delay in the draft opinion she was writing,

> It's a tricky thing to write, and I'm being held up in writing my "parade of horribles" section by the absence of a rather important "firetruck"— the evil nino has yet to circulate. . . . Perhaps I'm too suspicious, but I wonder if the CJ is pushing for a Friday deadline to make this case look less important. Friday cases always get less initial publicity, and his absence may reinforce the contention in his revised opinion that this case is "no big deal" b/c *Roe* has been effectively overruled. But then again, a Friday deadline gives them less time to respond to us. . . . Just in case you think I'm being "too" suspicious, I should note that [co-clerk] Jeff [Meyers] first mentioned this "idea" that it looks like the CJ is being "political." Perhaps we should pow-wow on this at Monday's breakfast.[97]

Two weeks after the joint opinion was circulated, Dangel wrote her justice,

> Here is a *rough* draft of what I've been able to complete in *Casey*. It needs some cutting and polishing. The final section is also incomplete, as AS has yet to circulate, thus continuing to hold up my parade of horribles. . . . GOOD NEWS—JPS' clerk informs me that the Justice has again changed his mind—he's writing a concurrence/dissent setting out the equal protection argument![98]

Two days later, and working on a more complete first draft, Dangel wrote the justice, "I will get a draft to you and the clerks by the end of the day. I will then incorporate the clerks' comments so that you will have a 'final' draft ready for circulation first thing tomorrow. If AS' draft has not come in by then, we will just have to attack him in a subsequent draft."[99] On Dangel's first complete draft of *Casey*, she typed on page 29, in reference to Chief Justice Rehnquist, "the Chief Judge cites," crossed out the word "Judge," inserted "Justice," and noted at the bottom of the page, "I guess I got so angry by the end of the draft that I subconsciously demoted him."[100] Blackmun edited the thirty-page draft for grammar, made some word changes, and deleted one paragraph.

Two days later, in the first of her four memos to the justice that day, she wrote,

> I am working on some revisions . . . nothing very substantive. Perhaps a few remarks at the end about AS. The one "substantive" decision you will have to make is whether you want to go with an ending that links the future of reproductive rights to the upcoming election (or confirmation process) in the manner that my earlier draft did. It's pretty radical—although AS has once again greased the skids by bringing it up in his dissent.[101]

In a separate memo the same day she wrote,

> I have three minor changes to suggest . . . I think they are necessary to distance ourselves from AS. . . . I suggest inserting "apparently" before "held," since AMK, one of the four in *Webster*, has obviously abandoned that position. There's no need to jump on board AS' attack on

AMK's inconsistency. . . . I think we should omit fn 4. AS makes these identical points in his draft. We should take advantage of his willingness to criticize the undue burden test—who knows, maybe it will eventually drive the joint opinion writers to adopt strict scrutiny. In any event, no need to pile on. . . . DHS' clerk called last night and asked if we could join Part VI of their opinion. . . . I see no harm in this.[102]

Dangel's third memo of the day on *Casey* shifted gears to the politics of the head note, which determines the order the opinions are read from the bench and printed in the *United States Reports*:

> While the headnote seems a little strange, I think it is correct. In short, we *joined* all the sections in which we make up the majority, so there is no need to summarize our concurrence. The CJ (joined by White) and AS only *concurred in judgment* on the other sections. Frank informs me that it is the "tradition" of the Reporter's Office to include all concurrences in judgment when there is not a majority opinion for the relevant section. I guess this tradition saves them the awkwardness of having to choose between concurrences in judgment. If however, AS joins the CJ, then AS' separate opinion should go. In any event, Frank has obviously given AS as little print as possible. I guess it all works out in the end, since our decision to join means that our opinion is included before the CJ and AS, thus allowing us to spin them before people read them. Moreover, if you decide to read your opinion from the bench, you would be before them.[103]

Dangel's fourth and final memo of the day on *Casey* continued the discussion of head note politics:

> JPS' clerk just called me about the head note and he was livid. He says that it is highly *unusual* to give so much attention to a concurrence in judgment. Using *Cippollone* as a model, the clerk claims that the norm is to treat these opinions as AS' opinion has been treated, i.e. in a couple of sentences. I pass this along for your consideration—you are certainly in a better position to know what the tradition is around here. I'm not sure, however, how much "standing" we have to object to the headnote since we're not included. I have passed along my concerns to the joint opinion clerks—hopefully, their Justices will say something since they have cause to complain.[104]

Not to be outdone, the next day Dangel sent Blackmun the first of five memos: "I have one more substantive addition I would like to make —I would like to conclude Section II with a reference to JPS' approach, as it does a good job of handling the only unanswered criticism levied by the joint opinion: the trimester framework's so-called unfulfilled promise of protecting potential human life."[105] In the next memo she wrote,

> After conferring with the clerks, I have offered you a more muted ending. "I am confident" is gone, and "I fear" is replaced with "I regret"— thus, it now reads less as a battle cry, and more as a lament that an issue as important as this should be decided in such a circus atmosphere. Now the sentence is one that even AS could join—in fact, he makes the same point in his dissent.[106]

In her third memo Dangel wrote, "AMK asked his clerk to pass along that he's a little concerned about the references to the Chief Justice as 'the Chief.' While I have my doubts as to whether he deserves to be call[ed] 'Justice' on this one, I guess there's no need to ruffle feathers needlessly—we ruffle enough with our criticism already."[107] In the fourth memo, Dangel returned to the head note controversy: "Frank Wagner called. . . . He is no longer sure how to do the headnote, nor am I."[108] Finally, in Dangel's record fifth memo of the day she returned to her own feelings on the case and delivered a scathing indictment of Justice Stevens (see appendix F):

> I cannot help be disappointed with JPS. Not only has he reversed without explanation his position on some of the issues in this case, but he has continued to distance himself from you in other opinions, specifically his last minute failure to join you in *Lucas* and *Sawyer*, when both opinions set out views he previously had put forth himself! I can't help but think that JPS sees that there's power in the middle, and therefore that's where he's moving. In short, I think JPS is taking for granted that you will always be here to make the principled argument, so he's free to go off and build coalitions in the middle.[109]

On June 27, Justice Stevens phoned Justice Blackmun to discuss the case. After discussing the phone call with his clerks, Blackmun wrote

Stevens, "I appreciate your call . . . about Part IV of my second draft. After lengthy discussion here, we have decided to leave that paragraph in. This does not mean that I do not appreciate your call."[110]

The day the opinion was handed down, a number of Blackmun's former clerks phoned his chambers. Secretary Wanda Martinson took messages for the justice. For example, she summarized 1985 clerk Pamela Karlan's call as follows:

> thinks AS's writing is "near hysteria" and thinks pro-choice people ought not to be saying negative things about the majority opinion. "This is more than we ever could have hoped for out of this Court." As for CT's voting with AS, she said: "First we have the Minnesota Twins, then we have the Arizona Twins, and now we have Ebony and Ivory."[111]

Though the case had been announced and Blackmun's opinion released, Dangel once again wrote the justice about the case and suggested still further revisions:

> I just wanted to let you know that (in case you haven't noticed) I'm feeling much better about our efforts in *Casey*. In addition to the end-of-terms blues, I was just frustrated by not being able to put more time into such an important opinion. But I guess law is the art of the possible, and we certainly did all that was humanly possible in the short time available to respond to the avalanche of paper in this case. . . . I also think you made the correct decision about the conclusion. It's too bad that some people have tried to transform your expression of regret into a "call to arms." . . . While it may be too late, I do have two suggested "revisions" to your opinion. You certainly know better whether these are permissible, but as they're on my mind, I thought I should give them to you to consider: 1) in footnote 4 we list a number of commentators who have recognized the equal protection basis for the abortion right. There is one obvious author missing from the list: Kitty MacKinnon, the pioneer in this area. . . . 2) While it is implicit in Section II, I think that you should consider making explicit your hope that the joint opinion authors will someday return to strict scrutiny. I therefore suggest that you add the following sentence to the end of Section IIB: "I therefore remain hopeful that the principles set forth in the joint opinion will in the future lead these Justices to reaffirm this aspect of *Roe* as well."[112]

On July 2, Blackmun wrote to the Court's reporter of decision, "I realize that it may be too late, but I wonder if I could insert an additional cite in footnote 4, where we list a number of commentators. Could the following be added: C. MacKinnon, 'Reflections on Sex Equality under Law,' 100 Yale L.J. 1281, 1308–1324 (1991)."[113] While the change was too late for the slip opinions handed out the day of the decision, the change was made for the final version in the *United States Reports*.

Our research suggests that the level of clerk activism, as exhibited here, depends on the type of case. Clerks, like justices, tend to be more active in the most important cases, such as those involving controversial constitutional issues such as abortion. Ten years after her term at the Court, Stephanie Dangel recognized this: "It was an unusual case and an unusual issue, because in the vast majority of cases politics doesn't come into play. But with an issue that confirmation hearings had focused on, and which could be affected by the next election, it would be disingenuous of us not to think about politics."[114]

Overall Clerk Influence

We asked clerks about their overall influence on the decision making of the justice they clerked for. Specifically, we asked if clerks often disagreed with their justice on case outcomes, whether they expressed their personal beliefs about cases, and whether clerks tried to convince the justice of their position on a case. We also wondered whether clerk perceptions changed over time regarding these decision-making variables. Overall, Figure 4.1 shows that there has been a steady rise from the Warren Court to the Rehnquist Court for each of these factors.

Did clerks give their personal beliefs about cases to their justice? The data show that Rehnquist Court clerks were more likely than their predecessors to express personal views of cases to their justice, though some clerks in all eras did so. For example, a Marshall clerk from the 1970s said that he did with regard to whether "the lower court was correct" but "very seldom" with regard to "whether I was pro-choice or anti-abortion." A Rehnquist clerk from the 1990s said, "I have no idea what 'personal beliefs' about a case are. I would offer my view of the *law* in every case."

Did clerks attempt to convince justices about their positions on cases

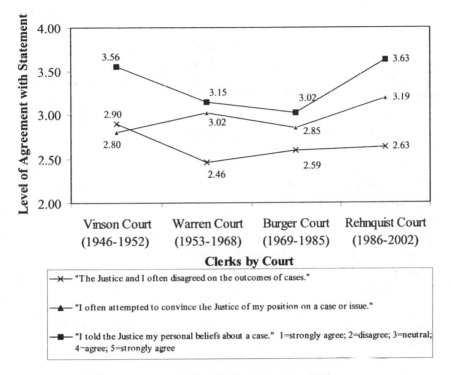

Figure 4.1. Clerk Perceptions of Their Role in Decision Making

or issues? The data show this phenomenon is also on the rise, with Rehnquist Court clerks more willing to convince their justices than clerks from previous eras. Still, some clerks in all eras took on this role. Julian Burke, who, with Rod Hills, clerked for Justice Reed in 1955, said,

> Rod was much more focused on trying to change the justice's mind than I was. . . . Rod was very interested in trying to change his mind. . . . A great number of the clerks who were there were more of the disposition of Rod than to my disposition, in that regard. . . . That's not to say that I didn't occasionally try to change his mind. I was not terribly interested in that whole set of conversations, actually.[115]

Harlan clerk Norman Dorsen wrote his justice regarding *In Re Groban*, "I have had a change of heart about the *Groban* case and now believe the dissent is right. . . . I urge that you consider changing your mind about the case."[116] A Rehnquist clerk from the 1970s said, "I told him what I thought—and then he decided." A Marshall clerk from the 1970s told us, "We discussed the cases as legal professionals. I did not attempt to manipulate him but I discussed the issues honestly and then wrote the opinion he would have written." A Burger clerk from the 1980s said, "Sometimes I did. Clerks could select which cert. granted case they wanted to work on, so you would avoid cases where you knew you would disagree with the Justice."

In general, clerks in all eras did not often disagree with their justice on case outcomes, though there was slightly more disagreement in the Rehnquist Court. This is largely because clerks said they rarely discussed outcomes with their justice. A Douglas clerk from the 1960s said, "I actually didn't form opinions as to most argued cases because I didn't read the briefs (unless WOD wrote an opinion)." A Clark clerk from the 1960s said, "We never discussed my views on outcomes." Taken together, these responses suggest that when clerks did disagree on outcomes with their justice, they did not always express their disagreement. They were more likely to express their disagreement when it concerned more subtle forms of decision making, such as in legal interpretation and the general reasoning of opinions.

We asked the clerks how frequently they were able to change their justice's mind about a particular case or issue. Table 4.1 shows that for the most part, clerks were not influential on their justice's decisions in most cases, with 51 percent answering "seldom" and 24 percent responding "never." For example, a Black clerk from the 1940s said "never" but "keep in mind that by the time of decision making, the judge had studied briefs, heard oral arguments, and discussed [the] case with other justices at conference and with informal visits." Another Black clerk from the 1960s said that he "never tried" to change Black's mind. Similarly, a Clark clerk from the 1950s said, "Not sure whether any of the research I did ever changed his views—and it was not our role to argue the case—we did the research we were instructed to do." A Warren clerk from the 1950s said, "Never that I know of; that is, through discussion. I have no way of measuring the impact of my initial memos, if any." A Marshall clerk from the 1970s said, "I did not believe that was my function—he was the justice, not I." But another Marshall clerk from the 1980s noted, "there was never a disagreement." A Powell clerk from the 1970s responded similarly that he "did

TABLE 4.1
*Percentage of Clerks Who Changed Their
Justice's Mind on Cases or Issues*

Frequency	N =	Percentage
Never	30	24%
Seldom	63	51%
Sometimes	29	24%
Frequently	1	1%
Always	0	0%
Total =	123	100%

Question: How frequently were you able to change your justice's mind about a particular case or issue?

not often disagree" with the justice. A Blackmun clerk from the 1970s said, "We did bench memos and recommended a result without consulting him. So I can't assume [that we changed his mind]. Mostly my influence was on the reasoning process after [the] decision. I counted up cases after the Term and found great agreement on civil cases and little agreement on criminal cases." A Blackmun clerk from the 1980s stated, "Since the justice would receive our views as part of his review of the case, it's not possible to say what his 'mind' was beforehand. The question assumes he knew the way he'd vote before he studied the issue, which isn't accurate. [I] don't know when I influenced his vote and when I simply mirrored his views." A White clerk from the 1980s said, "Who knows. Discussion was wide-open, but it was difficult to know where he was coming from going into the discussion. I suspect the right answer is seldom if ever." A Brennan clerk from the 1980s said that he was "seldom" able to change the justice's mind, adding, "We were usually in agreement." A Burger clerk from the 1970s told us, "That's not how it worked. [The] Chief made a decision and we implemented it."

Still, one out of four clerks (25 percent) said that they were able to change their justice's mind at least some of the time. This suggests that at least some clerks see their role as persuaders and find that they can make a difference in the way their justice views a case or issue. For example, a Black clerk from the 1940s said, "Stone's clerk changed his mind in *Martin v. Struthers.*"[117] Another Black clerk from the 1940s responded that he changed Black's mind "once or twice." A Rehnquist clerk from the 1970s said, "Justice Rehnquist always makes up his own mind—but he wants his clerks to tell him what they think before he does—he doesn't expect you to tell him what you think he wants to hear." A Burger clerk from the 1980s said, "Never, except on cert. petitions" and added, "sometimes on analysis or to dissent or not dissent." Similarly, Thomas C. Grey, a Marshall clerk from 1969, wrote a note to the justice concerning *Dutton v. Evans*: "Judge: [Law clerk] Gary [Wilson] worked on this one. You, along with Brennan + Douglas, voted to affirm. It seems to me this is quite vulnerable to a strong dissent, and you may want to do one."[118]

We asked the clerks whether certain clerks were more influential than others with their justice. A Warren clerk from the 1950s told us that he

> strongly agreed—that is, to the slight extent that any clerk might have influenced the Chief Justice on a substantive issue on very rare occasions, those clerks were very few in number. I kept in close contact with the C.J. after my clerkship, being charged with evaluating clerk applicants and recommending two of the three he chose each year. Accordingly, I had some insight into the C.J.'s relationship with his clerks over the years.

A Marshall clerk from the 1970s said that he "agreed" and added, "Usually the ones who tried to be the clerk rather than trying to be the justice were more influential." A Blackmun clerk from the 1970s said, "Not in our chambers. But Dan Fischel wrote several (i.e. 3, 4, 5?) dissents for Justice Stewart that became majority opinions—see [the] erroneous footnote in *Gannett v. DePasquale* they missed when converting it to a majority. 'Not until today has the Court. . . .'"[119] A Brennan clerk from the 1980s told us, "Our year there were 2 conservative clerks and 2 liberal clerks, one of whom was me. The other liberal clerk had a very special relationship with the justice and could influence him to some extent. The rest of us could not and, in my view, should not."

Were modern law clerks more successful at changing their justices' minds than clerks from previous eras? Figure 4.2 shows that over time, clerks have had more of an effect.[120] The average response of Vinson Court clerks was 0.56, between "never" and "seldom." The average response increased for Warren Court clerks to 1.05, just above "seldom." While Burger Court clerks responded on average similarly to Warren Court clerks, the average response of Rehnquist Court clerks was 1.31, between "seldom" and "sometimes." While these results still show that most of the time clerks were not able to change their justices' minds, recent clerks have been twice as influential as clerks were fifty years ago.

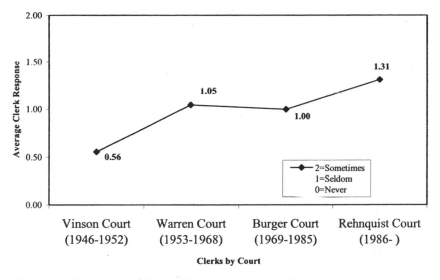

Figure 4.2. Frequency of Clerks Changing Justices' Minds on Cases or Issues over Time

Many former clerks have recognized this transformation. For example, a former clerk from the 1950s told us,

> If I am to judge from the occasional writings and published comments of a handful of clerks in recent years, things have changed a great deal since I served as Chief Law Clerk for Chief Justice Earl Warren. . . . Why not? Lots of other things have changed as well. Most not for the better, grumps the crotchety old man. It would seem that the typical law clerk now is a self-absorbed, self-important, mission-inspired crusader, whether for liberal or conservative causes, set upon forming the Court in his own image. And, to judge by their accounts, they (or, alternatively, the cabal of opposing clerks) are notably successful, primarily because of their brilliance and persuasive powers. I can assure you that, in my time and for a number of years thereafter, a clerkship was by no means so powerful a position, nor were Supreme Court law clerks the eloquent legal giants that they evidently are today. . . . While my colleagues were, by and large, quite talented and, indeed, better trained in disciplined writing and analysis than the typical graduates and law clerks with whom I have worked in recent years, they regarded themselves as, essentially, research assistants rather than Junior Justices.

There were a few Justices who felt that they benefited from rather frequent discussions with their law clerks, and that was, of course, a special bonus for those clerks. And it was gratefully received as a gift, not an entitlement.

Areas of Clerk Influence

If the clerks were ever able to change their justice's mind, we asked when would this be most likely to occur? While some clerks said that there was no one area where they felt they had more influence than another—for example, a Harlan clerk from the 1960s said there was "no pattern"—most clerks felt their influence was greater in some areas than in others.

Table 4.2 shows that the decision to grant or deny cert is where clerks felt they had the most influence on their justice's decision. Thirty-four percent of the clerks we surveyed said that they were able to change their justice's mind on certiorari decisions. Since the primary responsibility of clerks is reviewing cert petitions, it is not surprising that they perceive their influence as greatest in this area. But what makes this so difficult to measure is that clerks, rather than justices, make the initial decisions on whether a petition should be granted or denied. As we discussed in chapter 3, clerks are expected to make recommendations on cert memos. For example, Powell wrote his incoming clerks for the 1973 Term, "I am not likely to follow your recommendation all of the time, but I nevertheless want to know what you think."[121] There is evidence that justices look to clerks for help when they are unsure of whether to grant a case or not. For example, Justice Powell wrote 1972 clerk Larry A. Hammond, "Please take a brief look at the attached petition. . . . What do you think about taking this one? I don't want any great long memorandum from you, as you have more important things to do. Why don't you spend five minutes talking to me about it."[122]

Although a Blackmun clerk from the 1970s told us that he "never did a pool recommendation to deny [that was] granted," in an opposite example, the cert memo for the Eighth Amendment case, *Furman v. Georgia*, written by 1970 Blackmun clerk Mike LaFond, recommended "Deny" although the Court granted the case.[123] A Clark clerk from the 1960s told us, "Never—as far as I know. We did memos for him on all the certiorari cases and I have no idea whether we changed his mind on

TABLE 4.2
Most Likely Occurrence of Clerks Changing Their Justice's Mind

Occurrence	Number of Clerks Who Were Able to Change Their Justice's Mind	Percentage of Clerks Who Were Able to Change Their Justice's Mind*
Certiorari Decisions	50	34%
Legal, Substantive Content of an Opinion	43	29%
Stylistic Content of an Opinion	29	20%
Other	6	4%
Outcome of a Case	5	3%
Total =	133	90%*

Question: If you were ever able to change your justice's mind, when would this be most likely to occur?

* Percentages derived from total number of clerks surveyed (n = 148) as some clerks said they never changed their justice's mind. Therefore, the total does not equal 100%.

any of those because he didn't tell us what his views were before we did the memos."

One reason why clerks may feel they have influence in the decision to grant cert is that there are occasions when a clerk assigned to review the pool memo will disagree with the recommendation of the pool clerk. For example, in *Church of the Lukumi Babalu v. City of Hialeah*, 1991 Scalia clerk Brian D. Boyle recommended to deny the petition in his pool memo.[124] But two days later, Blackmun clerk Molly McUsic marked up Boyle's pool memo for her justice: "The dct's reasoning is clearly wrong here, and the Court needs to consider the Free Exercise Clause in the post-*Smith* world. Accordingly, I recommend a grant."[125] This case is an example where both Scalia and Blackmun voted against the recommendations of their clerks. Scalia voted to grant the case, along with Justices Stevens and Thomas. Justices O'Connor and Kennedy were willing to "join 3," i.e., grant a borderline case because it presents important issues that three justices strongly believe should be heard. Justice Blackmun voted to deny along with Chief Justice Rehnquist and Justices White and Souter.[126]

In another example of a clerk disagreeing with a pool clerk's recommendation, 1991 Thomas clerk Arnon Siegel wrote a pool memo recommending to grant the Tenth Amendment federalism case *New York v. United States*.[127] Four days later, Blackmun clerk Jeff Meyer marked up the memo: "I recommend denial. . . . The poolwriter's bias is evident when he wonders whether *Baker* is still good law and when he speculates that the SG's fulfillment of his duty to inform the Court of like cases pending signifies that he secretly wants a grant. The pool writer also has a lousy jump shot—like his pool memos, it has *no touch*."[128]

After certiorari decisions, the second highest response was in the area of the legal/substantive content of an opinion. Twenty-nine percent of clerks said that this was the area in which changing their justice's mind was likely to occur. Some justices allowed clerks considerable freedom in this area. For example, a Douglas clerk from the 1960s said, "I didn't try [to change the justice's mind] as to [the] outcome on argued cases. I did (1) make recommendations on cert. petitions and (2) occasionally influence the legal substantive rationale of a majority opinion when his first draft made that appropriate." A Brennan clerk from the 1980s said that he was able to change Brennan's mind on the "approach to [a] decision." Another Brennan clerk from the 1980s said that he changed Brennan's mind on "adding responses to [a] dissent." A Powell clerk from the 1970s said, "I could influence him on rationale, seldom; never on outcome."

Table 4.2 shows that the next highest category of likely changes was in the stylistic content of opinions, with 20 percent of clerks responding that their justice could be persuaded in this area of opinion writing. For example, a Clark clerk from the 1960s said that he was only able to change Clark's mind on the "stylistic content of an opinion." The clerk explained, "He drafted his own opinions and asked the clerks to review them—we might suggest a minor word change or add or subtract citations."

The area where clerks said they were least likely to change their justice's mind was in the outcome of cases, with only 3 percent saying it was most likely to occur at this point.[129] Whether a clerk is influential with a justice can depend on both the strengths and weaknesses of the justice and the clerk with regard to specific areas of the law. For example, a Clark clerk from the 1960s said, "Perhaps once the clerks affected the Justice's view on [an] outcome. Justice Clark had an extensively developed view in antitrust law, criminal law, etc. In other areas—patent law, administrative law, etc., he was more susceptible to the views of others." A Rehnquist clerk from the 1970s told us that he was able to change Rehnquist's mind on "business, antitrust, [and] tax cases."

There is some evidence that persuading a justice on the merits was more or less likely depending on the type of case. Death penalty cases, for example, comprised a unique category for certain justices. Justice Lewis Powell was often the swing vote on taking death penalty cases.

Vanderbilt law professor Rebecca Brown, a 1985 Marshall clerk, said, "[Powell] would want to be persuaded on the merits. Some clerks were more inclined to make the case [against execution] to him than others. It might have made the difference."[130] Perhaps one reason why last-minute death-row appeals are more susceptible to clerk influence is their urgency. A clerk said, "The papers come in late at night, when the justices are not in the building. You have a few minutes to decide whether there is enough merit in an appeal to really push a case. It's very difficult at 2 a.m."[131] Clerks must make a quick decision and then either phone or fax their justice for a vote. For example, Justice O'Connor was awakened three times in one night by one of her clerks on a single death-row appeal.[132]

Clerk influence on the outcome of cases also depended on whether it was a landmark or important case that was at stake. For example, a Stewart clerk from 1971 told us that he could change his justice's mind on the outcome of a case, "but not major cases." While this suggests that a handful of clerks were influential with their justices in deciding cases on the merits, nearly all the clerks were not.

Still, it is plain that there are justices who are open to and even welcome clerk input and advocacy. For example, Justice Powell told his clerks, "Our Chambers operate quite informally with a maximum of interchange of views and with each of you always free to talk to me at any time about anything."[133] Clerks take such freedom to heart, and it is not uncommon for some clerks to continue to aid their justice in deciding cases even after they leave their clerkship. The most common way of doing this is through general support for their justice's positions and opinions on cases. For example, three years after his clerkship ended, 1980 Powell clerk Paul Cane wrote his justice,

I just read *INS v. Delgado*, and I compliment you on hitting the nail on the head. I thought Justice Rehnquist's opinion (as did Justice Brennan in dissent) ignored the realities of what the INS euphemistically refers to as "survey." On the other hand, Justice Brennan's dissent ignores the significant governmental interest in rounding up undocumented workers. Your approach correctly gives primacy to that governmental interest and permits the necessary, brief detentions that simply must be performed if our already-feckless immigration laws are to be enforced at all. I am sorry no other Justice joined you. There is, obviously, some tension between your analysis in this case and the Court opinion in

Brignoni-Ponce, but—as you pointed out—the two decisions can be harmonized.[134]

Powell replied, "I . . . am glad to know you approve of my *Delgado* views—even though none of the other Justices perceived their merit."[135]

Another common way former clerks keep up with their justice is through published work, such as forwarding a law review article the former clerk or someone else wrote. In one instance, 1980 Powell clerk Paul W. Cane sent Powell a law review piece he had just completed, even though Cane was a year away from beginning his clerkship and had only been selected one month prior. He wrote Powell, "The Supreme Court will hear argument in *Carbon Fuel Co. v. United Mine Workers* (No. 78-1183) on November 5, 1979. I hope you will find the paginated proofs of this law review article useful in your consideration of that case."[136] Powell replied, "My thanks for your thoughtfulness in sending me the copy of your note that will indeed by helpful in the *Carbon Fuel* case. If I should write in that case, and want to cite your note, I will circulate copies of it to other members of the Court unless it has then been printed."[137]

It appears that justices even cultivate this extra-clerkship activity. For example, one year after their clerkships with Justice Powell concluded, Bob Comfort and Sam Estreicher, who worked on *Bakke*, received the following letter from their justice: "I have requested [my secretary] to send each of you the slip opinions in *Fullilove*. . . . I will be interested in your reactions to the opinions."[138]

Decision-Making Factors

The above analysis shows that law clerks believe that they have an effect on the decisions the justices make. But how influential are clerks in relation to other factors that justices consider in deciding cases? We asked the clerks to rate the importance of various factors that may have influenced their justice in his or her decisions regarding cases. Table 4.3 shows that according to the clerks, the most important factors for justices were the justice's jurisprudential philosophy, specific case facts, and previous case precedent. For example, a Clark clerk from the 1950s said that Clark's jurisprudential philosophy was a "very important" factor in Clark's decision making: "His philosophy reflected his long career as a

TABLE 4.3
Clerk Perception of Factors Influencing Justice's Decisions Regarding Cases

Factor	Average Score	Standard Deviation
Justice's Jurisprudential Philosophy	4.26	0.79
Specific Case Facts	4.15	0.68
Precedent of Previous Case(s)	4.07	0.80
Justice's View of What Is Proper Policy	3.95	1.04
Parties' Written Briefs	3.34	0.82
Persuasiveness of Lower Court Opinion	3.20	1.06
Other Justices' Views	3.04	0.89
Law Clerk's Research	2.87	0.89
Justices Negotiating with Other Justices	2.74	1.13
Attorneys' Oral Arguments	2.35	0.76
Law Clerk's Persuasiveness	2.09	0.83
Justice's Awareness of Public Sentiment	1.69	0.84

Question: Listed below are a number of factors that may have influenced your justice in his or her decisions regarding cases. Please circle the number indicating what you perceived to have been the importance of each factor for the justice for whom you clerked when deciding cases.
5 = very important; 4 = important; 3 = moderately important; 2 = seldom important; 1 = never important.

government lawyer and prosecutor; and as a southerner, his awareness of and sympathy for the plight of blacks in a segregated society." In an example of how specific case facts might be deemed important to a justice, 1984 Brennan clerk Michael Rips commented on Justice O'Connor's decision-making process, "The issues before the Court touch her personally on a profound level. Justices tend to become anesthetized both emotionally and intellectually, to the issues. O'Connor has escaped that."[139]

Moderately important factors, according to clerks, were the justice's policy views, written briefs of the parties, persuasiveness of lower court opinion, and the views of other justices. For example, a Clark clerk from the 1950s said that the views of "particularly Justice Jackson" had an influence on Clark's decision making. Similarly, a Burton clerk from the 1950s told us that the views of other justices were "very important, some much more than others."

Seldom important were law clerk research, negotiations among justices, oral argument, and law clerk persuasiveness. The justices' awareness of public sentiment was, for the most part, never important. On negotiations among justices, a Warren clerk from the 1950s said that it "depended on the case; e.g. as to *Brown* [it was] very important." But what is most interesting about this last group is that law clerks recognized that their own research and persuasiveness were of little value to their justices when compared to other decision-making factors. This data contradicts claims that clerks inflate their own importance.

Has the importance of these factors changed over time? Figure 4.3 shows the seven factors that have declined over time. Vinson Court clerks reported that the most important factor was their justices' jurisprudential philosophy (4.63). For Rehnquist Court clerks this factor had declined to 4.19 in importance. The policy views of the justices declined from 4.43 during the Vinson Court to 3.50 during the Rehnquist Court. Specific case facts declined in importance from 4.29 during the Vinson Court to 3.63 during the Rehnquist Court. The importance of lower court opinions declined from 3.33 during the Vinson Court to 2.88 during the Rehnquist Court. Negotiations between justices declined in importance from 3.00 during the Vinson Court to 2.13 during the Rehnquist Court. Public opinion from the Vinson Court to the Rehnquist Court declined in importance from 2.86 to 1.50. Finally, the oral arguments made by attorneys declined from 2.57 during the Vinson Court to 2.19 during the Rehnquist Court.

Figure 4.4 shows the five factors that have increased over time. Precedent has been important throughout the Court's history and has in-

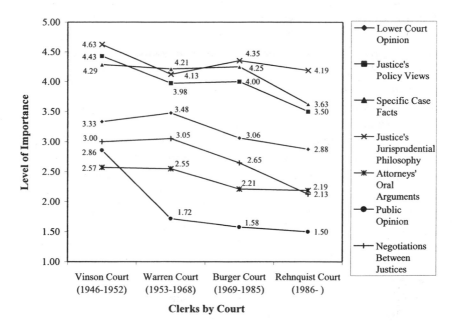

Figure 4.3. Clerk Perceptions of Influences on Justices' Decision Making: Declining Factors

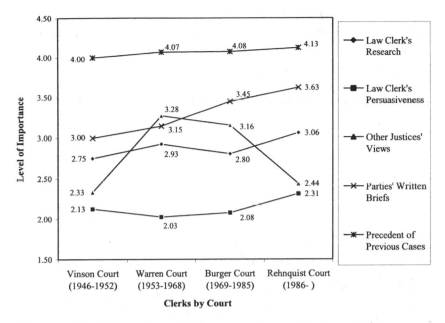

Figure 4.4. Clerk Perceptions of Influences on Justices' Decision Making: Increasing Factors

creased from 4.00 during the Vinson Court to 4.13 during the Rehnquist Court. The written briefs of the parties have increased in importance from 3.00 during the Vinson Court to 3.63 during the Rehnquist Court. Perhaps the most interesting change has been the effect of the views of the justices on each other. Vinson Court clerks reported this factor as seldom to moderately important (2.33). Its peak influence came during the Warren Court (3.28). And though it declined slightly through the Burger Court (3.16) and more significantly through the Rehnquist Court (2.44), it still remains higher than it was under Chief Justice Vinson. In 1976, Justice Powell described the lack of personal interaction among the members of the Court: "The informal interchange between chambers is minimal, with most exchanges of views being by correspondence or memoranda. Indeed, a justice may go through an entire term without being once in the chambers of all of the other eight members of the Court."[140] Yet members of the Court do phone and meet with each other in chambers on occasion for the purpose of discussing a case. For example, as we discussed earlier, after he voted in conference to overturn *Roe v. Wade*, Justice Kennedy sent a note to *Roe*'s author, Justice Blackmun, requesting a face-to-face meeting. After the meeting, Kennedy was persuaded to change his mind.

It is interesting to note from Figure 4.4 that, although less important than almost all other influences on the decision making of the justices, both law clerk factors have increased in importance in the last fifty years. According to the clerks, the effect of their research increased from 2.75 during the Vinson Court to 3.06 during the Rehnquist Court. Law clerk persuasiveness increased from 2.13 during the Vinson Court to 2.31 during the Rehnquist Court.

Conclusion

In all, clerks have played an important, and often hidden, role in the decision-making process of the justices. Though clerks seldom changed the minds of the justices, it has happened. Clerks are most influential in the certiorari process, though they are also able to change their justices' minds about the content and style of opinions—not surprising given that they are the principle drafters. They are also very active in coalition formation and use their contacts in other chambers through the clerk network to make substantive and strategic recommendations to their justices. Many of these findings are consistent with previously published accounts of the individual behavior of particular justices and judicial decision-making generally.[141]

Perhaps the most important finding from this data, however, is that the influence of clerks on the decision-making process of the justices has changed considerably over time. On the whole, clerks from the Vinson Court had less influence on their justices than did clerks during the Warren Court. In turn, Warren Court clerks had less effect than Burger Court clerks. Rehnquist Court clerks had the most influence over the decisions their justices made, and when compared to the responses of clerks from the Vinson Court, the changes in the last fifty years have been dramatic. The rise of clerk influence in the decision-making process has mirrored other institutional changes, such as the rise in the number of clerks working at the Court, their formal responsibility through the cert pool for reviewing cases petitioned to the Court, and their increasing use in writing the opinions issued by their justices.

Still, even former clerks remain skeptical. A clerk for Justice Minton in the 1950s told us, "Justice Minton had a very firm mind. He was not moved by law clerk's opinions very much." Did he encourage clerks to give their views? "Yes, he had no problem there, but basically he decided." A Douglas clerk told us,

> I believe there is a tendency on the part of many law clerks to overestimate and inflate their own importance to the decisions of the judges they serve. Law clerks are people often chosen because of academic and other success, and usually have a strong sense of self-confidence. It is perhaps natural for many such people to believe that their own intellectual power is very important to the decisions of the judges they serve. It is, I think, somewhat easy for such individuals to think that a judge or justice's tolerant listening to their views is the same as influence, which is something entirely different.

Though there is room for debate, we suggest that these results demonstrate that former clerks are able to tell the difference between tolerant listening and influential discussion. We do not argue that clerks are the primary force in judicial decision making. Indeed, the data show that most of the time, clerks are not able to change their justices' minds about cases or issues. This finding is significant when one considers that it is based on the perceptions of the clerks themselves. Still, as the data in this chapter, and particularly the case study on abortion, demonstrates, there is no doubt that particular clerks have played important decision-making roles at particular times and in particular cases. Interestingly, the Court's internal memoranda paint a more activist picture than the survey and interview responses suggest. On the whole, we suggest that clerks do not inflate their importance but are sincere about their effect on the decision-making process. Clerks do have influence at the Court and we submit that their influence is increasing.

5

Opinion Writing
From Research Assistants to Junior Justices

Brain surgeons are delegating the entire performance of delicate operations to nurses, orderlies and first-year medical students.
—Judge Richard Posner, U.S. Court of Appeals and
former clerk to William J. Brennan,
on the growing use of clerks

The justices work very hard. The idea that the clerks do all the work is nutty. —Justice John Paul Stevens, former clerk to
Justice Wiley Rutledge

There is considerable controversy about the role law clerks play in crafting the opinions handed down by the Court. When opinions are released to the public, they formally bear the authorship of one or more of the justices: "Justice O'Connor delivered the opinion of the Court" or "Justice Scalia, with whom Justice Thomas joins, dissenting." But it has been the admitted practice of the justices for some time to assign the drafting of opinions to their law clerks. Indeed, in his first year on the Court, Justice Lewis F. Powell, Jr., recognized this critical function. With three months left in the term, he wrote his clerks,

For the remainder of this term, writing opinions—for the Court, concurring and in dissent—will be the priority work. I can think of only two ways—both relatively minor I am afraid—to free up more of your time for the necessary research and drafting of opinions. I suggest: (i) that you write no more bench memos unless specifically requested by me; and (ii) that your cert memos, on the average, be a little briefer than those you have been writing.[1]

Are the clerks deciding cases, interpreting the Constitution, and constructing their own jurisprudence? Or, are the justices merely using the clerks as instruments to construct the opinions that they would write if they were to do it themselves?

On one side of the debate, critics suggest that clerks have far too much influence. Edward Lazarus, who clerked for Justice Harry Blackmun in 1988, wrote in his controversial book *Closed Chambers*, "Justices yield great and excessive power to immature, ideologically driven clerks, who in turn use that power to manipulate their bosses and the institution."[2] But the Court's defenders are many, not surprisingly including the justices themselves. Justice Louis Brandeis said, "The justices are almost the only people in Washington who do their own work."[3] Harold Koh, Yale law professor and a Blackmun clerk during the 1981 Term, remarked about the role of clerks in the opinion-writing process, "They are like the students of Michelangelo. They may put the ink on paper, but it is according to the justices' design."[4]

In the following analysis, we argue that the opinion-writing process can take place in differing ways, with justices giving clerks greater or lesser responsibility for the actual writing of the finished product. Also, we suggest that the process has changed over time, with justices ceding greater responsibility to clerks in recent years. Furthermore, drafts written entirely by clerks have been released as opinions with little or no changes made by justices. Also, practices vary from chambers to chambers, with certain justices ceding greater authority to clerks than others. At the same time, clerks have increasingly acted as surrogates in this process by attempting to draft opinions as if their justice were writing the opinion. Ultimately, these findings raise a number of important questions concerning the role that clerks play in this process, and we discuss these in light of what clerks and justices say about the process.

Historical Development

On some level, clerks have nearly always played some role in the opinion-writing process. Dean Acheson, a clerk for Justice Louis Brandeis during the 1919 and 1920 Terms, said, "When I finished my work on a draft which had been assigned to me or got as far as I could, I gave it to him. He tore it to pieces, sometimes using a little, sometimes none."[5] It was reported that Justice Harlan Fiske Stone, who joined the Court in

1925, wrote the general outlines of his opinions on yellow legal pads, dictated facts and arguments to a stenographer, and then charged his clerk with writing the drafts.[6] But Stone's secretary wrote,

> In preparing opinions the Justice prepares a draft opinion in typewritten form. When he has gotten it into final shape, a carbon is given to the law clerk. The law clerk goes over the opinion. . . . It will be the law clerk's responsibility to check the accuracy of all citations, both as to the name of the case and its citation, and as to its holding; to criticize the form of the opinions, so that so far as possible it may be expressed in terse, lucid English, accurately expressing the thought which is intended to be conveyed. . . . and then he and the Justice go over it together.[7]

This is in sharp contrast to comments of more recent justices who now see themselves and their clerks as comprising an opinion-writing team. In 1986 Justice Lewis F. Powell, Jr., wrote his clerks, "Apparently the Chief Justice does not like my law clerks, as again it seems to me that we have been 'short changed' on cases to write."[8] In a 1979 speech, Justice William J. Brennan described his opinions as "opinions that came from the Brennan chambers over the past twenty-three years. I say from 'the Brennan chambers' because, as Bentham said, the 'Law is not the work of judge alone but of judge and company.' The company in this case consisted of the sixty-five law clerks who have been associated with me on the Court."[9] But just exactly what role did the clerks of Powell and Brennan play, and did their role differ from those of clerks in other chambers?

As with the other areas of a law clerk's duties, the clerk's role in opinion writing has changed over time. Originally, clerks were not the primary opinion drafters they are today. A Black clerk from the 1940s said of the justice, "He always wrote the first draft of an opinion. He would give me the draft for my input." A clerk for Justice Charles Whittaker told us, "I rarely drafted any opinions." Clerks provided little more than research assistance for their justices, helping to check citations to past cases, fill out footnotes to opinions, and research points of law. But even footnotes can be controversial. For example, 1953 Earl Warren clerk Richard Flynn inserted references in footnote 11 to seven different works of social scientists, including Gunnar Myrdal's sociological study of racism, in *Brown v. Board of Education*.[10] The references were essentially ignored by the members of the Court but hotly debated by the public.[11] Footnote 4 of *United States v. Carolene Products Co.*,[12] which sparked a transformation of equal protection jurisprudence, was largely written by Louis Lusky, clerk to Chief Justice Harlan Fiske Stone in 1937.[13] Herbert Wechsler, Stone's clerk from 1932, likened Stone's penchant for footnotes to "a squirrel storing nuts to be pulled out at some later time."[14]

As part of their "apprenticeship," early clerks were occasionally given the task of drafting an opinion. But they soon found out that this was largely an exercise in learning the law and not for use by their justice. John Knox, who clerked for Justice James McReynolds in 1936, recalled the fate of the sole opinion he drafted for the justice: "He quietly reached across the desk and silently, almost gently let my opinion glide downward into his wastebasket."[15]

Over time, clerks were given more responsibility by an increasing number of justices. John Francis Cotter, a long-time clerk for Justice Pierce Butler in the 1920s, said that he wrote first drafts of many opinions and often did such a thorough job that Butler made few changes.[16] During his tenure on the High Court from the 1940s to the early 1950s, Chief Justice Fred Vinson completely delegated opinion writing to his clerks.[17] Chief Justice Rehnquist, who clerked for Justice Robert Jackson, wrote in 1957,

> On a couple of occasions each term, Justice Jackson would ask each clerk to draft an opinion for him along lines which he suggested. If the clerk were reasonably diligent in his work, the Justice would be quite charitable with his black pencil and paste pot. The result reached in these opinions was no less the product of Justice Jackson than those he drafted himself; in literary style, these opinions generally suffered by comparison with those which he had drafted.[18]

Justice Stevens, who clerked for Justice Rutledge over fifty years ago, remarked on the changes, "I had a lot less responsibility than some of the clerks now. They are much more involved in the entire process now."[19]

By the time of the Warren Court, most clerks were drafting entire opinions. Clerks were doing so much work, in comparison with past years, that one of Justice Sherman Minton's clerks from the 1950s told us, "Most of the justices at least did the major part of the work on their opinions." We suggest that the shift toward clerk-written opinions was largely due to Chief Justice Warren's opinion-assignment practice of equally dividing the cases among his colleagues.[20] Justice Brennan remarked that Warren "bent over backwards in assigning opinions to assure that each Justice, including himself, wrote approximately the same number of Court opinions and received a fair share of the more desirable opinions."[21] The norm began to develop during the last four years of Chief Justice Fred Vinson's tenure.[22] Prior to this time, opinions were largely assigned according to the speed at which the justices completed them.

The equality principle produced significant changes. Justice Douglas commented on the new system, "It has disadvantages to those of us who get out our work promptly because there is practically nothing to do from the first of May on. And judges who work more slowly are working long hours, Sundays, until the whole thing comes to a halt sometimes near the end of June."[23] In an attempt to cut down on these long hours, clerks took on an increased role. Judge Richard Posner, who clerked for Justice Brennan in 1962, said, "By 1959, a majority of the Supreme Court's opinions were being written by law clerks."[24]

Justice Frank Murphy's clerks drafted his opinions in longhand on yellow legal pads, and then typed the results for Murphy to review. For example, Eugene Gressman, who served as Murphy's clerk for five terms, wrote the first draft of Murphy's famous dissent in *Korematsu v. United States*,[25] including the charge that the internment of Japanese Americans during World War II "goes over the very brink of constitutional power and falls into the ugly abyss of racism." Gressman was modest about his contributions: "I certainly wouldn't say I'm the author of any of the opinions, although I am still proud of quite a few of the ones I worked on. Murphy was responsible for all the decisions that carried his name."[26] But Court insiders sarcastically referred to Murphy's clerks as "Mr. Justice Huddleson" and "Mr. Justice Gressman."[27] A clerk for Justice Stanley Reed who worked at the Court with Gressman said that Gressman did "most of the thinking for Murphy and, in certain areas, turned Murphy opinions into quite good opinions."[28] Even the other justices knew that Murphy relied heavily on his clerks. Douglas wrote Black about Murphy's dissent in the 1946 case *Mabee v. White Plains Pub. Co.*,[29] "Frank [Murphy] sa[id] Sat[urday] that he did not write the dissent in Mabee but was impressed when he saw it."[30]

Justice Douglas remarked on the increasing use of clerks in opinion writing, "As the years passed, it became more and more evident that the law clerks were drafting opinions. Brandeis, I think, was correct in believing that the totality of one decision should rest wholly on the Justice. That simply could not happen unless he was the architect, carpenter, mason, plumber, plasterer and roofer who put the whole structure together."[31] Douglas wrote most of his own opinions and in general kept his clerks at arm's length. For example, Gordon B. Davidson, who clerked for Justice Stanley Reed in 1954, recalled, "Douglas almost never talked to his clerks. Everything was by written communication. And I would say the worst clerkship at the Supreme Court was Douglas's because the clerk was made to feel less a part of the team and so forth."[32] In 1961, Douglas said,

> I have written all my own opinions. I use my law clerk to do research for me. I often send him to the library to prepare a footnote to an opinion that I am writing, telling him the cases pro and con that I want him to collect. Sometimes I ask him to prepare a digest for me that I'll put in a footnote. My law clerk has the responsibility of approving all my opinions for accuracy.[33]

Some of Justice Felix Frankfurter's most famous opinions were almost entirely the handiwork of his clerks, like his dissent in *Baker v. Carr*.[34] Anthony G. Amsterdam clerked for Frankfurter in 1960 and often prepared opinions in which Frankfurter only made minor changes. After Amsterdam submitted a dissent in *Elkins v. United States* to the justice, Frankfurter returned it with the attached note: "If you approve of my revisions send to printer and duly circulate."[35] A year later, Justice Douglas recalled the term:

> One year, Frankfurter brought on a man as a third law clerk and he tried to get Warren to put him on [the] Federal payroll but Warren refused to do it.[36] But this man wrote, worked in the library, and he wrote some of Frankfurter's long opinions. The law clerk wrote Frankfurter's opinion in the Sunday Law cases that were decided.[37] He wrote Frankfurter's opinion in the civil rights case, where I wrote for the Court coming out of Illinois as to what the meaning of under color of state law [was] in the Civil Rights Act.[38] The trend to develop in the Court sort of law-review articles as opinions, I think has been due to the extensive use by some justices, particularly Frankfurter, of law clerks in preparation of opinions.[39]

Frankfurter himself, however, was keenly aware of the extent to which his colleagues used their clerks in opinion writing and thought that he had struck the proper balance. He remarked, "The problem with Stanley [Reed] is that he doesn't let his law clerks do enough of the work. The trouble with Murphy is that he lets them do too much."[40]

A clerk from the 1960s told us that he would be told in a typical assignment from Justice Tom Clark,

> "Here's what was decided, here's the theories we've used. Come up with a draft for me to review." Along that lines, and I would do it. In a few of them he would say, "I don't know about this, I don't know about that, I'd like you to look into that," and so forth. It's the kind of a collaborative process between a writer and an editor that goes on in many fields. . . . Sometimes he knew just what he wanted to do, and in that situation my role would be much more limited.

One of Justice Potter Stewart's opinions, *Schneckloth v. Bustamonte*, an important Fourth Amendment case holding that individual searches could be lawfully conducted with the consent of a third party, was written by one of his clerks, with little revision from the justice.[41] A Stewart clerk from the 1970s told us,

> He would tell you to go start the opinion and sometimes he would tell you what the opinion should say, I mean he would tell you how it should come out, and sort of generally about what the reasoning was but basically not a lot. . . . [The instructions] were never very long. He might say, "Write an opinion following the lines we talked about yesterday," or it might be, "Write an opinion along the lines of the United States brief," or "the petitioner's brief." It might be as short as that. It might be, "Write an opinion, let's put this on due process grounds, not equal protection grounds."

Not only has the opinion-writing process changed over time, but we also found that often justices drafted their own opinions earlier in their tenures and relied more heavily on their clerks for drafts in later years. For example, a Blackmun clerk from the 1970s told us,

> In my Term, he did most of his drafting himself. My understanding is that that was unusual and it became unusual for him. My understand-

ing is that within a year or so of the year I clerked he was using his clerks more the way other justices historically used them and that involved a lot of drafting. . . . When I would talk to clerks a few years later they were doing all kinds of opinion drafting, which we hadn't done. So it changed dramatically.

Our review of Blackmun's case files confirms this. Another former clerk told us that Justice Rehnquist followed a similar pattern, writing many of his own opinions when he first joined the Court "because he was new." Rehnquist later delegated opinion drafting to his clerks. After five years on the Court, Powell wrote his clerks, "During my early Terms on the Court I . . . originated several drafts of Court opinions, but experience demonstrated that this is an improvident commitment of my time."[42] A clerk for then 78-year-old Justice Thurgood Marshall during the 1986 Term said, "He didn't write anything my year, but I still think he could."[43]

Clerks were also given more responsibility for writing opinions near the end of the term when the pressure was greater to finish the Court's work before summer recess. This often led to a decrease in the quality of the opinions. A Blackmun clerk from the 1970s told us,

He felt he was a little bit behind in his opinion drafting assignments and so we did do some drafting of opinions at the end of the Term. We, primarily a co-clerk and I, spoke to him quite strongly at the end of the year and said, "You have to use your clerks because you can't do all this on your own. It's a big job and you need help and you have to trust your clerks and you must use them more."

Powell wrote his clerks, "We are witnessing the usual June-end 'rush to judgment' that often leads to poorly written opinions and even errors."[44]

It was also not uncommon for certain clerks to write more opinions than did their fellow clerks in the same chambers. This disparity was usually due to the speed at which clerks completed a draft or the clerk's level of interest in opinion writing. Justice Powell wrote his clerks, "As Larry [Hammond] hopes to deliver *Rodriguez* to the printer today (for a rough first printing), and *Chambers* to the printer no later than Thursday, he appears to be free to write the first draft of *Basye*."[45] A Clark clerk from the 1960s told us, "The most interesting part was the role in the opinion writing process—the most interesting to me. Whereas my co-clerk, for example, had less interest in that aspect of it, which was good for me because I got to do more writing."

Clerk Collaboration

Clerks communicate and often collaborate with each other on opinions. This is most common for the co-clerks of a single justice but also occurs across chambers and even if the justices are on opposing sides of a case. One reason why within-chambers collaboration is practiced is that it fosters consistent opinion writing among the various clerks for a particular justice. Justice Powell explained to his clerks,

> Our Chambers is working on four opinions involving equal protection claims: Rodriguez, McGinnis, Rosario, and Griffiths. Each of you has a hand in at least one of these opinions. It is obviously important that my opinions are reasonably consistent both in doctrinal position and in the terminology employed. There has been enough confusion in equal protection terminology in recent years to confound everyone, and I would like to avoid adding to this—especially by manifest inconsistencies in my own opinions and at the same term of Court. As busy as we are, I still hope that no opinion from our Chambers will be handed down until each of you has read it. In addition, we must continue the policy initiated last year of having each opinion reviewed more carefully (not just a simple informational reading). In this process, I hope that each of you will be alert to the need for reasonable consistency in terminology. I think we have been consistent in doctrine.[46]

Despite his concern for consistency, Powell also recognized that the nature of forming coalitions made that difficult. He wrote, "The problem, of course, is not quite this simple as one often has to accept variations in language to retain or acquire the necessary consensus for a Court opinion."[47]

An example of within-chambers collaboration is Blackmun clerk Andrea Ward's 1990 memo to her justice: "I am finishing up a draft of *Indopco*. It needs to be citechecked by one clerk and read over by the others before it goes to you. The clerks are busy on bench memos for next week's cases, and would prefer, all things being equal, to citecheck it Wednesday instead of tomorrow."[48] Justices have encouraged this collaborative effort. Powell wrote his clerks, "I would like to follow our usual practice of swapping opinions so that each receives a review by a clerk who did not work with me on it."[49] Another example of within-chambers collaboration is a memo from 1993 Blackmun clerk Michelle Alexander to her justice on what would become his dissent from the denial of cert in the death penalty case *Callins v. Collins*:

> You are probably wondering what ever happened to the death penalty dissent you asked me to write. The answer is that I have been waiting for all of my co-clerks to finish their bench memos, pool work, etc., so that they can give the dissent a final edit. You should be pleased to hear that everyone feels very good about it and looks forward to the day it is announced. I am sure you will want to add your personal touch and will have suggestions for alternative approaches. I am writing now only to assure you that the draft is virtually in final form. I have just received the last edit from one of my co-clerks and I will give you the final draft as soon as my last bench memo for October is complete. I know that the process has taken longer than you or I would like, but I think it is particularly important that all of my co-clerks have the opportunity to contribute to the project and suggest revisions they think appropriate.[50]

An example of across-chambers collaboration among justices who are at least partially on the same side of an issue occurred during *Planned Parenthood v. Casey*, when 1991 Blackmun clerk Stephanie Dangel wrote her justice, "If you'd like, I can work with the clerks for [Justices O'Connor, Kennedy, and Souter] and JPS to draft a suitable proviso."[51]

Across-chambers collaboration among opposition justices also takes place. For example, a Clark clerk from the 1960s told us that he participated in "the argument, [the] back and forth about issues with the justice and the co-clerk, and very often the clerks for other justices." Julian Burke, who clerked for Justice Reed during the 1955 Term, described one such exchange involving himself and one of Justice Sherman Minton's clerks, Bob Cole:

> The case was *Shields vs. Atlantic Coast Line Railroad Company*, in which [Reed] was the dissenter. That case was a very minor, unimportant case in the term of the Court, although for reasons that are not

clear to me at this distant time, I believe it came out 5–4, and it was unclear, until it was finally published, which way it was going to go. I think at one time Reed was assigned to write the majority opinion, and Minton in dissent. And he indicated he was going to write the dissenting opinion. As a matter of fact, Minton's opinion became the majority opinion and I cannot recall who switched. . . . Minton's law clerk, who was just two doors from our office, and I kept exchanging drafts, where he was writing, he and Minton were writing one side and Reed and I were writing the other side. And before the justices were circulating to each other, Minton's clerk and I would compare notes. And it wasn't a game, although it certainly was intellectually challenging and did have a level of amusement about it, but we tried our damnedest to make the opinions meet exactly the same issues in the same order. And so it became somewhat of a crossword puzzle. We clearly wanted to see where the crucial sentence would come, which would shift one person to one side and one person to the other side. I was convinced that Reed's side was right, and he was convinced that Minton's side was right. We were bound and determined to try to discover where the single sentence was which shifted you from one side to the other side. I have not, since that opinion was published, ever gone back to read [it] to see whether it still works that way.[52]

In another example, Lewis D. Sargentich, a clerk during the 1970 Term, wrote his boss, Justice Marshall, "Justice Black has apparently changed his opinions somewhat in the direction of your views—i.e., he has made the opinions less tied to the particular facts of the 2 cases. (I am told this by his clerks—the opinions haven't come around a second time.)"[53] A more recent example of across-chambers collaboration with opposition justices occurred in the free-exercise peyote case, *Employment Division v. Smith*. Blackmun clerk Martha Matthews wrote her justice, "I am really happy about this. I have been working very closely with J. O'Connor's clerk, trying to ensure that her concurrence will say most of what the [Blackmun] dissent would otherwise have to say, and this draft is exactly what I hoped for."[54]

But some justices were wary of their clerks collaborating or even discussing cases with clerks from other chambers. As we discussed in the previous chapter, Chief Justice Warren regularly reminded his clerks that they worked for him and not the Court. He was particularly concerned about his clerks having contact with Justice Frankfurter or Frankfurter's clerks. A former Warren clerk recalled, "We were enjoined from falling under [Frankfurter's] sway. [Warren] as much as said, 'I know you're all quite young fellows from law school, and here's the great professor, but don't let him sell you any beans.' And it took the form of a mild paranoia about contacts between his law clerks and Frankfurter, or even Frankfurter's law clerks."[55] Frankfurter suspected Warren had such a policy. Frankfurter regularly held informal scholarly conversations with the Court's law clerks and in 1957, when he invited one of Warren's clerks to have a chat, he added, "unless, of course, I've been quarantined."[56]

A Warren clerk from the 1950s told us, "It was strictly between us and the Chief. We were early on instructed in the Chief's views about communicating those things to others. He very much did not want us talking out of school." When asked if lobbying went on across chambers, a Warren clerk from the 1950s told us,

If there was I don't remember it. Is seemed to me that we were not alone in the Chief's office as viewing our jobs as being clerks not being justices. These are cases that have some important issues sometimes and if you are a bright young lawyer with the sort of record to get you into that job, you are going to have views of your own . . . and sometimes you like to argue. The clerks would argue with each other. It wasn't so much trying to proselytize as it was that they were just arguing as bright young lawyers will about interesting legal issues. And there is a lot of exchanging of notes. One of the things that's I think good about the Supreme Court's work product is that "at the clerk level," which doesn't control the way the votes go, probably doesn't have as much to do with what's in the opinions as some people outside the Court think, and at the justices' level the cases that are argued get a lot of attention and some of them in which cert is not granted get a lot of attention. You've got nine offices with very good young lawyers going over them and you've got the justices who take their jobs very seriously going over—in my career there was not a lazy or unconscientious judge on that bench. And then they talk and if you missed a point, someone else would pick it up. And so even in our own conversations we would come out of those conversations knowing more about the cases than when we went in and I think that went on with the justices too.

Typology

Our research suggests that the opinion-writing process takes place in three different methods (see Table 5.1). Currently, the most common form is *delegation*, which involves a justice assigning the first draft of an opinion to a clerk and then revising the clerk's original draft. The second form was more common in past years and has been more rare in recent times. This process can be termed *retention*, and it involves a justice drafting his or her own opinion and using clerks to supplement the draft with editing, citations, and footnotes. The third way in which opinions are constructed can be termed *collaboration*, and it involves both the justice and his or her clerks working equally toward the creation of an opinion.

Historically, the retention approach was most common. Justices wrote draft opinions, and clerks reviewed and edited as well as provided footnotes and citations for the justice's draft. If a clerk was allowed to draft an opinion, it was rare, and the opinion was substantially revised by the justice. Under retention, opinion drafting by clerks was part of their advanced apprenticeship in the law. It was largely a learning exercise for the clerks. Justices considered drafting opinions as solely their responsibility. An example of the retention method is found in the chambers of Justice Hugo Black. A former clerk from the 1940s told us, "Justice Black did 1st drafts, [and] I revised and edited." A second Black clerk from the 1940s said that he worked on "2nd drafts." Another Black clerk from the 1950s said that he "drafted only one opinion. The Justice wrote opinions and gave drafts to the clerks (2) to review." A clerk from the 1960s told us, "Justice Black drafted nearly every one of his opinions himself. When a clerk did the first draft, [which was] very rare, it was worked over many times." Another Black clerk from the 1960s responded similarly: "almost all opinions were drafted by Justice Black himself." Our examination of Black's papers confirms these reports.[57]

Like Black, other justices have followed the retention approach. A clerk for Justice Sherman Minton from the 1950s told us that Minton's clerks "didn't draft opinions." Another Minton clerk said that the justice wrote his own first draft "almost always" and gave it to his clerks for editing. They filled out the fact situation and citations. "We would make suggestions about additional points." Each Minton clerk was allowed to write one dissent per term that Minton would then substan-

TABLE 5.1
Opinion-Writing Process Typology

Method	Process
Delegation	Justice assigns opinion to clerk and revises draft.
Retention	Justice writes opinion and clerk provides citations, footnotes, and editing.
Collaboration	Both justice and clerk work in tandem, or relatively equally, toward the construction of a single opinion.

tially revise. A clerk for Justice Charles Evans Whittaker from the 1950s said, "I drafted very, very few opinions." A clerk for Justice Tom C. Clark from the 1960s said that as a clerk he "did not draft opinions." Another clerk from the 1960s said, "Justice Clark drafted opinions and his clerks reviewed them." Furthermore, a third clerk from the 1960s remarked, "Justice Clark always prepared his own first draft. Law clerks were instructed to never prepare first drafts." A fourth clerk from the 1960s confirmed, "Mr. Justice Clark never allowed clerks to do the first draft." But Clark may have deviated from this practice on occasion as another Clark clerk from the 1960s told us that "it would depend on whether it was an opinion for the Court."

Though he only practiced retention on some opinions in the first few years of his tenure on the Court, Justice Powell wrote his clerks about their role regarding "Authorities and Cite Checking":

> My clerks are responsible for the basic research that precedes opinion writing. If a Supreme Court decision is cited, and I am not familiar with it, I will read it as a part of my own preparation for work on the opinion. But normally I simply do not have time to do research, to read decisions from other courts, or to read secondary authorities unless they are especially important to the issue before us. I do not like to clutter an opinion with an array of marginal citations, either in the text or notes. But when there are relevant Supreme Court precedents they *should* be cited, if for no other reason, to assure counsel and courts in the federal system that we have not overlooked pertinent prior decisions of this Court. I respect the scholarship of the leading law reviews, and want my clerks to include them within the scope of their legal research and bring the best ones to my attention. Where we are writing a criminal case, I also expect my clerks to check the ABA Criminal Justice Standards, the ALI Model Criminal Code, and other pertinent ALI

publications (e.g., Model Pre-Arraignment Code). The report, including the Task Force Reports, of the National Commission on Law Enforcement and the Administration of Justice (on which I served) also is a helpful source in some cases. As you know from your prior clerking experience, the clerk assigned to an opinion is responsible for the accuracy and relevance of all citations, references and quotations. There is a final checking by Mr. Putzel's office as to accuracy, but the basic responsibility is yours.[58]

Over time, retention largely gave way to delegation. While a few justices in the early years of clerks, like Pierce Butler and James F. Byrnes, delegated opinion writing to their clerks, this method became more common when opinions were distributed more equally during the final years of the Vinson Court. Furthermore, when the cert pool was created, clerks had greater institutional responsibility yet more time to devote to other tasks as the number of cert petitions each had to review decreased dramatically.

Under the delegation approach, a justice assigns the first draft of an opinion to the clerk, often instructing the clerk on what should be said and how it should be said. These instructions are usually given to the clerk orally after the justice emerges from the conference discussion with the other justices and after he or she has been assigned an opinion. For example, a Clark clerk from the 1960s told us, "He would usually come and tell us that he had been assigned the opinion in x case and would ask one of us to either do a first draft and chat with us about what he had in mind or sometimes he would do a first draft and we would take it from there." Similarly, a Blackmun clerk from the 1970s told us, "I remember being told something. It was orally and then I would go off and draft it."

In his first full term on the Court, Justice Powell wrote his clerks,

In my limited experience on the bench, I have been impressed by the importance of several characteristics of judicial opinion writing: (i) meticulous care in understanding and stating the facts; (ii) adherence to "principled analysis"; (iii) scrupulously honest citation and quotation from prior decisions of this Court; (iv) thorough research; (v) honest confrontation of the principle arguments against the position we take; and (vi) recognition that the form and style of the opinion, while obviously subordinate to the substance, is nevertheless important.[59]

Justice Powell outlined his requirements in a lengthy "confidential" memo distributed to his clerks at the start of each term:

> The clerk at the outset—based on our discussions and his familiarity with the case—will have a good idea as to how I wish the opinion to be drafted. But there is usually further discussing; sometimes I will request a topical outline or prepare one myself; and after we get into the case more deeply, there will be numerous discussions. A precise and condensed statement of the facts and the proceedings below must be the beginning of any opinion for the Court. In addition to recourse to the briefs and appendix, the clerk should review such additional exhibits and portions of the records as may be available in the Clerk's office. He also should review a copy of the transcript of the oral argument. Of course, such additional research as may seem desirable should be completed. We do not simply rely on the briefs.[60]

But opinion writing does not always take place after conference discussion and voting. Indeed, one can consider the original cert memo, and particularly the lengthy bench memo, as laying the groundwork for an opinion. In this sense, opinions are not necessarily written from scratch. For example, after reading law clerk Annmarie Levins's bench memo in *Garcia v. San Antonio Metropolitan Transit Authority*, Powell noted, "Well reasoned and exceptionally well written. This would be the basis for a scholarly dissent if, as I expect, I'll be on the 'losing' end."[61] Powell proved prophetic and did indeed issue a dissent in the case.

Sometimes a justice may decide to have an opinion drafted on a case or issue before oral argument or even before considering a specific case. One example is the death penalty dissent of Justice Blackmun in *Callins* where he instructed his clerks to draft an opinion expressing his views and search for an appropriate case to issue it in.[62] Justice Powell was always looking ahead to opinion writing, even before oral argument took place. He thought about which issues he might like to make his views known on and which cases he might be assigned to write in. He communicated these views, as well as the substance of what he was thinking, to his clerks. His clerks in turn prepared memoranda that would be the basis for later opinions. For example, before the Court convened for its first oral argument of the term, Powell wrote 1972 clerk Larry Hammond about the upcoming cases:

It is clear that I will not be assigned the opinions in either the abortion or obscenity cases. It is therefore probable—especially since I do not possess any expertise in either of these areas—that I will write no separate opinions in these cases. . . . I view the San Antonio case in a different light. All nine Justices are starting out "from scratch," and in view of my years of experience in public education, I think it probable that I will write an opinion—whether it be for the Court, in concurrences or in dissent. . . . As always, I am anxious to have the benefit of your views. If they differ from my tentative thinking, I will be happy to discuss the case with you next week before we start the Term on October 2. My hope is that you will be able to write a memorandum—not in the usual bench memo form—but one that can serve as a rough outline of an opinion, and thereby save valuable time at a later date.[63]

After he or she receives an assignment, the time it takes a clerk to draft an opinion varies and depends on numerous factors, including the type of opinion, i.e., whether it is a majority or separate opinion, within-chambers review procedures, and the time during the term when the opinion is written, with end-of-term pressures often dictating hurried efforts. For example, with two and a half months left in the 1972 Term, Powell wrote his clerks,

At the Conference today, for the first time this Term, Mr. Justice Brennan gave his status report on a per chambers basis as to assigned but uncirculated Court opinions. Contrary to the euphoria of my friend [clerk] Jay [Harvie Wilkinson] (who keeps telling me that we are in "great shape"), we rank at the bottom. . . . I have no feeling whatever that we are working less hard than other Chambers. We may have some built-in restraints against expeditious action, such as printing Chambers copies, having a second clerk review every opinion before it is released, and my own determination to work meticulously on each opinion.[64]

While the equality principle generally dictates that each justice receives an equal number of majority opinion assignments, speed can account for some variation. In order to guarantee that he would receive the number of assignments he wanted, Justice Powell explained to his clerks that they should work quickly:

We are not "quick draws" in circulating opinions, but we usually do better than the average. The Chief Justice . . . keeps a large tally sheet. I like to write 16 Court opinions per Term. This would mean four apiece for each of you to work with me on, if the workload can be divided that way. But if the Chief assigns only two cases per argument period, we end up with only 14 Court opinions. In order to have extra cases assigned, we must keep ahead of most of the Chambers and also hope to pick up an unassigned case where the vote is close.[65]

As our discussion of *Casey* in the preceding chapter demonstrates, clerks may also have to work more quickly or more slowly depending on the circulation of other opinions in the case and the strategic calculation about the most fortuitous time to circulate in order to form coalitions and insulate against criticism.[66] Some justices impose strict deadlines on their clerks. For example, Justice Byron White and Chief Justice Rehnquist expected their clerks to furnish them with drafts ten days after they were given an assignment.[67] Justice Powell explained to his clerks how strategy and timing would affect the speed at which they needed to complete dissents and concurrences:

> In many instances, work can commence on a dissenting opinion without awaiting the circulation of the majority opinion. Indeed, where the vote in Conference is close, and there may be some chance of winning over another Justice whose vote was genuinely tentative, it is desirable to have a dissenting opinion drafted, in print and substantially ready to circulate as promptly as possible following the circulation of the majority opinion. A concurring opinion almost always awaits the circulation of the Court opinion, as one hopes he may be able to join it without writing separately.[68]

After the clerk completes the draft, the justice usually revises it. But the extent of initial direction and subsequent revision provided by the justice varies according to the justice in question and often the case being decided. For example, a clerk for Justice John Marshall Harlan from the 1960s told us that Harlan only wanted "minor word changes in most opinions, but the result was that the product was his—with consistency from year to year. Drafts were done after substantial discussion [and] so were written with [the] Justice's views in mind." A clerk for Potter Stewart from the 1970s said that Stewart revised the clerk's draft opinions "more [for] style than structure [or] substance." A former Brennan clerk from the 1980s said that Brennan did "little revision" of the clerk's draft opinions. A Marshall clerk from the 1960s said, "I drafted any opinion with his views in mind and according to his direction or outline." Another former clerk for Marshall said that the justice revised her draft opinions in most cases "to a greater or lesser extent." A clerk for Justice White said, "He revised almost all opinions quite heavily." A White clerk from the 1970s said that White revised the clerk's opinions "when my draft didn't suit him."

Justice Powell explained his procedure to his clerks: "When a first draft is delivered to me, I do such editing, revising and rewriting as seems necessary. Sometimes I will conclude that we must make a fresh start, or at least substantially rewrite portions of the opinion."[69] But Powell's level of review could be hampered by end-of-term pressures and also depended on the type of case. He wrote his clerks,

> One of the problems which we encountered last term was that I became the "bottle neck" the last week in May, when several draft opinions hit my desk at about the same time. This makes it a bit difficult for me to do the type of reviewing, revising, rewriting and—above all—careful thinking about each opinion, which I wish to be free always to undertake, a task which varies with the case for all of the obvious reasons.[70]

Interestingly, at least one justice, William O. Douglas, practiced a combination of both retention and delegation, depending on whether he was writing for the Court or not. A Douglas clerk from the 1960s said, "I only wrote first drafts for concurring or dissenting opinions; WOD did *all* 1st drafts of opinions for the Court." Another Douglas clerk from the 1970s similarly responded that the "Justice did drafts of all, or nearly all, majority opinions; clerks did drafts of some dissents, orders of Circuit Justice, etc."

The third method of opinion writing, collaboration, is less common than either delegation or retention but has still been practiced by a number of justices in differing ways. At base, this method puts clerk and justice on equal ground in the drafting process. Both give an equal amount of effort in order to achieve a final opinion. The distinction between clerk and justice becomes less sharp as the traditional roles are replaced by a small working group of legal professionals functioning as a team to draft a document. For example, Justice Harold Burton explained his approach:

> On each case assigned to me for an opinion, I shall want the assistance of one of the law clerks. I shall expect him to study it thoroughly from a separate set of briefs and records and to prepare his idea of a draft of an opinion along the lines which are to be followed by the Court. This should cover issues rather fully so that I can use it as a check list. I shall draft an opinion in my own language and, as to it, I shall welcome suggestions of every sort from each law clerk, although one will have the initial responsibility for the case. Usually the clerk who wrote the cert. memo. will handle the bench memo. and also the assigned opinion on that case.[71]

A former Burton clerk told us, "Justice and clerk each wrote separate draft opinions without seeing the other draft. The review by each of the other's draft began. We probably worked more often from [the] Justice's first draft, but he might take portions from [the] clerk's draft." Another clerk said, "Justice Burton didn't like the direct confrontation with the law clerk, and so you would write something and he would rewrite it, but it all came back to you through the in-box and the out-box."[72]

Justice Stanley Reed struggled with opinion writing and once said, "Wouldn't it be nice if we could write the way we think."[73] One former clerk called the working relationship between Reed and his clerks a "cooperative endeavor."[74] They wrote the opinions and he inserted paragraphs throughout. A former clerk described the opinions they produced: "He didn't like to start from the beginning and write to the end. He much preferred to edit. . . . [t]he [opinions] are really a dialogue . . . their voice changes from paragraph to paragraph."[75]

When he did not do his own drafting, Chief Justice Warren practiced another form of collaboration. A Warren clerk from the 1950s told us,

> He would talk about the case and outline his ideas. Then the clerk who had worked on the case prior to the argument would go to work getting the materials ready for the Chief because the Chief and the clerk would work on the opinion together. . . . He would not always assign a first draft to a person. He would assign pieces. He would want me to write up this or write up that. He might write up certain things or he might give you the opinion in sort of rough form orally. You would take it

down literally—you didn't take shorthand—but you take notes and execute that. So it was a give and take process. He wanted us to make sure that the citations were right, that he cited cases correctly. He contributed. In whatever we wrote we were writing down what he had told us. It was what he wanted. We weren't out there freelancing. We didn't think we were justices. He didn't think we were justices. He would give us quite detailed views about how the case should go. . . . Looking back to mechanics. We would fill in the blanks. But we never went off and just dreamed stuff up.

A clerk for Chief Justice Warren Burger described another collaborative approach: "The drafting process was constantly back-and-forth from bench memo (clerk) to holding notes (Justice) to outline (clerk), etc. At each stage, [the] Justice made modifications." Another of Burger's clerks described the process: "kids could draft facts [and] procedural history. The Chief drafted [and] edited legal analysis and reasoning of [the] decision." A Burger clerk from the 1980s added, "Remember: each clerk had only about 3–4 majority opinions."

There is some evidence that justices varied their approach according to the type of case. For example, in landmark cases, justices are more likely to retain the opinion for themselves rather than delegate the drafting to their clerks. Pamela Karlan, Stanford University law professor and 1985 clerk to Justice Blackmun, explained that the clerks could not have written *Roe v. Wade*: "Justice Blackmun wrote *Roe* from the heart. The little beasts don't have them."[76] Indeed, Blackmun's case file confirms that he drafted the opinion. However, he did have substantial help from his clerks along the way.

The discussion between Blackmun and his clerks during *Roe*, and its companion case *Doe v. Bolton*, was lengthy and detailed.[77] Of course the clerks made the usual analysis and recommendations at the certiorari and bench memo stages. But it was when Blackmun circulated his drafts to his colleagues that the clerks became very specific in their critiques, in terms of both style and substance. For example, 1971 clerk George T. Frampton, Jr., wrote Blackmun,

Attached is a list of suggested revisions in the Georgia Abortion case. I feel even more strongly now that you should make explicit what the opinion presupposes by approving the decision of the court below as far as it went. Not only would that make this opinion more "complete" and logical; I am afraid without it your footnote still permits the CA 5 to undercut everything this Court does on the state's appeal there. At best, the present draft leaves the CA 5 and other lower courts in something of a quandary, and unnecessarily so. I think you need not endorse the Dist Ct's holding . . . I cannot believe that the other three (hopefully four or more) Justices who have so rapidly joined wouldn't be happy to go along with this, or even urge it.[78]

When the other justices responded to a circulated Blackmun draft, one of Blackmun's clerks wrote a memorandum commenting on the critique, suggesting a response, or commenting on a proposed response already written by Blackmun. For example, 1972 clerk Randy Bazanson wrote Justice Blackmun, "I see no problems in your response to Mr. Justice Rehnquist. I wonder, however, if another reason for not invalidating the Texas Statute only with respect to a litigant in the first trimester is that you are not now prepared to say that immediately after the first trimester such a restrictive statute would pass constitutional muster."[79] In another memo to Blackmun, Bazanson wrote,

With respect to the cut-off point issue upon which you solicited remarks from the Court, I think Mr. Justice Brennan's thoughts are very similar to those of Mr. Justice Marshall as expressed in his letter of last week. The point is that there are two potential state interests—one re; safety of the mother in the operation, etc.; and one re: the state's interest in potential life—and a single "cut-off" point cannot be drawn for both interests. As I have stated in earlier memos on this issue, I do not read your opinions to say that after the 1st trimester the states can enact a Texas-type statute. Rather, in the manner described by Justices Brennan and Marshall, state regulation can be "staged-in," so to speak. While I am in agreement with the Marshall letter, I think it would still be appropriate, as Justice Brennan suggests, to define some sort of threshold cutoff—"quickening," the end of the 1st trimester, or "somewhere between 16 and 24 weeks"—before which the state must leave the matter entirely within the medical judgment of the physician. . . . Mr. Justice Stewart has also written a short memo. . . . I am not sure what he is getting at. Perhaps the sort of balancing rule suggested by Justice Marshall and Justice Brennan would satisfy him. . . . However, if Justice Stewart is suggesting that the cut-off should be left completely vague, I would disagree with his position, for this Court must give some fairly certain guidance to the patients and doctors, as well as the legislatures who will be spending much time drafting new legislation, who will be placing substantial reliance on this Court's opinion.[80]

After Justice Rehnquist circulated his dissent in *Roe*, Bazanson wrote Blackmun,

> I do not think the dissent needs any response. Indeed, I think the dissent misses the point. Your opinion does not apply a substantive due process test in the *Williamson v. Lee Optical Co.* sense. Nor does it find a "fundamental right" in the equal protection sense—this is not an equal protection case. Rather, the opinion enunciates and defines an independent constitutional right, found before in Griswold, Stanley, and other opinions, which is very much akin to the First Amendment speech and press right.[81] The fact that that right rests in the "liberty" portion of the 14th amendment due process clause does not make the equal protection or "substantive due process" tests applicable. "Liberty" is a core value protected by the right, and the due process clause is therefore an appropriate source for the right. I should finally note that rather than confusing, as Justice Rehnquist suggests, this privacy right clears up a very muddled area. Indeed, in my view it is substantive due process and equal protection which are the more confusing areas.[82]

There is also some evidence that retention is also more common early in a justice's tenure, particularly if he or she lacks judicial experience. There appears to be a learning curve wherein new justices are more likely participate in opinion writing and other functions than their more experienced colleagues. For example, during his first term, Justice Powell wrote his clerks, "In view of my late arrival on the Court, and the necessity of contributing to my education, we have been somewhat behind other chambers (based on my conversations with other Justices) in having our cert notes available for my review."[83]

How does the current Court fit into the opinion-writing typology? Former Stevens clerk Sean Donahue reported that "well over half the text the Court now produces was generated by law clerks."[84] Currently, every justice, except Justice Stevens, largely uses the delegation method, assigning the first drafts of opinions to law clerks. In contrast, Stevens generally practices the retention approach.[85] A clerk from the 1980s told us, "Justice Stevens always did his own first drafts." Stevens said,

"Part of the reason I do first drafts myself is for self-discipline. I don't really understand a case until I write it out."[86] But even Stevens does not always write all of his own opinions. In the 1997 case of *Reno v. American Civil Liberties Union*, where the Court struck down key provisions of the Communications Decency Act, the first effort to regulate indecent material on the internet, it was reported that Stevens's clerks wrote key sections of the Court's opinion.[87] Of the remaining eight justices, only Justices David Souter and Antonin Scalia regularly draft some of their own opinions. Justice Souter, who does not use a word processor, writes substantial parts of his opinions in longhand. Justice Scalia's often witty and sarcastic opinions suggest that he writes many of his first drafts too. Former Blackmun clerk Edward Lazarus wrote, "Only Justices Scalia and Stevens made it a regular practice to participate in first drafts."[88]

Chief Justice Rehnquist, and Justices O'Connor, Kennedy, Ginsburg, and Thomas more often than not give their clerks considerable leeway in drafting opinions. Still, this does not mean that these justices are unaware of the pitfalls of delegating this important responsibility to the clerks. In a 1994 *New York Times* article, Ginsburg said that law clerks may be "highly intelligent. . . . But most of them are young and in need of the seasoning that experiences in life and in law practice afford."[89] A clerk for then Justice Rehnquist from the 1970s said, "if he liked what we wrote, he would use it—if not, he might rewrite it entirely." Another Rehnquist clerk from the 1970s said that the justice revised "most" of the draft opinions written by clerks. But a clerk from the 1990s said that of his opinions for Chief Justice Rehnquist, "none were substantially revised." Rehnquist described in some detail the process by which he delegated the process of opinion drafting:

> The law clerk is given, as best I can, a summary of the conference discussion, a description of the result reached by the majority in that discussion, and my views as to how a written opinion can best be prepared embodying that reasoning. The law clerk is not off on a frolic of his own, but is instead engaged in a highly structured task which has been largely mapped out for him by the conference discussion and my suggestions to him. This is not to say that the clerk who prepares a first draft does not have considerable responsibility in the matter. The discussion in conference has been entirely oral . . . nine oral statements of position suffice to convey the broad outlines of the views of the justices

but do not invariably settle exactly how the opinion will be reasoned through.[90]

What is perhaps most revealing about the above passage is the complete lack of coyness or reticence from a sitting Chief Justice regarding the degree of delegation to the law clerk in opinion writing. Indeed, Rehnquist has described the justices' chambers as "opinion writing bureaus."[91] "In my case," Rehnquist continued,

> the clerks do the first draft of almost all cases to which I have been assigned to write the Court's opinion. When the caseload is heavy, [I] help by doing the first draft of a case myself. [This] practice . . . may undoubtedly . . . cause raised eyebrows. I think the practice is entirely proper: The Justice must retain for himself control not merely of the outcome of the case, but of the explanation of the outcome, and I do not believe this practice sacrifices either."[92]

Contrast Rehnquist's remarks with Justice Charles Evans Hughes's earlier fear that "it might be thought that [the law clerks] were writing our opinions," and it is plain that the opinion-writing process has been completely transformed from its earlier incarnation.[93] Indeed, an O'Connor clerk from the 1990s told us that the justice "never" revised his draft opinions. Though Justice Breyer uses the delegation method like nearly all of his colleagues, he reportedly picks apart his clerks' first drafts line by line until the entire draft is changed.

But how often do justices revise the draft opinions written by their clerks?

Data: Drafting and Revising Opinions

Table 5.2 shows how often justices were said to revise the draft opinions written by their clerks. Seventy percent of clerks said that their justice revised every draft that was written. For example, a Blackmun clerk from the 1970s said that draft opinions were always submitted to the justice: "He always edited and, as is well-known, cite checked." Justice Powell checked his clerk's draft opinions very carefully, not only editing throughout but also suggesting substantive changes. For example, he wrote 1986 clerk Leslie S. Gielow regarding *Edwards v. Aguillard*,

TABLE 5.2
Frequency of Justices' Revisions of
Clerk's Draft Opinions

Frequency	Percentage of Clerks Responding That Their Justice Made Revisions in . . . (n =)
All Cases	70%
	(85)
Most Cases	19%
	(23)
Some Cases	7%
	(9)
Few Cases	2%
	(3)
No Cases	2%
	(2)

Question: If you wrote draft opinions for your justice, please
indicate how often your justice revised or modified those draft
opinions: all cases, most cases, some cases, few cases, no cases.
NOTE: 122 clerks responded to this question (n = 122).

"You also have done quite well in incorporating many of my views in Part II, as we have discussed. I think, however, that some additions— either in the text or in notes—would strengthen the discussion of what properly can be taught and why. I now identify *possible* ideas or facts that may be included in the revision of Part II."[94] After the clerk revised and sent Powell a second draft, he wrote, "This now reflects my views very well . . . let's move this through the Chambers normal process."[95] In another example, he wrote 1984 clerk Annmarie Levins regarding *Garcia v. San Antonio Metro. Transit Auth.*,

> I have now had an opportunity to read your first draft of a dissent in this case. . . . I now record random thoughts in the memorandum both for you and me as reminders to myself. I identify possible points to be made in our opinion. I state them in no particular order, and suggest no particular priority. In the end, some may merit including in a draft and others perhaps not. . . . This memorandum implies no criticism of your draft. I think the essence of your draft is sound and well written.[96]

We also found that 19 percent of the clerks said that their justice made revisions in most cases. Seven percent said that their justice only changed clerk written first drafts in some cases, and 4 percent said that revisions were made in few or no cases. What is striking from these results is that 30 percent of clerks had their drafts issued without modification, as opinions by their justice, at least some of the time.

This confirms what has been previously reported in anecdotal accounts of the Court's opinion-writing process: opinions written entirely by clerks have been released under their justice's name. And while it is seen as inappropriate at the Court, it is not uncommon for some clerks to recount with pride how a first draft of an opinion was ultimately released virtually unchanged. For example, early in his career, before the equality norm in opinion assignment developed, Justice Reed drafted most of his own opinions. Still, he did allow his clerks to write occasionally. A clerk from the 1954 Term recalled, "I drafted three or four opinions. . . . But there's really only one in the Term [that I clerked] that he almost didn't change a word of. It was a very unimportant case [*Opper v. United States*] . . . it's always been a nice thing to see my hand in the Supreme Court Reports."[97] Another clerk recalled that when the clerks wrote the first drafts, Reed "would reorganize, rewrite, restructure the opinion" but "there was one case in which I wrote an opinion for him. It wasn't a very important case, but he accepted it with, I think very, very few changes at all."[98] Similarly, a former clerk recalled, "Earl Warren's opinions change voice every year because, I mean, the Chief never made any bones about it—he didn't write most of his opinions. The clerks certainly did the major drafting effort."[99] Chief Justice Rehnquist said of his clerks' first drafts, "I may revise it in toto [but] I may leave it relatively unchanged."[100] In a May 1991 memorandum to Justice Thurgood Marshall, one of his clerks said that he was so busy writing several of Marshall's dissents that the justice ought to assign the case to Justice Blackmun instead.[101] Justice Powell reminded his clerks, "In the [opinion writing] process, there is no room for 'pride of authorship'—by me or any clerk."[102]

But we suspect that not all cases are created equal. Indeed, after the first round of opinions was assigned at the start of the 1972 Term, Justice Powell wrote his clerks, "I feel some sense of disappointment in the first cases which we will write."[103] We were interested in the types of cases that were revised. Because we found that every justice makes revisions of their clerk's drafts in at least some cases, we wondered whether this occurred only in landmark cases, whether it occurred only on cases addressing a particular issue, or whether there was no particular pattern of revision that the clerk could discern. Table 5.3 provides the overall results. The most common response from the clerks was that there was

TABLE 5.3
Justices' Revision of Clerk's Draft Opinions
by Type of Case

Type of Case	Number of Responses from Clerks That Their Justice Made Revisions in . . .
No Particular Pattern	56
All Cases	38
Landmark or Important Cases	16
Cases on a Particular Issue	13
Other	11

Question: If the justice did revise your draft opinions, please indicate when the justice substantially modified or revised the draft opinions (you may check more than one answer).

no particular pattern to the revising practice of their justice. The next most common response was that the justice made revisions in all cases. Still, there is some evidence that justices only substantially revised their draft opinions when particular issues were involved.

Also, a number of clerks said that their justice only substantially revised drafts in landmark or important cases. For example, a Stewart clerk from the 1970s told us,

> He would edit it. It varied as to how much he would edit it. Sometimes he would edit it very little and sometimes he would edit it very much. The most important cases he would edit the most. There were cases, which I'm sure he regarded as not that important where hardly any words would be changed and it would get circulated and get a Court and that would be the opinion. There would be other cases, big high-profile cases where—I know this one where he left in my first paragraph and rewrote the whole rest. And so sometimes he would do that if he cared a lot and wanted to say it his way. So it varied.

Because it is most common that justices revise in no particular pattern as to the type of case, we wondered whether justice revision has more to do with the quality of the opinion written and whether the clerk did a good job of reflecting the justice's views. Time constraints may also play a role here. If the justice is particularly busy, such as near the end of a term, he or she may be less willing or able to spend time revising a clerk's draft. Also, if a justice does not revise a clerk's draft opinion, does that mean that the justice agrees with everything in it? It may just be that the clerks for justices who are less likely to revise are simply better at drafting opinions to their justice's specifications. It may also be that those justices are not as stringent when it comes to the details of an opinion as long as the holding and reasoning are consistent with their views. This administrative view of opinion writing was suggested by one of Chief Justice Vinson's clerks, who said, "The fact that [Vinson] wasn't going to sit down with a blank yellow pad and start from scratch was the characteristic of an administrator."[104] Another clerk said that Vinson "was not a legal scholar who takes great delight in the intellectual approach to the law for its own sake."[105] Of course, it is possible that the justice simply agreed with the result and paid little or no attention to the reasoning. Such possibilities have given ammunition to those critical of the growing importance of clerks.

In a 1986 article, *The Times* (of London) reported, "In the United States judges have 'clerks,' i.e., assistants who prepare and frequently write judgments which their masters often merely adopt and which a qualified observer can easily recognize as the work of a beginner."[106] Do clerk-written opinions differ substantially than those written by justices? Court of Appeals Judge Richard Posner called law clerks "in many situations, 'para-judges.' In some instances, it is to be feared, they are indeed invisible judges, for there are appellate judges whose literary style appears to change annually."[107] Do clerks make an effort to draft opinions in the style of their justice to avoid this concern? We asked them how they saw their role in this process and were curious as to whether this perception has changed over time as opinion writing has become more commonplace.

Figure 5.1 shows the law clerks' perceptions of their role in opinion writing. Specifically, we asked clerks if they attempted to draft opinions as if the justice were writing the opinion him- or herself. As the nature of opinion writing changed from the Vinson Court, where clerk-written opinions were less common and sometimes done as exercises or foils for a justice, to the Rehnquist Court, where opinion writing was virtually the exclusive province of clerks, there was an increasing trend for clerks to draft opinions as if their justice was doing the drafting. For example, a Black clerk from the 1940s said, "Of course," he (as a clerk) would attempt to draft as if Black was writing himself "as to revisions." A Rehnquist clerk from the 1970s told us, "Yes, in opinion drafts, you were trying to express the Justice's articulation of how he had decided."

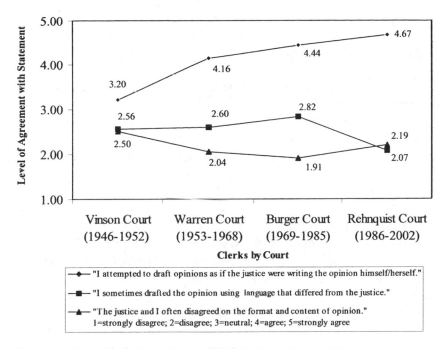

Figure 5.1. Law Clerk Perceptions of Their Role in Opinion Writing

A Stewart clerk from the 1970s told us, "In the opinion, you try to write it the way you think he went at it. You try to be a surrogate."

Did clerks sometimes draft opinions using language that differed from their justice? In general clerks did not, but Rehnquist Court clerks are even more careful than their predecessors not to use language that differed from their justice. For example, a Clark clerk from the 1950s said, "My drafts initially were always my language, not his. That's why he revised them if he didn't like my choice of words." Similarly, a Clark clerk from the 1960s explained to us how he came up with an important legal principle that Clark and the other justices agreed to:

Sometimes my role would be somewhat more important in terms of structure. In fact in one of the cases that we had in that Term was a school prayer case and he was assigned the opinion. And the Court knew, in terms of the vote, how it wanted to come out, and in general terms "why" but then we had to work out a structure. And basically, I worked out a structure that he liked, which was we had to deal with things that could be done that impacted religion. Because all kinds of governmental action could have some impact on religion that could be argued as being either establishment or prohibition, I worked out the structure, the concept that it couldn't have the purpose or a purpose or primary effect. . . . That was the structure that worked and that people bought. And so there in that case I probably had more of an impact. But again, if he had said, as he might well have, "That's the stupidest thing I have ever heard," I could take one shot at arguing but if he said "No, I don't want to hear it," then that was it. There was no question who the boss was.

We asked clerks whether they often disagreed with their justice on the format and content of opinions. In general, the clerks said that they did not. For example, a Blackmun clerk from the 1970s told us that the content of opinions "was [the justice's] job." But, as our archival data suggests, clerks do suggest substantive changes. A Clark clerk from the 1960s recalled how he discussed his drafts with the justice:

Sometimes it might be simply being sure that the cases stood for what he said, or putting in a case when he wanted one, but sometimes a lot more. Sometimes I would say, "Mr. Justice I just have a real problem with this. It doesn't work for this reason or that reason." And sometimes he would say, "Well, let's look at that," or sometimes he would say, "Well, maybe so and I appreciate your comment but that's my judgment about this and let's float it by circulating the opinion and we'll see what people say."

Taken together, these responses reflect the increasing responsibility given to law clerks for opinion writing. As clerks have become the primary drafters of opinions, they have become more conscientious in carrying out the wishes of their justice. In short, the modern law clerk endeavors to act as a surrogate for his or her justice in the opinion-writing process. But while clerks see themselves as surrogates, they still have considerable discretion over the word choice, structure, and sometimes even the substance of the opinions they write. A former clerk to Justice Thurgood Marshall said of a Marshall clerkship, "It's the best job in the building. You have enormous discretion and no authority."[108]

Conclusion

What is plain from the above analysis is that the opinion-writing process on the Supreme Court has undergone a dramatic transformation in
recent years, with justices ceding the task of composing their words to
their clerks. What started out as a learning exercise developed into necessary work when the Court equalized opinion assignment in the 1950s.
Not surprisingly, clerks have endeavored to write opinions that their
justices find satisfactory and therefore need little or no revision. As a
result, justices have issued wholly clerk-written opinions as their own.
Many suggest that the rise of clerk involvement in this process has contributed to the dramatic increase in the number of separate opinions
issued by the justices and a loss of quality in those opinions. Of course,
justices are ultimately responsible for the words that are issued under
their names, whether written by themselves or by one of their clerks.

As clerks have taken over a larger share of the opinion-writing process, has the language and doctrine of opinions also changed? It has been
suggested that the use of inexperienced, unsure clerks has resulted not
only in longer opinions but also in opinions that are less clear and are
filled with tentative language and every conceivable argument, citation,
and authority, leaving the opinions more difficult for lower courts to interpret. Former Yale Law School Dean Anthony T. Kronman remarked,
"Opinions written by law clerks tend to be longer because their authors
have not yet acquired the conciseness that comes with experience and
practice. Being new to the law, moreover, they lack confidence in their
own insight and judgment, and therefore tend to include every conceivable argument for their position."[109]

Justice Powell was concerned about this issue. On opinion length, he
wrote his clerks, "It will be tempting in . . . these cases to write long
opinions, as each presents issues that cannot be addressed in eight or
ten pages. I reiterate my concern about unduly long opinions."[110] Three
months later, he again wrote his clerks,

I found my in-basket weighted down with opinions from other Chambers. The first five that I picked up ranged in length as follows: 19,
27, 28, 30, and 31!! The one case I have read, the shortest of the half-
a-dozen is at least 50% longer than necessary to say everything that
was said. Indeed, the use of different language at different places to say

pretty much the same thing is the sort of opinion that generates uncertainty and further litigation.[111]

Similarly, he cautioned his clerks on the problem of excessive citations:

> Now that we are in the intensive opinion writing phase of our responsibility, one thing I have wanted to mention is the need for care and restraint in citing secondary authorities in our opinions. I respect scholarship and documentation, but even Frankfurter's early influence did not persuade me that one must cite every known authority and every decision, however tangential, in the footnotes to a brief, law review article or an opinion. Or, putting it differently, let us concentrate on the relevant cases and scholarship and avoid the marginal ones. A second point, perhaps of greater importance, is the danger of weakening an opinion by citing some controversial or unrecognized secondary authority. Here, I am not thinking of the law reviews but of writers who may not lend strength to a point or to an opinion. The use as an authority of some hack, could detract from an opinion. I hardly need say that, whenever time is available, I hope that we can canvass the leading law reviews and refer to such articles, comments or notes as may be relevant.[112]

Still, Powell praised his clerks when he felt they did a particularly good job. He wrote two of his clerks, "In a telephone talk Tuesday afternoon with Dean Phil Neal of the University of Chicago Law School, he complimented me warmly on the quality of my opinions last term. As the two of you had a major hand in those that have received the most attention, I pass the compliment on to you—with my appreciation for your scholarly assistance."[113]

Because Supreme Court opinions are interpreted for years after they are written, key words, phrases, constructions, and even footnotes play a crucial role in the formation of law. Author Bernard Schwartz derided the use of law clerks in opinion writing: "For the law, it is a disaster, since it will inevitably lead not only to a dilution in the quality but also in the reputation of the court." Kennedy clerk and Columbia law professor Michael Dorf explained, "In the broad sweep of the law, the effect of clerks is negligible. But it is true that, sometimes, you will see lower courts deciding a case, basing a decision on their interpretation of a phrase that was written by a clerk." But like the justices, the president and members of Congress also rely on their staffs for most of what they say and write. Ronald Klain, a former clerk for Justice White who has also held posts as chief of staff for Vice President Al Gore and counsel to the Senate Judiciary Committee, remarked, "Supreme Court law clerks have less impact on the Supreme Court than do the staff of Congress and the White House. The difference is that the law clerks are so young and inexperienced. The fact that any power at all is vested in someone who is one or two years out of law school is incredible."

For their part, clerks are eager to draft opinions, seeing this as the apex of their contribution. Kevin Worthen, who clerked for Justice White in 1983, explained, "A Supreme Court clerk's daily regimen includes several different writing assignments such as cert memos, bench memos, and draft opinions. Some of these—draft opinions, for example—are more interesting and 'prestigious' than others. Work on draft opinions, after all, might actually be published in a somewhat recognizable form for the world to see."[114]

The number of separate opinions per case has almost doubled in the last five decades, and there has been much speculation as to the cause. Because clerks are almost totally responsible for opinion writing and view opinions as the most prestigious part of their work, it should not be surprising that as the number of clerks has increased, there has been a dramatic rise in the number of separate concurring and dissenting opinions issued by the Court. Bradley J. Best and others have argued that the number of clerks is a contributing factor.[115]

We asked clerks from previous eras, when there were fewer clerks per chambers, whether their justices would have produced more separate opinions if they had had more clerks. A former clerk for Justice Minton responded,

> I don't think so. I wouldn't want to say for certain but he was not one who thought just because he didn't agree, he needed to write a dissent. Occasionally he did but occasionally he would join someone else's. Many times, although he didn't really agree with the majority opinion, he didn't see any reason—since it clearly was a majority opinion—not to go along with them.

A Stewart clerk from the 1970s told us,

> He wasn't driven by the number of clerks. Where he wanted to write he would tell you. I mean I wrote plenty of concurring and dissenting

opinions too and he would tell you and I don't think he would say, "Oh God, you guys are too busy. I'm not going to burden you, never mind." I mean he didn't think like that. We weren't overworked. We worked very hard but because we didn't do bench memos, although we had to do all the cert petitions, we worked hard but I don't think he felt like it would be some imposition if he wanted to write.

A former clerk to Justice Clark told us that having more clerks would not have encouraged his justice to write more opinions. Instead, he suggested a different cause:

A substantial part—it's ego that drives the proliferation. And another aspect of it, and ego's never absent from it, but some judges happen to have strong views about an issue, which they happen to be on the losing side all the time. But more it's that there are some judges like there are some board members in a board meeting that just can't resist being heard.

Whether it is ego driven or not, some justices are interested in some cases more than others and feel a corresponding need to make their views known. With two months left in the 1971 Term, Justice Powell wrote his clerks,

There probably will be additional concurring and dissenting opinions from our chambers. I am particularly interested, for example, in *Caldwell, Gravel* (not enough to want to be assigned the opinion) and *Gelbard*. I believe that Mr. Justice Rehnquist expects to write in *Gelbard* and so we will await what he does. Whether we concur separately or dissent in other cases will depend upon the acceptability of opinions written by the Justices to whom they have been assigned. Although I do not expect to write separately, I am interested in the Emporia School case. If Phil can do it, I hope he will find time in May to revise and tighten up the Chief's preliminary memorandum on Emporia.[116]

Still, Powell recognized the need for restraint. He told his clerks,

It is clear that I will have to join opinions as to which I may have doubts or reservation, especially with respect to keeping some of my options for the future. I have discussed this problem with two or three

Justices. They say that all members of the Court have the problem and find that they simply cannot (except Justice Douglas) state their personal views on every case. Accordingly, I will tend to join opinions in accordance with my Conference vote, but will continue to welcome suggestions.[117]

Another often-cited answer for the rise in separate opinions has to do with the increasing use of technology at the Court. For example, the Court's data systems director writes each justice when the new clerks arrive in the summer,

> Training for your law clerks on using the personal computer and the Supreme Court Opinion Writing System has been scheduled. . . . Each law clerk has been scheduled for two days of training, as close as possible to his or her arrival date. . . . This training is essential to a law clerk's successful use of the Court's SCOWS, WordPerfect systems, and the Automated Docket Systems.[118]

Word processors make it easier for justices and clerks to churn out opinions. In 1977, Justice Powell explained, "The great new interest of our Chambers is the Wang equipment. . . . Its product is sensational! The only negative is that apparently it induces all of us to write longer, more frequently, and to feel freer to make changes."[119] In a recent conversation with Justice Scalia, he recognized this change as well as the increase in the number of clerks available to a justice—currently four each.[120] But Scalia also made the point that he only joins an opinion when he agrees with every word in it. If he does not, then he said that he always writes a separate opinion to make his views clear—or at least has a clerk draft his separate opinion.

Scalia's comments suggest that it may simply be that the more ideological or jurisprudential differences there are among the justices, and the more divided the Court generally is, the more likely that separate opinions will be issued. In 1976 Justice Powell wrote his clerks about the decision to write separately:

> I wrote more concurring opinions last Term than I would like to write. The force of a Court opinion is sometimes weakened by concurrences. But there are times when I have been willing to join an opinion (usually to "make a Court") only because I could record my own position. I did

this last Term in *Spock* and *Mini-Theatres* to preserve my position on the First Amendment as I perceive it. We must bear in mind, however, that each Justice has a responsibility to the Court as an institution to help form a majority wherever this can be done without sacrifice of principle or conviction. The Court is not best served by plurality or fractioned opinions.[121]

Still, the fact remains that, unlike clerks from previous eras, modern law clerks are largely responsible for opinion writing. Justice Powell remarked, "Quality in opinion writing on this Court—overloaded as we are—depends in major part upon the ability, pride, and dedication of the law clerks."[122] And despite the direction Powell provided to his clerks each term, he still conceded, "Do not be too self-conscious about your opinion drafting. Go ahead and draft the opinion the way you think it should be written."[123] Chief Justice Rehnquist defended this dramatic change in the process:

I don't think people are shocked any longer to learn that an appellate judge receives a draft of a proposed opinion from a law clerk. I think they would be shocked, and properly shocked, to learn that an appellate judge simply "signed off" on such a draft without fully understanding its import and in all probability making some changes in it. The line between having law clerks help one with one's work, and supervising subordinates in the performance of their work, may be a hazy one, but it is at the heart . . . [of] the fundamental concept of "judging."[124]

The most damaging aspect, however, of having judicial opinions written by clerks is the potential loss of authority that these opinions carry. Indeed, it is only respect for the Court's legitimacy that gives its judgments weight with both the public and lower court judges who are expected to follow its mandates.

6

Conclusion
Sorcerers' Apprentices

We couldn't get our work done without the clerks. But I don't
think they influence the results here all that much.
—Justice Byron R. White, U.S. Supreme Court

The less that lawyers and especially other judges regard judicial
opinions as authentic expressions of what the judges think, the less
they will rely on judicial opinions for guidance and authority. . . .
The more the thinking embodied in opinions is done by law clerks
rather than by judges, the less authority opinions will have.
—Judge Richard A. Posner, U.S. Court of Appeals

In 1955, Justice Robert H. Jackson wrote, "It is often suggested that the Court could create a staff of assistants like those of
administrative tribunals to take much of the drudgery of judicial work
from the Justices."[1] Since Jackson's comments, the Court has done precisely that and more. With their increase in number and responsibility,
law clerks have become more than simply the Court's revolving staff of
assistants. Over time, law clerks have come to play an increasingly crucial role in the certiorari process, decision making, and opinion writing.

The preceding chapters provide an historical portrait of the Supreme
Court law clerk. We discussed the genesis of the institution and the way
it was transformed over time. We examined how clerks were selected
and the roles they played in reviewing the thousands of cases petitioned
to the Court, in drafting the opinions issued by their justices, and in the
decision-making process. In each area, we found dramatic changes in
the institution. In this chapter, we discuss these transformations, our
key findings, and the implications they raise for the future role of law
clerks. In the end, we suggest that clerks are neither merely surrogates

nor scheming usurpers. Their role falls somewhere in between. Still, institutional changes have made them a growing part of, and increasingly influential in, the daily work of the Court. We suggest that both the justices and, particularly, the clerks adopt new standards to limit the potential dangers that have arisen as more and more responsibility has been delegated to the clerks.

Findings and Avenues for Future Research

Our analysis shows that the rise of the law clerk was largely caused by institutional changes in the way the justices chose to conduct their work. Initially, clerks wrote certiorari memos and drafted the occasional opinion for their justice as part of an advanced apprenticeship in learning the law. Rarely were these memos or opinions given much weight by the justices. But important institutional changes caused the role of clerks to change from that of apprentices in learning the law to that of practitioners without whom the Court could not function. We explained how the creation of the "dead list" under Chief Justice Hughes encouraged justices to rely on clerk-written memos of the cases petitioned to the Court. The "cert pool," created under Chief Justice Burger, further cemented the position of the clerks as the initial gatekeepers and primary decision makers in the agenda-setting process. The equalization of opinion assignment under Chief Justice Vinson precipitated the transformation of the opinion-writing process from retention to delegation. The addition of a second, third, and fourth clerk per chambers caused an explosion in the number of applicants for clerkships. This resulted in increased ideological divisions among co-clerks within each chambers and increased attempts by clerks to influence the decision-making process.

The institution of the Supreme Court law clerk was a byproduct of the apprentice model of legal education. Justices perpetuated the system of young lawyers-to-be learning the law at the foot of the master. The first clerks studied the law just as much as they aided their justices in legal research and other nonlegal tasks. While the clerk as an institution is now largely justified by the Court's growing caseload, there has always been a strong mentoring component to the justice-clerk relationship. Simply put, justices like having law clerks in the same way professors like having students: they have a desire to teach and derive some benefit from passing on what they have learned. Indeed, many justices were law professors before coming to the Court and some continued to teach, albeit during the summer recess, while on the Court. Hence the justices need and want law clerks, not just to aid them in their work but also as apprentices in the study and practice of law.

Our analysis of the selection process shows that these coveted apprenticeships have largely been the province of white males who graduated from a handful of elite law schools and clerked for certain "feeder" judges on the courts of appeals. On one level, the process has changed from a largely haphazard one wherein justices received relatively few applications and often allowed certain law schools to supply them with clerks to a much more formalized one wherein prospective clerks plan far in advance to spend a year on the courts of appeals and increasingly apply to all nine justices for highly competitive High Court clerkships. A review of the application files of the justices shows that through the 1940s, justices only received a handful of applications and had only a few students recommended to them by at most two or three law schools. As Congress increased the number of clerkships, the number of applicants began to climb in the 1950s and through the 1960s, but it was not until the Burger and Rehnquist Courts that the number of applicants exploded. Justices now have more than one thousand applicants to choose from each year.

But on another level, the selection process has changed little. Three out of every four clerks were graduates of only seven law schools: Harvard, Yale, Chicago, Columbia, Stanford, Virginia, and Michigan. While nearly every clerk has had experience clerking on a lower court, more than one-third of all Supreme Court clerks come from the Court of Appeals for the D.C. Circuit. Furthermore, a small group of appeals court judges routinely supply clerks for the High Court. The most successful "feeder" judge has been J. Michael Luttig of the Fourth Circuit, who places nearly three of his clerks at the Supreme Court each year.

We also examined sex, race, and ideology in the selection process. We found that women have made steady inroads since the 1970s and now comprise nearly 40 percent of Supreme Court clerks. This was largely due to the hiring practices of individual justices such as Justices Breyer, O'Connor, and Ginsburg, who routinely select as many female clerks as male clerks. But, since 1971, only 7 percent of clerks were minorities, and pressure has been placed in recent years on the justices to improve those numbers. We also found that, in general, clerks have been ideologically aligned with their justices. This was particularly true through the Warren Court, when prospective clerks were more likely to limit their applications to selected justices. Beginning with the Burger Court, and most dramatically into the Rehnquist Court, clerks were much less ideologically aligned with their justice and as a result, certain clerks were more influential than others. This is probably a result of the increasing trend of applicants blanketing all nine chambers.

The master-apprentice relationship explains the genesis of clerk participation in the certiorari process. Through the Hughes Court, most justices personally reviewed the relatively small number of petitions they received: approximately eight per week. When clerks were given the task of reviewing the petitions and preparing memos for their justices, the clerks recognized that this task was purely an exercise in learning the law and did not aid their justice much in deciding what to decide. Because every petition was discussed in conference, in those early years, justices who had not examined the record could rely on the comments, recommendations, and discussions of the other justices. But Chief Justice Hughes felt that not all cases were worthy of discussion and started placing cases on a "dead list" to save time. As more and more cases appeared on the dead list, justices were forced to turn to their clerks to help insure that worthy cases were not inadvertently left off the agenda. In order to keep pace with the Court's growing docket, a group of justices devised a scheme to pool their clerks and divide the petitions up among them.

The cert pool had a dramatic effect on the Court's functioning. Not only did the cert pool end the duplication by clerks across chambers, but it also freed up the clerks to spend more time on the cert memos they did write and gave them more time to concentrate on opinion writing. We found that while the cert pool diluted the influence of individual clerks, it dramatically increased the influence of clerks collectively. The addition of a third and fourth clerk per chambers facilitated the increasing responsibility given to clerks in the agenda-setting process. We suggest that the expansion of the cert pool is largely responsible for the steady decrease during the Rehnquist Court of the number of cases granted review and subsequently decided.

We also found that while clerks felt their influence was greatest in the certiorari process, this influence has been on the decline since the creation of the cert pool, when their work in this area was cut in half. As more clerks have joined the pool, more chambers have had to rely on memos written by clerks from other chambers, thereby lessening the degree to which clerks for a particular justice felt they could be influential with their justice in the agenda-setting process.

We found that in the area of decision making, the arguments of clerks were less important to the justices than the more traditional factors of the justices' jurisprudential philosophy, specific case facts, and precedent. Nevertheless, clerks have on occasion been able to change the minds of their justices on particular cases and issues. Furthermore, such attempts are on the rise, with recent clerks more likely than their predecessors to give their personal beliefs about cases to their justice, to attempt to convince their justice about cases or issues, and to disagree with their justice. This may be a result of the recent increases in the number of clerks who are not ideologically aligned with their justice. Clerks are most persuasive in the certiorari process, in fashioning the legal and substantive content of opinions, as well as in the more stylistic aspects of opinion writing. Where clerks have less influence is in changing their justices' minds on the outcomes of cases. Yet, clerks play a prominent role as informal ambassadors across chambers in aiding the decisions their justices make in forming coalitions.

In the controversial area of opinion writing, we found that the process can take place in three ways. Historically, the most common approach was retention, where justices wrote draft opinions themselves and used clerks to check citations and add footnotes. In the 1950s, retention gave way to delegation, with clerks drafting the opinions according to the oral instructions of their justice. This transition was largely precipitated by a change in the opinion assignment policy by Chief Justice Vinson. Rather than assign opinions according to how quickly the justices finished their assignments, Vinson equalized the process by endeavoring to assign the same number of opinions to each justice. This forced more methodical and deliberate justices such as Frankfurter to delegate to their clerks the initial drafting of opinions in an attempt to keep pace with their speedier colleagues like Douglas and Black. The final opinion-writing method is the collaborative approach, with clerk and justice working together to construct drafts. This approach describes the drafting practice often employed by Chief Justice Burger and Justices Burton and Reed.

We found that drafts written entirely by clerks have been released as opinions with little or no changes made by their justice. Clerks reported that there was no discernible pattern as to the type of case the justice might revise or let stand, with landmark cases being as likely to be unchanged or revised as noncontroversial cases. At the same time, clerks have increasingly acted as surrogates for their justice in drafting opinions.

But in many ways, these findings only scratch the surface, and suggest numerous avenues for further research. Our conclusions on the role that partisanship plays in clerk selection can certainly be further explored. While our initial work in this area suggests that there is generally an ideological congruence between the justices and their clerks, and that justices are conscious of partisanship during the selection process, further study could help identify the extent to which clerks are self-selective in applications and acceptances, versus the justices themselves screening for partisanship. Also, it is unclear whether justices are concerned about ideology because they seek like-minded clerks or because they want to avoid selecting activist clerks with partisan agendas.

Our findings on clerk influence in the cert process suggest a need to delve even deeper into the politics of this process. We found evidence of pool writers injecting partisanship and strategy into a function that was designed to be objective. While we showed a number of manifestations of this partisanship, such as in the omission of dissenting views and the names of judges participating, editorializing when labeling the parties in the case, and the timing of circulating the memos, our discussion suggests that a more in-depth analysis could answer questions of how frequent and widespread these practices are. Furthermore, more research needs to be done on the substance of the memos and whether pool clerks attempt to manipulate information through slanting and omissions.

Much more research needs to take place in the area of decision making. In particular, we have shown how the clerk network is used and how clerks are often the conduits for information about the justices, particularly in the area of coalition formation. Furthermore, this ambassadorial role appears to be largely political. If clerks are constantly networking across chambers to glean information that may be helpful to their justice, lobbying on behalf of their justice, and generally acting as surrogates for their justice in dealings with other chambers, then to what extent do clerks act on their own behalves as opposed to acting on behalf of the justices they are supposed to be representing? And perhaps even more troubling, to what extent are clerks acting on their own behalves in their within-chambers dealings with their own justices?

While it is plain that clerks draft opinions, more research needs to be done on the extent to which clerks, as opposed to their justices, are influencing the law through both the style and substance of opinions. The reality is that in the legal world, even "stylistic changes," which we found were for the most part the prerogative of clerks, can have a dramatic effect on the direction of the law. Research showing the extent to which the choices that are made by clerks in opinions either affect or do not affect doctrinal development and even outcomes on the merits will be useful here.

The Law Clerk and Its Critics

This overview of our findings serves to highlight the dramatic changes in the institution of the Supreme Court law clerk. In the past one hundred years, clerks were transformed from primarily clerical assistants to key staffers with influence on the Court's agenda, judicial opinions, and decision making. This significant change illustrates one of the principle arguments of this book: the institution of the law clerk has been dramatically transformed over time, and the results of these changes have in turn transformed aspects of the Court itself.

Yet these changes in the role of the clerk have not been without controversy. In the era of the modern law clerk, allegations of undue clerk influence have periodically surfaced as commentators assert that the law clerks wield excessive power. These criticisms coincided with the rise of the modern clerks in the 1950s and their increasing responsibility in the certiorari process and opinion writing. But they were also part of larger inquiries into the Supreme Court, mainly prompted by the Court's involvement in civil rights and liberties cases such as 1954's *Brown v. Board of Education*.[2] It was suggested that young, liberal-minded law clerks were unduly influencing the justices.

Interestingly, one of the first salvos against clerks came from a former clerk, William H. Rehnquist, who went on to become Chief Justice. In his 1957 article for *U.S. News and World Report*, Rehnquist, who had clerked for Justice Robert Jackson in 1952, suggested that there was some "unconscious slanting of material by clerks" and that the power to select clerks should not be left in the hands of the justices alone.[3] Rehnquist's charge of clerk influence was covered by both the Associated Press and the *New York Times*.[4] A former Reed clerk from 1952,

William D. Rogers, responded to the Rehnquist piece two months later in his own *U.S. News and World Report* article. Rogers said that during his term, no justice changed his vote because of clerk influence and that Rehnquist's allegation of clerk slanting would provide further ammunition for Court critics who felt that law clerk appointments should have congressional approval.[5]

Sensing a brewing storm, Justice Felix Frankfurter suggested to his former clerk from the 1952 Term, Alexander Bickel, that he take on Rehnquist's claims. In April 1958, Bickel's article appeared in the *New York Times*.[6] In it, he downplayed clerk influence: "The law clerks are in no respect any kind of kitchen cabinet. [They] generally assist their respective justices in researching the law books and other sources for materials relevant to the decision of cases before the Court."[7]

A month later, Senator John Stennis of Mississippi, who was a critic of the Warren Court, brought the issue up on the Senate floor. He quoted Rehnquist's article at length, advocated for a return to career appointments for clerks, for minimum qualifications to be set via legislative statute, and for Congress to "determine whether or not Senate confirmation should be required for these positions of ever-increasing importance and influence."[8] He argued that clerks were more influential than many executive branch undersecretaries and assistant secretaries. "To the extent that they participate in shaping the work of the Court," Stennis said, "they are deciding vital questions of national effect. Within the judicial branch, these are equivalent to policy-level decisions in the executive branch."[9] As with Rehnquist and Rogers, Stennis's remarks were reprinted in *U.S. News and World Report* as well as the *New York Times*.[10] But despite this flurry of public debate on the role of law clerks, Congress failed to take up the matter and the issue died. The role of clerks was not considered again for over a decade.

In the late 1970s, the publication of *The Brethren* by Bob Woodward and Scott Armstrong renewed allegations of excessive law clerk influence and also raised questions regarding confidentiality of justice-clerk communications.[11] In 1998, another critique of clerk influence was levied with the publication of the book *Closed Chambers*, written by former Blackmun clerk Edward Lazarus.[12] One of the author's targets was what he reported to be the self-proclaimed "cabal" of conservative clerks who worked behind the scenes to manipulate justices and other clerks in order to achieve conservative outcomes on cases.

Throughout these controversies, the justices were rarely critical of law clerks. At nearly every turn, the justices were quick to downplay clerk influence and defend the institution. Justice John Paul Stevens remarked, "An interesting loyalty develops between clerks and their Justices. It is much like a lawyer-client relationship, close and confidential. Like a lawyer, a clerk can't tell his client, the Justice, what to do. He can only suggest what can happen if he does or doesn't do something."[13] Justice Byron White said,

> We couldn't get our work done without the clerks. But I don't think they influence the results here all that much. I like 'em around to hear their various views. When I served as a clerk, I don't think anything I ever did or said influenced my Justice. 1 felt 1 was doing Chief Justice Vinson a service by making sure that relevant considerations were placed before him, such as opinions from other courts, law journals, ideas of my own—things he wouldn't have time to dig up on his own.[14]

Despite some of the claims he made to the contrary, Rehnquist asserted in his 1957 article, "The specter of the law clerk as a legal Rasputin, exerting an important influence on the cases actually decided by the Court, may be discarded at once.[15]

But on occasion, some justices did question the role of law clerks. Perhaps the most vocal critic from within the Court was Justice William O. Douglas. On several occasions, Douglas questioned the increasing use of law clerks by his colleagues. For example, Douglas recalled,

> Under Earl Warren the demand for more law clerks continued. There were to be four, instead of three, for the Chief, and three, instead of two, for the Justices. One day when the matter was discussed at Conference I made a countermotion to abolish all law clerks. "For one year," I pleaded, "why don't we experiment with doing our own work? You all might like it for a change." My proposal was met by a few smiles but mostly stony silence.[16]

Conclusion: The Sorcerers' Apprentices

These recurring controversies, however they are framed, all pose the same question: how influential are law clerks? Are they merely agents for the justices or are they influential political actors in their own right?

We suggest that the data presented in this book show that clerks are not merely surrogates or agents, but they are also not the behind-the-scenes manipulators portrayed by some observers. On the whole, clerks are extremely bright, ambitious young women and men, eager to succeed in their positions. Yet a danger exists that ambition coupled with passion could lead to self-serving partisanship.

What keeps clerks from abusing their position? Certainly a sense of loyalty to their subordinate role is plain from much of our discussion. Also, the justices themselves provide an obvious check against potential abuses. Indeed, the members of the Court are not entirely naïve about their clerks. For example, Justice Blackmun wrote about one of his clerks, "She writes and works with a certain passion."[17] Furthermore, clerks are just beginning their promising careers in the law and therefore are unlikely to risk incurring the wrath of their justices by stepping beyond the accepted boundaries of their jobs.

Despite these safeguards, we have demonstrated that the changes in the institution have extended those boundaries and empowered the clerks in ways wholly unanticipated. Specifically, the power of the clerks collectively is greatest in the agenda-setting process. The creation of the dead list and the cert pool have resulted in justices ceding clerks the responsibility to do the initial review and make recommendations on the thousands of cases petitioned to the Court each year. Yet the justices retain the prerogative to review cases themselves and have the ultimate say on whether a case will be decided.

The role of the clerk in the opinion-writing process is perhaps more problematic. Equalization of opinion assignment and the shift from clerks as editors and cite-checkers to clerks as drafters opened the door for potential abuses. In most cases, the role of the justice is to outline the parameters of the opinion and act as final editor of the clerk-written draft. Yet this system poses a real danger if justices delegate too much authority to clerks with little, if any, direction and oversight. It also raises the important question of clerk influence on the law as they make structural, stylistic, and even substantive choices as they write.

Overall, then, we take a middle path—we suggest that the influence of the clerk is neither negligible nor total. There is no question that the clerks provide a vital role in assisting the Court with its workload. However, it seems equally plain to us that some aspects of the role of the modern law clerk tread perilously close to what many critics see as an unconstitutional abdication of the justices' duties.

A number of proposals have been suggested to reduce clerk influence, ranging from outright abolition of clerks to a permanent law clerk staff. However, we suggest that it is highly unlikely that any significant reforms will take place in the near future, given institutional and bureaucratic inertia. Indeed, one major reform effort that was widely studied, debated, and ultimately failed was the debate over an intermediate National Court of Appeals to help relieve the Court from its crushing number of petitions.[18] We will not attempt to revisit that issue here. Instead, we make only a modest proposal: that the justices and particularly the clerks themselves place limits and further checks on the role that clerks play in the cert process, decision making, and opinion writing. Specifically, one way to help guard against undue clerk influence would be through increased disclosure of the Court's internal operations and, at the same time, of the role that clerks play.

For example, in the cert process, when the Court denies a petition, the only information they release is a short statement: "The petition for writ of certiorari is denied." But we know that a pool clerk prepared a pool memo with a recommendation and that the pool memo was marked up by an additional clerk in each chambers who also made a recommendation. If the case was placed on the discuss list, it was either listed by the Chief Justice or through a request by another justice. If on the discuss list, it was voted on by the nine justices in conference and, because it was denied, did not receive the four votes necessary to grant cert. Yet, none of this information is disclosed to either the litigants in the case or the public. Releasing the pool memo, at the very least, could help ensure that pool writers are providing the kind of objective analysis that they are supposed to provide.

Along these lines, attorney and former federal appeals court clerk Nadine J. Wichern has suggested a number of proposals, the most drastic being her call for the justices to once again write the first drafts of their opinions and only use clerks for editing.[19] She also suggests that short of this fundamental retreat, the role of clerks could be referenced more candidly and more frequently in opinions. Perhaps one way to move toward such disclosure in the opinion-writing process would be for the Court to do what Justice Brennan made reference to in his 1979 speech. Namely, opinions could be issued as coming from the chambers of a particular justice as opposed to coming from the justice him- or herself, as is the practice now.

Another small reform that could help minimize the potential for clerk activism would be to prohibit "case swapping" at each stage of the process. As we discussed in the chapter on certiorari, Chief Justice Rehnquist banned the practice for pool writers.

But we recognize that expecting the justices themselves to reform practices they have engaged in for decades is probably unrealistic. Yet this is where the clerk's role in the decision-making process can make a difference. For example, Wichern offers that clerks can use their influence to change the nature of opinions through consensus building within the Court, thereby decreasing the number of separate opinions that need to be written, and through brevity in the opinions themselves. While clerks have often spoken with pride about the opinions they authored, and particularly those that were issued by the Court virtually unchanged, perhaps future clerks will recognize the dangers inherent in this practice.

We have shown that clerks are active ambassadors for their justices in dealing with clerks from other chambers. And while using this role to build consensus, as Wichern suggests, may or may not have an effect on the opinion-writing process, bolstering this informal role could create new dangers. It may be that Chief Justice Warren's initial embargo on his clerk's interactions with the Frankfurter clerks is the best way to guard against clerk activism in coalition forming and opinion writing. Of course, such a step would require the justices themselves to replace their clerks in performing this political role, and that is something justices will understandably be reluctant to do.

Also, it should be recognized that the president must nominate and the Senate must confirm prospective justices before they ascend the bench. These popular institutions provide a unique opportunity for the public to express concerns about the role that law clerks will play for a prospective justice. Questioning the nominee about his or her views on these matters, whether in the executive branch during the screening process or in the Senate during confirmation hearings, could prove influential.

In summary, the institution of the law clerk has been transformed into a permanent bureaucracy of influential legal decision makers, scarcely resembling its original incarnation. Today, voting and editing largely defines the role of a Supreme Court justice. Clerks are now responsible for the raw material that goes into the Court's opinions. And while the outcomes in cases—who wins and who loses—are important to litigants and the general public, for the legal world, the legal support for the outcome is just as crucial. Attorneys, lower court judges, and even future Supreme Courts scrutinize the reasoning, language, and general details of opinions. It is these details that clerks have tremendous discretion over. As one clerk put it, "You go back to your office, you stare at your computer screen, and you go, 'Holy shit, I'm going to write the law of the land.'"[20]

But we suggest that this is turning the process of judging on its head. Judges, and only judges, have the constitutional authority to do the work of judging. That includes reviewing petitions, doing legal research, writing opinions, and making decisions. Former Solicitor General Wade McCree described the judicial function as uniquely individual: "The traditional understanding of the judicial office [is] an office whose duties are defined in terms of the actions, judgment and explanations not of a committee, but of an individual. That the Founders of our Republic recognized this fact is evidenced by their efforts to guarantee 'judicial independence.'"[21] In his 1981 article, McCree decried the increasing "depersonalization" of the judicial function through the bureaucratization of federal courts—including the heavy reliance on law clerks. In the two decades since McCree's warning, judges have become only more dependent on staff. In this light, the transformation of the law clerk appears less benign.

In the 1779 poem by Johann Wolfgang von Goethe, the sorcerer's apprentice could not resist the temptation to put on the robes of the master and try his hand at sorcery:

> That old sorcerer has vanished
> And for once has gone away!
> Spirits called by him, now banished,
> My commands shall soon obey.
> Every step and saying
> That he used, I know,
> And with sprites obeying
> My arts I will show.

While the temptation may only be natural, and to some extent encouraged by the master, the apprentice has a responsibility to be true to his or her role. In the context of law clerks, that responsibility is a great one, for it is only the justices who have the legitimate authority to discharge the duties of their offices. If both justices and clerks continue to blur the distinction between their very different commissions, not only will public confidence in the Court be jeopardized but also, like the apprentice in von Goethe's poem, the clerks may find themselves unable to quell increasing threats to the Court's legitimacy that their institution has fostered.

Appendix A

"Memorandum for the Law Clerks" from the Chambers of Chief Justice Earl Warren

A. *Principal Duties*

  1. *The Appellate Docket*

The Appellate Docket is comprised of all paid petitions for certiorari, all paid appeals, all cases originally on the Miscellaneous Docket in which certiorari has been granted or probable jurisdiction noted, and certain miscellaneous items such as petitions for rehearing.

Your primary responsibility with respect to the appellate docket cases is (1) to prepare a memorandum on each petition for cert and each jurisdictional statement, and (2) to prepare a memorandum on each argued case.

  a. Memoranda on Cert Petitions and on Jurisdictional Statements.

  (1) Mechanics.

  (a) Vacation-Time.

During the summer, the Clerk's Office continues to distribute petitions for cert and jurisdictional statements. They must all be processed by the law clerks far enough in advance of the first Conference of the Term so that they can be studied by the Chief Justice a reasonable time before Conference. The deadline for these memoranda will fluctuate from year to year; you should ask Mrs. McHugh about this matter. Of course, regardless of the particular deadline date, you should process these cases regularly during the summer in order to avoid a last minute rush.

Undated and unsigned memorandum from the chambers of Chief Justice Earl Warren, Warren Papers, Box 398.

(b) Term-Time.

During the Term, the Clerk's Office continues the weekly distribution of petitions for cert and jurisdictional statements. A total of approximately 15–25 will arrive each Wednesday, together with a Conference List scheduling these cases for discussion by the Court. Frequently the Conference date will be a week from the following Friday, although during recesses usually there will be no Conference until the last recess week. Memoranda on these cases must be completed by the time the Chief Justice leaves the building on the Tuesday before the Conference, inasmuch as he studies the cases Tuesday evening. During session weeks, this allows a maximum of 5½ days from receipt of these cases until the deadline. And even during recess weeks when there is no Tuesday deadline, it is best to keep current by finishing by Tuesday anyway.

It is most important that this deadline be met, and you should bear in mind that these memoranda must be typed after you finish writing them. Thus, if all of the clerks wait until late Monday or Tuesday morning to do the bulk of their work, or even if each clerk begins his final case early Tuesday afternoon, it is extremely unlikely that the secretary will be able to finish them all in time. The secretary must begin typing cert memos by at least Monday noon, and must be supplied with a steady flow from that time on, if the deadline is to be met. And in weeks where there are 20–25 cases on the list, she should begin typing the memos on Monday morning.

(2) Nature of the Memoranda.

The purpose of these memoranda is to save the Chief Justice's time by enabling him to perceive quickly the character of the case without having to cull through every word of the often poorly drafted petitions and responses. The purpose is not merely to give your opinion on a case, or to identify the cases you believe are most important. Consequently, the memos should be internally complete, i.e., they should be understandable without reference to materials contained in the petitions or responses. The relevant facts should be stated, the issues identified, and the legal arguments of both parties set forth and briefly analyzed. This will enable the Chief Justice to use the "raw material" of the petitions and responses to best advantage.

Check some old memos for the form which is to be used. You will see that the first standard element is a heading which gives (a) the docket number and term; (b) the name of the case; (c) the court to which cert is asked or from which the appeal is taken; (d) a notation as to whether or not the case is timely. The second standard element is a conclusion which contains (a) your recommendation and (b) a citation to the places where the opinions of the lower courts can be found. All memos which are "X DENIED" should begin at the top of the first page. All memos carrying other recommendations should begin in the middle of the first page, so that the Chief Justice will have room at the top to write his conference notes.

Length is variable. Since the memoranda are designed to be time-savers, they should be kept as short as is consistent with a clear and sufficiently complete statement of the case. They may range in length from 1 page on up, depending upon the case. The average memo seems to run about 5 pages. While no effort should be made to comply with any arbitrary page limitation, conciseness should be a constant goal.

b. Miscellaneous Items.

The Conference Lists will contain a variety of miscellaneous items, such as petitions for rehearing, motions to retax cost, etc. A memorandum must be prepared on each of these items also, and the deadline is the same as for cert petitions. On petitions for rehearing, if there is nothing new of any consequence, the standard memo simply says "Nothing new." These memos should not be done until after the cert and appeal memos are completed.

c. Bench Memoranda.

Memoranda on each case set for argument must be completed on the Friday preceding the week in which the case is to be heard. The general purpose of these memos is the same as the purpose of the cert memos, though naturally they normally will be somewhat longer. Again, it is impossible to suggest any page limitation. In very simple cases, the memo may be as short as 6 or 7 pages; but the average memo probably runs about 10–15 pages. You will receive the briefs the week preceding the Friday deadline, and, as with cert memos, it is important that the secretary be able to begin the bench memos immediately on the day after the cert memos are completed, i.e., on Wednesday morning, so that there will not be a typing problem at the end of the week.

2. *The Miscellaneous Docket.*
   a. General.

The Misc. Docket is composed of all *in forma pauperis* (IFP) applications (certs and appeals), and all applications for extraordinary remedies (original habeas corpus, mandamus, etc.).

You will initially process all cases appearing on the Misc. Docket. The files are sent to the Chief Justice's Office each Friday at a rate of about 20–25 per week. To a certain extent, the rate at which they are disposed of by the Court will depend upon the rate at which you process them, since these cases are not listed for Conference until you have finished them. The procedure is set forth in detail below.

b. Mechanics.

There will normally be only one copy of the relevant papers in these cases. When that is true, you will prepare a memorandum which is typed in 11 copies for distribution to each office. Where there *are* 9 copies of each relevant paper (petition, response, and opinion of the lower court), you will prepare a memorandum which states (a) that there are 9 copies of the petition and response which will be distributed with the memorandum, (b) that consequently no memorandum will be prepared by the Office of the Chief Justice, (c) that the file will be in the Office of the Chief Justice, and (d) that the case will be listed for Conference on ———— date. The date will be that of the next scheduled Conference. You will also prepare a full memorandum on such a case for the Chief Justice. Thus, such a 9-copy case is handled in precisely the same way as ordinary certs after the papers are distributed to each office. Consequently, much of the following discussion will not pertain to 9-copy cases. But whatever is said with respect to preparing a case for circulation is applicable, as will be specifically noted.

In Misc. cases, you may make various recommendations to the Chief Justice, which have various consequences:

(1) If your recommendation to the Chief Justice is X Deny, and the Chief Justice so decides, only your memo will circulate to the Court. The file, of course, will be in Mrs. McHugh's office, so that it is available to everyone. If all of the Justices agree, the case will be disposed of at the Friday Conference after the Tuesday circulation of Misc. memos.

(2) If your recommendation is against X Denying the case, and the Chief Justice so decides, the entire file in the case will circulate to each office, and the case will be disposed of when every Justice has seen the file.

(3) If a case appears to have substance (and this includes 9-copy cases) normally you will recommend to the Chief Justice that a response be called for. No memo on such a case is distributed to the Court until the response has been received. There are certain things to bear in mind with respect to call for response memos.

(a) Their purpose is not to discuss the case completely, but rather to indicate to the Chief Justice why a response is warranted. Consequently, you need to set forth only the arguments of petitioner which appear meritorious, and the fact statement need include only those facts which are relevant to those arguments. Such elimination of non-essential material is most desirable because it saves the Chief Justice's time and also the secretary's time.

(b) On the other hand, since normally you will have studied a case thoroughly before you recommend a call for response, you will save yourself time in the long run if you draft a full memo so that, when the response comes in, you need not start from scratch. Before you give this memo to the secretary, then, you should excise the material which is extraneous to a call for response memo.

(c) Some states become irritated by calls for response. Moreover, calls for response naturally involve work for the Clerk's Office. Consequently, it is advisable to keep such memos to a minimum consistent with proper disposition of the cases. This is to say only, however, that a call for response is not the *ordinary* course of action, not that you should avoid recommending such action in any case where you deem it advisable.

(d) One way of saving the states useless labor in responses is, where possible, to limit the request to the issues which may be cert worthy. But when you do this, make absolutely sure that your manner of framing the questions is clear and comprehensive enough so that you will not have to ask for a further response.

(e) Normally, a call for response is a necessary preliminary to circulating a case. However, this is not invariably true. Upon occasion, you may believe that a case appears fairly substantial but that, for one reason or another, it should be circulated without calling for a response. In such a case, you should, at some point in the memo, indicate that no response has been requested. If the Court is interested in the case, the Court will then call for a response after Conference discussion.

(f) If the first response is incomplete in some important respect, you may recommend a call for a further response.

(4) In some cases (including 9-copy cases) you may find that a record is essential for disposition of the case, e.g., where it is necessary to ascertain precisely what the petitioner's habeas corpus allegations were in a lower court. Moreover, a record is normally a prerequisite for affirmative action by the Court. Consequently, you will from time to time recommend calling for a record as well as a response. And where you circulate a case in which a record has not been secured, you should so note in your memorandum.

As has been stated, you will receive about 20–25 Misc. cases a week from the Clerk's Office. The Vacation-Time schedule is the same as for appellate docket cases. During the term, you should make every effort to process 20–25 cases each week and send them to the Chief Justice on Monday. It may be noted parenthetically that the secretary will have to be able to type many of them at the end of the week, since she will have little time on Monday. The Chief Justice will study the cases on Monday night, and those in which the files do not circulate will be disposed of the next Friday at Conference. Also, as has been indicated, all 9-copy cases will be disposed of that Friday. However, the single copy cases in which the file does circulate will not be disposed of until each office has processed the case independently.

Since there are no specific deadlines for completing the memoranda on Misc. cases, there is a tendency to let these cases accumulate. However, you should not permit this to happen, since a backlog at the end of the term makes the Court's work more difficult and prevents prisoners from obtaining a prompt disposition of their petitions. Therefore, you should impose upon yourselves regular deadlines for cleaning up the Misc. docket. The best procedure would be to complete all the cases received on a given week before the following week's cases are distributed. However, it may occasionally be difficult to meet a weekly deadline of this nature during those weeks when bench memos are prepared. Consequently, a certain amount of flexibility will be necessary. This can be achieved if you do as many Misc. cases as is possible every

week, and then catch up on the backlog during the second week of an argument period, which is anon-bench memo week. In this manner, the Misc. docket will be up to date at least once a month.
e. Capital Cases.*

Capital cases are expedited. Those which are received on Thursday must be done by the Monday deadline. They will appear on the Conference List for the following Friday. Always check to see whether a stay has been granted, and when it expires.
f. Business with the Clerk's Office with respect to Misc. cases.

Your principal contact in the Clerk's Office with respect to the Misc. docket will be Mr. Rodak. The Clerk's Office is very cooperative and relations between the law clerks and the Clerk's Office have been excellent.

During the course of the year, it will be necessary at fairly frequent intervals to coordinate the efforts of your office and the Clerk's Office. For example, Mr. Rodak may ask you whether a response which has been requested is sufficiently complete so that the case may be distributed to the Chief Justice's Office for preparation of a memo. The Clerk's Office strongly desires cooperation of this type, and the Chief Justice wants you to extend it. On the other hand, while it is part of your job not to bother the Chief Justice with unimportant administrative details, it is also part of your job not to exercise any authority in areas where the action should be that of the Chief Justice. Putting this in the concrete terms of the example given above, you should give Mr. Rodak your opinion as to whether he should ask the state for additional material *if* this would merely be carrying out the direction of the Chief Justice's original call for response. On the other hand, you should not suggest that Mr. Rodak ask for additional material if this would be in effect calling for a new response. You will have to exercise your judgment in each situation as it arises.
g. Nature of the Memoranda.

Where there are 9 copies of the relevant papers, the memo for the Chief Justice serves precisely the same function as the appellate docket cert memos.

Where your memo is the only memo seen by every Justice, however, your task is somewhat modified. Your primary function

---

* Original document contained no 2.c or 2.d.

is to set forth accurately, as they appear from the papers, the facts, the issues, and the legal arguments which *any* Justice might regard as relevant. Your secondary function is to present the arguments which petitioner *could* make based upon the facts of the case. That is, inasmuch as the IFP petitioners generally do not have counsel, it is necessary for you to be their counsel, in a sense. Your final function is to include whatever evaluation is necessary to focus the attention of the Court, and of other law clerks, upon the most significant aspects of a case.

Your principal difficulties in discharging these functions will arise from the fact that, to some degree, they are conflicting. It is not easy to present an objective-appearing statement of a case in the same memo in which you are acting as petitioner's counsel by figuring out arguments for him while at the same time evaluating the merits of both his and the other party's arguments. And it is very important that your memos not only be objective, but appear to be objective, for otherwise some Justices who might consistently disagree with your evaluations might also be inclined to discount other portions of your memos.

There is a related problem, which arises from the fact that some Justices might not react favorably to consistently evident expressions of the memo writer's views on the merits of the case. As has been indicated, however, your task cannot be performed without some evaluation in order (a) to identify the principal issues and (b) to present the arguments the petitioner could make; and as long as this is kept within reasonable limits, there can be no legitimate objection. But if you frequently exceed this necessary minimum, it is possible that some Justices might regard your work as being affected by "over-advocacy," and this might redound to the disadvantage of the petitioners rather than to their advantage.

The most that can be said in this area, which involves problems mainly of degree, is that you should avoid "over-advocacy" both in your own mind, so that your presentation of the facts and the arguments of *both* sides is not affected by your view of the merits, and in the phrasing of your memorandum. Where this restriction makes it necessary for you to state your own views with more clarity in order to perform your duty as personal clerk to the Chief Justice, you should add an evaluation post-script underneath your recommendation, which, along with your recommendation, will appear only on this office's copies of the memos.

There are certain facts which you should put in every memo, including relevant dates (date of conviction, date of collateral attack, etc.); nature of crime and length of sentence; representation by counsel both at trial and on collateral attack; nature of proceeding (state collateral, state direct, federal collateral, federal direct); previous applications for relief and the issues there raised; timeliness as cert of applications for original habeas.

Finally, a word about the format of the Misc. memos. Memos in cases where there are 9 copies of the relevant papers are prepared in the same way as the appellate docket memos. In cases where you have prepared a memo for the entire Court, the memo should always begin at the top of the first page. If you believe that the case should be discussed by the Conference, you should write the word "CIRCULATE" at the end of the memo. That word, along with your recommendation to the Chief Justice, will appear only on this office's copies of the memo. In cases which are recommended for circulation, the typist should prepare a cover sheet for the Chief Justice's copy of the memo. This cover sheet should contain, at the top of the page, the normal memorandum heading, and the rest of the page should be left blank, since it will be used by the Chief Justice for his conference notes.

B. *Responsibilities of the Chief Clerk.*

1. The Chief Clerk's major responsibility is to administer the work of the office so that it is finished on time.

2. For general purposes, he should keep a complete record in the docket books for the recommendations of all clerks on the various cases and of the final disposition of all cases. He should also check each item on the Conference List when it is sent to Mrs. McHugh to insure that all cases are finished and that all memos are properly marked.

3. Before the Chief Justice gives the orders to the Clerk's Office on Fridays, the Chief Clerk should familiarize himself with the cases that the Conference has discussed so that he may be of assistance to the Chief Justice.

4. In general, the Clerk's Office channelizes its contacts with the law clerks through the Chief Clerk. This type of centralization promotes efficient administration of this office.

5. So far as the other Justices' law clerks are concerned, the Chief Clerk's responsibilities are relatively few. His major job is to arrange luncheons at periodic intervals. The major task in this connection is to secure speakers. There is a file in one of the cabinets which contains past correspondence with invitees which will be of assistance in selecting candidates and in drafting letters. Once a speaker is secured, the Chief Clerk's only remaining task is to inform George Hutchinson of the Marshall's Office sufficiently ahead of time so that the table in the Clerk's dining room will be set, and to circulate a memorandum to the law clerks giving them biographical data on the speaker.

It is customary to have all of the Justices to lunch during the year. The invitations should be extended in order of seniority—though you will no doubt find that acceptances will not come in that order. Justice Frankfurter, for example, may wish to postpone his appearance until the Spring, and Justice Douglas is a hard man to pin down because he leaves the City during so many of the recess periods. Inasmuch as there is always a heavy backlog of work in the Spring, it is advisable to have as many Justices to lunch as possible during the first half of the Term. .

Other traditional guests are the Solicitor General and Dean Acheson. Also, an invitation is always extended to the Attorney General, who may or may not come. Worthwhile speakers during the 1959 Term included Senator Morse, Representative Bowles, Judge Bazelon and Judge Fahy.

The Chief Clerk also arranges football, basketball, and softball games with other groups in the City (usually Covington and Burling and the law clerks from the Court of Appeals,) and takes care of whatever other administrative matters are brought to his attention by other clerks. For the last two years, into the latter category has fallen the job of having a picture of the law clerks taken. Each year the clerks were fortunate to number among them a photographer. In future years, the clerks may want to put the project on a more formalized basis.

C. *Miscellaneous Matters*

1. You will be running on a very tight schedule all year, and will find that you will not have enough time to do as thorough a job as you would like on most cases. You will also find that it is necessary to put in a very long work day every day, and that you will have to do a good deal of work on the weekends.

2. In order to meet your deadlines, it is helpful to set some kind of *average* time limitation for each batch of cases of the various types. After the Term begins, you will have gained enough experience so that you should not spend, on the average, more than one full day per bench memo, more than 3 hours per cert memo, and more than 1½ hours per Misc. memo (excluding capital cases). These averages are very rough, of course, and in any event will be inapplicable to any given case.

3. The greatest source of temptation to let work pile up will be in the area of opinion work, since there you will normally not be working under any strict deadline. Consequently, the Chief Clerk should work out with the other clerks some sort of self-imposed schedule for completing opinion assignments. In general, you should be able to complete a draft for submission to the Chief Justice in two weeks of relatively uninterrupted work. The problem, of course, is to find those weeks somewhere. *If* you are doing your Misc. cases regularly so that there is not a serious jam-up every deadline week, you will have at least two weeks each month in which you will have a "minimal" work load. The ideal system, then, would work out as follows: The Chief Justice will normally take an average of one majority opinion after every argument period. One clerk will be assigned to work on that opinion, and he should be relieved of all responsibility for either Misc. memos or cert memos or bench memos for two relatively free weeks, with the understanding that he will have a draft prepared by the end of that period. It is most important, of course, that the opinion writer keep his end of the "bargain," for otherwise the entire schedule will collapse immediately.

Even if this program were to operate ideally, you would find yourself with opinion work undone, since the Chief Justice will take two opinions after some argument sessions. And, of course, there will be a certain number of dissents to work on. Nonetheless, there will be times during the year, notably the Christmas period and the end of the year, when you will have time to take up the slack.

4. Some hints on opinion work:
   a. You should be particularly careful in this phase of your work, since it is perhaps the most important.
   b. Each law clerk should carefully go over every draft opinion before it is sent to the Chief Justice and contribute what he can in terms of editing and substantive criticism.
   c. You should do a complete source-check on a copy of the final

draft you send to the Chief Justice before you submit it to him. Then, before the final circulation of the printed opinion, you should use your checked draft to check the print.

    d. Use the Reporter's handbook as a reference on questions of form, and, where that source does not provide the answer, the law journals' manual on uniform citations.

    e. Keep together all of the source books which you obtain from the library. The Reporter's Office will collect them after the opinion is handed down. This saves that office the trouble of getting the books from the library. Of course, if the library calls for books, you need not get them back to save them for the Reporter.

    5. You will find the library most helpful in getting you whatever books you need and in doing research of limited types, e.g., finding a state statute covering a particular subject or providing you with the legislative history on a particular act. Of course, if the research bears upon a point which is critical to an opinion, you should check the library's research.

    6. You will frequently need records in cases. You may call for records in appellate docket cases yourself, but do it through your secretary and have her keep a record of those you request and those you return. But when you call for Misc. records, have your secretary do so through Mrs. McHugh so that Mrs. McHugh can keep her records straight.

    7. Never permit the Clerk's Office—or any other office—to send you any papers or borrow any papers directly. All such transactions should be done through Mrs. McHugh, who keeps a complete record of all papers for which the Chief Justice's Office is responsible. It is permissible, of course, for someone like Mr. Rodak to bring a paper up and show it to you, but don't let him get away without taking it with him.

    8. You will find in the office the following important facilities:

    a. Files on all office memos from past years.

    b. An index of relevant cases and memos, mainly bearing on the Misc. cases. This index was begun some time in the past, but apparently was not used. We have added to it this year, and you should supplement the index during the year, for you and your successors will find it a valuable aid.

    c. A card (in your desk) identifying the various responsibilities of the persons in the Clerk's Office, and giving their phone numbers.

9. The Chief Justice wants you to feel entirely free to attend oral argument, and whether you do so in any case is entirely up to you. You will find that the pressure of work will keep you from hearing a number of the arguments.

10. When questions arise—as they will with some frequency—consult Mrs. McHugh.

Appendix B

*Letter from Stephen G. Breyer to
Earl Warren, October 6, 1963*

October 6, 1963

The Chief Justice
The Supreme Court
Washington 25, DC

Sir,

    May I take the liberty of submitting this application for a clerkship with you next year? I am Articles Editor of the *Harvard Law Review* and in my last year at the Harvard Law School. I took my A.B. at Stanford in 1959 and after that spent two years as a Marshall Scholar at Magdalen College, Oxford, where I received first class honors in Philosophy, Politics, and Economics. I plan to return eventually to San Francisco to practice law. I am enclosing a curriculum vitae and would be pleased to arrange for recommendations from faculty members if you desire. Sensible as I am of the honor and opportunity that being your clerk affords, I should greatly appreciate an interview at any time that suits your convenience, though I may add that I plan to be in Washington on October 22 and 23.

Yours faithfully,
Stephen G. Breyer

Stephen G. Breyer to Earl Warren, October 6, 1963, Warren Papers, Box 398.

Appendix C

Letter from John Minor Wisdom to Hugo Black, October 15, 1965

John Minor Wisdom
United States Circuit Judge
Fifth Circuit
New Orleans, Louisiana

October 15, 1965

Dear Mr. Justice Black:

Lamar Alexander, one of my law clerks, is very anxious to clerk for you next year.

All law clerks, of course, are able, attractive fellows with fine records in college and in law school. Lamar is something more. He is clerking for me on a messenger's salary of $3600. (The "Messenger" title is a gimmick to enable us to have two clerks; I had a previous commitment for the other clerkship.)

Lamar was raised in Maryville, Tennessee. In his senior year in High School he was elected Governor of Tennessee's Boys' State and Senator to Boys' Nation. At Vanderbilt Lamar put himself through school but managed to earn his letter in track, edit the college newspaper, and make Phi Beta Kappa and Omicron Delta Kappa (leadership society). At N.Y.U. Law School he was a Root-Tilden scholar and was on the law review. He has written a very fine two-part comment, *En Banc Hearings in the Federal Courts of Appeals: Accommodating Institutional Responsibilities.*

I am glad to say that he has made up his mind to return to Tennessee, practice law, accept an offer to teach (part-time) at the University of Tennessee, and go into politics.

John Minor Wisdom to Hugo Black, October 15, 1965, Black Papers, Box 444.

I recommend Lamar Alexander highly on his ability, character, and record.

With warm personal regards to you and Elizabeth,

Sincerely,
John Wisdom
The Honorable Hugo Black
Supreme Court of the United States
Washington, D.C.

Appendix D

Justice Harry A. Blackmun's Talking Points for Interviewing Prospective Law Clerks

LAW CLERK APPLICANT INTERVIEWS

1. Why does he want a clerkship?
2. Attitudes toward the lower courts.
3. *Military service*
4. What I expect.   *Sal*
5. Hours. *long*   *Roe*
6. Typing.
7. Confidence.   *Salary*
8. Rule 7.
9. No memo or other item leaving the building.
10. Where else applied.
11. Favorite branch of law.
12. No comment about the Justices or their division.
13. Parking. *1 space to a chamber.*
14. Room tidiness.   *Messenger:*
15. Division of work.   *Helps secs*
16. Health.   *Driving*
17. Compatibility   *Volunteer*
18. *2 years.*
19. Dependent on me.
20. *Exposure*
21. *No interviews.*

"Law Clerk Applicant Interviews," undated, Blackmun Papers, Box 1568. Note: Blackmun's handwritten changes are italicized.

22. *lecture–teaching–other?*
23. *Ever in trouble?*
    Travel.
    Bar exams.
    Smoking.
    Get along.

Appendix E

Memorandum from Molly McUsic to Harry A. Blackmun, re: Certiorari Petition, Planned Parenthood v. Casey, January 4, 1992

The prospect of this case being heard has gripped the attention of the outside world, both pro and anti-*Roe* groups. I will briefly describe here the legal and political issues, as I understand them, that are being advanced.

As the poolwriter describes, under the strict scrutiny test that would apply if a woman's right to control her own body were still deemed fundamental, these laws would fail. The State's only interest in most of these provisions is to dissuade women from exercising their constitutional rights, obviously not a compelling interest. Nor are the statutory provisions narrowly tailored to any legitimate state interest, such as the health of the mother. Thus, if *Roe* were still good law, this Pennsylvania law would be unconstitutional. Accordingly, CA3's decision must be viewed as a serious undermining of *Roe*.

However, it is not a complete refutation. Pennsylvania's law still permits a woman to choose an abortion. Although Justice O'Connor's "undue burden" test seems to assume the conclusion, it is preferable to no scrutiny. In other words, things could be worse. Other states such as Louisiana have passed far more offensive laws, and it is likely that any CA5 decision will be less measured and reasonable.

That being said, if this case were not about abortion, it would be a grant. CA3 blatantly refused to follow this Court's decisions, and it is an issue of national importance.

This "Attachment" was given to Justice Blackmun with the original pool memo on Casey. Molly McUsic to Harry A. Blackmun, January 4, 1992, Blackmun Papers, Box 602.

The "political" picture is mixed. The pro-women's groups believe that the Court should hear *Roe* now. Echoing your dissent in *Rust v. Sullivan*, III S.Ct. 1759, 1786 (1991), the petitioners argue that this constant chipping away at the right has "rendered the right's substance nugatory" while technically leaving it intact. *Id.*, at 1786. "This is a course nearly as noxious as overruling *Roe* directly, for if a right is found to be unenforceable, even against flagrant attempts by government to circumvent it, then it ceases to be a right at all." *Id.* If the substance of the right is nearly gone away, the logic goes, better to overturn it directly and gain the political capital.

There is some sense to this position. If you believe that there are enough votes on the Court now to overturn *Roe*, it would be better to do it this year before the election and give women the opportunity to vote their outrage. The only harm would be that *Roe* would be overturned sooner rather than later. While under usual circumstances that harm would be enough to avoid hearing the case for as long as possible, the November Presidential elections may tip the scale in favor of hearing this case.

The advantage of this course, rests on one crucial assumption: the overturning of *Roe* is inevitable, so the only issue is timing. There may also be a possibility that the Court will change again in a *favorable* way before the next case challenging Roe comes up. Assuming DHS sits on the fence and declines to vote to overrule, there are now just 5 votes to do so. But CJ and/or BRW could decide to step down. (BRW has yet to select clerks for next year.) With the worsening economy a new President could also be elected next year, or, even if a new President is not elected, the next appointment to the Court (to fill a seat left open by CJ or BRW) could be moderate enough that he would opt for modifying *Roe* (a la SOC's 'undue burden' approach) rather than outright overruling *Roe*. This scenario is not tremendously likely. But it is also not inconceivable.

In a slightly different vein, I think there are other "political" considerations. The Court's authority is in the long run limited by popular will. The Court can protect people against the popular will for some time, but not forever. Eventually the Court's authority comes from the popular acceptance and understanding of its opinions. *Brown v. Board of Education* is illustrative. Although *Brown* was highly controversial initially and desegregating schools is still hotly debated, *Brown* is popularly accepted. Nobody could win national office or seek Senate confirmation espousing the view that *Brown* was wrongly decided.

Roe is different. *Roe* was initially controversial, but the political support and acceptance did not follow. While the 1950s and *Brown* were followed by a period of greater tolerance in the 1960s, the 1970s and *Roe* were followed by a period of political conservatism and religious fundamentalism. Women, unlike African-Americans were unable to capitalize politically on the justice they gained in the courts. *Roe* has been continually challenged and provided immense political advantage to the Republicans. It is an easy source of fundraising and passion for the right wing.

Perhaps the Court has done all it can do. It protected women for as long as it could against the forces of the majority. Perhaps the only way for women's concerns to gain popular support is for women to take control of their own destiny and become politically empowered. At the same time *Roe* was decided women were disempowered, both economically and politically. Women desperately needed the Court's protection, and the Court courageously and correctly responded. 1991 was a horrific year for women, considering Clarence Thomas and the William Kennedy Smith trial alone, but women indisputably have more power today than they did in 1973.

The end of this Court's roles as both protector and scapegoat may in fact lead to the creation of rights that are rooted in the necessary popular support. Certainly that may not be the result; I fear that women may still be far too disenfranchised, and disempowered to claim their most basic right to physical integrity. But if so, in a real sense this Court is powerless to stop it.

The arguments of the pro-choice groups has appeal to me—the Court is already inhospitable to those without power. Once the CAs start rejecting *Roe* on their own, as CA3 has done here, the harm to women already exists. But the delay in this Court's decision allows the political right to keep focusing on *Roe* to their benefit.

Jeff disagrees, and his position too has appeal. He believes that the advantages of throwing the issue to the voters before the election are ephemeral in comparison to the possibility—by putting off decision now—of preserving *Roe*, or at least a part of it, for the many years to come. To Jeff, the benefits to the women who will be helped by delaying along with the chance that *Roe* might be preserved are too important.

I am not so presumptuous as to offer you any advice on *Roe v. Wade*. I simply offer this description of the various competing views in the hope that it will be of some use.

MM

1/4/92

Appendix F

Memorandum from Stephanie A. Dangel to Harry A. Blackmun, June 26, 1992

Mr. Justice,

I hope you don't feel that we were pressuring you too much on the final section of this opinion. You certainly should not include it if you feel uncomfortable. I thought, however, that it might be helpful to put in writing my views and what I perceive to be JPS' views.

From speaking to JPS' clerk, I gather that his concern is that your ending undermines the attempt by the joint opinion to say "SCt Justices are above politics, Mr. Pres., so why don't you stop trying to influence us." He also thinks it's important to encourage the troika.

I admire what the troika has done, and I think your opinion expresses that admiration. But I find it difficult to believe that this is going to end the politicization of the appointment process—indeed, with the vote at 5–4, I think it highly likely that *Casey* will only push the Pres. to get a commitment to overrule *Roe* from the next nominee.

I can also understand why JPS has done his best to form an alliance with the SOC/AMK/DHS group (although I do not agree with his decision to uphold provisions in this case which he previously has struck down). Like it or not, they are the swing votes on the Court, and therefore they carry a lot of power.

But at some point, on some issues, some people have to end the compromises and perpetuation of myths. Some issues are just too important—abortion is one of them, and like it or not, you are the person American women look to in order to find out what is really happening in this case. I can't help but fear that without that last paragraph

Stephanie A. Dangel to Harry A. Blackmun, June 26 (d), 1992, Blackmun Papers, Box 602.

women are going to think they can rest easy, because *Roe* has been reaffirmed once and for all.

And, quite honestly, this is not just about abortion or this Term. Justices who oppose *Roe* have a constricted view of most liberty interests. And the Justices who get appointed in the next few years are going to make up the Court *for most of my life*!

Finally, while this is completely inappropriate, I cannot help be disappointed with JPS. Not only has he reversed without explanation his position on some of the issues in this case, but he has continued to distance himself from you in other opinions, specifically his last minute failure to join you in *Lucas* and *Sawyer*, when both opinions set out views he previously had put forth himself! I can't help but think that JPS sees that there's power in the middle, and therefore that's where he's moving. In short, I think JPS is taking for granted that you will always be here to make the principled argument, so he's free to go off and build coalitions in the middle.

Regardless of my disappointment with JPS, the important point is that we've already got plenty of Justices in this case willing to compromise and perpetuate myths. The people of America need someone to tell them the truth. And as the author of *Roe*, I think you're the only person who can do it.

Steff

P.S. If you like we can change 83 yrs old to "getting along in years" a la INDOPCO.

Appendix G

United States Supreme Court
Law Clerk Questionnaire

Please respond to each item on this questionnaire by circling the appropriate answer code or writing your answer, although you may skip any item that you do not wish to answer. YOU ARE INVITED TO ADD COMMENTS OR EXPAND UPON ANY ANSWER ON THE BACK OF THIS FORM.

1. What is your gender?
_____ Male   _____ Female

2. What is your race?
_____ Caucasian
_____ African-American
_____ American Indian
_____ Hispanic
_____ Asian
_____ Other (please specify)

3. What is your religious orientation?
_____ Catholic
_____ Protestant
_____ Jewish
_____ Islamic
_____ Buddhist
_____ None
_____ Other (please specify)

4. *At the present time*, do you consider yourself politically to be:
_____ Strong Republican
_____ Moderate Republican

_____ Independent
_____ Moderate Democrat
_____ Strong Democrat
_____ Other (please specify)

5. *When you were a law clerk*, where would you have placed yourself on this political scale?
_____ Extremely liberal
_____ Slightly liberal
_____ Moderate
_____ Slightly conservative
_____ Extremely conservative

6. What years/term did you clerk on the Supreme Court?

7. Which Justice did you clerk for?

8. Did you clerk for another judge before clerking at the Supreme Court?
_____ Yes _____ No

9. What factors regarding your selection as a law clerk do you believe were most important to your justice? Please rank the three most important, with one being the most important.
_____ Prior clerking experience
_____ Law school academic performance
_____ Quality of law school
_____ Similar political views as justice
_____ Recommendation of professor or judge
_____ Rapport with justice during initial interview
_____ Other (please specify)

10. Were you a member of any of these organizations during law school? Please check all that apply.
_____ Law review membership (primary law journal)
_____ Law journal membership (secondary journal)
_____ Student Bar Association or equivalent
_____ Participant in student legal clinic
_____ Moot court participant
_____ Federalist Society

_____ Other policy or political organization (please specify)
_____ Other (please specify)

11. During your interview with the justice for your selection as law clerk, did you discuss policy or political issues?
_____ Yes _____ No

12. If you wrote draft opinions for your justice, please indicate how often your justice revised or modified these draft opinions:
_____ All cases
_____ Most cases
_____ Some cases
_____ Few cases
_____ No cases

13. If the Justice did revise your draft opinions, please indicate when the Justice *substantially* modified or revised the draft opinions (you may check more than one answer):
_____ Landmark or important cases
_____ Cases on a particular issue
_____ All cases
_____ No particular pattern of revision
_____ Other (please specify)

14. How frequently were you able to change your justice's mind about a particular case or issue?
_____ Never
_____ Seldom
_____ Sometimes
_____ Frequently
_____ Always

14a. If you were ever able to change your justice's mind, when would this be most likely occur?
_____ Certiorari decisions
_____ Outcome of a case
_____ Legal, substantive content of an opinion
_____ Stylistic content of an opinion
_____ Other (please specify)

Listed below are a number of factors that may have influenced your justice in his or her decisions regarding cases. Please circle the number indicating what you perceived to have been the importance of each factor *for the Justice* for whom you clerked when deciding cases:

5—very important   4—important   3—moderately important
2—seldom important   1—never important

Persuasiveness of lower court opinion	5	4	3	2	1
Law clerk's research	5	4	3	2	1
Justice's view of what is proper policy	5	4	3	2	1
Specific case facts	5	4	3	2	1
Justice's jurisprudential philosophy	5	4	3	2	1
Other justices' views	5	4	3	2	1
Attorney's oral arguments	5	4	3	2	1
Law clerk's persuasiveness	5	4	3	2	1
Justice's awareness of public sentiment	5	4	3	2	1
Parties' written briefs	5	4	3	2	1
Justice negotiating with other Justices	5	4	3	2	1
Precedent of previous case(s)	5	4	3	2	1

Listed below are a number of statements regarding your role as a clerk on the Court. Please circle the number indicating the degree of agreement with the statement:

5—strongly agree   4—agree   3—neutral   2—disagree   1—strongly disagree

My role as a law clerk was to act as a surrogate (that is, write legal documents just as my justice would) for the Justice at all times.

   5   4   3   2   1

My role as a law clerk was to play devil's advocate (that is, provide opposing viewpoints) when discussing issues with the Justice.

   5   4   3   2   1

My role as a law clerk was to provide the justice with current intellectual and legal ideas that I had just been exposed to at law school.

   5   4   3   2   1

I attempted to draft opinions as if the Justice were writing the opinion himself/herself.

5   4   3   2   1

I sometimes drafted the opinion using language that differed from the Justice.

5   4   3   2   1

The Justice and I often disagreed on the outcomes of cases.

5   4   3   2   1

The Justice and I often disagreed on the format and content of opinions.

5   4   3   2   1

The Justice and I often disagreed on when certiorari should be granted.

5   4   3   2   1

My fellow clerks in my chamber shared the same general political and legal convictions as myself.

5   4   3   2   1

I often attempted to convince the Justice of my position on a case or issue.

5   4   3   2   1

I told the Justice my personal beliefs about a case.

5   4   3   2   1

Certain clerks were more influential than others with the Justice.

5   4   3   2   1

Thank you very much for your participation in this project!

Notes

NOTES TO THE PREFACE

1. Sheldon H. Elsen to Harry A. Blackmun, September 22, 1982, Box 1568, Blackmun Papers.

2. Jim Browning to the Law Clerks, September 29, 1982, Box 1568, Blackmun Papers.

3. See, e.g., G. Edward White, *Alger Hiss's Looking-Glass Wars: The Covert Life of a Soviet Spy* (New York: Oxford University Press, 2004).

4. James McReynolds served as secretary to Howell Jackson when Jackson was a U.S. senator and not after Jackson joined the High Court, as has occasionally been reported.

5. Bernard Schwartz, *Decision: How the Supreme Court Decides Cases* (New York: Oxford University Press, 1996), 48.

6. Bernard Schwartz, *Super Chief: Earl Warren and His Supreme Court* (New York: NYU Press, 1984), 63. For details on the 1963 brunch, see Warren Papers, Box 392.

7. Robert von Mehren Interview, Stanley Forman Reed Oral History Project, University of Kentucky.

8. Tony Mauro, "For Lawyers, Clerkship Is Ultimate Job," *USA Today*, June 5, 1998.

9. Ibid.

10. Schwartz, *Super Chief*, 59.

11. Harry A. Blackmun to Harry M. Caldwell, October 5, 1982, Box 1568, Blackmun Papers.

12. William H. Rehnquist, "2003 Year-End Report on the Federal Judiciary," www.supremecourtus.gov.

13. Donna Murasky to Harry A. Blackmun, August 14, 1976, Box 1564, Blackmun Papers.

14. Lewis F. Powell, Jr., to Eugene J. Comey, Tyler A. Baker, Charles C. Ames, and David A. Martin, June 3, 1977, Powell Papers, Box 130b.

15. Lewis F. Powell to Warren E. Burger, Byron R. White, Harry A. Blackmun, and William H. Rehnquist, June 11, 1974, Blackmun Papers, Box 1374.

16. William H. Rehnquist to Lewis F. Powell, June 8, 1973, Box 1374, Blackmun Papers.

17. Eugene Gressman, "Celebration of the Life of Robert L. Stern," Remarks presented at Sheraton North Shore Hilton, Northbrook, Illinois, June 10, 2000.

18. Lewis F. Powell, Jr., to Eugene J. Comey, Tyler A. Baker, Charles C. Ames, and David A. Martin, September 1976, Powell Papers, Box 130b.

19. *New York v. United States*, 505 U.S. 144 (1992); *Garcia v. San Antonio Metropolitan Transit Authority*, 469 U.S. 528 (1985); *South Carolina v. Baker*, 485 U.S. 505 (1988); Andrea Ward to Harry A. Blackmun, March 27, 1992, Blackmun Papers, Box 600.

20. John T. Rich to Harry A. Blackmun, February 8, 1972, Blackmun Papers, Box 136.

21. Molly McUsic to Harry A. Blackmun, December 20, 1991, Blackmun Papers, Box 586.

22. See, for example, Jeffrey A. Segal and Harold J. Spaeth, *The Supreme Court*

and the Attitudinal Model Revisited (New York: Cambridge University Press, 2002), and Lee Epstein and Jack Knight, *The Choices Justices Make* (Washington, DC: CQ Press, 1997).

23. Bob Woodward and Scott Armstrong, *The Brethren* (New York: Simon and Schuster, 1980); Edward Lazarus, *Closed Chambers: The First Eyewitness Account of the Epic Struggles inside the Supreme Court* (New York: Times Books, 1998).

24. In addition, there is a recent dissertation published on the topic of law clerks: Todd C. Peppers, "Courtiers of the Marble Palace: The Rise of the Supreme Court Law Clerk," diss., Emory University, 2003.

25. John B. Oakley and Robert S. Thompson, *Law Clerks and the Judicial Process: Perceptions and Functions of Law Clerks in American Courts* (Berkeley: University of California Press, 1980).

26. H. W. Perry, *Deciding to Decide: Agenda Setting in the United States Supreme Court* (Cambridge: Harvard University Press, 1991).

27. Ibid., 69.

28. Bradley J. Best, *Law Clerks, Support Personnel, and the Decline of Consensual Norms on the United States Supreme Court, 1935–1995* (New York: LFB Scholarly Publishing, 2002).

29. Toward this end, there have been a number of important articles that have furthered our understanding of certain aspects of clerking at the U.S. Supreme Court, the role of clerks on lower U.S. courts, and law clerks outside the United States. See, e.g., Stephen L. Wasby, "Clerking for an Appellate Judge: A Close Look," presented at the annual meeting of the Midwest Political Science Association, Chicago, IL, April 3–6, 2003; Corey Ditslear and Lawrence Baum, "Selection of Law Clerks and Polarization in the U.S. Supreme Court," *Journal of Politics* 63 (2001): 869; Lorne Sossin, "The Sounds of Silence: Law Clerks, Policy Making, and the Supreme Court of Canada," *University of British*

Columbia Law Journal 30 (1996): 279; Charles H. Sheldon, "The Evolution of Law Clerking with the Washington Supreme Court: From 'Elbow Clerks' to 'Puisne Judges,'" *Gonzaga Law Review* 24 (1988/89): 45; Charles H. Sheldon, "Law Clerking with a State Supreme Court: Views from the Perspective of the Personal Assistants to the Judges," *Justice System Journal* 6 (1981): 346; Arthur D. Hellman, "Central Staff in Appellate Courts: The Experience of the Ninth Circuit," *California Law Review* 68 (1980): 937.

30. *Planned Parenthood v. Casey*, 505 U.S. 833 (1992).

31. Of the initial sample of six hundred, there were 579 valid addresses. Five surveys were returned by clerks who did not work at the Supreme Court but instead clerked on lower U.S. courts. We received 160 completed or partially completed surveys out of 574, for a response rate of 28 percent and a margin of error of +/- 7.33 percent, at a 95 percent confidence interval.

32. It should also be pointed out that our data includes responses from only twelve former clerks who worked at the Court after the Code of Conduct was established.

33. Tony Mauro, "For Lawyers, Clerkship Is Ultimate Job," *USA Today*, June 5, 1998.

34. Harry A. Blackmun "Note for the File," February 28, 1984, Blackmun Papers, Box 1553.

35. Alex Kozinski, "Conduct Unbecoming," *Yale Law Journal* 108 (1999): 845 n.47.

36. William H. Rehnquist to the Conference, March 5, 1993, Blackmun Papers, Box 1374.

37. Embry technically "resigned" after the Court found out that he took part in a scheme to garner stock market profits based on information in the case of *United States v. Southern Pacific Co.*, 251 U.S. 1 (1919). See, e.g., John B. Owens, "The Clerk, the Thief, His Life as a Baker: Ash-

ton Embry and the Supreme Court Leak Scandal of 1919," *Northwestern University Law Review* 95 (2000): 271; David J. Garrow, "Book Review—'The Lowest Form of Animal Life'? Supreme Court Clerks and Supreme Court History," *Cornell Law Review* 84 (March 1999): 859; Drew Pearson and Robert S. Allen, *The Nine Old Men* (Garden City, NY: Doubleday, Doran, 1936), 40.

38. Dennis J. Hutchinson and David J. Garrow, eds., *The Forgotten Memoir of John Knox* (Chicago: University of Chicago Press, 2002), 85.

39. Warren E. Burger to the Conference, March 25, 1971, Harlan Papers, Box 490.

40. Warren E. Burger to Potter Stewart and William H. Rehnquist, March 5, 1973, Powell Papers, Box 130b.

41. Lewis F. Powell, Jr., to William C. Kelly, Jr., March 6, 1973, Powell Papers, Box 130b.

42. Harry A. Blackmun to Warren E. Burger, July 18, 1974, Blackmun Papers, Box 1568.

43. Lewis F. Powell, Jr., to Eugene J. Comey, Tyler A. Baker, Charles C. Ames, and David A. Martin, September 1976, Powell Papers, Box 130b.

44. Lewis F. Powell to Law Clerks, Secretaries, and Messenger, April 27, 1977, Powell Papers, Box 130b.

45. Samuel Estreicher to Paul B. Stephan, III, Eric G. Andersen, James Bruce Boisture, and David L. Westin, July 21, 1978, Powell Papers, Box 130b.

46. Justice Powell's files show that he spoke with Woodward, Powell Papers, Box 136. Justice Blackmun's files reveal that he spoke in person with Scott Armstrong on July 6, 1978, and September 15, 1978, Shirley A. Bartlett to Harry A. Blackmun, June 30, 1978, September 15, 1978, Blackmun Papers, Box 1435. Also, Armstrong spoke with numerous former Blackmun clerks without any objection from Blackmun, though he did make sure his former clerks were informed "not [to] underestimate him," see, e.g., Shirley A. Bartlett to Harry A. Blackmun, July 7, 1978, Black-

mun Papers, Box 1435. David Garrow has concluded that the other two justices to speak with Woodward and Armstrong were Rehnquist and White. David J. Garrow, "The Supreme Court and *The Brethren*," *Constitutional Commentary* 18 (Summer 2001): 55.

47. Lewis F. Powell, Jr., to James D. Alt, December 12, 1979, Powell Papers, Box 129a.

48. Lewis F. Powell, Jr., to the Conference, December 31, 1979, Blackmun Papers, Box 1435.

49. Harry A. Blackmun to C. Stanley McMahon, March 26, 1980, Blackmun Papers, Box 1435.

50. Warren E. Burger to the Conference, June 18, 1979, Blackmun Papers, Box 1568. On Burger's nearly identical 1984 memo, Blackmun wrote "Pure defensiveness." Warren E. Burger to the Conference, June 8, 1984, Box 1568, Blackmun Papers.

51. Bob Carlson, "Ex-Clerks Downplay *The Brethren*," *Virginia Law Weekly*, February 1, 1980, 1.

52. Ibid.

53. Ibid.

54. Lewis F. Powell, Jr., to David F. Levi, Richard H. Fallon, John S. Wiley, Jr., and Mary Ellen Becker, June 28, 1982, Powell Papers, Box 130b.

55. William H. Rehnquist to the Law Clerks, September 21, 1988, Blackmun Papers, Box 1568.

56. Code of Conduct for Law Clerks of the Supreme Court of the United States, Canon 2, 3(C), 1989. The code is largely based on the more general Judicial Conference's Code of Conduct for Law Clerks, which was adopted March 13, 1981, Blackmun Papers, Box 1553. Justices Brennan, White, and O'Connor were appointed to draft the code. Their initial draft was revised to incorporate suggestions by Chief Justice Rehnquist and Justice Stevens, resulting in the final document, Blackmun Papers, Box 1568. See also Alex Kozinski, "Conduct Unbecoming," *Yale Law Journal* 108 (1999): 835, 843.

57. Blackmun Papers, Box 1405.

58. William H. Rehnquist to the Conference, December 1, 1993, Blackmun Papers, Box 1568.

59. William H. Rehnquist to the Law Clerks, December 10, 1993, Blackmun Papers, Box 1568.

60. *Bush v. Gore*, 531 U.S. 98 (2000); David Margolick, Evgenia Peretz, and Michael Shnayerson, "The Path to Florida," *Vanity Fair*, October 2004, 310–23, 355–67, 369.

61. See, e.g., Charles Lane, "In Court Clerks' Breach, a Provocative Precedent," *Washington Post*, October 17, 2004, D01.

62. Wanda Martinson to Harry A. Blackmun, September 10, 1979, Box 1568, Blackmun Papers.

63. Because there are so many first-person accounts, we have not attempted to incorporate every recollection in this book. Instead, we have used many such accounts to help explicate our data and generally illustrate the historical development of the institution. For a discussion of all past accounts, see David J. Garrow, "Book Review—'The Lowest Form of Animal Life'? 855. Garrow's review covers Edward Lazarus, *Closed Chambers: The First Eyewitness Account of the Epic Struggles inside the Supreme Court* (New York: Times Books, 1998), and Dennis J. Hutchinson, *The Man Who Once Was Whizzer White: A Portrait of Justice Byron R. White* (New York: Free Press, 1998).

64. Tony Mauro, "Corps of Clerks Lacking in Diversity," *USA Today*, June 5, 1998.

65. Karen Nelson Moore to Harry A. Blackmun, October 10, 1975, Box 1563, Blackmun Papers.

66. Paul W. Cane, Jr., to Lewis F. Powell, Jr., October 23, 1981, Powell Papers, Box 129a.

67. Lewis F. Powell, Jr., to Paul W. Cane, Jr., October 27, 1981, Powell Papers, Box 129a.

68. From interview correspondence with authors.

69. This is certainly true when compared to former clerk authors such as Edward Lazarus, who reaped some measure of fame and fortune with their published accounts.

NOTES TO CHAPTER 1

1. See, for example, Bradley J. Best, *Law Clerks, Support Personnel, and the Decline of Consensual Norms on the United States Supreme Court, 1935–1995* (New York: LFB Scholarly Publishing, 2002); Dennis J. Hutchinson and David Garrow, eds., *The Forgotten Memoir of John Knox: A Year in the Life of a Supreme Court Clerk in FDR's Washington* (Chicago: University of Chicago Press, 2002); Edward Lazarus, *Closed Chambers: The First Eyewitness Account of the Epic Struggles inside the Supreme Court* (New York: Times Books, 1998); Bernard Schwartz, *Decision: How the Supreme Court Decides Cases* (New York: Oxford University Press, 1996); Alex Kozinski, "Making the Case for Law Clerks," *The Long Term View* 3 (1995): 55.

2. See, for example, Chester A. Newland, "Personal Assistants to Supreme Court Justices: The Law Clerks," *Oregon Law Review* 40 (1961): 299; Best, *Law Clerks, Support Personnel, and the Decline of Consensual Norms*.

3. For a discussion of the development of law clerks on the lower federal courts, see J. Daniel Mahoney, "The Second Circuit Review—1986–1987 Term: Foreword: Law Clerks: For Better or for Worse?" *Brooklyn Law Review* 54 (1988): 321.

4. See, e.g., Rogers Smith, "Political Jurisprudence, the 'New Institutionalism,' and the Future of Public Law," *American Political Science Review* 82 (1988): 89; Karen Orren and Stephen Skowronek, "Beyond the Iconography of Order: Notes for a 'New' Institutionalism," in *The Dynamics of American Politics: Approaches and Interpretations*, Lawrence C. Dodd and Calvin Jillson, eds. (Boulder, CO: Westview Press, 1994); Howard Gillman, "The New Institutionalism, Part I," *Law and Courts* (Winter 1996–97): 6.

5. Stephen Skowronek, "Order and Change," *Polity* 28 (1995): 94.

6. David L. Weiden, "Law Clerks," in *Legal Systems of the World*, Herbert Kritzer, ed. (Santa Barbara, CA: ABC-CLIO Publishers, 2002); David L. Weiden, "The New Institutionalism and the Supreme Court Law Clerk: Notes for a Theory," presented at the American Political Science Association annual meeting, 1998.

7. For a discussion of the impetus for the Law Clerk Manual, see the Memorandum from the Administrative Assistant to the Chief Justice to the Conference, June 12, 1992, Blackmun Papers, Box 1568.

8. Elder Witt, *Guide to the U.S. Supreme Court*, 2nd ed. (Washington, DC: CQ Press, 1990), 769.

9. Newland, "Personal Assistants to Supreme Court Justices," 301.

10. Act of Aug. 4, 1886, ch. 902, 24 Stat. 222.

11. Paul R. Baier, "The Law Clerks: Profile of an Institution," *Vanderbilt Law Review* 26 (1973): 1132; see also Todd C. Peppers, "Courtiers of the Marble Palace: The Rise of the Supreme Court Law Clerk," diss., Emory University, 2003.

12. See, e.g., Richard R. Nelson and Sidney G. Winter, *An Evolutionary Theory of Economic Change* (Cambridge: Harvard University Press, 1985).

13. A. A. Berle, Jr., "Legal Profession and Legal Education," in *The Legal Profession: Responsibility and Regulation*, Geoffrey C. Hazard, Jr., and Deborah L. Rhode, eds. (Westbury, NY: Foundation Press, 1933), 9.

14. Lawrence Friedman, *A History of American Law* (New York: Simon and Schuster, 1973).

15. Robert Stevens, *Law School: Legal Education from the 1850s to the 1980s* (Chapel Hill: University of North Carolina Press, 1983), 3.

16. Ibid., 11.

17. Ibid., 7.

18. Melvin I. Urofsky, *A March of Liberty: A Constitutional History of the United States* (New York: Knopf, 1988), 508.

19. Samuel Williston, "Horace Gray," in *Great American Lawyers*, William Draper Lewis, ed. (Philadelphia: Winston, 1907–1909; South Hackensack, NJ: Rothman Reprints, 1971), 137, 158–59.

20. Joan Biskupic and Elder Witt, *The Supreme Court at Work*, 2nd ed. (Washington, DC: CQ Press, 1997), 179.

21. Newland, "Personal Assistants to Supreme Court Justices," 306.

22. John M. Landis to Hugo L. Black, February 15, 1938, Black Papers, Box 442.

23. Ibid.

24. Edward S. Widdifield to Hugo L. Black, August 12, 1937, Black Papers, Box 442.

25. Nield's tenure was Justice White's response to Chief Justice Burger's 1974 proposal that each member of the Court have one permanent clerk. But because a majority of the justices was strongly opposed, no institutional change took place. Henry J. Abraham, *The Judicial Process*, 3rd ed. (New York: Oxford University Press, 1975), 241.

26. Alexander Bickel, *The Judiciary and Responsible Government: 1910–1921* (New York: Macmillan, 1964), 82.

27. Williston, "Horace Gray"; John B. Oakley and Robert S. Thompson, "Law Clerks in Judges' Eyes: Tradition and Innovation in the Use of Legal Staff by American Judges," *California Law Review* 67 (1979): 1286.

28. Leonard Baker, *Brandeis and Frankfurter: A Dual Biography* (New York: Harper and Row, 1984), 131.

29. 41 Stat. 209, July 19, 1919.

30. Dean Acheson, "Recollections of Service with the Federal Supreme Court," *Alabama Lawyer* 18 (1957): 355.

31. Baker, *Brandeis and Frankfurter*, 197.

32. Silas Bent, *Justice Oliver Wendell Holmes: A Biography* (Garden City, NY: Garden City Publishing, 1932), 306.

33. 281 U.S. 389 (1930).

34. Bent, *Justice Oliver Wendell Holmes*, 306.

35. Dennis J. Hutchinson and David Garrow, eds., *The Forgotten Memoir of John Knox* (Chicago: University of Chicago Press, 2002), 86.

36. Hugo L. Black to Rev. C. B. Arendall, December 13, 1937, Black Papers, Box 442.

37. Hugo L. Black to M. B. Grace, June 6, 1944, Black Papers, Box 442.

38. www.uscourts.gov, Federal Law Clerk Information System.

39. William O. Douglas to Harry W. Jones, November 5, 1965, Douglas Papers, Box 1102.

40. Hugo L. Black to Howard R. Sack, March 11, 1948, Black Papers, Box 442.

41. Robert von Mehren Interview, Stanley Forman Reed Oral History Project, University of Kentucky.

42. Newland, "Personal Assistants to Supreme Court Justices."

43. "Chief Justice Vinson and His Law Clerks," *Northwestern Law Review* 49 (1954): 27.

44. Bernard Schwartz and Stephan Lesher, *Inside the Warren Court: 1953–1969* (Garden City, NY: Doubleday, 1983), 38–39.

45. Memorandum of Mr. Justice Frankfurter on In Forma Pauperis Petitions, November 1, 1954, Warren Papers, Box 399.

46. Schwartz and Lesher, *Inside the Warren Court*, 39.

47. F. Aley Allen Interview, Stanley Forman Reed Oral History Project, University of Kentucky.

48. David M. O'Brien, *Storm Center: The Supreme Court in American Politics*, 2nd ed. (New York: Norton, 1990).

49. Arthur Rosett Interview, Stanley Forman Reed Oral History Project, University of Kentucky.

50. Bernard Schwartz, *Decision: How the Supreme Court Decides Cases* (New York: Oxford University Press, 1996), 52.

51. John T. Rich to Harry A. Blackmun, February 19, 1972, Blackmun Papers, Box 139.

52. Barbara Gamarekian, "O'Connor's Agonizing Search for Law Clerks," *New York Times*, November 3, 1989, B7.

53. See, e.g., Lewis F. Powell, Jr., to Larry G. Alexander, July 18, 1973, Powell Papers, Box 130b.

54. Stuart Taylor, Jr., "When High Court's Away, Clerks' Work Begins," *New York Times*, Sept. 23, 1988, B7.

55. *Plessy v. Ferguson*, 163 U.S. 537 (1896); O'Brien, *Storm Center*, 162.

56. O'Brien, *Storm Center*, 168.

57. Baker, *Brandeis and Frankfurter*, 415.

58. Ibid., 416.

59. Charles Nesson, "Mr. Justice Harlan," *Harvard Law Review* 85 (1971): 390.

60. O'Brien, *Storm Center*, 161.

61. Transcriptions of conversations between Justice William O. Douglas and Professor Walter F. Murphy, Cassette No. 14: April 5, 1963, Princeton University Library, 1981.

62. The data compiled by Palmer and Brenner illustrate this effect. After Vinson began equalizing opinion assignment, the Court's slowest opinion writers actually finished their opinions more quickly. Frankfurter went from 104 days to seventy-seven, Burton from ninety-nine days to seventy-three, and Vinson from ninety-nine to seventy-five. Though the authors argue that this was due to the criticism by Douglas that the process was taking too long, we suggest it is probably the result of the rise of equality in opinion assignment and the resultant increased role of law clerks in opinion writing by these justices. Jan Palmer and Saul Brenner, "The Time Taken to Write Opinions as a Determinant of Opinion Assignments," *Judicature* 72 (1988): 183.

63. Lewis F. Powell, Jr., to Hamilton Fox, Lawrence A. Hammond, Covert Parnell, and J. Harvie Wilkinson, III, April 25, 1972, Powell Papers, Box 130b.

64. *Regents of the University of California v. Bakke*, 438 U.S. 265 (1978);

DeFunis v. Odegaard, 416 U.S. 312 (1974); *Lafayette v. Louisiana Power and Light Co.*, 435 U.S. 389 (1978); Robert D. Comfort to Lewis F. Powell, Jr., February 8, 1978, Powell Papers, Box 46.

65. The Supreme Court's decision to create permanent staff attorney units was modeled on the staff attorneys who worked at the U.S. courts of appeals and at state high courts. See, for example, John B. Oakley and Robert S. Thompson, *Law Clerks and the Judicial Process: Perceptions and Functions of Law Clerks in American Courts* (Berkeley: University of California Press, 1980); Arthur D. Hellman, "Central Staff in Appellate Courts: The Experience of the Ninth Circuit," *California Law Review* 68 (1980): 937; Charles H. Sheldon, "Law Clerking with a State Supreme Court: Views from the Perspective of the Personal Assistants to the Judges," *Justice System Journal* 6 (1981): 346; Charles H. Sheldon, "The Evolution of Law Clerking with the Washington Supreme Court: From 'Elbow Clerks' to 'Puisne Judges,'" *Gonzaga Law Review* 24 (1988/89): 45.

66. See, e.g., William H. Rehnquist, "Who Writes Decisions of the Supreme Court," *U.S. News and World Report*, December 13, 1957; Newland, "Personal Assistants to Supreme Court Justices"; Alexander Bickel, *Politics and the Warren Court* (New York: Harper and Row, 1965); Bob Woodward and Scott Armstrong, *The Brethren* (New York: Simon and Schuster, 1980); Joseph Vining, "Justice, Bureaucracy, and Legal Method," *Michigan Law Review* 80 (1981): 248; Harry T. Edwards, "A Judge's View on Justice, Bureaucracy, and Legal Method," *Michigan Law Review* 80 (1981): 248; William H. Rehnquist, *The Supreme Court: How It Was, How It Is* (New York: Morrow, 1987); Alex Kozinski, "Making the Case for Law Clerks," *The Long Term View* 3 (1995): 55; Richard A. Posner, *The Federal Courts: Challenge and Reform* (Cambridge: Harvard University Press, 1996).

67. John Oakley, "Defining the Limits of Delegation," *The Long Term View* 3 (1995): 86.

68. O'Brien, *Storm Center*, 322.

69. Earl Warren to Herbert Wechsler, December 12, 1955, Warren Papers, Box 387.

70. Lewis F. Powell to Warren E. Burger, September 11, 1974, Blackmun Papers, Box 1374.

71. Gamarekian, "O'Connor's Agonizing Search for Law Clerks."

72. Robert von Mehren Interview, Stanley Forman Reed Oral History Project, University of Kentucky.

73. Drew Pearson and Robert S. Allen, *The Nine Old Men* (Garden City, NY: Doubleday, Doran, 1936), 178.

74. Lewis F. Powell, Jr., "An Overburdened Supreme Court," remarks to the Fourth Circuit Judicial Conference, June 30, 1972, 10; Blackmun Papers, Box 1406.

75. Lewis F. Powell, Jr., to Samuel E. Gates, October 3, 1972, Powell Papers, Box 129a.

76. Lewis F. Powell, Jr., to Eugene J. Comey, Tyler A. Baker, Charles C. Ames, and David A. Martin, September 1976, Powell Papers, Box 130b.

77. Gamarekian, "O'Connor's Agonizing Search for Law Clerks."

78. See, e.g., Sally J. Kenney, "Puppeteers or Agents? What Lazarus's Closed Chambers Adds to our Understanding of Law Clerks at the U.S. Supreme Court," *Law and Social Inquiry* (Winter 2000): 185.

79. Saul Brenner, "The Memos of Supreme Court Law Clerk William Rehnquist: Conservative Tracts, or Mirrors of His Justice's Mind?" *Judicature* 76.2 (August/September 1992): 77, 81.

80. Ibid., 77.

81. Lewis F. Powell, Jr., to James D. Alt, September 15, 1976, Powell Papers, Box 129a.

82. *Regents of the University of California v. Bakke*, 438 U.S. 265 (1978); Robert D. Comfort to Lewis F. Powell, Jr., August 29, 1977, Powell Papers, Box 46.

NOTES TO CHAPTER 2

1. See, e.g., Robert M. Agostini and Brian P. Corrigan, "Do As We Say or Do As We Do? How the Supreme Court Law Clerk Controversy Reveals a Lack of Accountability at the High Court," *Hofstra Labor and Employment Law Journal* 18 (Spring 2001): 625; Mark R. Brown, "Gender Discrimination in the Supreme Court's Clerkship Selection Process," *Oregon Law Review* 75 (1996): 359; Tony Mauro, "Corps of Clerks Lacking in Diversity," *USA Today*, June 5, 1998.

2. Barbara Gamarekian, "O'Connor's Agonizing Search for Law Clerks," *New York Times*, November 3, 1989, B7.

3. Harry A. Blackmun to Bruce A. Brown, October 13, 1976, Box 1568, Blackmun Papers.

4. Interview notes on Tyler Baker, August 6, 1975, Powell Papers, Box 129a.

5. Gamarekian, "O'Connor's Agonizing Search for Law Clerks."

6. Howard is a traditionally African-American university. Thurgood Marshall earned his law degree there, but Howard has had only one Supreme Court law clerk in its history. Tony Mauro, "Corps of Clerks Lacking in Diversity," *USA Today*, June 5, 1998.

7. Not all justices hire this far in advance. For example, over a year after he received their letters, Justice Harry Blackmun typically wrote recommenders, "A long time ago you wrote a letter in warm support of the application of Michelle Alexander for a clerkship here for October Term 1993. I defer my appointments until late, because I wish to have input from the judges for whom the applicants are presently working." Letter from Harry A. Blackmun to Thomas C. Grey, May 10, 1993, Blackmun Papers, Box 1553. For a detailed analysis of the federal law clerk hiring process, based on survey responses from judges, clerks, and law students, see Christopher Avery, Christine Jolls, Richard Posner, and Alvin E. Roth, "The Market for Federal Judicial Law Clerks," *University of Chicago Law Review* 68 (Summer 2001): 793. It is also important to note that there has been a new trend on the part of some justices to hire more experienced attorneys as clerks. For example, Justice Ginsburg selected 52-year-old William Hodes, a professor at Indiana University School of Law, to be one of her clerks in 1996. See, e.g., Ken Myers, "Law Professor Opens New Book: Clerking for U.S. Supreme Court," *The National Law Journal*, April 22, 1996, A20; Ellen Wayne, "It's Not Too Late to Clerk," *The National Law Journal*, December 10, 2001, B14.

8. Michelle Alexander to Harry A. Blackmun, undated, received March 6, 1992, Blackmun Papers, Box 1553.

9. Robert M. Lubin to William O. Douglas, October 21, 1971, Douglas Papers, Box 1102.

10. Hugo L. Black to Robert O. Lesher, June 29, 1949, Black Papers, Box 442.

11. Wesley A. Sturges to Hugo L. Black, November 26, 1947, Black Papers, Box 442.

12. Hugo L. Black to Wesley A. Sturges, November 28, 1947, Black Papers, Box 442.

13. Black Papers, Box 443.

14. Warren Papers, Box 387.

15. Warren Papers, Box 390.

16. Douglas Papers, Box 444.

17. Black Papers, Box 446.

18. Hugo L. Black to John K. McNulty, October 30, 1968, Black Papers, Box 446.

19. Harlan Papers, Box 559.

20. William O. Douglas to Neil Robblee, November 13, 1971, Douglas Papers, Box 1102.

21. Harry A. Blackmun to George T. Frampton, May 15, 1974, Blackmun Papers, Box 1568.

22. Lewis F. Powell, Jr., to Dallin H. Oaks, June 30, 1977, Powell Papers, Box 129a.

23. Gamarekian, "O'Connor's Agonizing Search for Law Clerks."

24. Stephen M. Tennis to Thurgood Marshall, October 25, 1967, Marshall Papers, Box 571.

25. John K. McNulty to Hugo L. Black, October 16, 1968, Black Papers, Box 446.

26. Joan Biskupic, "Clerks Gain Status, Clout in the Temple of Justice," *Washington Post*, January 2, 1994, A23.

27. Paul R. Dean to Earl Warren, November 9, 1966, Warren Papers, Box 390.

28. Thomas C. Grey to Thurgood Marshall, October 18, 1967, Marshall Papers, Box 571.

29. "Nancy J. Bregstein Memorandum on Interview," September 9, 1976, Powell Papers, Box 129a.

30. John Greenya, "Super Clerks," *Washington Lawyer* 6 (May–June 1992): 40.

31. Tony Mauro, "Corps of Clerks Lacking in Diversity," *USA Today*, June 5, 1998.

32. Debra M. Strauss, *Behind the Bench: The Guide to Judicial Clerkships* (Chicago: BarBri Group, 2002), 199.

33. Blackmun Papers, Box 1562.

34. Strauss, *Behind the Bench*, 199.

35. Louis H. Pollak to Hugo L. Black, October 21, 1968, Black Papers, Box 446.

36. John Marshall Harlan, II, to William J. Brennan, October 2, 1956, Harlan Papers, Box 554.

37. Lewis F. Powell, Jr., to Warren E. Burger, September 28, 1984, Powell Papers, Box 129.

38. Harlan selected Prettyman for the 1954 Term. Bill Matteson to John Marshall Harlan, II, November 8, 1954, Harlan Papers, Box 553.

39. Mike Wishnie to Harry A. Blackmun, March 15, 1996, Blackmun Papers, Box 1567.

40. Ibid.

41. In one instance, after reviewing files, each current clerk wrote his or her initials on the corner of the file folder. See, e.g., file for Mary F. Becker, Powell Papers, Box 129a. See also Notes on "Robert D. Comfort, Memorandum on Interview," Powell Papers, Box 129a.

42. Lewis F. Powell, Jr., to Paul B. Stephan, III, June 12, 1981, Powell Papers, Box 129a.

43. Notes on interview with "Eugene Comey," June 11, 1975, Powell Papers, Box 129a.

44. Lewis F. Powell, Jr., to David R. Boyd, Julia P. Clark, and Ronald G. Carr, August 21, 1974, Powell Papers, Box 130b.

45. Lewis F. Powell, Jr., to David F. Levi, Richard H. Fallon, John S. Wiley, Jr., and Mary Ellen Becker, June 2, 1982, Powell Papers, Box 130b.

46. Julian Burke Interview, Stanley Forman Reed Oral History Project, University of Kentucky.

47. Lewis F. Powell, Jr., to Eugene J. Comey, Tyler A. Baker, Charles C. Ames, and David A. Martin, June 3, 1977, Powell Papers, Box 130b.

48. Morrison did interview with Blackmun and was selected as one of his clerks for the 1985 Term. Wanda Martinson phone conversation notes, "Re: Helane Morrison–clerkship applicant," January 31, 1985, Blackmun Papers, Box 1563.

49. Though Justice Blackmun did not respond to Streisinger's request, she was eventually interviewed and selected for the 1982 Term. Wannett Smith Ogden to Harry A. Blackmun, undated, Blackmun Papers, Box 1566.

50. Dennis J. Hutchinson and David J. Garrow, eds., *The Forgotten Memoir of John Knox* (Chicago: University of Chicago Press, 2002), 56.

51. Felix Frankfurter to John Marshall Harlan, II, December 7, 1956, Harlan Papers, Box 553.

52. William O. Douglas to Lino A. Graglia, January 4, 1956, Douglas Papers, Box 1101.

53. William O. Douglas to Michael D. DeVito, November 18, 1964, Douglas Papers, Box 1101. Douglas first delegated the selection to Max Radin and upon his death recruited Sparrowe for the task. William O. Douglas to Harry W. Jones, November 5, 1965, Douglas Papers, Box 1102. Following Sparrowe, a three-person committee of ex-clerks, including Jerome B. Falk, former clerk to Justice Abe Fortas,

and ex-Douglas clerks Charles Ares and William Cohen, took on the assignment. William O. Douglas to Lee Kanon Alpert, December 13, 1971, Douglas Papers, Box 1102; William O. Douglas to Regina McGranery, November 26, 1971, Douglas Papers, Box 1102; Nan Burgess to Raymond A. Diaz, September 14, 1972, Douglas Papers, Box 1102; William O. Douglas to Michael E. Stevenson, January 3, 1972, Douglas Papers, Box 1102.

54. William O. Douglas to Tom Triplett, June 13, 1964, Douglas Papers, Box 1101.

55. See Warren Papers, Box 389.

56. Bernard Schwartz and Stephan Lesher, *Inside the Warren Court: 1953–1969* (Garden City, NY: Doubleday, 1983), 43–44.

57. Earl Warren to William E. Orr, September 17, 1961, Warren Papers, Box 388.

58. Earl Warren to Fred L. Biester, November 16, 1961, Warren Papers, Box 388.

59. See, e.g., Warren Papers, Box 398.

60. Earl Warren to Arthur M. Sammis, September 2, 1966, Warren Papers, Box 390.

61. Earl Warren to Samuel D. Thurman, January 23, 1967, Warren Papers, Box 390. Prior to Heyman and Steinman, Warren enlisted the help of Thurman and Adrian Kragen for the West Coast committee. See Samuel D. Thurman to Earl Warren, January 17, 1967, Warren Papers, Box 390. The Washington, D.C., committee was composed of former Warren clerks Murray H. Bring and William H. Dempsey, Jr. See for example, Walter E. Dellinger to William H. Dempsey, Jr., November 8, 1967, and Murray H. Bring to William H. Dempsey, Jr., January 8, 1971, Warren Papers, Box 392.

62. On the number of interviews, see, e.g., Lewis F. Powell, Jr., to Walter J. Blum, April 7, 1980, Powell Papers, Box 129a; Lewis F. Powell, Jr., to Mary E. Becker, September 13, 1984, Powell Papers, Box 129a.

63. Handwritten notation, Lewis F.

Powell, Jr., to Charles C. Ames, May 31, 1975, Powell Papers, Box 129a.

64. Lewis F. Powell, Jr., to Samuel E. Gates, October 3, 1972, Powell Papers, Box 129a.

65. "James D. Alt, Memorandum on Interview," September 2, 1976, Powell Papers, Box 129a.

66. Gamarekian, "O'Connor's Agonizing Search for Law Clerks."

67. Ibid.

68. Harry A. Blackmun to Betty B. Fletcher, April 28, 1981, Blackmun Papers, Box 1566.

69. John E. Nolan, Jr., to Earl Warren, February 15, 1955, Warren Papers, Box 387.

70. William S. Eggeling to William O. Douglas, September 27, 1974, Douglas Papers, Box 1103.

71. Thomas F. Bergin to William O. Douglas, September 13, 1974, Douglas Papers, Box 1103.

72. There was even some nepotism in early clerk selection. Justice John Marshall Harlan's first clerk was his son, John Maynard Harlan. Another of Harlan's sons, James S. Harlan, clerked for Chief Justice Melville Weston Fuller. Like Harlan, Justice William R. Day selected his two sons as law clerks.

73. Tony Mauro, "Corps of Clerks Lacking in Diversity," *USA Today*, June 5, 1998.

74. See, for example, Harry W. Jones to Earl Warren, October 28, 1966, Warren Papers, Box 390, and Mark A. Jacoby to Earl Warren, November 7, 1966, Warren Papers, Box 390.

75. Russell D. Niles to Earl Warren, November 2, 1955, Warren Papers, Box 387.

76. Earl Warren to Gerald Gunther, January 25, 1962, Warren Papers, Box 388.

77. Edward H. Levi to Earl Warren, January 6, 1954, Warren Papers, Box 387.

78. Harold C. Havighurst to Earl Warren, January 19, 1955, Warren Papers, Box 387.

79. Dennis J. Hutchinson and David J. Garrow, eds., *The Forgotten Memoir of John Knox* (Chicago: University of Chicago Press, 2002), 70.

80. Notes on "Interview with David Boyd," September 26, 1973, Powell Papers, Box 129a.

81. Earl Warren to Gerald Gunther, January 25, 1962, Warren Papers, Box 388.

82. Undated clerk committee recommendation, Warren Papers, Box 390.

83. Hugo L. Black to W. Lee McLane, Jr., December 8, 1950, Black Papers, Box 442.

84. The other clerk-producing schools and the number of clerks are Cornell 7, North Carolina 7, Arizona 6, Minnesota 6, Illinois 5, Washington and Lee 5, Boston University 4, Catholic University 4, Georgia 4, Kansas 4, Boston College 3, Colorado 3, Iowa 3, Loyola–Los Angeles 3, Mississippi 3, Missouri 3, Ohio State 3, Southern Methodist University 3, Utah 3, Vanderbilt 3, Arizona State 2, Alabama 2, Case Western 2, Denver 2, Detroit 2, Fordham 2, Loyola–New Orleans 2, Miami 2, National Law 2, SUNY Buffalo 2, Temple 2, Tulane 2, Union University 2, Villanova 2, American University 1, Dickinson 1, Drake 1, Emory 1, Houston 1, Howard 1, Kentucky 1, Louisville 1, Maine 1, Maryland 1, Nebraska 1, New Mexico 1, Northeastern 1, University of the Pacific 1, Pepperdine 1, Puget Sound 1, Rutgers 1, Saint Mary's San Antonio 1, Santa Clara 1, Texas A & M 1, Washburn 1, William and Mary 1, Yeshiva 1.

85. Floyd A. Wright to Hugo L. Black, May 19, 1938, Black Papers, Box 442.

86. Hugo L. Black to Floyd A. Wright, May 24, 1938, Black Papers, Box 442.

87. Lewis F. Powell, Jr., to Tyler A. Baker, September 22, 1983, Powell Papers, Box 129a.

88. William O. Douglas to J. L. Cundiff, December 5, 1959, Douglas Papers, Box 1101.

89. William O. Douglas to Harry W. Jones, November 5, 1965, Douglas Papers, Box 1102.

90. John Jay Dystel to William O. Douglas, October 15, 1971, Douglas Papers, Box 1102.

91. Earl Warren to Eugene V. Rostow, October 31, 1960, Warren Papers, Box 398.

92. Jerome Frank to William O. Douglas, March 5, 1943, Douglas Papers, Box 1101.

93. William O. Douglas to Jerome Frank, March 8, 1943, Douglas Papers, Box 1101.

94. F. Aley Allen Interview, Stanley Forman Reed Oral History Project, University of Kentucky.

95. Jerome N. Frank to Hugo L. Black, May 1, 1945, Black Papers, Box 442.

96. Robert von Mehren Interview, Stanley Forman Reed Oral History Project, University of Kentucky.

97. Lewis F. Powell, Jr., to Nancy J. Bregstein, August 13, 1975, Powell Papers, Box 129a. Bregstein went on to clerk on the court of appeals and then was selected by Blackmun the following term.

98. Harry A. Blackmun to Bruce A. Brown, October 13, 1976, Box 1568, Blackmun Papers.

99. Earl Warren to Harry L. Freeman, April 10, 1956, Warren Papers, Box 387.

100. David Hittner to Harry A. Blackmun, October 18, 1988, Blackmun Papers, Box 1568.

101. Harry A. Blackmun to David Hittner, October 21, 1988, Blackmun Papers, Box 1568.

102. In 1978, Congress authorized ten new judgeships, raising the number from thirteen to twenty-three. Five more judgeships were added in 1984, bringing the total to twenty-eight.

103. Paul Cane to Lewis F. Powell, Jr., May 3, 1980, Powell Papers, Box 129a.

104. Lewis F. Powell, Jr., to Paul Cane, May 12, 1980, Powell Papers, Box 129a.

105. Our findings support the conclusion of Corey Ditslear and Lawrence Baum, "Selection of Law Clerks and Polarization in the U.S. Supreme Court," *Journal of Politics* 63 (2001): 869.

106. David M. O'Brien, *Storm Center*, 2nd ed. (New York: Norton, 1990), 161. See also Marcia Coyle, "31 New Law Clerks Begin at Supreme Court," *National Law Journal*, October 12, 1987, 3, 43; D. Lauter, "Clerkships: Picking the Elite," *National Law Journal*, February 9, 1987, 1.

107. Tony Mauro, "Corps of Clerks Lacking in Diversity," *USA Today*, June 5, 1998.

108. William O. Douglas to David R. Eccles, March 26, 1965, Douglas Papers, Box 1102.

109. See, e.g., Adrian A. Kragen to Earl Warren, October 4, 1960, Warren Papers, Box 398.

110. Hugo L. Black to Ruth Street Pedigo, November 14, 1945, Black Papers, Box 442.

111. Hugo L. Black to Erwin Griswold, March 27, 1952, Black Papers, Box 442.

112. Hugo L. Black to Edmond Cahn, December 13, 1957, Black Papers, Box 442.

113. O'Brien, Storm Center, 160.

114. Tony Mauro, "Supreme Court Renovations Set to Start," *American Lawyer Media*, April 21, 2003.

115. Ibid.

116. See generally Mark R. Brown, "Gender Discrimination in the Supreme Court's Clerkship Selection Process," *Oregon Law Review* 75.2 (1996): 380.

117. William O. Douglas to Judson F. Falknor, March 13, 1943, Douglas Papers, Box 1101.

118. Judson F. Falknor to William O. Douglas, March 22, 1943, Douglas Papers, Box 1101.

119. William O. Douglas to Judson F. Falknor, March 24, 1943, Douglas Papers, Box 1101.

120. Judson Falknor to William O. Douglas, March 29, 1943, Douglas Papers, Box 1101.

121. Sarah Livingston Davis to Hugo L. Black, October 4, 1950, Black Papers, Box 442.

122. Hugo L. Black to Sarah Livingston Davis, October 17, 1950, Black Papers, Box 442.

123. Adrian A. Kragen to Earl Warren, December 3, 1959, Warren Papers, Box 398.

124. 404 U.S. 71 (1971).

125. 411 U.S. 677 (1973).

126. Malcolm R. Wilkey to Harry A. Blackmun, October 12, 1973, Blackmun Papers, Box 1563.

127. Karen Nelson Moore to Harry A. Blackmun, February 26, 1998, Blackmun Papers, Box 1563.

128. Harry A. Blackmun to Karen Nelson Moore, March 2, 1998, Blackmun Papers, Box 1563.

129. Lewis F. Powell, Jr., to Tyler A. Baker, September 22, 1983, Powell Papers, Box 129a.

130. William T. Coleman, Jr., to Hugo L. Black, June 20, 1946, Black Papers, Box 442.

131. Hugo L. Black to William T. Coleman, Jr., June 24, 1946, Black Papers, Box 442.

132. Bernard Schwartz and Stephan Lesher, *Inside the Warren Court: 1953–1969* (Garden City, NY: Doubleday, 1983), 69.

133. Ibid.

134. Leonard Baker, *Brandeis and Frankfurter: A Dual Biography* (New York: Harper and Row, 1984), 417.

135. 347 U.S. 483 (1954).

136. Thurgood Marshall to the Conference, April 13, 1978, Powell Papers, Box 46.

137. James C. Duff to the Conference, October 7, 1998, Blackmun Papers, Box 1568.

138. Cheryl Thompson to William H. Rehnquist, October 1, 1998, Blackmun Papers, Box 1568.

139. Tony Mauro, "Justices Give Key Role to Novice Lawyers," *USA Today*, June 5, 1998.

140. Tony Mauro, "Congress Grills Justices on Clerks," *USA Today*, March, 11, 1999.

141. Ibid.

142. See Tony Mauro, "High Court Hires More Minorities," *USA Today*, September 9, 1999.

143. Tony Mauro, "Sentencing, Clerkships Discussed at High Court Budget Hearing," www.law.com, April 10, 2003.

144. Tony Mauro, "Scalia Defends Clerk Hiring Record," *USA Today*, February 22, 1999.

145. Tony Mauro, "Corps of Clerks Lacking in Diversity," *USA Today*, June 5, 1998.

146. Ibid.

147. Ibid.

148. Mauro, "Sentencing, Clerkships Discussed at High Court Budget Hearing," www.law.com, April 10, 2003.

149. Tony Mauro, "Court Justices Defend Hiring Record," *USA Today*, December 8, 1998.

150. Tony Mauro, "Congress Grills Justices on Clerks," *USA Today*, March 11, 1999.

151. Tony Mauro, "Scalia Defends Clerk Hiring Record," *USA Today*, February 22, 1999.

152. Tony Mauro, "Rehnquist Won't Discuss Minority Clerks," *USA Today*, June 10, 1998.

153. Tony Mauro, "Court Justices Defend Hiring Record," *USA Today*, December 8, 1998.

154. Paul Brest to Harry A. Blackmun, October 7, 1992, Box 1553, Blackmun Papers.

155. Gerald P. Lopez to Harry A. Blackmun, March 11, 1992, Box 1553, Blackmun Papers.

156. Barbara Allen Babcock to Harry A. Blackmun, March 3, 1992, Box 1553, Blackmun Papers.

157. Mauro, "Sentencing, Clerkships Discussed at High Court Budget Hearing," www.law.com, April 10, 2003.

158. *Bowers v. Hardwick*, 478 U.S. 186 (1986); Joyce Murdoch and Deb Price, *Courting Justice: Gay Men and Lesbians v. the Supreme Court* (New York: Basic Books, 2001), 23. For a detailed discussion

of *Bowers v. Hardwick*, Justice Powell, and his clerks, see 271–354.

159. Blackmun Papers, Box 451.

160. Transcript: The Justice Harry A. Blackmun Oral History Project, Library of Congress, Washington, DC.

161. Murdoch and Price, *Courting Justice*, 416.

162. Ibid., 417.

163. Ibid., 418.

164. Tony Mauro, "Scalia Defends Clerk Hiring Record," *USA Today*, February 22, 1999.

165. Tony Mauro, "Justices Give Key Role to Novice Lawyers," *USA Today*, June 5, 1998.

166. Notes of phone conversation between Harry A. Blackmun and Herbert Y. C. Choy, February, 18, 1983, Blackmun Papers, Box 1556.

167. Gamarekian, "O'Connor's Agonizing Search for Law Clerks."

168. Peter W. Low to Lewis F. Powell, Jr., May 30, 1979, Powell Papers, Box 129a.

169. Stanley Bucksbaum to Hugo L. Black, September 24, 1937, Black Papers, Box 442.

170. Arthur R. Miller to Hugo L. Black, November 18, 1957, Black Papers, Box 442.

171. Learned Hand to Hugo L. Black, April 26, 1945, Black Papers, Box 442.

172. David L. Bazelon to Hugo L. Black, January 28, 1958, Black Papers, Box 442.

173. William O. Douglas to Max Radin, May 27, 1946, Melvin I. Urofsky, ed., *The Douglas Letters* (Bethesda, MD: Adler and Adler, 1987), 47.

174. Arthur Rosett Interview, Stanley Forman Reed Oral History Project, University of Kentucky.

175. Hugo L. Black to William Hughes Mulligan, October 22, 1956, Black Papers, Box 442.

176. Lewis F. Powell, Jr., to Samuel E. Gates, October 3, 1972, Powell Papers, Box 129a.

177. Notes on "Interview with Penny

Clark on September 20, 1973," Powell Papers, Box 129a.

178. Notes from "Interview with Ronald Carr on September 21, 1973," Powell Papers, Box 129a.

179. Terry Eastland, "While Justice Sleeps," *National Review*, April 21, 1989, 25.

180. For reliability purposes, Figure 2.3 includes only those justices for which five or more surveys from clerks were returned: Black, Blackmun, Brennan, Burger, Clarke, Douglas, Frankfurter, Marshall, Powell, Rehnquist, Stewart, Warren, and White.

181. William H. Rehnquist to Danny Davis, November 17, 1998. See "Text of Rehnquist Letter," *USA Today*, December 8, 1998.

NOTES TO CHAPTER 3

1. *Hearings on S. 2060 and 2061 before a Subcomm. of the Committee on the Judiciary*, 68th Cong., 1st sess. (1924), 8.

2. Bernard Schwartz and Stephan Lesher, *Inside the Warren Court: 1953–1969* (Garden City, NY: Doubleday, 1983), 37.

3. Julian Burke Interview, Stanley Forman Reed Oral History Project, University of Kentucky.

4. Samuel Williston, "Horace Gray," in *Great American Lawyers*, W. Lewis, ed. (Philadelphia: Winston, 1907–1909; South Hackensack, NJ: Rothman Reprints, 1971), 158–59.

5. C. Dickerman Williams, "The 1924 Term: Recollections of Chief Justice Taft's Law Clerk," *Supreme Court Historical Society Yearbook* (1989), www.supremecourthistory.org.

6. This is in contrast to the standard account that clerks began reviewing cert memos because of the Court's increasing workload. See, e.g., Bradley J. Best, *Law Clerks, Support Personnel, and the Decline of Consensual Norms on the United States Supreme Court, 1935–1995* (New York: LFB Scholarly Publishing, 2002), 96.

7. Undated and unsigned "office procedure" memorandum, Stone Papers, Box 81.

8. William Howard Taft to the Brethren, March 24, 1926, Stone Papers, Box 76.

9. Charles Evans Hughes to Harlan Fiske Stone, October 1, 1931, Stone Papers, Box 75. See also Charles Evans Hughes to Harlan Fiske Stone, October 1, 1933, ibid.

10. David J. Danelski and Joseph S. Tulchin, eds., *The Autobiographical Notes of Charles Evans Hughes* (Cambridge: Harvard University Press, 1973), 323.

11. Dennis J. Hutchinson and David J. Garrow, eds., *The Forgotten Memoir of John Knox* (Chicago: University of Chicago Press, 2002), 29–30. Knox's description of the conference procedure of discussing cases in order of seniority and then voting in reverse order is accurate for the Hughes Court. In the conferences of the current Supreme Court, justices state their views and their votes simultaneously and by order of seniority, with the Chief Justice first and the most junior justice last. Apparently, the process changed at some point after the Hughes Court. Hughes explained,

> It is frequently and mistakenly said that in these conferences the Chief Justice gives his verbal opinion last. On the contrary, it is the tradition and regular practice for the Chief Justice to lead the discussion of each case by stating his opinion first and then to call for the views of the other Justices in the order of seniority. The mistaken notion is due to a confusion of the order of discussion with the order of voting. When the discussion has reached the point where the Justices are ready to vote, the Chief Justice calls the roll in the inverse order of seniority and thus casts the vote last.

Danelski and Tulchin, eds., *The Autobiographical Notes of Charles Evans Hughes*, 301–2. Justice Douglas confirmed, "As soon as the last man had spoken, [Hughes] said, 'Now we will vote.' And he would open the docket book to the sheet where this case was listed and starting with the junior judge he would call for a vote."

Transcriptions of Conversations between Justice William O. Douglas and Professor Walter F. Murphy, Cassette No. 1: December 20, 1961, Princeton University Library, 1981. Chief Justice Rehnquist described the current process:

> With respect to petitions for certiorari, if the Chief Justice has put the case on the discuss list, he leads off the discussion with a statement of why he thought the case should be brought to the attention of the conference, and usually will indicate that he thinks certiorari should be granted. The discussion then proceeds around the table from senior associate justice to the junior justice, with each indicating a vote to either grant review or to deny review. . . . In discussing cases that have been argued, the Chief Justice begins by reviewing the facts and the decision of the lower court, outlining his understanding of the applicable case law, and indicating either that he votes to affirm the decision of the lower court or to reverse it. The discussion then proceeds to Justice Brennan (as senior associate justice) and in turn down the line to Justice Scalia (as the most junior justice). For many years there has circulated a tale that although the discussion in conference proceeds in order from the Chief Justice to the junior justice, the voting actually begins with the junior justice and proceeds back to the Chief Justice in order of seniority. I can testify that, at least during my fifteen years on the Court, this tale is very much of a myth; I don't believe I have ever seen it happen at any of the conferences that I have attended. . . . At the end of the discussion, I announce how I am recording the vote in the case, so that others may have the opportunity to disagree with my count if they believe I am mistaken.

William H. Rehnquist, *The Supreme Court: How It Was, How It Is* (New York: Morrow, 1987), 289–90, 293. Clearly the process changed either under Chief Justice Stone, Chief Justice Vinson, or Chief Justice Warren—or perhaps Chief Justice Burger, despite Rehnquist's recollection. Though Supreme Court scholars disagree on exactly when this change took place, it is likely that the change occurred at some point during the Warren Court, though the order of the justices listed in their own docket books went from junior to senior until 1974, when it was reversed.

12. Transcriptions of conversations between Justice William O. Douglas and Professor Walter F. Murphy, Cassette No. 2: December 20, 1961, Princeton University Library, 1981.

13. Transcriptions of conversations between Justice William O. Douglas and Professor Walter F. Murphy, Cassette No. 5: December 27, 1961, Princeton University Library, 1981.

14. This is the first indication of the presence of a dead list. Charles Evans Hughes to Willis Van Devanter, September 30, 1935, Van Devanter Papers, Box 37; Charles Evans Hughes to Harlan Fiske Stone, September 30, 1935, Stone Papers, Box 75. Such a memo does not appear in the papers of either Van Devanter or Stone in prior years.

15. Charles Evans Hughes to Hugo Black, September 27, 1938, Black Papers, Box 255. Now, whichever justice moves a case to the discuss list leads the discussion for that case in conference.

16. Transcriptions of conversations between Justice William O. Douglas and Professor Walter F. Murphy, Cassette No. 2: December 20, 1961, Princeton University Library, 1981.

17. Hutchinson and Garrow, eds., *The Forgotten Memoir of John Knox*, 56.

18. Drew Pearson and Robert S. Allen, *The Nine Old Men* (Garden City, NY: Doubleday, Doran, 1936), 222–23.

19. Hutchinson and Garrow, eds., *The Forgotten Memoir of John Knox*, 10–11.

20. Edwin M. Zimmerman interview, March 19, 1981, Stanley Forman Reed Oral History Project, University of Kentucky Libraries.

21. Doris Marie Provine, *Case Selection*

in the United States Supreme Court
(Chicago: University of Chicago Press,
1980), 28–29.

22. Bernard Schwartz, *Decision: How
the Supreme Court Decides Cases* (New
York: Oxford University, Press, 1996), 51.

23. Schwartz and Lesher, *Inside the
Warren Court*, 32.

24. Transcriptions of conversations
between Justice William O. Douglas and
Professor Walter F. Murphy, Cassette No.
3: December 20, 1961, Princeton University Library, 1981.

25. Lewis F. Powell, Jr., to John J.
Buckley, John C. Jeffries, Jr., and Jack B.
Owens, June 26, 1973, Powell Papers,
Box 130b.

26. Robert E. Gooding, Jr., to Harry A.
Blackmun, August 28, 1970, Blackmun
Papers, Box 135.

27. Michael S. Davis to Thurgood Marshall, June 23, 1991, Thurgood Marshall
Papers, Box 523.

28. Wiley Rutledge to Fred Vinson, May
17, 1948, Rutledge Papers, Box 166.

29. F. Aley Allen Interview, Stanley Forman Reed Oral History Project, University
of Kentucky.

30. Rehnquist, *The Supreme Court*, 263.

31. Lewis F. Powell, Jr., to Hamilton
Fox, Lawrence A. Hammond, Covert Parnell, and J. Harvie Wilkinson, III, March
20, 1972, Powell Papers, Box 130b.

32. Lewis F. Powell, Jr., to J. Harvie
Wilkinson, III, December 27, 1972, Powell
Papers, Box 130b.

33. Warren E. Burger to the Conference,
July 12, 1972, Blackmun Papers, Box
1374.

34. Doug Floyd, Jim Scarboro, John
Rich, and Larry Hammond to Warren E.
Burger, July 12, 1972, Blackmun Papers,
Box 1374.

35. "Recurring Issues In Cert Petitions,"
July 13, 1972, Blackmun Papers, Box
1374. One year later, Blackmun clerk
Ralph Miller drafted a similar document
for use by Blackmun's own clerks on cert
petitions. It is titled "Possible Dispositions
for Petitions for Review" and contains a

list of dispositions, such as "AFFIRM,"
"CALL FOR A RESPONSE (CFR)," and
"PROBABLE JURISDICTION NOTED (NOTE)"
and their meaning. Blackmun Papers,
Box 1442.

36. William O. Douglas to Warren E.
Burger, July 13, 1972, Blackmun Papers,
Box 1374.

37. Julian Burke Interview, Stanley Forman Reed Oral History Project, University
of Kentucky.

38. William O. Douglas to William H.
Alsup, Richard L. Jacobson, and Kenneth
R. Reed, April 22, 1971, Melvin I. Urof-
sky, ed., *The Douglas Letters* (Bethesda,
MD: Adler and Adler, 1987), 53–54.

39. Warren E. Burger to the Conference,
July 13, 1972, Blackmun Papers, Box
1374.

40. Potter Stewart to Warren E. Burger,
September 5, 1972, Blackmun Papers, Box
1374.

41. William J. Brennan to Warren E.
Burger, September 26, 1972, Blackmun
Papers, Box 1374.

42. Tony Mauro, "Justices Give Key
Role to Novice Lawyers," *USA Today*,
June 5, 1998.

43. William J. Brennan, Jr., "The
National Court of Appeals: Another Dissent," *University of Chicago Law Review*
40 (1973): 40.

44. Schwartz, *Decision*, 50.

45. Lewis F. Powell to Participants in the
Cert Pool, November 22, 1972, Blackmun
Papers, Box 1374.

46. Lewis F. Powell to Warren E. Burger,
June 7, 1973, Blackmun Papers, Box 1374.

47. William H. Rehnquist to Warren E.
Burger, June 8, 1973, Blackmun Papers,
Box 1374.

48. Harry A. Blackmun to Warren E.
Burger, June 8, 1973, Blackmun Papers,
Box 1374.

49. Warren E. Burger to Lewis F.
Powell, June 8, 1973, Blackmun Papers,
Box 1374.

50. See, e.g., "flimsies" from the 1955
Term, Harlan Papers, Box 16.

51. Lewis F. Powell to Kenneth F. Rip-

ple, September 24, 1973, Blackmun Papers, Box 1374.

52. Doug Floyd, Jim Scarboro, John Rich, and Larry Hammond to Warren E. Burger, July 12, 1972, Blackmun Papers, Box 1374.

53. "Preliminary Memo," *Gooch v. Skelly Oil Co.*, 73–221, October 21, 1974, Blackmun Papers, Box 822.

54. "Preliminary Memorandum," *Hasty v. United States*, 74–223, December 3, 1974, Blackmun Papers, Box 822.

55. Jan Horbaly to Law Clerks in the Cert Pool, September 19, 1984, Blackmun Papers, Box 1374.

56. Lewis F. Powell, Jr., to Larry A. Hammond, J. Harvie Wilkinson, III, and William C. Kelly, Jr., November 29, 1972, Powell Papers, Box 130b.

57. Barbara Gamarekian, "O'Connor's Agonizing Search for Law Clerks," *New York Times*, November 3, 1989, B7.

58. While the number may fluctuate throughout the term, the average is derived from dividing the number of yearly petitions, currently over eight thousand, by the number of weeks and the number of pool clerks, currently thirty-two.

59. Dan T. Coenen, "Book Review— Deciding to Decide: Agenda Setting in the United States Supreme Court," *Constitutional Commentary* 10 (1993): 183 n.10.

60. William H. Rehnquist to Pool Memo Law Clerks, February 17, 1989, Blackmun Papers, Box 1374.

61. Michael F. Sturley, "Cert Pool," in *The Oxford Companion to the Supreme Court of the United States*, ed. Kermit L. Hall (New York: Oxford University Press, 1992); H. W. Perry, *Deciding to Decide: Agenda Setting in the United States Supreme Court* (Cambridge: Harvard University Press, 1991).

62. John Paul Stevens, "Some Thoughts on Judicial Restraint," *Judicature* 66 (1982): 177, 179.

63. Lewis F. Powell, Jr., to Larry A. Hammond, J. Harvie Wilkinson, III, and William C. Kelly, Jr., December 19, 1972, Powell Papers, Box 130b.

64. Lewis F. Powell, Jr., to John J. Buckley, John C. Jeffries, Jr., and Jack B. Owens, June 26, 1973, Powell Papers, Box 130b.

65. Lewis F. Powell, Jr., to Lynda G. Simpson, Annmarie Levins, Arthur L. Bentley, III, and Daniel R. Ortiz, April 1, 1985, Powell Papers, Box 130b.

66. Sean Donahue, "Behind the Pillars of Justice: Remarks on Law Clerks," *The Long Term View* 3 (1995): 79.

67. Tony Mauro, "Justices Give Key Role to Novice Lawyers," *USA Today*, June 5, 1998.

68. Rehnquist, *The Supreme Court*, 264–65.

69. Perry, *Deciding to Decide*; Sturley, "Cert Pool."

70. Coenen, "Book Review," 185.

71. On this point, we differ from David M. O'Brien's assertion: "Clerks' memos do not fully explore whether an alleged conflict is 'real,' 'tolerable,' or 'square' and must be decided. The workload usually precludes such an examination until a case has already been granted and set for oral argument." David M. O'Brien, *Storm Center: The Supreme Court in American Politics*, 2nd ed. (New York: Norton, 1990), 216. While this may have been true in the late 1960s, the emergent structure of the cert pool has drastically decreased the number of cases that each clerk reviews. This allows modern clerks not only more time for opinion writing and other tasks but also additional time to explore cert petitions more fully and make more thoughtful recommendations. Furthermore, on the basis of our interviews with former clerks, we conclude that the institutionalization of the clerk culture has created an atmosphere in which the clerks will perform significant research when they identify a case, which may present a conflict.

72. Mauro, "Justices Give Key Role to Novice Lawyers."

73. Lewis F. Powell, Jr., to John J. Buckley, John C. Jeffries, Jr., and Jack B. Owens, June 26, 1973, Powell Papers, Box 130b.

74. *Brown v. Board of Education*, 347 U.S. 483 (1954).

75. Deb Price, "Civil Rites: Arguments against Same-sex Marriage Mirror Those That Kept the Races Apart," *Detroit News*, April 18, 1997.

76. Ibid.

77. Ibid.

78. Lewis F. Powell, Jr., to John J. Buckley, John C. Jeffries, Jr., and Jack B. Owens, August 20, 1973, Powell Papers, Box 130b.

79. *Webster v. Reproductive Health Services*, 492 U.S. 490 (1989).

80. *Roe v. Wade*, 410 U.S. 113 (1973); "Preliminary Memorandum," Kevin M. Kearney to the cert pool, December 28, 1988, Blackmun Papers, Box 536.

81. Ibid.

82. *Lee v. Weisman*, 505 U.S. 577 (1992); *Lemon v. Kurtzman*, 403 U.S. 602 (1971); "Preliminary Memorandum," Iman Anabtawi to the cert pool, March 6, 1991, Blackmun Papers, Box 586.

83. Ibid. The Court granted cert 5–4 with Justices Marshall, Blackmun, Stevens, and O'Connor voting to deny. Docket No. 90-1014, Blackmun Papers, Box 719.

84. Harry A. Blackmun to Kenneth F. Ripple, September 25, 1973, Blackmun Papers, Box 1374.

85. Warren E. Burger to Byron R. White, Harry A. Blackmun, Lewis F. Powell, and William H. Rehnquist, June 11, 1974, Blackmun Papers, Box 1374.

86. *McClesky v. Kemp*, 481 U.S. 279 (1987); *Giglio v. United States*, 405 U.S. 150 (1972); *Sandstrom v. Montana*, 442 U.S. 510 (1979); "Preliminary Memo," Samuel J. Dimon, July 29, 1985, Powell Papers, Box 132.

87. *Regents of the University of California v. Bakke*, 438 U.S. 265 (1978).

88. James P. Ginty to the cert pool, January 13, 1977, Powell Papers, Box 46.

89. See, e.g., David Crump, "Law Clerks: Their Roles and Relationships with Their Judges," *Judicature* 69 (1986): 236.

90. Ibid. But see Stephen L. Wasby, "Clerking for an Appellate Judge: A Close Look," presented at the Midwest Political Science Association, Chicago, IL, April 3–6, 2003, for a discussion of how some clerks prefer subjects they studied in law school, including constitutional law.

91. See, e.g., Robert H. Stern, "Denial of Certiorari Despite a Conflict," *Harvard Law Review* 66 (1953): 465; Robert H. Stern, Eugene Gressman, and Stephen M. Shapiro, *Supreme Court Practice*, 6th ed. (Washington, DC: Bureau of National Affairs, 1986).

92. Sidney S. Ulmer, "The Supreme Court's Certiorari Decisions: Conflict as a Predictive Variable," *American Political Science Review* 78 (1984): 901.

93. Sturley, "Cert Pool," 624.

94. Kevin J. Worthen, "Shirt-Tales: Clerking for Byron White," *Brigham Young University Law Review* 349 (1994): 355.

95. Perry, *Deciding to Decide*.

96. Joyce Murdoch and Deb Price, *Courting Justice: Gay Men and Lesbians v. the Supreme Court* (New York: Basic Books, 2001), 17.

97. Harry A. Blackmun to Warren E. Burger, Byron R. White, Lewis F. Powell, and William H. Rehnquist, October 28, 1977, Blackmun Papers, Box 1374.

98. Warren E. Burger to the chambers of Byron R. White, Harry A. Blackmun, Lewis F. Powell, and William H. Rehnquist, August 3, 1978, Blackmun Papers, Box 1374.

99. Harry A. Blackmun to Jan Horbaly, September 18, 1984, Blackmun Papers, Box 1374.

100. Jan Horbaly to Law Clerks in the Cert Pool, September 15, 1984, Blackmun Papers, Box 1374.

101. Certiorari Memoranda, *In Forma Pauperis*, 83-5809 to 83-5853, Blackmun Papers, Box 1021.

102. *R.A.V. v. St. Paul*, 505 U.S. 377 (1992); "Preliminary Memorandum," Jeffrey L. Bleich to the cert pool, May 21, 1991, Blackmun Papers, Box 596.

103. *Kemp v. Drake*, No. 85-556;

Pamela Karlan to Harry A. Blackmun, November 4, 1985, Blackmun Papers, Box 1560.

104. Lewis F. Powell, Jr., to Warren E. Burger, October 2, 1984, Powell Papers, Box 129.

105. Andrea Ward to Harry A. Blackmun, June 16, 1992, Blackmun Papers, Box 1567.

106. Samuel Estreicher to Paul B. Stephan, III, Eric G. Andersen, James Bruce Boisture, and David L. Westin, July 21, 1978, Powell Papers, Box 130b.

107. See, e.g., Blackmun Papers, Box 1093.

108. Blackmun Papers, Box 1289.

109. That term the Court's docket consisted of 809 petitions for certiorari, excluding the sixty in forma pauperis petitions handled solely by Chief Justice Hughes.

110. Hutchinson and Garrow, eds., *The Forgotten Memoir of John Knox*, 14.

111. Transcriptions of Conversations between Justice William O. Douglas and Professor Walter F. Murphy, Cassette No. 1: December 20, 1961, Princeton University Library, 1981.

112. Arthur Rosett Interview, Stanley Forman Reed Oral History Project, University of Kentucky.

113. William O. Douglas to James T. Brady, November 2, 1962, Urofsky, ed., *The Douglas Letters*, 62–63.

114. Warren E. Burger to Hugo L. Black, William O. Douglas, John Marshall Harlan, William J. Brennan, Potter Stewart, Byron R. White, and Thurgood Marshall, August 26, 1969, Harlan Papers, Box 490.

115. Warren E. Burger to the Conference, July 16, 1970, Harlan Papers, Box 490.

116. Ibid.

117. Ibid.

118. Ibid.

119. See William O. Douglas to Warren E. Burger, July 21, 1970, Harlan Papers, Box 490.

120. William O. Douglas to Warren E. Burger, August 19, 1970, Urofsky, ed., *The Douglas Letters*, 140.

121. Donahue, "Behind the Pillars of Justice," 79.

122. See, e.g., Bradley J. Best, *Law Clerks, Support Personnel, and the Decline of Consensual Norms on the United States Supreme Court* (New York: LFP Scholarly Publishing, 2002).

123. On this point, see David M. O'Brien, "The Rehnquist Court's Shrinking Plenary Docket," *Judicature* 81 (Sept.–Oct. 1997): 58.

124. Harry A. Blackmun to Warren E. Burger, June 11, 1974, Blackmun Papers, Box 1374.

125. See Lewis F. Powell to Warren E. Burger, June 24, 1975, Blackmun Papers, Box 1374.

126. Mauro, "Justices Give Key Role to Novice Lawyers."

127. Ibid.

128. Ibid.

129. Ibid.

130. For a complete analysis of this question, see chapter 5 on decision making.

131. Mauro, "Justices Give Key Role to Novice Lawyers."

132. Anthony Kennedy to William H. Rehnquist, August 1, 1991, Blackmun Papers, Box 1374.

133. Harry A. Blackmun to William H. Rehnquist, August 6, 1991, Blackmun Papers, Box 1374.

134. Ibid.

135. Handwritten note of October 1, 1991, Anthony Kennedy to the Conference, August 5, 1991, Blackmun Papers, Box 1374.

NOTES TO CHAPTER 4

1. Quoted in Kevin J. Worthen, "Shirt-Tales: Clerking for Byron White," *Brigham Young University Law Review* 349 (1994): 351.

2. *Girouard v. United States*, 328 U.S. 61 (1946); Alpheus T. Mason, *Harlan Fiske Stone: Pillar of the Law* (New York: Viking Press, 1956), 804–5.

3. *O'Connor v. Donaldson*, 422 U.S. 563 (1975); Bob Woodward and Scott Armstrong, *The Brethren: Inside the Supreme Court* (New York: Random House, 1979), 3–4.

4. *Patterson v. McLean Credit Union*, 491 U.S. 164 (1989); Edward Lazarus, *Closed Chambers: The First Eyewitness Account of the Epic Struggles inside the Supreme Court* (New York: Times Books, 1998), 119.

5. *Planned Parenthood v. Casey*, 505 U.S. 833 (1992).

6. John P. Frank, *The Marble Palace* (New York: Knopf, 1958), 119.

7. David M. O'Brien, *Storm Center*, 2nd ed. (New York: Norton, 1990), 161.

8. Robert von Mehren Interview, Stanley Forman Reed Oral History Project, University of Kentucky.

9. Julian Burke Interview, Stanley Forman Reed Oral History Project, University of Kentucky.

10. Tony Mauro, "Insiders' Book Breaks Code of Silence," *USA Today*, March 13, 1998.

11. Lewis F. Powell, Jr., to William C. Kelly, Jr., September 21, 1972, Powell Papers, Box 130b.

12. *Regents of the University of California v. Bakke*, 438 U.S. 265 (1978); Lewis F. Powell, Jr., to Aleta Estreicher, July 10, 1978, Powell Papers, Box 129a.

13. Lewis F. Powell, Jr., to Samuel Estreicher, September 4, 1978, Powell Papers, Box 129a.

14. Samuel Estreicher to Lewis F. Powell, Jr., September 27, 1977, Powell Papers, Box 46.

15. *Bowers v. Hardwick*, 478 U.S. 186 (1986); Michael W. Mosman to Lewis F. Powell, Jr., April 2, 1986, Powell Papers, Box 129. Coughlin has denied that she supported this position. Powell read the memo and was the deciding vote in conference. He recorded his vote, "Affirm. Viewing the case as presenting a facial challenge, I'd find a violation of 8th Amend. See my notes. Not persuaded there is any fundamental D/P right." Bowers v. Hardwick conference notes, April 2, 1986, Powell Papers, Box 129. The next day, in a two-page letter Chief Justice Burger lobbied Powell to change his vote. It worked and Powell noted on the letter, "There is both sense and non-sense in the letter— mostly the latter. I have changed my vote to Reverse, but I adhere to my 8th Amend position." Warren E. Burger to Lewis F. Powell, Jr., April 3, 1986, Powell Papers, Box 129.

16. Leslie S. Gielow to Lewis F. Powell, Jr., October 14, 1986 (b), Powell Papers, Box 132.

17. Edwin M. Zimmerman interview, March 19, 1981, Stanley Forman Reed Oral History Project, University of Kentucky.

18. William H. Rehnquist, "The Supreme Court's Conference," in *Judges on Judging: Views from the Bench*, ed. David M. O'Brien (Chatham, NJ: Chatham House Publishers, 1997), 90.

19. *Edwards v. Aguillard*, 482 U.S. 578 (1987); Powell notes from November 21, 1986, on "Bench Memorandum, No. 85-1513, Edwards v. Aguillard," Leslie S. Gielow to Lewis F. Powell, Jr., November 17, 1986.

20. Bernard Schwartz and Stephan Lesher, *Inside the Warren Court: 1953–1969* (Garden City, NY: Doubleday, 1983), 38.

21. Lewis F. Powell, Jr., to Larry A. Hammond, William C. Kelley, Jr., and J. Harvie Wilkinson, III, February 9, 1973, Powell Papers, Box 130b.

22. Lewis F. Powell, Jr., to James O. Browning, Mark E. Newell, Michael F. Sturley, and Daniel Rives Kistler, November 1, 1982, Powell Papers, Box 130b.

23. Samuel Estreicher to Paul B. Stephan, III, Eric G. Andersen, James Bruce Boisture, and David L. Westin, July 21, 1978, Powell Papers, Box 130b.

24. Lewis F. Powell, Jr., to Samuel Estreicher, June 7, 1978, Powell Papers, Box 129a.

25. Eugene Gressman to Wiley Rutledge, undated, Rutledge Papers, Box 166.

26. Robert D. Comfort to Lewis F. Powell, Jr., January 2, 1978, Powell Papers, Box 46.

27. Robert D. Comfort to Lewis F. Powell, Jr., June 9, 1978, Powell Papers, Box 46.

28. Lewis F. Powell, Jr., to Robert D. Comfort, June 17, 1978, Powell Papers, Box 46.

29. *Roe v. Wade*, 410 U.S. 113 (1973).

30. Harry A. Blackmun to the Conference, November 21, 1972, Powell Papers, Box 5.

31. William O. Douglas to Harry A. Blackmun, December 11, 1972, Powell Papers, Box 5; *United States v. Kras*, 409 U.S. 434 (1973); Lawrence A. Hammond to Lewis F. Powell, Jr., December 12, 1972, Powell Papers, Box 5.

32. Lawrence A. Hammond to Lewis F. Powell, Jr., January 16, 1973, Powell Papers, Box 5.

33. Bradley J. Best concluded, "The analysis of quantitative opinion writing data tentatively indicates that the law clerks have some effect on the justices' decision to draft dissenting, concurring, and separate opinions," *Law Clerks, Support Personnel, and the Decline of Consensual Norms on the United States Supreme Court, 1935–1995* (New York: LFB Scholarly Publishing, 2002), 232. See also David O'Brien, *Storm Center: The Supreme Court in American Politics*, 2nd ed. (New York: Norton, 1990), 170; Richard A. Posner, *The Federal Courts: Challenge and Reform* (Cambridge: Harvard University Press, 1996), 357.

34. Lewis F. Powell, Jr., to Larry A. Hammond, J. Harvie Wilkinson, III, and William C. Kelley, Jr., December 19, 1972, Powell Papers, Box 130b.

35. See, e.g., Bob Woodward and Scott Armstrong, *The Brethren: Inside the Supreme Court* (New York: Simon and Schuster, 1979), 34–36.

36. Tony Mauro, "For Lawyers, Clerkship Is Ultimate Job," *USA Today*, June 5, 1998.

37. On the politics and strategy involved in coalition formation, see Forrest Maltzman, James F. Spriggs, II, and Paul J. Wahlbeck, *Crafting Law on the Supreme Court: The Collegial Game* (New York: Cambridge University Press, 2000).

38. *Nilva v. United States*, 352 U.S. 385 (1957); Norman Dorsen to John Marshall Harlan, II, February 9, 1957, Harlan Papers, Box 553.

39. Dennis J. Hutchinson and David J. Garrow, eds., *The Forgotten Memoir of John Knox* (Chicago: University of Chicago Press, 2002), 12.

40. Alpheus T. Mason, *Harlan Fiske Stone: Pillar of the Law* (New York: Viking Press, 1956), 406; see also O'Brien, *Storm Center*, 149.

41. Lewis F. Powell, Jr., to the law clerks, October 11, 1983, Powell Papers, Box 130b.

42. Lewis F. Powell, Jr., to Eugene J. Comey, Tyler A. Baker, Charles C. Ames, and David A. Martin, September 1976, Powell Papers, Box 130b.

43. *McClesky v. Kemp*, 481 U.S. 279 (1987); Leslie S. Gielow to Lewis F. Powell, Jr., October 14, 1986 (a), Powell Papers, Box 132.

44. Internal Burger Chambers Memo of August 12, 1969, Woodward and Armstrong, *The Brethren*, 34–35.

45. Lewis F. Powell, Jr., to Jack B. Owens, John C. Jeffries, Jr., and John J. Buckley, January 21, 1974, Powell Papers, Box 130b.

46. *New York v. United States*, 505 U.S. 144 (1992); Andrea Ward to Harry A. Blackmun, April 2, 1992, Blackmun Papers, Box 600.

47. Bernard Schwartz, *Super Chief: Earl Warren and His Supreme Court* (New York: NYU Press, 1984), 62.

48. Julian Burke Interview, Stanley Forman Reed Oral History Project, University of Kentucky.

49. Bernard Schwartz and Stephan Lesher, *Inside the Warren Court: 1953–1969* (Garden City, NY: Doubleday, 1983), 5.

50. William O. Douglas, *The Court*

Years (New York: Random House, 1980), 173.

51. *Renegotiation Board v. Bannercraft Co.*, 415 U.S. 1 (1974); Benjamin S. Sharp to Harry A. Blackmun, January 17, 1974, Blackmun Papers, Box 175.

52. *J.E.B. v. Alabama ex rel. T.B.*, 511 U.S. 127 (1994); Michelle L. Alexander to Harry A. Blackmun, March 31, 1994, Blackmun Papers, Box 636.

53. *United States v. Fordice*, 505 U.S. 717 (1992); Andrea Ward to Harry A. Blackmun, March 23, 1992, Blackmun Papers, Box 590.

54. Stuart Taylor, Jr., "When High Court's Away, Clerks' Work Begins," *New York Times*, September 23, 1988, B7.

55. *Regents of the University of California v. Bakke*, 438 U.S. 265 (1978); Lewis F. Powell, Jr., to Robert D. Comfort, January 9, 1978, Powell Papers, Box 46.

56. *Machinists v. Street*, 367 U.S. 740 (1961); John Marshall Harlan, II, to Charles Fried and Phillip B. Heymann, June 28, 1960, Harlan Papers, Box 554.

57. Lewis F. Powell, Jr., to Gerald Gunther, September 10, 1975, Powell Papers, Box 129a.

58. Lewis F. Powell, Jr., to Eugene J. Comey, Tyler A. Baker, Charles C. Ames, and David A. Martin, September 1976, Powell Papers, Box 130b.

59. *Boddie v. Connecticut*, 401 U.S. 371 (1971). See Tinsley E. Yarbrough, *John Marshall Harlan: Great Dissenter of the Warren Court* (New York: Oxford University Press, 1992), 314–15.

60. Robert D. Comfort to Lewis F. Powell, Jr., September 6, 1977, Powell Papers, Box 46.

61. *Edwards v. Aguillard*, 482 U.S. 578 (1987); Leslie S. Gielow to Lewis F. Powell, Jr., January 8, 1987, Powell Papers, Box 135.

62. Ibid.

63. Lewis F. Powell, Jr., to C. Cabell Chinnis, Jr., Ann Marie Coughlin, William J. Stuntz, and Michael W. Mosman, December 19, 1985, Powell Papers, Box 130b.

64. William J. Brennan, Jr., to John Marshall Harlan, II, January 8, 1957, Harlan Papers, Box 486.

65. John Marshall Harlan, II, to Hugo Black, January 12, 1965, Harlan Papers, Box 484.

66. William H. Rehnquist to Cert Pool Law Clerks, February 13, 1996, Blackmun Papers, Box 1374.

67. Lewis F. Powell, Jr., to John J. Buckley, John C. Jeffries, Jr., and Jack B. Owens, June 26, 1973, Powell Papers, Box 130b.

68. *San Antonio School District v. Rodriguez*, 411 U.S. 1 (1973); *Neil v. Biggers*, 409 U.S. 188 (1972); *United States v. Fuller*, 409 U.S. 488 (1973); Lewis F. Powell, Jr., to Lawrence A. Hammond, William C. Kelly, Jr., and J. Harvie Wilkinson, III, October 25, 1972, Powell Papers, Box 130b.

69. *District of Columbia v. Greater Washington Board of Trade*, 506 U.S. 125 (1992); William S. Dodge to Harry A. Blackmun, October 20, 1992, Blackmun Papers, Box 1556.

70. *Kraft General Foods v. Iowa Dept. of Revenue*, 505 U.S. 71 (1992); *Lee v. Weisman*, 505 U.S. 577 (1992); *Lucas v. South Carolina Coastal Council*, 505 U.S. 1003 (1992); Molly McUsic to Harry A. Blackmun, May 26, 1992, Blackmun Papers, Box 599.

71. Lewis F. Powell, Jr., to Christina Brooks Whitman, Carl R. Schenker, Jr., Gregory K. Palm, and Phillip J. Jordan, January 30, 1976, Powell Papers, Box 130b.

72. William C. Kelly, Jr., to Lewis F. Powell, Jr., February 9, 1973, Powell Papers, Box 130b.

73. Paul W. Cane, Jr., to Peter J. Byrne, Paul M. Smith, and Richard G. Morgan, July 7, 1980, Powell Papers, Box 130b.

74. Paul W. Cane, Jr., to David F. Levi, Richard H. Fallon, John S. Wiley, Jr., and Mary Ellen Becker, June 16, 1981, Powell Papers, Box 130b.

75. *Lloyd Co. v. Tanner*, 407 U.S. 551 (1972); Lewis F. Powell, Jr., to Hamilton

Fox, Lawrence A. Hammond, Covert Parnell, and J. Harvie Wilkinson, III, April 25, 1972, Powell Papers, Box 130b.

76. *Planned Parenthood v. Casey*, 505 U.S. 833 (1992).

77. *Roe v. Wade*, 410 U.S. 113 (1973).

78. Molly McUsic to Harry A. Blackmun, January 4, 1992, Blackmun Papers, Box 602.

79. Stephanie A. Dangel to Harry A. Blackmun, January 10, 1992, Blackmun Papers, Box 602.

80. David H. Souter to the Conference, January 15, 1992, Blackmun Papers, Box 601.

81. Molly McUsic, Stephanie A. Dangel, Jeffrey A. Meyer, Andrea M. Ward, and Hugh W. Baxter to Harry A. Blackmun, January 16, 1992, Blackmun Papers, Box 602.

82. 1st Draft, *Planned Parenthood v. Casey*, 91–744, Chief Justice Rehnquist delivered the opinion of the Court, May 27, 1992, Blackmun Papers, Box 602.

83. Ibid.

84. Byron R. White to William H. Rehnquist, May 28, 1992, Blackmun Papers, Box 601.

85. Harry A. Blackmun to William H. Rehnquist, May 28, 1992, Blackmun Papers, Box 601.

86. Anthony M. Kennedy to Harry A. Blackmun, May 29, 1992, Blackmun Papers, Box 601.

87. Harry A. Blackmun Oral History, Library of Congress; Anne Gearan, "Blackmun's Papers Tell Tale of '92 Ruling on Abortion," Associated Press, March 5, 2004.

88. Harry A. Blackmun's Notes on Meeting with Anthony M. Kennedy, May 30, 1992, Blackmun Papers, Box 601.

89. 1st Draft, *Planned Parenthood v. Casey*, 91–744, Justices O'Connor, Kennedy, and Souter delivered the opinion of the Court" marked up by Justice Blackmun, June 3, 1992, Blackmun Papers, Box 602.

90. John Paul Stevens to Sandra Day O'Connor, Anthony M. Kennedy, and

David H. Souter, June 3, 1992, Blackmun Papers, Box 601.

91. Stephanie A. Dangel to Harry A. Blackmun, June 8, 1992, Blackmun Papers, Box 602.

92. William H. Rehnquist to all Law Clerks, June 10, 1992, Blackmun Papers, Box 601.

93. Stephanie A. Dangel to Harry A. Blackmun, June 16, 1992, Blackmun Papers, Box 602.

94. Ibid.

95. John Paul Stevens to Sandra Day O'Connor, Anthony M. Kennedy, and David H. Souter, June 18, 1992, Blackmun Papers, Box 601.

96. Anthony M. Kennedy to John Paul Stevens, June 18, 1992, Blackmun Papers, Box 601.

97. Stephanie A. Dangel to Harry A. Blackmun, June 20, 1992, Blackmun Papers, Box 602.

98. Stephanie A. Dangel to Harry A. Blackmun, June 21, 1992, Blackmun Papers, Box 601.

99. Stephanie A. Dangel to Harry A. Blackmun, June 23, 1992, Blackmun Papers, Box 602.

100. Stephanie A. Dangel's draft of *Planned Parenthood v. Casey*, 91–744, June 24, 1992, Blackmun Papers, Box 601.

101. Stephanie A. Dangel to Harry A. Blackmun (a), June 25, 1992, Blackmun Papers, Box 602.

102. Stephanie A. Dangel to Harry A. Blackmun (b), June 25, 1992, Blackmun Papers, Box 602.

103. Stephanie A. Dangel to Harry A. Blackmun (c), June 25, 1992, Blackmun Papers, Box 602.

104. *Cipollone v. Liggett Group, Inc.*, 505 U.S. 504 (1992); Stephanie A. Dangel to Harry A. Blackmun (d), June 25, 1992, Blackmun Papers, Box 602.

105. Stephanie A. Dangel to Harry A. Blackmun (a), June 26, 1992, Blackmun Papers, Box 602.

106. Stephanie A. Dangel to Harry A. Blackmun (b), June 26, 1992, Blackmun Papers, Box 602.

107. Stephanie A. Dangel to Harry A. Blackmun (c), June 26, 1992, Blackmun Papers, Box 602.

108. Stephanie A. Dangel to Harry A. Blackmun (d), June 26, 1992, Blackmun Papers, Box 602.

109. *Lucas v. South Carolina Coastal Council*, 505 U.S. 1003 (1992); *Sawyer v. Whitley*, 505 U.S. 333 (1992); Stephanie A. Dangel to Harry A. Blackmun, June 26, 1992 (e), Blackmun Papers, Box 602.

110. Harry A. Blackmun to John Paul Stevens, June 27, 1992, Blackmun Papers, Box 601.

111. Wanda Martinson to Harry A. Blackmun, June 30, 1992, Blackmun Papers, Box 601.

112. Stephanie A. Dangel to Harry A. Blackmun, July 1, 1992, Blackmun Papers, Box 602.

113. Harry A. Blackmun to Frank D. Wagner, July 2, 1992, Blackmun Papers, Box 601.

114. Anne Gearan, "Blackmun's Papers Tell Tale of '92 Ruling on Abortion," Associated Press, March 5, 2004.

115. Julian Burke Interview, Stanley Forman Reed Oral History Project, University of Kentucky.

116. *In Re Groban*, 352 U.S. 330 (1957); Norman Dorsen to John Marshall Harlan, II, February 9, 1957, Harlan Papers, Box 553.

117. *Martin v. Struthers*, 319 U.S. 141 (1943). Stone provided the fifth vote to strike down a city ordinance prohibiting door-to-door distribution of leaflets. The ordinance was used to convict a Jehovah's Witness who distributed flyers advertising a religious meeting.

118. *Dutton v. Evans*, 400 U.S. 74 (1970); Thomas C. Grey to Thurgood Marshall, undated note, 1969 Term, Marshall Papers, Box 69.

119. *Gannett v. DePasquale*, 443 U.S. 368 (1979).

120. While the data shows that more recent clerks said they had more influence than past clerks, it is possible that the results could be a function of the recency with which the Rehnquist Court clerks worked at the Court. It may be that the sense of one's importance in a clerkship may fade, or be put into perspective, as one grows older and gains more legal experience. Future research could test this hypothesis by repeatedly surveying clerks over time.

121. Lewis F. Powell, Jr., to John J. Buckley, John C. Jeffries, Jr., and Jack B. Owens, June 26, 1973, Powell Papers, Box 130b.

122. Lewis F. Powell, Jr., to Larry A. Hammond, May 1, 1973, Powell Papers, Box 130b.

123. *Furman v. Georgia*, 408 U.S. 238 (1972); Mike LaFond to Harry A. Blackmun, April 14, 1971, Blackmun Papers, Box 135.

124. *Church of the Lukumi Babalu v. City of Hialeah*, 508 U.S. 520 (1993); "Preliminary Memorandum," Brian D. Boyle to the cert pool, February 26, 1992, Blackmun Papers, Box 611.

125. *Employment Division, Department of Human Resources of Oregon v. Smith*, 494 U.S. 872 (1990); ibid.

126. Docket No. 91-948, Blackmun Papers, Box 722.

127. *New York v. United States*, 505 U.S. 144 (1992); "Preliminary Memorandum," Arnon Siegel to the cert pool, January 3, 1992, Blackmun Papers, Box 600.

128. *Baker v. Carr*, 369 U.S. 186 (1962); Jeffrey A. Meyer to Harry A. Blackmun, January 7, 1992, Blackmun Papers, Box 600. Justices Blackmun, White, and Stevens voted to deny cert while Justice Thomas and the other justices voted to grant. Docket No. 91-543, Blackmun Papers, Box 720.

129. See also Jan Palmer and Saul Brenner, "The Law Clerks' Recommendations and the Conference Vote on-the-Merits," *The Justice System Journal* 18 (1995): 187.

130. Tony Mauro, "Justices Give Key Role to Novice Lawyers," *USA Today*, June 5, 1998.

131. Ibid.

132. Ibid.

133. Lewis F. Powell, Jr., to John J. Buckley, John C. Jeffries, Jr., and Jack B. Owens, June 26, 1973, Powell Papers, Box 130b.

134. *INS v. Delgado*, 466 U.S. 210 (1984); *United States v. Brignoni-Ponce*, 422 U.S. 873 (1975); Paul W. Cane, Jr., to Lewis F. Powell, Jr., May 2, 1984, Powell Papers, Box 129a.

135. Lewis F. Powell, Jr., to Paul W. Cane, Jr., May 15, 1984, Powell Papers, Box 129a.

136. *Carbon Fuel Co. v. United Mine Workers*, 444 U.S. 212 (1979); Paul W. Cane, Jr., to Lewis F. Powell, Jr., undated, received October 29, 1979, Powell Papers, Box 129a.

137. Lewis F. Powell, Jr., to Paul W. Cane, Jr., November 2, 1979, Powell Papers, Box 129a.

138. *Regents of the University of California v. Bakke*, 438 U.S. 265 (1978); *Fullilove v. Klutznick*, 448 U.S. 448 (1980); Lewis F. Powell, Jr., to Robert D. Comfort and Samuel Estreicher, July 8, 1980, Powell Papers, Box 129a.

139. Barbara Gamarekian, "O'Connor's Agonizing Search for Law Clerks," *New York Times*, November 3, 1989, B7.

140. Lewis F. Powell, "What the Justices Are Saying . . . ," *American Bar Association Journal* 62 (1976): 1454.

141. See, e.g., Jeffrey Segal and Harold Spaeth, *The Supreme Court and the Attitudinal Model* (New York: Cambridge University Press, 1993).

NOTES TO CHAPTER 5

1. Lewis F. Powell, Jr., to Hamilton Fox, Lawrence A. Hammond, Covert Parnell, and J. Harvie Wilkinson, III, March 20, 1972, Powell Papers, Box 130b.

2. Edward P. Lazarus, *Closed Chambers: The First Eyewitness Account of the Epic Struggles inside the Supreme Court* (New York: Times Books, 1998), 6.

3. Tony Mauro, "Justices Give Key Role to Novice Lawyers," *USA Today*, June 5, 1998.

4. Ibid.

5. Henry J. Abraham, *The Judicial Process*, 3rd ed. (New York: Oxford University Press, 1975), 238.

6. Drew Pearson and Robert S. Allen, *The Nine Old Men* (Garden City, NY: Doubleday, Doran, 1936), 109.

7. Undated and unsigned "office procedure" memorandum, Stone Papers, Box 81.

8. Lewis F. Powell, Jr., to C. Cabell Chinnis, Jr., Ann Marie Coughlin, William J. Stuntz, Robert Stack, and Michael W. Mosman, April 8, 1986, Powell Papers, Box 130b.

9. William J. Brennan, Dean's Day Address, New York University Law School, 1979.

10. *Brown v. Board of Education*, 347 U.S. 483, 494 n.11 (1954).

11. In 1971, seventeen years after the decision, Justice Clark said, "I questioned the Chief's going with Myrdal in that opinion. I told him—and Hugo Black did, too—that it wouldn't go down well in the South and he didn't need it." But author Bernard Schwartz argued that the only reason Clark brought this footnote up was to change one of the citations from simply the last name "Clark" to "K. B. Clark" so that no one would confuse the justice with sociologist Kenneth Clark. Bernard Schwartz and Stephan Lesher, *Inside the Warren Court: 1953–1969* (Garden City, NY: Doubleday, 1983), 5–6, 46–47.

12. *United States v. Carolene Products Co.*, 304 U.S. 144, 152 n.4 (1938).

13. See Louis Lusky, *Our Nine Tribunes: The Supreme Court in Modern America* (Westport, CT: Praeger, 1993); Louis Lusky, "'Footnote Redux': A *Carolene Products* Reminiscence," *Columbia Law Review* 82 (1982): 1093; Stone Papers, Box 67.

14. Stone Papers, Box 48.

15. *P.J. Carlin Construction Co. et al. v. Heaney et al.*, 299 U.S. 41 (1936); Dennis J. Hutchinson and David J. Garrow, eds., *The Forgotten Memoir of John Knox* (Chicago: University of Chicago Press, 2002), 130–36.

16. Chester A. Newland, "Personal Assistants to Supreme Court Justices: The Law Clerks," *Oregon Law Review* 40 (1961): 312.

17. See, e.g., Philip B. Kurland, "Book Review," *University of Chicago Law Review* 22 (1954): 297; Dennis J. Hutchinson, *The Man Who Once Was Whizzer White: A Portrait of Justice Byron R. White* (New York: Free Press, 1998), 206.

18. William H. Rehnquist, "Who Writes Decisions of the Supreme Court?" *U.S. News and World Report*, December 13, 1957, 74.

19. Mauro, "Justices Give Key Role to Novice Lawyers."

20. This is in contrast to the standard account that opinion writing was delegated to clerks in response to general workload pressure and justices being forced to take on a more administrative role in managing paper flow and a small workforce of secretaries, messengers, and clerks. See, e.g., David M. O'Brien, *Storm Center*, 2nd ed. (New York: Norton, 1990), 124; Bradley J. Best, *Law Clerks, Support Personnel, and the Decline of Consensual Norms on the United States Supreme Court, 1935–1995* (New York: LFB Scholarly Publishing, 2002), 96.

21. William J. Brennan, "Chief Justice Warren," *Harvard Law Review* 88 (1974): 1, 2, 5.

22. See, e.g., Elliot Slotnick, "The Equality Principle and Majority Opinion Assignment on the United States Supreme Court," *Polity* 12 (1979): 318; Jan Palmer and Saul Brenner, "The Time Taken to Write Opinions as a Determinant of Opinion Assignments," *Judicature* 72 (1988): 179.

23. Transcriptions of conversations between Justice William O. Douglas and Professor Walter F. Murphy, Cassette No. 14: April 5, 1963, Princeton University Library, 1981. Douglas was so perturbed by the glacial pace of some of his colleagues that he proposed a rule change at the end of the 1948 Term. Specifically, Douglas suggested that an opinion should be reassigned if the opinion writer did not complete his assignment within three months. Sidney Fine, *Frank Murphy: The Washington Years* (Ann Arbor: University of Michigan Press, 1984), 254.

24. Richard Posner, *Overcoming Law* (Cambridge: Harvard University Press, 1999).

25. 323 U.S. 214 (1944).

26. David Williamson, "Leading Expert on U.S. Supreme Court Practice Publishes Latest 'Bible,'" University of North Carolina News Services, September 2, 2002, www.newswire.com.

27. Fine, *Frank Murphy*, 161.

28. Robert von Mehren Interview, Stanley Forman Reed Oral History Project, University of Kentucky.

29. 327 U.S. 178 (1946).

30. Bernard Schwartz, *Decision: How the Supreme Court Decides Cases* (New York: Oxford University Press, 1996), 53.

31. William O. Douglas, *The Court Years* (New York: Random House, 1980), 173.

32. Gordon B. Davidson Interview, Stanley Forman Reed Oral History Project, University of Kentucky.

33. Transcriptions of Conversations between Justice William O. Douglas and Professor Walter F. Murphy, Cassette No. 3: December 20, 1961, Princeton University Library, 1981.

34. *Baker v. Carr*, 369 U.S. 186 (1962).

35. *Elkins v. United States*, 364 U.S. 206 (1960); Schwartz and Lesher, *Inside the Warren Court*, 38.

36. Frankfurter's three clerks for the 1960 Term were Anthony G. Amsterdam, John D. French, and Daniel K. Mayers.

37. *McGowan v. Maryland*, 366 U.S. 420 (1961). Frankfurter's concurrence totaled ninety-three pages, including a ten-page appendix. By contrast, Douglas's dissent totaled twenty pages.

38. *Monroe v. Pape*, 365 U.S. 167 (1961). Frankfurter's dissent totaled fifty-seven pages while Douglas's majority opinion totaled twenty-four pages.

39. Transcriptions of Conversations

between Justice William O. Douglas and Professor Walter F. Murphy, Cassette No. 3: December 20, 1961, Princeton University Library, 1981.

40. F. Aley Allen Interview, Stanley Forman Reed Oral History Project, University of Kentucky.

41. *Schneckloth v. Bustamonte*, 412 U.S. 218 (1973); Bob Woodward and Scott Armstrong, *The Brethren* (New York: Simon and Schuster, 1980), 320.

42. Lewis F. Powell, Jr., to Eugene J. Comey, Tyler A. Baker, Charles C. Ames, and David A. Martin, September 1976, Powell Papers, Box 130b.

43. David Savage, *Turning Right: The Making of the Rehnquist Supreme Court* (New York: Wiley, 1992), 73.

44. Lewis F. Powell, Jr., to Cammie R. Robinson, David A. Charny, Joseph E. Neuhaus, and Robert M. Couch, June 23, 1984, Powell Papers, Box 130b.

45. *San Antonio Independent School District v. Rodriguez*, 411 U.S. 1 (1973); *Chambers v. Mississippi*, 410 U.S. 284 (1973); *United States v. Basye*, 410 U.S. 441 (1973); Lewis F. Powell, Jr., to Larry A. Hammond, J. Harvie Wilkinson, III, and William C. Kelly, Jr., December 19, 1972, Powell Papers, Box 130b.

46. *San Antonio Independent School District v. Rodriguez*, 411 U.S. 1 (1973); *McGinnis v. Royster*, 410 U.S. 263 (1973); *Rosario v. Rockefeller*, 410 U.S. 752 (1973); *In Re Griffiths*, 413 U.S. 717 (1973); Lewis F. Powell, Jr., to Larry A. Hammond, J. Harvie Wilkinson, III, and William C. Kelly, Jr., January 18, 1973, Powell Papers, Box 130b.

47. Lewis F. Powell, Jr., to Larry A. Hammond, February 18, 1973, Powell Papers, Box 130b.

48. *INDOPCO, Inc. v. CIR*, 503 U.S. 79 (1992); Andrea Ward to Harry A. Blackmun, January 6, 1991, Blackmun Papers, Box 1567.

49. This is not to be confused with our discussion of "case swapping" in the previous chapter. Lewis F. Powell, Jr., to Hamilton Fox, Lawrence A. Hammond, Covert

Parnell, and J. Harvie Wilkinson, III, June 2, 1972, Powell Papers, Box 130b.

50. *Callins v. Collins*, 510 U.S. 1141 (1994); Michelle L. Alexander to Harry A. Blackmun, October 5, 1993, Box 1553.

51. *Planned Parenthood v. Casey*, 505 U.S. 833 (1992); Stephanie A. Dangel to Harry A. Blackmun, June 16, 1992, Blackmun Papers, Box 602.

52. *Shields v. Atlantic Coast Line Railroad Company*, 350 U.S. 318 (1956); Julian Burke Interview, Stanley Forman Reed Oral History Project, University of Kentucky.

53. Lewis D. Sargentich to Thurgood Marshall, undated note, 1970 Term, Marshall Papers, Box 69.

54. Martha A. Matthews to Harry A. Blackmun, February 9, 1990, Blackmun Papers, Box 547.

55. Schwartz and Lesher, *Inside the Warren Court*, 44.

56. Ibid.

57. See, e.g., Black Papers, Manuscript Division, Library of Congress, Washington, D.C.

58. Lewis F. Powell, Jr., to Eugene J. Comey, Tyler A. Baker, Charles C. Ames, and David A. Martin, September 1976, Powell Papers, Box 130b.

59. Lewis F. Powell, Jr., to Larry A. Hammond, William C. Kelly, Jr., and J. Harvie Wilkinson, III, October 25, 1972, Powell Papers, Box 130b.

60. Lewis F. Powell, Jr., to Eugene J. Comey, Tyler A. Baker, Charles C. Ames, and David A. Martin, September 1976, Powell Papers, Box 130b.

61. *Garcia v. San Antonio Metropolitan Transit Authority*, 469 U.S. 528 (1985); Powell notes from September 25, 1984, on "Bench Memorandum," September 22, 1984, Powell Papers, Box 117.

62. *Callins v. Collins*, 510 U.S. 1141 (1994), Blackmun Papers, Boxes 648–49.

63. *San Antonio Independent School District v. Rodriguez*, 411 U.S. 1 (1973); Lewis F. Powell, Jr., to Larry A. Hammond, September 21, 1972, Powell Papers, Box 130b.

64. Lewis F. Powell, Jr., to Larry A. Hammond, J. Harvie Wilkinson, III, William C. Kelly, Jr., Thomas W. Reavley, April 13, 1973, Powell Papers, Box 130b.

65. Lewis F. Powell, Jr., to James O. Browning, Mark E. Newell, Michael F. Sturley, and Daniel Rives Kistler, November 1, 1982, Powell Papers, Box 130b.

66. *Planned Parenthood v. Casey*, 505 U.S. 833 (1992).

67. Kevin J. Worthen, "Shirt-Tales: Clerking for Byron White," *Brigham Young University Law Review* 349 (1994): 349; Savage, *Turning Right*, 74.

68. Lewis F. Powell, Jr., to Eugene J. Comey, Tyler A. Baker, Charles C. Ames, and David A. Martin, September 1976, Powell Papers, Box 130b.

69. Lewis F. Powell, Jr., to Eugene J. Comey, Tyler A. Baker, Charles C. Ames, and David A. Martin, September 1976, Powell Papers, Box 130b.

70. Lewis F. Powell, Jr., to Larry A. Hammond, William C. Kelly, Jr., Thomas W. Reavley, and J. Harvie Wilkinson, III, April 2, 1973, Powell Papers, Box 130b.

71. Harold Burton to Thomas N. O'Neill, Jr., and William B. Matteson, July 1, 1954, Harlan Papers, Box 561.

72. Arthur Rosett Interview, Stanley Forman Reed Oral History Project, University of Kentucky.

73. Quoted in Felix Frankfurter to Stanley Reed, December 3, 1941, David M. O'Brien, *Storm Center*, 2nd ed. (New York: Norton, 1990), 163.

74. Robert von Mehren Interview, Stanley Forman Reed Oral History Project, University of Kentucky.

75. Arthur Rosett Interview, Stanley Forman Reed Oral History Project, University of Kentucky.

76. Mauro, "Justices Give Key Role to Novice Lawyers."

77. *Roe v. Wade*, 410 U.S. 113 (1973); *Doe v. Bolton*, 410 U.S. 179 (1973).

78. George T. Frampton, Jr., to Harry A. Blackmun, May 26, 1972, Blackmun Papers, Box 151.

79. Randall P. Bazanson to Harry A. Blackmun, November 27, 1972, Blackmun Papers, Box 151.

80. Randall P. Bazanson to Harry A. Blackmun, December 14, 1972, Blackmun Papers, Box 151.

81. *Griswold v. Connecticut*, 381 U.S. 479 (1965); *Stanley v. Georgia*, 394 U.S. 557 (1969).

82. *Williamson v. Lee Optical Co.*, 348 U.S. 483 (1955); Randall P. Bazanson to Harry A. Blackmun, January 11, 1973, Blackmun Papers, Box 151.

83. Lewis F. Powell, Jr., to Hamilton Fox, Lawrence A. Hammond, Covert Parnell, and J. Harvie Wilkinson, III, April 25, 1972, Powell Papers, Box 130b.

84. See, e.g., Sean Donahue, "Behind the Pillars of Justice: Remarks on Law Clerks," *The Long Term View* 3 (1995): 81.

85. Ibid.

86. Mauro, "Justices Give Key Role to Novice Lawyers."

87. *Reno v. American Civil Liberties Union*, 521 U.S. 844 (1997); ibid.

88. Edward Lazarus, *Closed Chambers: The First Eyewitness Account of the Epic Struggles inside the Supreme Court* (New York: Times Books, 1998), 271.

89. Schwartz, *Decision*, 54.

90. William H. Rehnquist, *The Supreme Court: How It Was, How It Is* (New York: Morrow, 1987), 300.

91. William H. Rehnquist, "Are the Old Times Dead?" Mac Swinford Lecture, University of Kentucky, September 23, 1983.

92. Schwartz, *Decision*, 52.

93. Alexander Bickel, *The Judiciary and Responsible Government: 1910–1921* (New York: Macmillan, 1964), 82.

94. *Edwards v. Aguillard*, 482 U.S. 578 (1987); Lewis F. Powell, Jr., to Leslie S. Gielow, March 10, 1987, Powell Papers, Box 135.

95. Powell notes from March 17, 1987, on "No. 85-1513, Edwards v. Aguillard, SECOND DRAFT," undated, Powell Papers, Box 135.

96. *Garcia v. San Antonio Metropolitan Transit Authority*, 469 U.S. 528 (1985); Lewis F. Powell, Jr., to Annmarie Levins,

October 18, 1984, Powell Papers, Box 117.

97. *Opper v. United States*, 348 U.S. 84 (1954); Gordon B. Davidson Interview, Stanley Forman Reed Oral History Project, University of Kentucky.

98. Robert von Mehren Interview, Stanley Forman Reed Oral History Project, University of Kentucky.

99. Arthur Rosett Interview, Stanley Forman Reed Oral History Project, University of Kentucky.

100. Schwartz, *Decision*, 52.

101. Ibid., 53. It should be noted, however, that it can be difficult to assess the amount of involvement a justice has in the opinion-writing process by solely examining case files. For example, the opinion drafts contained in the case files of Justice Marshall contain very few written edits from the justice, though there are often multiple drafts to many of his opinions. As a result, it is virtually impossible to know from this material alone the extent of the oral conversations Marshall and other justices had with their clerks about the initial drafts and subsequent revisions without interviewing the clerks as we have done here.

102. Lewis F. Powell, Jr., to Eugene J. Comey, Tyler A. Baker, Charles C. Ames, and David A. Martin, September 1976, Powell Papers, Box 130b.

103. Lewis F. Powell, Jr., to Larry A. Hammond, William C. Kelly, Jr., and J. Harvie Wilkinson, III, October 25, 1972, Powell Papers, Box 130b.

104. O'Brien, *Storm Center*, 162.

105. Ibid.

106. Schwartz, *Decision*, 50.

107. Ibid., 52.

108. Savage, *Turning Right*, 74.

109. Anthony T. Kronman, *The Lost Lawyer: Failing Ideals in the Legal Profession* (Cambridge: Harvard University Press, 1995).

110. Lewis F. Powell, Jr., to Cammie R. Robinson, David A. Charny, Joseph E. Neuhaus, and Robert M. Couch, December 12, 1983, Powell Papers, Box 130b.

111. Lewis F. Powell, Jr., to Cammie R. Robinson, David A. Charny, Joseph E. Neuhaus, and Robert M. Couch, March 14, 1984, Powell Papers, Box 130b.

112. Lewis F. Powell, Jr., to Hamilton Fox, Lawrence A. Hammond, Covert Parnell, and J. Harvie Wilkinson, III, May 11, 1972, Powell Papers, Box 130b.

113. Lewis F. Powell, Jr., to Larry A. Hammond and J. Harvie Wilkinson, III, September 27, 1972, Powell Papers, Box 130b.

114. Kevin J. Worthen, "Shirt-Tales: Clerking for Byron White," *Brigham Young University Law Review* (1994): 349.

115. See, e.g., Bradley J. Best, *Law Clerks, Support Personnel, and the Decline of Consensual Norms on the United States Supreme Court, 1935–1995* (New York: LFB Scholarly Publishing, 2002).

116. *United States v. Caldwell* (companion case to *Branzburg v. Hayes*), 408 U.S. 665 (1972); *Gravel v. United States*, 408 U.S. 606 (1972); *Gelbard v. United States*, 408 U.S. 41 (1972); *Wright v. Council City of Emporia*, 407 U.S. 451 (1972); Lewis F. Powell, Jr., to Hamilton Fox, Lawrence A. Hammond, Covert Parnell, and J. Harvie Wilkinson, III, April 25, 1972, Powell Papers, Box 130b.

117. Lewis F. Powell, Jr., to Hamilton Fox, Lawrence A. Hammond, Covert Parnell, and J. Harvie Wilkinson, III, May 11, 1972, Powell Papers, Box 130b.

118. James R. Donovan to Harry A. Blackmun, June 22, 1993, Blackmun Papers, Box 1568.

119. Lewis F. Powell, Jr., to Powell clerks and spouses, December 12, 1977, Powell Papers, Box 130b.

120. Remarks by Justice Antonin Scalia to the Institute for Constitutional Studies, Supreme Court Historical Society, June 27, 2002.

121. *Greer v. Spock*, 424 U.S. 828 (1976); *Young v. American Mini Theatres*, 427 U.S. 50 (1976); Lewis F. Powell, Jr., to Eugene J. Comey, Tyler A. Baker, Charles C. Ames, and David A. Martin, September 1976, Powell Papers, Box 130b.

122. Lewis F. Powell, Jr., to Larry A. Hammond, William C. Kelly, Jr., and J. Harvie Wilkinson, III, October 25, 1972, Powell Papers, Box 130b.

123. Lewis F. Powell, Jr., to C. Cabel Chinnis, Jr., Ann Marie Coughlin, William J. Stuntz, and Michael W. Mosman, October 25, 1985, Powell Papers, Box 130b.

124. William H. Rehnquist, Remarks, Ninth Circuit Conference, Coronado, California, July 27, 1982, 24.

NOTES TO CHAPTER 6

1. Bernard Schwartz, *Decision: How the Supreme Court Decides Cases* (New York: Oxford University Press, 1996), 257.

2. *Brown v. Board of Education*, 347 U.S. 483 (1954).

3. William H. Rehnquist, "Who Writes Decisions of the Supreme Court?" *U.S. News and World Report*, December 13, 1957, 275.

4. "'Sway' of Clerks on Court Cited," *New York Times*, December 10, 1957, 23.

5. William D. Rogers, "Do Law Clerks Wield Power in Supreme Court Cases?" *U.S. News and World Report*, February 21, 1958, 114.

6. Alexander M. Bickel, "The Court: An Indictment Analyzed," *New York Times*, April 27, 1958, 6.

7. Bernard Schwartz and Stephan Lesher, *Inside the Warren Court: 1953–1969* (Garden City, NY: Doubleday, 1983), 37.

8. John C. Stennis, Speech on the Senate Floor (May 6, 1958), reprinted in "Investigate Supreme Court's 'Law Clerk' System?" *U.S. News and World Report*, May 16, 1958, 117.

9. "Stennis Is Wary of Court's Clerks," *New York Times*, May 7, 1958, 27; see also Henry J. Abraham, *The Judicial Process*, 3rd ed. (New York: Oxford University Press, 1975), 238; Bernard Schwartz and Stephan Lesher, *Inside the Warren Court: 1953–1969* (Garden City, NY: Doubleday, 1983), 37.

10. "Stennis Is Wary," 27.

11. Bob Woodward and Scott Armstrong, *The Brethren: Inside the Supreme Court* (New York: Simon and Schuster, 1979).

12. Edward Lazarus, *Closed Chambers: The First Eyewitness Account of the Epic Struggles inside the Supreme Court* (New York: Times Books, 1998).

13. Richard L. Williams, "Justices Run 'Nine Little Law Firms' at Supreme Court," *Smithsonian*, February 1977, 88.

14. Ibid.

15. William H. Rehnquist, "Who Writes Decisions of the Supreme Court?" *U.S. News and World Report*, December 13, 1957, 74.

16. William O. Douglas, *The Court Years, 1939–1975: The Autobiography of William O. Douglas* (New York: Random House, 1980), 172.

17. Harry A. Blackmun to Judith W. Wegner, February 25, 1993, Blackmun Papers, Box 1562.

18. See, e.g., *Report of the Study Group on the Caseload of the Supreme Court* (Washington, DC: U.S. Government Printing Office, 1972); *Report of the Commission on Revision of the Appellate Court System* (Washington, DC: U.S. Government Printing Office, 1975); William H. Alsup, "A Policy Assessment of the National Court of Appeals," *Hastings Law Journal* 25 (1974): 1313; James F. Blumstein, "The Supreme Court's Jurisdiction: Reform Proposals, Discretionary Review, and Writ Dismissals," *Vanderbilt Law Review* 26 (1973): 895; Eugene Gressman, "The National Court of Appeals: A Dissent," *American Bar Association Journal* 59 (1973): 253; Douglas A. Poe, John R. Schmidt, and Wayne W. Whalen, "A National Court of Appeals: A Dissenting View," *Northwestern University Law Review* 67 (1973): 842; William J. Brennan, "The National Court of Appeals: Another Dissent," *University of Chicago Law Review* 40 (1973): 473; Roy W. McLeese, II,

"Disagreement in D.C.: The Relationship between the Supreme Court and the D.C. Circuit and Its Implications for a National Court of Appeals," *New York University Law Review* 59 (1984): 1048.

19. Nadine J. Wichern, "A Court of Clerks, Not of Men: Serving Justice in the Media Age," *DePaul Law Review* 49 (Winter 1999): 621.

20. Mary Ann Glendon, *A Nation under Lawyers: How the Crisis in the Legal Profession Is Transforming American Society* (Cambridge: Harvard University Press, 1996).

21. Wade H. McCree, Jr., "Bureaucratic Justice: An Early Warning," *University of Pennsylvania Law Review* 129 (April 1981): 777, 778–79.

Bibliography

MANUSCRIPT COLLECTIONS

Hugo Black Papers, Manuscript Division, Library of Congress, Washington, DC.

Harry A. Blackmun Papers, Manuscript Division, Library of Congress, Washington, DC.

William O. Douglas Papers, Manuscript Division, Library of Congress, Washington, DC.

John Marshall Harlan Papers, Princeton University Library, Princeton, NJ.

Thurgood Marshall Papers, Manuscript Division, Library of Congress, Washington, DC.

Lewis F. Powell, Jr., Papers, Washington and Lee University School of Law, Lexington, VA.

Stanley Forman Reed Oral History Project, Stanley Forman Reed Collection, Modern Political Archives, Division of Special Collections and Archives, University of Kentucky Libraries, University of Kentucky, Lexington, KY.

Wiley Rutledge Papers, Manuscript Division, Library of Congress, Washington, DC.

Harlan Fiske Stone Papers, Manuscript Division, Library of Congress, Washington, DC.

Earl Warren Papers, Manuscript Divison, Library of Congress, Washington, DC.

GOVERNMENT RECORDS AND DOCUMENTS

41 Stat. 209, July 19, 1919.
Act of Aug. 4, 1886, ch. 902, 24 Stat. 222.

Code of Conduct for Law Clerks of the Supreme Court of the United States, 1989.

Hearings on S. 2060 and 2061 before a Subcomm. of the Committee on the Judiciary, 68th Cong., 1st Sess. (1924).

Rehnquist, William H. "2003 Year-End Report on the Federal Judiciary," www.supremecourtus.gov.

"Report of the Commission on Revision of the Appellate Court System," Washington, DC: U.S. Government Printing Office, 1975.

"Report of the Study Group on the Caseload of the Supreme Court," Washington, DC: U.S. Government Printing Office, 1972.

MAGAZINE AND INTERNET ARTICLES

Bickel, Alexander M. "The Court: An Indictment Analyzed," *New York Times*, April 27, 1958, 6.

Biskupic, Joan. "Clerks Gain Status, Clout in the Temple of Justice," *Washington Post*, January 2, 1994, A23.

Carlson, Bob. "Ex-Clerks Downplay *The Brethren*," *Virginia Law Weekly*, February 1, 1980, 1.

Coyle, Marcia. "31 New Law Clerks Begin at Supreme Court," *National Law Journal*, October 12, 1987, 3.

Eastland, Terry. "While Justice Sleeps," *National Review*, April 21, 1989, 25.

Gamarekian, Barbara. "O'Connor's Agonizing Search for Law Clerks," *New York Times*, November 3, 1989, B7.

Gearan, Anne. "Blackmun's Papers Tell Tale of '92 Ruling on Abortion," Associated Press, March 5, 2004.

Lane, Charles. "In Court Clerks' Breach, a Provocative Precedent," *Washington Post*, October 17, 2004, D01.

Lauter, D. "Clerkships: Picking the Elite," *National Law Journal*, February 9, 1987, 1.

Margolick, David, Evgenia Pretz, and Michael Shnayerson, "The Path to Florida," *Vanity Fair*, October 2004, 310–23, 355–67, 369.

Mauro, Tony. "Congress Grills Justices on Clerks," *USA Today*, March, 11, 1999.

———. "Court Justices Defend Hiring Record," *USA Today*, December 8, 1998.

———. "For Lawyers, Clerkship Is Ultimate Job," *USA Today*, June 5, 1998.

———. "High Court Hires More Minorities," *USA Today*, September 9, 1999.

———. "Insiders' Book Breaks Code of Silence," *USA Today*, March 13, 1998.

———. "Rehnquist Won't Discuss Minority Clerks," *USA Today*, June 10, 1998.

———. "Scalia Defends Clerk Hiring Record," *USA Today*, February 22, 1999.

———. "Sentencing, Clerkships Discussed at High Court Budget Hearing," www.law.com, April 10, 2003.

———. "Supreme Court Renovations Set to Start," *American Lawyer Media*, April 21, 2003.

Myers, Ken. "Law Professor Opens New Book: Clerking for U.S. Supreme Court," *National Law Journal*, April 22, 1996, A20.

Price, Deb. "Civil Rites: Arguments against Same-sex Marriage Mirror Those That Kept the Races Apart," *Detroit News*, April 18, 1997.

Rehnquist, William H. "Who Writes Decisions of the Supreme Court?" *U.S. News and World Report*, December 13, 1957.

Rogers, William D. "Do Law Clerks Wield Power in Supreme Court Cases?" *U.S.*

News and World Report, Feb. 21, 1958.

Stennis, John C. Speech on the Senate Floor (May 6, 1958), reprinted in "Investigate Supreme Court's 'Law Clerk' System?" *U.S. News and World Report*, May 16, 1958.

"Stennis Is Wary of Court's Clerks," *New York Times*, May 7, 1958, 27.

"'Sway' of Clerks on Court Cited," *New York Times*, Dec. 10, 1957, 23.

Taylor, Jr., Stuart. "When High Court's Away, Clerks' Work Begins," *New York Times*, Sept. 23, 1988.

Wayne, Ellen. "It's Not Too Late to Clerk," *National Law Journal* 24 (December 10, 2001): B14.

Williams, Richard L. "Justices Run 'Nine Little Law Firms' at Supreme Court," *Smithsonian*, February 1977, 88.

Williamson, David. "Leading Expert on U.S. Supreme Court Practice Publishes Latest 'Bible,'" University of North Carolina News Services, September 2, 2002, www.newswire.com.

BOOKS

Abraham, Henry J. *The Judicial Process*, 3rd ed. New York: Oxford University Press, 1975.

Baker, Leonard. *Brandeis and Frankfurter: A Dual Biography*. New York: Harper and Row, 1984.

Bent, Silas. *Justice Oliver Wendell Holmes: A Biography*. Garden City, NY: Garden City Publishing, 1932.

Best, Bradley J. *Law Clerks, Support Personnel, and the Decline of Consensual Norms on the United States Supreme Court, 1935–1995*. New York: LFB Scholarly Publishing, 2002.

Bickel, Alexander. *The Judiciary and Responsible Government: 1910–1921*. New York: Macmillan, 1964.

Danelski, David J., and Joseph S. Tulchin, eds. *The Autobiographical Notes of Charles Evans Hughes*. Cambridge: Harvard University Press, 1973.

Douglas, William O. *The Court Years*,

1939–1975: The Autobiography of William O. Douglas. New York: Random House, 1980.

Epstein, Lee, and Jack Knight. *The Choices Justices Make.* Washington, DC: CQ Press, 1997.

Fine, Sidney. *Frank Murphy: The Washington Years.* Ann Arbor: University of Michigan Press, 1984.

Frank, John P. *The Marble Palace.* New York: Knopf, 1958.

Friedman, Lawrence. *A History of American Law.* New York: Simon and Schuster, 1973.

Glendon, Mary Ann. *A Nation under Lawyers: How the Crisis in the Legal Profession Is Transforming American Society.* Cambridge: Harvard University Press, 1996.

Hutchinson, Dennis J. *The Man Who Once Was Whizzer White: A Portrait of Justice Byron R. White.* New York: Free Press, 1998.

Hutchinson, Dennis J., and David J. Garrow, eds. *The Forgotten Memoir of John Knox: A Year in the Life of a Supreme Court Clerk in FDR's Washington.* Chicago: University of Chicago Press, 2002.

Kronman, Anthony T. *The Lost Lawyer: Failing Ideals in the Legal Profession.* Cambridge: Harvard University Press, 1995.

Lazarus, Edward. *Closed Chambers: The First Eyewitness Account of the Epic Struggles inside the Supreme Court.* New York: Times Books, 1998.

Lusky, Louis. *Our Nine Tribunes: The Supreme Court in Modern America.* Westport, CT: Praeger, 1993.

Maltzman, Forrest, James F. Spriggs, II, and Paul J. Wahlbeck. *Crafting Law on the Supreme Court: The Collegial Game.* New York: Cambridge University Press, 2000.

Mason, Alpheus T. *Harlan Fiske Stone: Pillar of the Law.* New York: Viking Press, 1956.

Murdoch, Joyce, and Deb Price. *Courting Justice: Gay Men and Lesbians v. the*

Supreme Court. New York: Basic Books, 2001.

Nelson, Richard R., and Sidney G. Winter. *An Evolutionary Theory of Economic Change.* Cambridge: Harvard University Press, 1985.

Oakley, John B., and Robert S. Thompson. *Law Clerks and the Judicial Process: Perceptions and Functions of Law Clerks in American Courts.* Berkeley: University of California Press, 1980.

O'Brien, David M. *Storm Center: The Supreme Court in American Politics,* 2nd ed. New York: Norton, 1990.

Pearson, Drew, and Robert S. Allen. *The Nine Old Men.* Garden City, NY: Doubleday, Doran, 1936.

Peppers, Todd C. "Courtiers of the Marble Palace: The Rise of the Supreme Court Law Clerk." Diss., Emory University, 2003.

Perry, H. W. *Deciding to Decide: Agenda Setting in the United States Supreme Court.* Cambridge: Harvard University Press, 1991.

Posner, Richard A. *The Federal Courts: Challenge and Reform.* Cambridge: Harvard University Press, 1996.

———. *The Federal Courts: Crisis and Reform.* Cambridge: Harvard University Press, 1985.

———. *Overcoming Law.* Cambridge: Harvard University Press, 1999.

Provine, Doris Marie. *Case Selection in the United States Supreme Court.* Chicago: University of Chicago Press, 1980.

Rehnquist, William H. *The Supreme Court: How It Was, How It Is.* New York: Morrow, 1987.

Savage, David. *Turning Right: The Making of the Rehnquist Supreme Court.* New York: Wiley, 1992.

Schwartz, Bernard. *Decision: How the Supreme Court Decides Cases.* New York: Oxford University Press, 1996.

———. *Super Chief: Earl Warren and His Supreme Court.* New York: NYU Press, 1984.

Schwartz, Bernard, and Stephan Lesher,

Inside the Warren Court: 1953–1969. Garden City, NY: Doubleday, 1983.

Segal, Jeffrey A., and Harold J. Spaeth. *The Supreme Court and the Attitudinal Model.* New York: Cambridge University Press, 1993.

———. *The Supreme Court and the Attitudinal Model Revisited.* New York: Cambridge University Press, 2002.

Stern, Robert H., Eugene Gressman, and Stephen M. Shapiro. *Supreme Court Practice,* 6th ed. Washington, DC: Bureau of National Affairs, 1986.

Stevens, Robert. *Law School: Legal Education from the 1850s to the 1980s.* Chapel Hill: University of North Carolina Press, 1983.

Strauss, Debra M. *Behind the Bench: The Guide to Judicial Clerkships.* Chicago: BarBri Group, 2002.

Urofsky, Melvin I. *A March of Liberty: A Constitutional History of the United States.* New York: Knopf, 1988.

———, ed. *The Douglas Letters.* Bethesda, MD: Adler and Adler, 1987.

White, G. Edward. *Alger Hiss's Looking-Glass Wars: The Covert Life of a Soviet Spy.* New York: Oxford University Press, 2004.

Witt, Elder. *Guide to the U.S. Supreme Court,* 2nd ed. Washington, DC: CQ Press, 1990.

Woodward, Bob, and Scott Armstrong. *The Brethren.* New York: Simon and Schuster, 1980.

Yarbrough, Tinsley E. *John Marshall Harlan: Great Dissenter of the Warren Court.* New York: Oxford University Press, 1992.

JOURNAL ARTICLES, BOOK CHAPTERS, AND CONFERENCE PRESENTATIONS

Acheson, Dean. "Recollections of Service with the Federal Supreme Court." *Alabama Lawyer* 18 (1957): 355–66.

Agostini, Robert M., and Brian P. Corrigan. "Do As We Say or Do As We Do? How the Supreme Court Law Clerk Controversy Reveals a Lack of Accountability at the High Court." *Hofstra Labor and Employment Law Journal* 18 (Spring 2001): 625–58.

Alsup, William H. "A Policy Assessment of the National Court of Appeals." *Hastings Law Journal* 25 (1974): 1313.

Avery, Christopher, Christine Jolls, Richard Posner, and Alvin E. Roth. "The Market for Federal Judicial Law Clerks." *University of Chicago Law Review* 68 (Summer 2001): 793–902.

Baier, Paul R. "The Law Clerks: Profile of an Institution." *Vanderbilt Law Review* 26 (1973): 1125–73.

Berle, Jr., A. A. "Legal Profession and Legal Education." In *The Legal Profession: Responsibility and Regulation,* Geoffrey C. Hazard, Jr., and Deborah L. Rhode, eds. (Westbury, NY: Foundation Press, 1933).

Blumstein, James F. "The Supreme Court's Jurisdiction: Reform Proposals, Discretionary Review, and Writ Dismissals." *Vanderbilt Law Review* 26 (1973): 895.

Brennan, William J. "Chief Justice Warren." *Harvard Law Review* 88 (1974): 1.

———. "The National Court of Appeals: Another Dissent." *University of Chicago Law Review* 40 (1973): 473–77.

Brenner, Saul. "The Memos of Supreme Court Law Clerk William Rehnquist: Conservative Tracts, or Mirrors of His Justice's Mind?" *Judicature* 76 (August/September 1992): 77–81.

Brown, Mark R. "Gender Discrimination in the Supreme Court's Clerkship Selection Process." *Oregon Law Review* 75 (1996): 359–88.

"Chief Justice Vinson and His Law Clerks." *Northwestern Law Review* 49 (1954): 26–35.

Coenen, Dan T. "Book Review—Deciding to Decide: Agenda Setting in the United States Supreme Court." *Constitutional Commentary* 10 (1993): 180–93.

Crump, David. "Law Clerks: Their Roles and Relationships with Their Judges." *Judicature* 69 (1986): 236–40.

Ditslear, Corey, and Lawrence Baum.

"Selection of Law Clerks and Polarization in the U.S. Supreme Court." *Journal of Politics* 63 (2001): 869–85.

Donahue, Sean. "Behind the Pillars of Justice: Remarks on Law Clerks." *The Long Term View* 3 (1995): 77–84.

Edwards, Harry T. "A Judge's View on Justice, Bureaucracy, and Legal Method." *Michigan Law Review* 80 (1981): 248–69.

Garrow, David J. "Book Review—'The Lowest Form of Animal Life'? Supreme Court Clerks and Supreme Court History," *Cornell Law Review* 84 (March 1999): 855–94.

———. "The Supreme Court and *The Brethren*." *Constitutional Commentary* 18 (Summer 2001): 55–82.

Gillman, Howard. "The New Institutionalism, Part I." *Law and Courts* (Winter 1996–97): 6–11.

Greenya, John. "Super Clerks," *Washington Lawyer* 6 (May–June 1992): 40.

Gressman, Eugene. "The National Court of Appeals: A Dissent." *American Bar Association Journal* 59 (1973): 253.

Hellman, Arthur D. "Central Staff in Appellate Courts: The Experience of the Ninth Circuit." *California Law Review* 68 (1980): 937–1003.

Kenney, Sally J. "Beyond Principals and Agents: Seeing Courts as Organizations by Comparing Referendaires at the European Court of Justice and Law Clerks at the U.S. Supreme Court." *Comparative Political Studies* 33 (2000): 593–625.

———. "Puppeteers or Agents? What Lazarus's Closed Chambers Adds to Our Understanding of Law Clerks at the U.S. Supreme Court." *Law and Social Inquiry* (Winter 2000): 185–226.

Kozinski, Alex. "Conduct Unbecoming." *Yale Law Journal* 108 (1999): 835.

———. "Making the Case for Law Clerks." *The Long Term View* 3 (1995): 55–59.

Kurland, Philip B. "Book Review." *University of Chicago Law Review* 22 (1954): 297.

Lusky, Louis. "Footnote Redux: A *Carolene Products* Reminiscence." *Columbia Law Review* 82 (1982): 1093.

Mahoney, J. Daniel. "The Second Circuit Review—1986–1987 Term: Foreword: Law Clerks: For Better or for Worse?" *Brooklyn Law Review* 54 (1988): 321–45.

McCree, Jr., Wade H. "Bureaucratic Justice: An Early Warning." *University of Pennsylvania Law Review* 129 (April 1981): 777–79.

McLeese, II, Roy W. "Disagreement in D.C.: The Relationship between the Supreme Court and the D.C. Circuit and Its Implications for a National Court of Appeals." *New York University Law Review* 59 (1984): 1048.

Nesson, Charles. "Mr. Justice Harlan." *Harvard Law Review* 85 (1971): 390.

Newland, Chester A. "Personal Assistants to Supreme Court Justices: The Law Clerks." *Oregon Law Review* 40 (1961): 299–317.

Oakley, John. "Defining the Limits of Delegation." *The Long Term View* 3 (1995): 85–93.

Oakley, John B., and Robert S. Thompson. "Law Clerks in Judges' Eyes: Tradition and Innovation in the Use of Legal Staff by American Judges." *California Law Review* 67 (1979): 1286–1317.

O'Brien, David M. "The Rehnquist Court's Shrinking Plenary Docket." *Judicature* 81 (Sept.–Oct. 1997): 58–65.

Orren, Karen, and Stephen Skowronek, "Beyond the Iconography of Order: Notes for a 'New' Institutionalism." In *The Dynamics of American Politics: Approaches and Interpretations*, Lawrence C. Dodd and Calvin Jillson, eds. (Boulder, CO: Westview Press, 1994).

Owens, John B. "The Clerk, the Thief, His Life as a Baker: Ashton Embry and the Supreme Court Leak Scandal of 1919." *Northwestern University Law Review* 95 (2000): 271–308.

Palmer, Jan, and Saul Brenner. "The Law Clerks' Recommendations and the

Conference Vote on-the-Merits." *Justice System Journal* 18 (1995): 187–97.

Palmer, Jan, and Saul Brenner. "The Time Taken to Write Opinions as a Determinant of Opinion Assignments." *Judicature* 72 (1988): 179–84.

Poe, Douglas A., John R. Schmidt, and Wayne W. Whalen. "A National Court of Appeals: A Dissenting View." *Northwestern University Law Review* 67 (1973): 842–56.

Powell, Lewis F. "What the Justices Are Saying . . . ," *American Bar Association Journal* 62 (1976): 1454.

Rehnquist, William H. "The Supreme Court's Conference." In *Judges on Judging: Views from the Bench*, David M. O'Brien, ed. (Chatham, NJ: Chatham House Publishers, 1997), 90.

Sheldon, Charles H. "The Evolution of Law Clerking with the Washington Supreme Court: From 'Elbow Clerks' to 'Puisne Judges.'" *Gonzaga Law Review* 24 (1988/89): 45–84.

———. "Law Clerking with a State Supreme Court: Views from the Perspective of the Personal Assistants to the Judges." *Justice System Journal* 6 (1981): 346–71.

Skowronek, Stephen. "Order and Change." *Polity* 28 (1995): 91–96.

Slotnick, Elliot. "The Equality Principle and Majority Opinion Assignment on the United States Supreme Court." *Polity* 12 (1979): 318–32.

Smith, Rogers. "Political Jurisprudence, the 'New Institutionalism,' and the Future of Public Law." *American Political Science Review* 82 (1988): 89–108.

Sossin, Lorne. "The Sounds of Silence: Law Clerks, Policy Making, and the Supreme Court of Canada." *University of British Columbia Law Journal* 30 (1996): 279–308.

Stern, Robert H. "Denial of Certiorari Despite a Conflict." *Harvard Law Review* 66 (1953): 465.

Stevens, John Paul. "Some Thoughts on Judicial Restraint." *Judicature* 66 (1982): 177–83.

Sturley, Michael F. "Cert Pool." In *The Oxford Companion to the Supreme Court of the United States*, Kermit L. Hall, ed. (New York: Oxford University Press, 1992).

Ulmer, Sidney S. "The Supreme Court's Certiorari Decisions: Conflict as a Predictive Variable." *American Political Science Review* 78 (1984): 901–11.

Vining, Joseph. "Justice, Bureaucracy, and Legal Method." *Michigan Law Review* 80 (1981): 248–69.

Wald, Patricia M. "Selecting Law Clerks." *Michigan Law Review* 89 (1990–91): 152–63.

Wasby, Stephen L. "Clerking for an Appellate Judge: A Close Look." Paper presented at the annual meeting of the Midwest Political Science Association, 2003.

Weiden, David L. "Law Clerks." In *Legal Systems of the World*, Herbert Kritzer, ed. (Santa Barbara, CA: ABC-CLIO Publishers, 2002).

———. "The New Institutionalism and the Supreme Court Law Clerk: Notes for a Theory." Paper presented at the American Political Science Association annual meeting, 1998.

Wichern, Nadine J. "A Court of Clerks, Not of Men: Serving Justice in the Media Age." *DePaul Law Review* 49 (Winter 1999): 621–71.

Williams, C. Dickerman. "The 1924 Term: Recollections of Chief Justice Taft's Law Clerk." *Supreme Court Historical Society Yearbook* (1989). www.supremecourthistory.org.

Williston, Samuel. "Horace Gray." In *Great American Lawyers*, W. Lewis, ed. (Philadelphia: J. C. Winston, 1907–1909; South Hackensack, NJ: Rothman Reprints, 1971), 158–59.

Worthen, Kevin J. "Shirt-Tales: Clerking for Byron White." *Brigham Young University Law Review* (1994): 349–61.

SPEECHES

Brennan, William J. Dean's Day Address, New York University Law School, 1979.

Gressman, Eugene. "Celebration of the Life of Robert L. Stern." Remarks presented at Sheraton North Shore Hilton, Northbrook, Illinois, June 10, 2000.

Rehnquist, William H. "Are the Old Times Dead?" Mac Swinford Lecture, University of Kentucky, September 23, 1983.

Scalia, Antonin. Remarks to the Institute for Constitutional Studies, Supreme Court Historical Society, June 27, 2002.

CASES

Baker v. Carr, 369 U.S. 186 (1962).

Boddie v. Connecticut, 401 U.S. 371 (1971).

Bowers v. Hardwick, 478 U.S. 186 (1986).

Brown v. Board of Education, 347 U.S. 483 (1954).

Bush v. Gore, 531 U.S. 98 (2000).

Callins v. Collins, 510 U.S. 1141 (1994).

Carbon Fuel Co. v. United Mine Workers, 444 U.S. 212 (1979).

Chambers v. Mississippi, 410 U.S. 284 (1973).

Church of the Lukumi Babalu v. City of Hialeah, 508 U.S. 520 (1993).

Cipollone v. Liggett Group, Inc., 505 U.S. 504 (1992).

Danovitz v. United States, 281 U.S. 389 (1930).

DeFunis v. Odegaard, 416 U.S. 312 (1974).

District of Columbia v. Greater Washington Board of Trade, 506 U.S. 125 (1992).

Doe v. Bolton, 410 U.S. 179 (1973).

Dutton v. Evans, 400 U.S. 74 (1970).

Edwards v. Aguillard, 482 U.S. 578 (1987).

Elkins v. United States, 364 U.S. 206 (1960).

Employment Division, Department of Human Resources of Oregon v. Smith, 494 U.S. 872 (1990).

Frontiero v. Richardson, 411 U.S. 677 (1973).

Fullilove v. Klutznick, 448 U.S. 448 (1980).

Gannett v. DePasquale, 443 U.S. 368 (1979).

Garcia v. San Antonio Metropolitan Transit Authority, 469 U.S. 528 (1985).

Gelbard v. United States, 408 U.S. 41 (1972).

Giglio v. United States, 405 U.S. 150 (1972).

Girouard v. United States, 328 U.S. 61 (1946).

Gravel v. United States, 408 U.S. 606 (1972).

Greer v. Spock, 424 U.S. 828 (1976).

Griswold v. Connecticut, 381 U.S. 479 (1965).

In Re Griffiths, 413 U.S. 717 (1973).

In Re Groban, 352 U.S. 330 (1957).

INDOPCO, Inc. v. CIR, 503 U.S. 79 (1992).

INS v. Delgado, 466 U.S. 210 (1984).

J.E.B. v. Alabama ex rel. T.B., 511 U.S. 127 (1994).

Korematsu v. United States, 323 U.S. 214 (1944).

Kraft General Foods v. Iowa Dept. of Revenue, 505 U.S. 71 (1992).

Lafayette v. Louisiana Power and Light Co., 435 U.S. 389 (1978).

Lee v. Weisman, 505 U.S. 577 (1992).

Lemon v. Kurtzman, 403 U.S. 602 (1971).

Lloyd Co. v. Tanner, 407 U.S. 551 (1972).

Lucas v. South Carolina Coastal Council, 505 U.S. 1003 (1992).

Mabee v. White Plains Pub. Co., 327 U.S. 178 (1946).

Machinists v. Street, 367 U.S. 740 (1961).

Martin v. Struthers, 319 U.S. 141 (1943).

McClesky v. Kemp, 481 U.S. 279 (1987).

McGinnis v. Royster, 410 U.S. 263 (1973).

McGowan v. Maryland, 366 U.S. 420 (1961).

Monroe v. Pape, 365 U.S. 167 (1961).

Neil v. Biggers, 409 U.S. 188 (1972).

New York v. United States, 505 U.S. 144 (1992).

Nilva v. United States, 352 U.S. 385 (1957).

O'Connor v. Donaldson, 422 U.S. 563 (1975).

Opper v. United States, 348 U.S. 84
(1954).
Patterson v. McLean Credit Union, 491
U.S. 164 (1989).
P.J. Carlin Construction Co. et al. v.
Heaney et al., 299 U.S. 41 (1936).
Planned Parenthood v. Casey, 505 U.S.
833 (1992).
Plessy v. Ferguson, 163 U.S. 537
(1896).
R.A.V. v. St. Paul, 505 U.S. 377 (1992).
Reed v. Reed, 404 U.S. 71 (1971).
Regents of the University of California v.
Bakke, 438 U.S. 265 (1978).
Renegotiation Board v. Bannercraft Co.,
415 U.S. 1 (1974).
Reno v. American Civil Liberties Union,
521 U.S. 844 (1997).
Roe v. Wade, 410 U.S. 113 (1973).
Rosario v. Rockefeller, 410 U.S. 752
(1973).
San Antonio Independent School District v.
Rodriguez, 411 U.S. 1 (1973).
Sandstrom v. Montana, 442 U.S. 510
(1979).
Sawyer v. Whitley, 505 U.S. 333 (1992).
Schneckloth v. Bustamonte, 412 U.S. 218
(1973).

Shields v. Atlantic Coast Line Railroad
Company, 350 U.S. 318 (1956).
South Carolina v. Baker, 485 U.S. 505
(1988).
Stanley v. Georgia, 394 U.S. 557 (1969).
United States v. Basye, 410 U.S. 441
(1973).
United States v. Brignoni-Ponce, 422 U.S.
873 (1975).
United States v. Caldwell, 408 U.S. 665
(1972).
United States v. Carolene Products Co.,
304 U.S. 144 (1938).
United States v. Fordice, 505 U.S. 717
(1992).
United States v. Fuller, 409 U.S. 488
(1973).
United States v. Kras, 409 U.S. 43 (1973).
United States v. Southern Pacific Co., 251
U.S. 1 (1919).
Webster v. Reproductive Health Services,
492 U.S. 490 (1989).
Williamson v. Lee Optical Co., 348 U.S.
483 (1955).
Wright v. Council City of Emporia, 407
U.S. 451 (1972).
Young v. American Mini Theatres, 427
U.S. 50 (1976).

Index

Abraham, Henry J., 285n25, 305n5, 310n9

Acheson, Dean, 1, 260, 285n30; and Louis Brandeis, 34–35, 201

Agostini, Robert M., 288n1

Ainsworth, Robert, A., 77

Alexander, Larry G., 286n53

Alexander, Michelle A., 95, 98, 165, 209, 288n8, 302n52, 307n50

ALI Model Criminal Code, 213

Allen, F. Aley, 39, 76, 286n47, 291n94, 296n29, 307n40

Allen, Robert S., 283n37, 287n73, 295n18, 305n6

Alpers, Ann, 130

Alpert, Lee Kanon, 290n53

Alschuler, Martha F., 89–90

Alt, Jim, 14, 66, 153, 283n47, 287n81, 290n65

Alsup, William, 296n38, 310n18

American Bar Association, 91, 213

American Civil Liberties Union, 89, 223

American University College of Law, 291n84

Ames, Charles C., 66, 281n14, 281n18, 283n43, 287n76, 288n47, 290n63, 301n42, 302n58, 307n42, 307n58, 307n60, 308n68, 308n69, 309n102, 309n121

Amsterdam, Anthony G., 205, 306n36

Anabtawbi, Iman, 130, 298n82, 298n83

Anderson, Eric G., 283n45, 299n106, 300n23

Appellate Docket, 251

Apprentice model of legal training, 22, 26–30, 53, 238

Arendall, C. B., 286n36

Ares, Charles, 290n53

Arizona University School of Law, 291n84

Armitage, Thomas C., 120

Armstrong, Scott, 6, 14, 16, 151, 244, 282n23, 283n46, 287n66, 300n3, 301n35, 301n44, 307n41, 310n11

Avery, Christopher, 288n7

Babcock, Barbara Allen, 98, 293n156

Baier, Paul, 25–26, 285n11

Baker, Leonard, 285n28, 285n31, 286n57, 286n58, 292n134

Baker, Tyler A., 281n14, 281n18, 283n43, 287n76, 288n4, 288n47, 291n87, 292n129, 301n42, 302n58, 307n42, 307n58, 307n60, 308n68, 309n69, 309n102, 309n121

Baker v. Carr, 205, 304n128, 306n34

Baldwin, Sharon, 90

Ball, Jesse C., 32

Bartkus v. Illinois, 119

Bartlett, Shirley A., 283n46

Baum, Lawrence, 282n29, 291n105

Baxter, Hugh W., 47, 172, 302n81

Bazanson, Randall P., 221–222, 308n79, 308n80, 308n82

Bazelon, David, 101, 260, 293n172

Becker, Mary Ellen, 283n54, 289n42, 289n45, 290n62, 302n74

Been, Vicki, 11

Bench memos, 3–4, 40–42, 52, 107, 155, 162–163, 208

Bent, Silas, 285n32, 286n34

Bentley, Arthur L., III, 297n65

Bergin, Thomas F., 68, 290n71

Berle, A. A., 285n13

Berzon, Marsha, 90

Best, Bradley J., 7, 233, 282n28, 284n1, 294n6, 299n122, 300n33, 306n20, 309n115

Bickel, Alexander, 1, 41, 244, 285n26, 287n66, 308n93, 310n6

About the Authors

Artemus Ward is Assistant Professor of Political Science at Northern Illinois University. He is the author of *Deciding to Leave: The Politics of Retirement from the U.S. Supreme Court*.

David L. Weiden is Assistant Professor of Politics and Government and Director of the Legal Studies Program at Illinois State University.